# Paris: An Architectural History

# Paris

An Architectural History

Anthony Sutcliffe

Yale University Press

New Haven and London 1993

Designed by John Trevitt
Set in Linotron Palatino by Best-set Typesetter Ltd., Hong Kong
Printed by C.S. Graphics Ltd., Singapore

**Library of Congress Cataloging-in-Publication Data**
Sutcliffe, Anthony, 1942–
        Paris: an architectural history / Anthony Sutcliffe.
            p.      cm.
        Includes bibliographical references and index.
        ISBN 0–300–05445–9
        1. Architecture, Modern—France—Paris.
        2. Architecture—France—Paris.   3. Paris (France)—
        Buildings, structures, etc.   I. Title.
        NA1050.S87   1993                            93–24
        720′.944′.36—dc20                            CIP

To my mother and in memory of my father

# Acknowledgments

The following holders of copyright are gratefully
acknowledged in respect of the following illustrations.

Bibliothèque Nationale    2, 25, 28, 45, 47, 49, 65, 87, 88,
89, 149
Documentation Française    29, 52, 57, 73, 91, 93, 117,
118, 121, 148, 191, 243, 246, 248, 254, 267
Fondation Le Corbusier © DACS 1993    213
Musée de France    42, 76
Musées d'Angers    152
Photothèque des Musées de la Ville de Paris © DACS
1993    1, 6, 8, 9, 12, 13, 19, 21, 23, 26, 27, 35, 36, 50, 51,
59, 60, 64, 66, 68, 70, 71, 79, 81, 84, 92, 95, 98, 99, 102,
138, 141, 142, 145, 153, 155, 156, 157, 158, 170, 195, 196,
197, 275
Samaritaine    233
Société Française des Architectes    173

# Contents

# Preface

Of all the world's great cities, Paris is probably the most noted for its architecture. It may seem inadequate or presumptuous therefore to offer an architectural history of Paris in one volume. Such treatments, even of less distinguished cities, are rare. Pictorial guides or compilations of interesting features designed mainly for the intelligent tourist may be found on every bookstall, but this book is not intended to serve such a function. Nor is it the kind of specialised architectural history which seeks to describe and comment upon all the representative buildings of a locality or of a period in time, or to identify and explain the works of a single architect, or of a school of architects. Such studies have been of great value in the preparation of the present volume, but something different is attempted here.

This book discovers in Paris a continuous architectural tradition which has produced an aesthetic harmony surpassing any other large city. Paris offers a visual equilibrium and homogeneity across both space and time which allow the historian to escape from individual buildings and architects and to present the evolution of an urban architecture of surprising continuity. A New York or a London would not permit such a treatment.

Parisian architectural continuity is more widely acknowledged in France than it is abroad, though it is often described in such rhetorical terms that incredulity may result. A recent formulation by René Huyghe, director of the Musée Jacquemart-André and member of the Académie Française, is a case in point:

> Do cities make sense? Paris certainly does! As for modern American cities, mechanical agglomerations of attached rectangles, I have my doubts. Their geometry is detached from historical circumstances, while Paris is the creation of the progression of the centuries. At Paris, the curve of time follows the curve – and the course – of a river. The Champs-Elysées provides the guiding axis of this progress.[1]

The drift of this passage into contradictory geometrical symbolism helps to explain why a more objective consideration is necessary of the Parisian 'eternal city' phenomenon. No American would readily accept that the gridiron plan of Philadelphia, dating back to 1682, deprived the city of a history. Nor would anyone aware of the importance of religious liberty in the history of the United States want to discount the significance of the generous grid of Salt Lake City, founded in 1849. Paris can be no more or less the product of history than any other urban settlement. The interest of Paris lies in the way in which history has shaped it, and not in any special status as a privileged 'city of history'.

History has, of course, shaped American cities as places of great visual diversity, with the gridiron providing the only component of visual homogeneity in most cases. Paris, without a geometrical street plan, offers a striking continuity, expressed mainly through the architecture of individual buildings, and the symmetry and perspective of many of its greater streets. While historical forces produced an increasingly ragged architectural individualism in New York City, in Paris traditional forms were hardly threatened until the 1960s. Perhaps only Washington DC, of all the cities of North America, offers a continuity of this type, but in Paris the time span is much longer and the harmonious aesthetic product is more extensive and more comprehensive.

It would be possible to multiply these ironies and paradoxes but this book is intended to achieve rather more than this. It seeks to identify the basic character of the continuity of Paris's physical environment, and to explain how and why it came into being and exercised its influence. The process, it will be argued, began in the sixteenth century, and it is still going on today.

The author's thanks are due to numerous friends and colleagues whose help and comprehension have shaped this study: Violette Andres, for constant help in the selection of the illustrations; Laure Beaumont-Maillet, for her comprehension and toleration of an unconventional approach to architectural history; Viviane Claude for constant guidance on Parisian debates; Marie-Geneviève Dezès for her early encouragement and her guidance on social housing; Jeffrey Diefendorf for the gift of a number of outstanding original photographs of modern architecture in Paris; Marie-Jeanne Dumont for her help with the Société Française des Architectes and its records; the Faculty of the Social Sciences, Leicester University, for a generous research grant; Michel Fleury, for his hospitality and unrivalled knowledge of Paris architecture; Jean-Pierre Gaudin, whose knowledge of the recent history of planning in Paris has contributed to a number of interpretations; Jean-Marc Léri, who sharpened my perception of the key visual sources; Mary McLeod, for advice on the definition of architectural styles; Bernard Marrey, for his help on Louis Bonnier; Maurice Aymard and the Maison des Sciences de l'Homme for generous hospitality in 1988; Luc Passion, for his lively insight into the way life was lived in a changing Paris; Shelley Rice, whose Paris homes are always of historic interest; Michel Roussier, whose help and advice still provide, as they always did, the foundation on which years of work on Paris have been built; Marcel Smets, who provided very helpful information on the Urban Art movement, and a number of clues to the almost invisible links between Paris and Belgium; Brian Brace Taylor, for crucial information and advice; Roger Taylor, for copies of original photographs from his collection; and Russell Walden, for original photographs.

Two contributions above all have made this book. John Nicoll, the publisher, spotted its potential as architectural history; and Donald Olsen, whose books on city architecture were an inspiration from the start, has set his mark on every page. No author could expect better advice.

Nottingham, September 1992

# 1     Architecture and the Capital City

THE ROLE OF THE CITY IN ARCHITECTURAL
DEVELOPMENT

Architectural history is mostly a tale of
men and buildings, not places. It presents a
succession of innovations, the best buildings
of the best designers. The spatial context is
international or national, not local or even
regional. In that minor variant, the social
history of architecture, design springs from
the human condition, but even here the
physical environment secures but a minor
role.[1]

Our perceptions of architecture on the
ground often differ from this academic view.
Even the most distinguished structures
merge with their surroundings. Groups of
quite ordinary buildings can have a common
character. Sometimes visual coherence marks
whole cities, with every street and building
sharing in a corporate aesthetic. This effect is
more common in smaller towns, and those
which have suffered a relative decline in
importance.[2] Venice is the classic example. In
Britain, Bath and Edinburgh qualify. So does
Washington DC. Throughout Europe the
smaller country town has this unified character, but North America has many such places
too. The small towns of upper New York
State, and of Quebec, retain the harmony of
their foundation years.

But what of the growing cities of our
own, industrial age? New York, Tokyo and
London do not have a common aesthetic
unless it be in the crude 'skyline' silhouette of
tall buildings, randomly sited. The world's
most fashionable 'skyline' of the early 1980s,
Houston, contained some of the most individualistic buildings ever built in a city
centre. Such 'battles of the styles' date back to
the middle of the nineteenth century, when
romanticism freed architects from classical
discipline in time to build for the new clients
of industrialism. Underlying the battles are
rapid economic change, population growth,
multiple functions, class formation, and a
lively property market.[3] This jungle chokes

any inherited city aesthetic and prevents the
birth of a new one.

In the sixteenth century the exemplary city
of the western world was Rome. Since the
1920s it has been New York. Most other large
cities now have much in common with it.
From Tokyo to Rio de Janeiro, from Frankfurt
to Sydney, towers and slabs dominate the
city. The layout and architecture reflect the
competitive pursuit of wealth. A handful of
large cities are nevertheless exceptions. One
of them is Paris.

Paris is no museum piece. Nor is it a
parasite, a leisure centre or a French plot
to take over Europe. On every count it is
a leading capital of the industrial world.
As a tertiary centre it ranks with London,
New York and Tokyo. Luxury and precision
industries within the city boundary are complemented by large-scale manufacturing in
the suburbs, making it France's biggest
industrial producer. The face of Paris thus
belies its status as a giant of the industrial
world. What, then, has shaped the face, and
how does it survive?

Like most European cities, Paris sprang
from the Middle Ages. Nor was it alone
in receiving a classical overlay from the
seventeenth century. Industrialisation did
not prompt an architectural revolution in
nineteenth-century Paris, but neither did
it do so in Berlin or London. The city's
adoption of modernism after 1918 was not
markedly more reluctant than elsewhere, and
the high-rise boom of the 1960s spared Paris
no more than other capitals. Paris architecture is therefore not unique simply because
the city itself is *sui generis*. The answer lies in
the Parisian classical tradition, the theme of
this book.

THE CITY AS A CREATOR OF ARCHITECTURE

Architects, who are the greatest of individ-
ualists and who rate their own abilities very
highly, believe that architecture is made

by architects working in the 'heroic' mode of endeavour. From Leonardo da Vinci to Howard Roark, architects have struggled against meanness, exploitation and bad taste. Above all, perhaps, they have struggled against being told what to do by ignorant clients or strait-jacketed by bathetic regulations. Architecture is made by architects. In this perspective, architectural history becomes a whirl of brilliant or influential projects by star performers. The client is scarcely visible. Architectural diffusion and evolution are the product of links between practitioners. Even the history of the Modern Movement, which is supposed to be the product of an irresistible 'Machine Age', is normally presented as a heroic struggle against convention by a small group of revolutionaries.

This book puts forward a very different view. The subject is Paris but there are many echoes in other cities. In Paris, architects have tended to conform more than they have struggled. The influence of powerful, corporate clients has done much to produce this effect. More important, however, has been the influence of the city itself. The royal example to the court, cautious promoters of rental housing, building regulations, a social structure conducive to emulation, and a universally admired aesthetic, discouraged competing or alternative architecture. The result has been a harmonious city evolving over the centuries. Architects have been proud to work in this context, and Paris has enjoyed a high standard of design and building which has compensated for any lack of variety or novelty. This is the reverse of the Modern Movement myth, a story that is rarely heard. It will be heard now.

THE EUROPEAN CITY AND THE GENESIS OF ARCHITECTURAL TRADITIONS

Paris is the product of a European city-building tradition. This tradition spread outside Europe from the sixteenth century in step with colonisation. Most of the cities of North and South America, Australasia and parts of Africa grow today on European lines. Only in Asia has history built an alternative city.

## The City of Medieval Europe

In the early Middle Ages urbanisation started to recover from the collapse of the western Roman Empire. Its cities, once a dense network west of the Rhine and south of the Danube, were decimated by the invasions, civil wars and epidemics which lasted into the seventh century. Their gridiron street patterns often survived, usually in a distorted form, but their buildings decayed. Their social structures, no longer sustained by administrative functions, military requirements and slavery, disappeared almost completely. Thus no Roman influences remained to guide the renewed urban growth which began uncertainly in the eighth century.

The imperial collapse spared one Roman institution nevertheless. It even strengthened it. This was the Christian Church, ultimately the most effective opponent of the invaders. Even in defeat, the Church had not been threatened by the new masters of Europe who, with the exception of the transient Mongol hordes, had been converted to Christianity before their incursions began. As the Empire collapsed, the Church clung to its urban bishoprics under the guidance of the ultimate urban episcopacy, the see of Rome. The survival and proliferation of rural monasteries thus did little to undermine the cities as the centres of Christian influence.

Urban revival from the eighth century thus included numerous towns of Roman origin. Many of the Roman gridiron plans now came back into service, as at Chester and Turin. However, Roman property rights and institutions had gone, and new buildings spread on to the streets with impunity. Nor did the boundaries of Roman sites have any validity. The street patterns therefore became increasingly distorted, while completely new sites were marked out. These new sites were crucial to the form of the medieval city, and they marked a sharp break with Roman colonial practice.

All but the older Roman cities had been laid out with shallow, rectangular sites. This shape reflected the absence of any need to cultivate some of their area, for the cities could concentrate on high-order functions and supplies could be cheaply imported from the countryside. In early medieval towns the weakness of market production and control by feudal lords required extensive cultivation within the town. The result was a standard form of site known as the 'burgage plot', a site with a narrow frontage and considerable depth. The house was always built directly on the street frontage, while the land behind supported various non-residential uses, including cultivation.

Burgage plots did not fit easily within the Roman grids. However, many blocks were merged and whole sections of street disappeared. Moreover, when urban growth accelerated around the end of the millennium as agriculture and trade revived, many towns started to grow outside the grids. Meanwhile, a new generation of towns was founded by lords and kings to encourage trade and then tax it. These new towns used the burgage plot *ab initio*. The evolving streets, rather than shaping the sites, responded to them in a process often described as 'organic growth'. The resulting towns had narrow, winding streets with plots of divergent dimensions.

Most of these new towns reached their peak in the early fourteenth century, before plague and economic depression cut back their populations in the later Middle Ages. By this time, many of the old Roman towns had been ringed by medieval growth, and few visitors would have noticed where the old Roman gridiron ended and the new districts began. Nearly all the original Roman buildings had gone, together with the flimsy structures of the early Middle Ages. Despite the frequent fires which caused much of this change, fourteenth-century constructions still relied heavily on wood, and the carpenters who built the timber frames were the main building designers of the day. There is little sign that urban authorities tried to impose a more solid form of construction before the later Middle Ages, except in the advanced commercial cities of northern Italy such as Florence and Milan.

Thus the later medieval city was not the creation of architects or master masons, except for a growing number of churches, chapels, abbeys, mansions and palaces, which were built in stone. A main feature was the narrow gable end facing the street, sometimes with a narrow lane separating it from the next house, but more often engaged with its neighbours on both sides. Almost everywhere north of the Alps, each house would have a heavy wooden frame, but the materials filling the gaps between the frame varied according to the region – wattle and daub, clay, mud, plaster, stucco or rubble. The roof was normally covered by thatch or reeds, and was very steep in order to run the water off before it could penetrate minor blemishes. Most houses did not exceed two or three storeys, except in the centres of the biggest cities such as London and Paris where houses of five storeys lined the main streets.

The resulting townscape was anarchic in that it had not been planned or designed, but it had a certain harmony resulting from the repetition of narrow frontages along the street. Churches and religious houses normally failed to pull the scene together because the dynamic evolution of the burgage plots, the paucity of public places and the fluid street pattern usually prevented them from acting as focal points. What the medieval city showed above all was that building houses for the burgesses tended to produce a standard house type, and that building directly on the street frontage was the natural result of pre-industrial urbanisation. Neither architects nor authorities did much to produce these effects, which have to be seen as consensual. They can also be seen as the first two ways in which the urban architecture of western Europe was shaped by the city itself, rather than by architects. An urban vernacular thus preceded any intervention by architects and designers.

The disruptions of the later Middle Ages, which reduced most city populations and accelerated migration towards them, complicated the development of urban form in Europe. More buildings survive from this than from earlier periods, partly because they are more recent and partly because greater per capita wealth produced a greater solidity of construction. However, it was not until the sixteenth century that a long surge in building, following a sustained growth in urban population from the later 1400s, created a more durable, permanent city which nevertheless retained the essentials of a medieval form.

## The City of the Sixteenth Century

The city of the sixteenth century was a larger and better-built version of its late medieval predecessor. Although population

3

growth, at a time of slow improvement in productivity, tended to undermine incomes, it also promoted a wave of new building. The resulting houses were more durable and comfortable than their predecessors, and their owners seem to have attached more importance to their exterior appearance. These qualities did not reflect effective demand among the poor, who normally lived in the older buildings. The new houses were built for an urban middle and upper class, mostly composed of the growing merchant and professional groups. However, in many parts of western Europe – and especially in the south – the landowning gentry and aristocracy kept town houses. Large numbers of these more grandiose residences were built, or rebuilt, during the sixteenth century.

The houses of the rich, and especially of the aristocracy, tended to differ from those of the middle classes. They sought a degree of spendthrift ostentation whereas the houses of the middle classes normally cherished a more modest conformity and comfort. The rich generally aped the architectural fashions of those whose status marginally exceeded their own, and the superior groups often emulated the styles of foreign countries noted for their taste. These features had already been present in the Middle Ages, when Italian and later French taste had been admired in northern and eastern Europe, but the gradual diffusion of Italian Renaissance design from the later 1400s was the main challenge to medieval building. This diffusion was the work of the rich and powerful, rather than of the solid burgesses who had shaped the medieval city. It incorporated different values and produced different results.

*The Renaissance City*

In complete contrast to the medieval city, the Renaissance city was at first a product of the intellect. It took the form of theoretical planning exercises undertaken mainly by intelligent young men during their education. Only slowly did it take shape on the ground, and even then it did little more than modify cities of medieval origin, rather than replace them completely, or take the form of completely new cities. With the European urban network complete by the sixteenth century, there was no place for new towns except for purposes of defence. Most of the latter were in any case too remote to

achieve much growth. The Renaissance thus engendered a struggle between the medieval forms already on the ground, and the trenchant concepts and images born of reason and the new love of Antiquity.

The new urban concepts sprang mainly from architectural innovations. A new style of architecture grew up in Italy from the later fifteenth century, drawing on Ancient examples. The dominant feature was the use of the three classical orders of columns and capitals. Lintels, arches, sculptures and pediments were incorporated as appropriate, using rough principles of proportion and perspective. Little attempt was made to simulate Ancient buildings in their entirety. Some churches went a long way towards reproducing the Christian basilica of the later Roman Empire, but their simple, elongated plan was generally superseded in the sixteenth century. The Renaissance architectural style, as developed in Italy, was nevertheless sufficiently novel to inspire the efforts of architects abroad who also wanted to draw on the Ancient example.

Renaissance urban buildings were thus, to begin with, mainly churches, palaces and the mansions of the rich. Inserted in the existing urban fabric, they made a striking contrast rather than bringing greater order to the cityscape. Built by the rich and powerful, their designers sought to stress the distinction and foresight of their owners. They even competed among themselves, though always within the Renaissance design constraints of reason and order. Constricted sites meant that most secular structures were built on the street frontage, and up to a height of three or four storeys. These features were nothing new, but in every other respect they were a striking departure from the existing vernacular.

By the middle of the sixteenth century attention was moving to the construction or reconstruction of cities on Renaissance lines. Although this was largely a conceptual matter, the development of persuasive principles and attractive images won many converts among rulers, clients and the growing profession of architects. This debate led on to a number of efforts to put these ideas into practice in the second half of the sixteenth century. This practical urban planning of the Renaissance centred on the creation of squares (*piazze*) and approach streets. These were always ambitious undertakings, and behind them lay the princely takeover of most of the previously merchant-controlled cities of northern and central Italy in the fifteenth century. They thus expressed power as much as reason.

The squares were the first effort to extend the Renaissance formula beyond individual buildings. Though most were built by a ruler, they were presented as a contribution to the life of the city and they were multi-functional. Normally rectangular but sometimes circular or triangular in shape, they offered an unencumbered open space for displays. A statue or other monument normally stood at the centre of the square to provide a visual focus. Trading, in contrast to the medieval market place, was concentrated on the sides of the square under an arcade. Merchants used the space under the arcades for the display of their goods, which were stored in their premises behind. Partly owing to the insertion of some of the squares in dense central areas, the sites were of limited depth and their frontages were correspondingly broad. The arcades, over which the upper floors projected, were normally supported by rows of arches, and the facades had regular fenestration and classical detailing.

The squares marked the first step in a popularisation of Renaissance urban architecture. The houses, expensive though their design was to build, were normally intended to attract traders, who could see the advantage of an attractive and well-frequented location. These virtues, it was hoped, would compensate for the imposition of a facade designed to meet the aesthetic requirements of the ruler, and often to express a political or dynastic message. Although the owner was normally free to modify the house behind the facade, or to build from scratch according to his own wishes, complaints about the compulsory facades were legion. However, in the long run the implicit compact between the princely developer (or his nominees) and the merchant owner or occupier was accepted.

The success of the piazza, both in reality and as an idea, had important implications for the evolution of building throughout the city. The arcades and the facade treatments grew in popularity, affecting a variety of new buildings in every district. However, the bulk of this architecture could not be in the expensive squares, which remained a minority form of development. As in the medieval city, the street remained the main context for building.

Renaissance architecture tended to spread first of all to the sections of street which approached the new piazzas. The stress on common facade designs was less pronounced here, but since the building of squares normally required the construction of short sections of access street, an opportunity was created for an integrated scheme. In these cases it was normal for the frontage architecture of the square to be extended along the street. Since part of the square, and sometimes the monument or statue in the middle, were visible at the end of the street, there were the makings of a perspective view which layout and architecture could enhance. At this point, however, the idea of urban perspective requires more discussion.

The concept of perspective was scarcely present in the Ancient and medieval worlds, either in art or in urban layout. In the later fifteenth century, history's greatest perceptual revolution occurred. Beginning in Italy, painters developed the technique of perspective, which created an illusion of distance in two-dimensional art. At first, urban scenes provided the best subjects for perspective techniques. Meanwhile, urban perspective views were used as theatre backdrops, with radiating, rectilinear streets lined by identical facades being particularly common. These *trompe l'oeil* were so popular that they fostered the idea that such perspective streets should be built in cities, allowing reality to match art. In approaching, or linking, the new squares they would create sections of townscape which had no equivalent in the medieval world, nor even in Antiquity.

By the middle of the sixteenth century, however, thinking had extended beyond the square and the adjoining street. The drafting of plans for ideal cities and military concerns had encouraged an integral view of the city based on street networks surrounded by extensive earthworks. Crucial to this development was the growth of long-range artillery. The gunnery and infantry tactics developed from around the turn of the fifteenth century required new fortifications in which geometrically planned earthworks replaced the masonry walls of the Middle Ages. The new military methods prompted plans for completely new strategic towns, while city extensions were normally fortified in the new style and equipped with street networks designed to promote the efficiency of the defence. Such extensions were common as cities grew rapidly in the sixteenth and early seventeenth centuries. The streets within them were usually of standard width, rectilinear, and geometrical in pattern, almost always using a grid system.

The ideal city plans normally included the modern fortifications, usually arranged in a circle. This maximised the area contained within a given length of wall, and often prompted a layout based on a central piazza with radiating streets. However, they were as much the product of idealism as of practicality. They presented the city not just as a meeting-point and the permanent home of people and work, but as the expression of political authority, knowledge and culture. The ideal city plans thus reflected the guiding values of the Renaissance. Shaped above all by reason, they provided a convincing blueprint for a new form of city, in which every square metre would form part of a logical whole.

The practical application of these ideal plans was, however, limited. As Europe had been fully urbanised in the Middle Ages, there was no scope for new cities. They were used in a number of new, defensive towns or naval bases. In the eighteenth century, following the example of Louis XIV's Versailles, a number of minor rulers built their capitals on these lines, as at Karlsruhe. During this phase, the liberating planning of the Renaissance became associated with Absolutism, but there was no real aesthetic change.

Even in the planned towns and districts, building design was normally left to those who purchased the sites, rather than imposed from above. Sites were wider and shallower than in the past, as the geometrical street network required. Facade design evolved only slowly away from medieval conventions. Building continued to reflect the wishes of the merchant for the most part, but classical principles remained the main influence on fashion as Mannerism, baroque and rococo succeeded one another into the Palladianism of the eighteenth-century Augustan Age. Meanwhile, the authorities extended building control in the interests

of public safety. Fireproof materials were gradually imposed and action was taken to protect natural lighting and ventilation. Together with the natural conformism of the middle classes, these controls were tending by the eighteenth century to generate a more conformist and harmonious urban architecture in the cities. In this way, most towns had come to reflect something of the Renaissance vision by 1789.

### The City of the Industrial Era

Since Lewis Mumford first published his influential stage theories of urban development before the last war, it has been widely assumed that industrialisation shattered this elegant harmony. However, this was not generally the case in those great European cities which had matured in earlier periods. Here, any mechanised processes and big service industries such as gas normally developed in remote suburbs where disorder could pass unnoticed. Established districts were little affected, and most of the new, residential areas were developed on traditional lines. The British architectural revolution initiated by the Gothic Revival in the 1840s and continued by other revivals, complicated by eclecticism, undermined the Renaissance ideal and generated an alternative cityscape which was perhaps appropriate to the home of the Industrial Revolution. Elsewhere in Europe, however, the industrial challenge was fragmented. Renaissance design remained in vigour, especially in mass residential construction and street improvements. The cityscape continued to evolve on the basis of a pre-industrial consensus, modified only by an increase in scale.

### The Modern Movement

In this evolutionary perspective, the main break-point of urban architecture comes in the twentieth century with the revolutionary Modern Movement. Although the Modern Movement prophets stressed its links with classical principles, the idealised urban forms developed by Le Corbusier and others from the 1920s were a radical departure from the Renaissance tradition. Seeking free movement for motor vehicles and a high standard of natural lighting and open space, they broke away from the traditional street, and built upwards. The resulting aesthetic of 'towers in a park' had no precedent in the history of cities, so its advocates equated it with natural forms and with an 'industrial aesthetic' which sometimes recalled the old nineteenth-century 'sublime'.

Although the Modern Movement was arguably a logical response to the urban requirements and potential of industrialisation, its rejection of established city form prevented its adoption as a vernacular comparable to medieval building and the long-lived classical tradition. Where it could be implemented in ideal conditions, as for instance at the city periphery or in big urban renewal schemes, the structures were normally so large and costly that only public finance could undertake them. Even where Modern Movement buildings were constructed individually, and on a smaller scale, for instance on central, commercial sites, the scale of investment excluded all but corporate enterprise.

Modern architecture was thus more of a challenge to the European cityscape than anything that preceded it, but it lacked the harmony and certainty of its great predecessors. After a big challenge from 'post-modernism' in the 1970s and the 1980s, it remained in place in the 1990s, but it took such a variety of forms that the future of modernism remained uncertain.


PARIS AS A SOURCE OF URBAN ARCHITECTURE

Much of the above applies to Paris. Paris has been too big since the Middle Ages to diverge greatly from European patterns. On the contrary, it has done more than any other city to shape them. However, as Europe's largest city from the Middle Ages to the end of the seventeenth century, the capital of Europe's most powerful monarchy until 1789, the second-largest city in Europe during the nineteenth century and a potential capital of Europe after 1945, Paris was distinctive in many ways. As we proceed, these distinctive features will be identified, and their contribution to a unique architectural result will be discussed. This study can now move, however, from the general features of urbanisation and architecture in large cities to the special alchemy of Paris.

THE MEDIEVAL INHERITANCE

The architectural history of Paris begins in the first century BC, when the Romans founded the city of Lutetia on what is now the Île de la Cité.[1] The Roman city spread southwards on to the Left Bank of the Seine, where most of its public facilities were built. This was an impressive city, the largest in northern Europe, but little of it survived into the Middle Ages, except for the baths of Julian and the amphitheatre. Lutetia appears to have had very little influence on the architecture of the medieval city when building resumed in the eighth century.

By the thirteenth century, Paris was the largest city in western Europe, mainly because it had been capital of Europe's greatest kingdom since the turn of the millennium.[2] Intensive building within cramping fortifications produced a congested, incoherent city. Paris was dominated by individualistic architectural forms representing religion, power, great wealth and military strength, while the houses of the people were built of such flimsy materials that lengthy survival rarely ensued.

It was not until Paris began to be influenced by the Italian Renaissance, at the close of the fifteenth century, that an alternative to incoherence came on the scene. During the new era in its architectural history which now began, Paris would develop its own version of classicism, a version which would shape the city until the twentieth century. However, the medieval heritage of streets, sites and buildings was so large that the initial effect was an amalgam of medieval and Renaissance design.

Perhaps the most important product of the early Renaissance was the emergence of the architect as a major figure in the building process, rather than as a shadowy associate of the master masons, carpenters and builders who had built the medieval city in almost complete anonymity. The architect used design principles rather than artisan experi-

ence, and he was prepared to discuss them. He was interested in design practice outside his own city, and he was often prepared to pursue a peripatetic career. His emergence created a potential conflict between the new architecture and the old vernacular.

Most out of tune with Renaissance design was the soaring, gabled house (Fig. 1). The majority of houses were the work of master carpenters, who built the timber frames and hired lesser artisans to complete the structures. The carpenters, even more than the master masons, clung to well-tried techniques. This produced a similarity between the houses but there was no deliberate harmony in this. On the contrary, the burgesses valued such distinctive features as the builders could provide as symbols of their individuality in a city where few had civic rights. The large, overhanging gables were cherished for this reason. The expression 'avoir pignon sur rue' is still used in France to describe a firm's proud presence in the High Street.

The construction of gabled houses advanced in the later Middle Ages. As early as the fourteenth century, masons were being asked to replace defective timber framing by dressed stone members held together with mortar.[3] This suggests that houses were also being built from scratch, using a stone frame. However, stone was more expensive than timber, and it probably made little difference to the appearance of the house. Meanwhile, timber frames were made more robust to sustain greater heights and to permit jettying (the construction of projecting upper floors) though this was already under attack by the Crown in the fifteenth century, as we shall see. The gaps between the spars were probably already being filled with rubble, which reduced fire risk and reinforced the entire structure. Facade decoration was very limited on these houses, perhaps because the timber frame was such a striking feature. However, many of the heavy lintel beams which often topped the ground floor may have been

1 Old houses on the Place de Grève in a painting by Raguenet, *c.* 1750. This, together with the Halles, was the most densely constructed area of Paris in the later Middle Ages.

carved or inscribed. Door frames probably received a similar treatment. This type of house had a future which the Renaissance could not undermine overnight.

Another important medieval building type had a greater potential for adaptation. This was the *hôtel*, the mansion residence of aristocracy and of the royal family. The *hôtel* emerged in the later Middle Ages from the miniature fortress of earlier times. *Hôtels* were normally designed by master masons just as fortifications and bridges were, but by the later Middle Ages certain master masons appear to have been specialising in *hôtel* design. Aware of the importance of comfort and fashion to their clients, they ceased to draw only on established practice and began to consider the principles on which the design should be developed. They also looked around for models in the work of other master masons in Paris and outside, and outside France. The result was a gradual movement towards designs which would not embarrass the client when compared with other new *hôtels*, and a constant search for

new features which would produce a distinctive design nevertheless. These motivations were a stimulus to architecture rather than mere building, and the *hôtel*, more than any other building type, provides a link between the building conventions of the Middle Ages, and the classicism of the Renaissance.

Most *hôtels* stood on large sites with gardens and ancillary buildings. They were generally closed off from the street by a curtain wall or by dour frontages with sparse fenestration. Their main rooms faced an interior courtyard or garden. The principal entry from the street was through a *porte cochère*, defined by massive masonry and heavy wooden doors. This required at the very least a small courtyard just inside the entrance where vehicles could unload and turn round. This link with the street, and the gradual arrangement of the buildings around an interior space, had created the essentials of the comfortable town house by the end of the fifteenth century.

At this time even the most advanced *hôtels* still used a secular variant of the Gothic style with pointed and ogee arches, stone window tracery and transoms, and carved decoration in the *flamboyant* style. Regularity and order were already valued, however, and there was great scope for the adoption of Renaissance features, which the aristocracy readily associated with comfort and fashion. However, the persistent desire to turn the main buildings away from the street, or to withdraw from it, restricted the power of the *hôtel* to help regularise the townscape. As late as the fifteenth century, owners were still building prominent turrets (*tourelles*) on the frontages or the curtain walls of their *hôtels*, often at street corners (Fig. 2). Most of them had tall pyramidal or conical roofs, and were corbelled out over the street as if to stress the unique status of the owner even within the crowded burgess city.[4]

The Hôtel de Sens (1475–1507), built as a Paris residence for the bishops of Sens, was in the vanguard of *hôtel* design (Fig. 3). It was apparently designed to be defended, and the outer wall was pierced with small, irregular windows. The gardens were undefended, but the house and courtyard could be sealed against an approach from that quarter (Fig. 4).[5] The Hôtel de Cluny, built for the abbots of one of France's biggest monasteries between 1485 and 1498, was larger and more comfortable in appearance. It had a rectangular plan and regular fenestration, but ogee arches, gargoyles and touches of flamboyant decoration held it firmly in the Middle Ages.

Religious houses, even more than *hôtels*, lowered behind their high walls. The biggest, like the abbey of Saint-Germain-des-Prés, covered larger areas than even the greatest *hôtels*. Their churches were among the grandest in Paris, but their conventual buildings were spartan. They were slow to adopt Renaissance fashion.[6] Parish churches and chapels, in contrast, were prominent in the townscape. By the end of the Middle Ages most were in the Gothic style, except on the island of the Cité where a number of small, Romanesque structures survived from the tenth and eleventh centuries. The rapid growth of Paris from the twelfth century had produced a wave of Gothic building,

resulting in a goodly number of large parish churches. As a powerful design statement with spiritual associations they were an obstacle to the popular adoption of Renaissance design. Inside, however, they offered scope for the application of Renaissance features in the form of altars, memorials, tombs and side chapels. This classicisation of the church from within was already under way at the end of the fifteenth century.

Whatever the architectural merits of all these major buildings, one thing was lacking – the open space from which to view them (Fig. 5). Few streets were wider than five metres (15 feet) and continuous frontages did not help the eye to roam. Widenings and junctions used for markets offered more space, but they were intermittent. Many churches retained their small graveyards, and there was a small open space (*parvis*) in front of some churches, but large, public spaces were few and far between. The Place de Grève, in front of the Maison des Piliers (now the site of the Hôtel de Ville), was the largest uninterrupted space (Fig. 6). The *parvis* of the cathedral of Notre-Dame was the largest in Paris, and there was a succession of open spaces in the markets area (Halles).

2 *Left*, turreted gateway at the Hôtel de Clisson, 1371, in a nineteenth-century print.

3 *Above*, main front of the Hôtel de Sens.

4 *Right*, the Hôtel de Sens, garden front.

5 *Far right*, tall gabled houses in the Rue François-Miron. Much restored in the 1970s, they are claimed to date from the fourteenth century.

6 *Above*, Raguenet's painting of the Hôtel de Ville and the Place de Grève, 1751.

7 *Right*, turret at the Hôtel Hérouet, 1510. The body of the building was partly reconstructed after bomb damage in the Second World War.

Views across the Seine were fleeting because banks and bridges were lined by buildings. This was a very claustrophobic environment, the only visual release being upwards to the turrets and dormers of the mansions, the towers of the churches and on to the heavens (Fig. 7). It was, at the same time, a very resistant environment, which the Renaissance could not sweep away overnight.[7]

In the fifteenth century Italy began to experience a surge of interest in the art, literature and thought of the Ancient world. Architecture was the most visible product of this 'rebirth'. Towards the end of the century the French court began to follow Italian fashion. Links with Italy were strengthened by the French intervention there in 1494. By the early sixteenth century, Renaissance design had begun to set its mark on Paris.

An important design episode exemplified the transitional character of the time. In 1499 the most important Seine bridge, the Pont Notre-Dame, collapsed.[8] Built of timber by the municipality in 1413, the bridge had carried thirty houses on each side. These houses had been uniform in construction, according to the record. Prudence alone could have dictated the decision to rebuild the bridge in stone. However, the impressive attention devoted to the reconstruction by an *ad hoc* investing group of burgesses, courtiers, officials and consultant builders was unprecedented. The Crown was clearly more interested in the welfare of Paris than in the past, so a more ambitious structure could be envisaged. An Italian master builder (*deviseur*), the Franciscan friar, Jean Gucundus from Verona, took charge of the reconstruction.[9] It was assumed from the start that houses would be built on the bridge, and the final decision to that effect was made by the Bureau de Ville (municipality).[10] Work started in 1507, and all the houses were finished in 1513 (Fig. 8).

The elegant lines of the bridge were matched by the houses. Thirty-four were built on each side, to an identical design determined by the Bureau de Ville. Each house had a single-bay, gabled facade of three floors, with an attic in the gable. An inset arcade at ground level was supported by piers set in line with the party walls. The facade was in brick, with dressed stone inserts marking the divisions between the houses, above the piers of the arcade. The design was nothing more than a regularised version of the medieval burgess house, but its repetition on a straight thoroughfare produced a perspective unprecedented in Paris. It appears to have been much admired by the citizenry, withal.

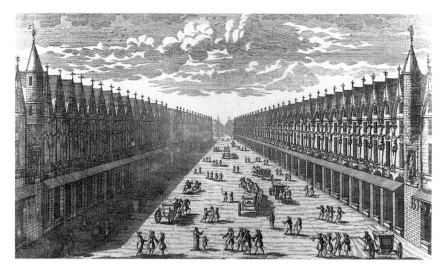

Before long, the houses and the roadway were adapted to the growing Renaissance fashion. At each end of the bridge, fussy masonry arches with some Renaissance details were built, perhaps as early as 1531.[11] They were probably inspired by the temporary arches set up in the main streets to honour the king's movements, and were not necessarily intended to reinforce the whole composition. A later print suggests that, probably before the end of the sixteenth century, the gables and the upper part of the facades were rebuilt with crude orders and bas-relief caryatids. These disguised the most obviously pre-Renaissance element of the design, the gable.

Especially valued were the arcades under the new houses, one arch per house. The Parlement even tried to extend them to the neighbouring streets, issuing an ordinance in 1508 requiring all new facades to adopt the same height and shape as those on the bridge.[12] Such arcades were not new. They may even have been very common in medieval Paris, at any rate in the form of set-back ground floors in individual houses, especially in the Halles area, to provide space for sheltered trading (Fig. 9).[13] What distinguished the arcades on the bridge was their length and symmetry. More than any other feature of the bridge, the arcades heralded the streetscape of classical Paris.

8 Perspective view of the Pont Notre-Dame by Avéline, 1507.

9 Open ground floors in the Rue de la Tonnellerie, Halles, in a print of 1866.

## TOWARDS A RENAISSANCE AESTHETIC

The Pont Notre-Dame was for many years an isolated achievement. The Renaissance made its mark in design details but the results were often strident or pathetic caricatures. The Crown appreciated this problem more than most and eventually took action.

François Ier (1515–47) made a concerted effort to bring Italian expertise directly into France. Leonardo da Vinci spent his last years in France at the invitation of Francois Ier, and other leading figures of the Italian Renaissance followed for stays of varying length.[14] The most important architectural personality in the early years was Sebastiano Serlio (1475–1554). As a practising architect who published his own designs with lengthy explanations, his Italian work was influential in France before he ever set foot there. In 1545 his *First* and *Second Books of Architecture* were published in Paris with a French translation. A *Fifth Book* followed in 1547. They were widely consulted, probably because their fidelity to the best Italian practice distinguished them from the bastardised architecture already emerging in France.[15]

Meanwhile, Serlio had come to the French court in 1540 or 1541 at the king's invitation. He stayed until 1547, when he may have been disappointed by the choice of Lescot as architect of the new Louvre.[16] In his later years Serlio prepared drawings for an unpublished 'Sixth Book of Architecture', which appears to have been intended to disseminate designs deemed especially appropriate for France.[17] His drawings were mainly for houses, some of them urban. A few modest, burgess types were shown but the collection quickly progressed to large *hôtels* and some grandiose and inventive chateaux and palaces. Some of the small houses are shown with both traditional and Renaissance elevations, probably in order to convince the French that Renaissance design need not be less convenient or more costly than French custom.

Nearly all Serlio's urban examples have broad, symmetrical facades, most of them apparently standing directly on the street frontage. Some have steeply pitched roofs parallel to the frontage, as though Serlio is suggesting that so beloved a feature need not be ruled out. Above all, Serlio achieves symmetry and proportion in a wide variety of situations and the overall effect was probably persuasive.[18] The aristocracy, in particular, must have been impressed by the palatial qualities of even the houses of moderate size. Serlio's reputation as the man who did most to introduce Renaissance architecture into France seems entirely justified.[19]

Whether the French extended their admiration into practice remains more questionable. Serlio's less distinguished French equivalent, Jacques Androuet du Cerceau, published his *Livre d'architecture* in 1559. He followed

Serlio in including numerous elevations for residential buildings, from burgess houses to large mansions and chateaux.[20] There was a strong emphasis on steep roofs, large dormers and very tall windows at the *piano nobile*. Enclosed courtyards were a feature of the larger houses. French tradition had the upper hand in many of these designs, and the exotic touches of a Serlio were rare. Du Cerceau's elevations sought an overall symmetry, but a strict balance could be sacrificed to permit the efficient lighting of the rooms.[21] Meanwhile, most of the Paris *hôtels* built in the second half of the sixteenth century used steep roofs and turrets even though Serlio had envisaged the former mainly for rows of burgess houses. Some turrets bore Renaissance detail but this did nothing to mask a mass and outline which recalled the fifteenth century.[22]

THE DESIGN OF THE *HÔTEL*

It would be misleading to dwell too long with the great sixteenth-century pattern books, whether Italian or French. Many of their designs were hypothetical exercises, some of them radiating whimsy or fantasy. Parisian architecture pursued its own course, with *hôtel* design proving especially innovative. The result was as much Parisian as it was classical.

In France as in other kingdoms, the aristocracy tended to follow the royal example. This was especially the case when they were building Paris mansions for use when attending court. The Crown's patronage of Renaissance design was clearly irrevocable by the 1540s, when work started on the new Louvre. The aristocracy responded with a somewhat motley version of Renaissance architecture which flourished from the 1540s. Their *hôtels* lacked Italian purity, but many were striking in appearance. Elaborate classical features such as capitals and pilasters were rare, perhaps following the view of Philibert de l'Orme, the architect of the Tuileries palace, that they were not necessary in domestic architecture.[23]

*Hôtel* building accelerated after 1550. Progress on the new Louvre prompted the construction of new *hôtels* to the north of the palace. Much building also took place in the older noble district of the Marais, to the east.

The owners emulated the Crown, and vied with one another. Contemporaries noted, and sometimes regretted, the ostentation of these buildings, which inevitably made older houses look spartan and severe, but such comparisons only encouraged further commissions in the new style.[24] Indeed, in the judgment of the leading authority on this obscure period, David Thomson, the development of *hôtel* building in Paris from the middle of the sixteenth century amounted to an architectural revolution, whatever its divergence from classicism as perceived in Italy.[25]

The most important innovation was one of plan rather than of elevation. In 1544–6 Serlio built the house of the Grand Ferrare at Fontainebleau, where François Ier had built a palace in the Renaissance style. Serlio's main building was fronted by a courtyard, with a garden behind. Parallel wings on either side linked the house to a screen on the street frontage, pierced by a *porte cochère*. This arrangement allowed the house to be designed as a palazzo, with two long frontages.[26] The courtyard allowed carriages to unload and turn with an ease which city streets did not permit. The garden could be laid out geometrically to enhance any symmetrical effects in the rear elevation.[27]

Parisian architects showed great interest in this arrangement. Philibert de l'Orme used a variant of it in the house which he built for himself in the Rue de la Cerisaie in about 1557, and Androuet du Cerceau published Serlio's plan in his *Livre d'architecture* in 1559.[28] Although the new plan was used only in the larger of the new *hôtels*, it soon acquired the status of an ideal and it contributed to a general acceleration of architectural change in the middle of the sixteenth century.[29] It also helped, together with the general use of symmetrical elevations, to focus the attention of architects and master masons on a small number of key design problems and to discourage Mannerism.

A good example of quality architecture at an early stage was the Hôtel de Carnavalet. Probably designed by Pierre Lescot shortly before he took up his Louvre commission, the Hôtel de Carnavalet dates from 1544. Located in the Marais, its scale and style made it the outstanding new mansion of its day. However, only its balustrade and the crude orders and pediments decorating its large dormers were obviously classical in inspiration. Its two main storeys were dominated by tall, rectangular windows divided into four sections by the heavy masonry transoms used at the Hôtel de Sens and the Hôtel de Cluny in the later fifteenth century. The storeys were separated by the projecting masonry strip which had been much used on medieval fortified buildings such as the turreted entrance to the Hôtel de Clisson. This strip was repeated in modified form at cornice level. The result was an elevation of strong grid lines. The steep roof topped by tall chimneys rising through the ridge prolonged the French medieval tradition of exuberant verticality.

Smaller projects were even less likely to be in touch with Renaissance fashion (Fig. 10). Elsewhere in Paris, specialists such as Lescot were rarely used in *hôtel* construction. The task was left to master masons and others with building skills who, while competent and in many cases creative, were probably only partially in touch with changing Italian fashions and the developing theory of classical architecture.[30] They must have made use of the rich copperplate engravings of Androuet du Cerceau and others which multiplied from the 1550s. The most respected of these collections was Androuet du Cerceau's *Les plus excellents bastiments de France*, a selection of royal and noble buildings. Published in 1576 and 1579, this book complemented his *Livre d'architecture* of 1559. However, the engravings included some medieval castles and some fussy transitional buildings such as François Ier's Château de Boulogne (Madrid). In untutored hands, they were bound to encourage eclecticism and Mannerism.

By the 1580s there was a move towards a bigger scale in *hôtel* design, and classical components were applied with greater confidence. The Hôtel Lamoignon, built in the Marais by J. Thiriot in 1584–6, used the giant order, for the first time in Paris, on the courtyard side (Fig. 11). This grand scheme was however offset by a fragmented arrangement of dormers, pediments and entablature. The towering, hipped roofs must be among the steepest in Paris. Serlio's recommended arrangement for the front courtyard was ignored, and the large garden behind the *hôtel* was not incorporated into the architectural scheme.[31] This was still a transitional style, for all its charm and grandeur.

## THE ROYAL CONTRIBUTION

The royal contribution has been kept in the background until now because it was discontinuous and independent of Parisian traditions. However, the Crown could have its pick of architects and, after François Ier's espousal of the Renaissance ideal, royal buildings could in theory rival the best Italian work.

In the mid-sixteenth century the royal family began to move from its cluster of old *hôtels* in the Marais to the west of the city near the fortress of the Louvre. At the end of his reign, François Ier decided to demolish Philip Augustus's old keep and replace it with a palace. After rejecting designs by Serlio, the

10 *Top*, garden front of the Hôtel de Donon, 1576. David Thomson detects the continuing influence of Philibert de l'Orme in this design.

11 *Above*, the Hôtel Lamoignon, main front. The lower building to the left is a later construction.

king appointed Pierre Lescot in 1546. Lescot designed a large, nine-bay structure facing a courtyard, with a plainer elevation on the other side. The inner facade had two tall storeys surmounted by a lower, attic floor. The two lower storeys made much use of Corinthian pilasters. The attic floor was separated from the first floor by a cornice, and above it an ornate balustrade partially hid the roof. Major entrances were marked by pedimented pavilions with statues in niches. The wall surfaces carried extensive decorative sculptures.

The new Louvre combined French and Italian features in a way which secured general approval at the time (Fig. 12).[32] As an example to the nobility, however, it suffered from its huge dimensions, and emulation in later *hôtels* is hard to trace. In the long term, it set major problems of articulation in the extension of the new palace. Meanwhile, Catherine de Medici, widow of Henri II, launched her Tuileries palace project, to the west of the Louvre, in the 1560s. Her initial architect, Philibert de l'Orme, produced a bolder exercise in classicism but on a smaller scale. Construction was rapid, and the Tuileries may well have been a stronger influence than Lescot's Louvre.

The clearest expression of classical purity was not to be found in any palace or *hôtel*. Lescot's associate at the Louvre, Jean Goujon, went on to build a public fountain, the Fontaine des Innocents, at the Halles in 1548–9. Though a municipal project, it was intended to honour the king, and in both style and dimensions the structure was out of the ordinary (Fig. 13). Goujon's three-bay loggia, with no interior rooms to light, permitted an elegant, classical design which foreshadowed some of the finest French architecture of the seventeenth century. Each of the three bays was dominated by an open arch flanked by pairs of fluted Corinthian pilasters, between which bas-reliefs were set. An attic decorated with friezes rose above a restrained but assertive cornice. D. Thomson thinks the design reflects debates at court over Lescot's Louvre plans.[33] However, Parisians probably noted a resemblance to contemporary church monuments, which used Ancient components to achieve classical authenticity, rather than inserting them in a traditional framework. Sited in the city's most crowded and commercial district, the

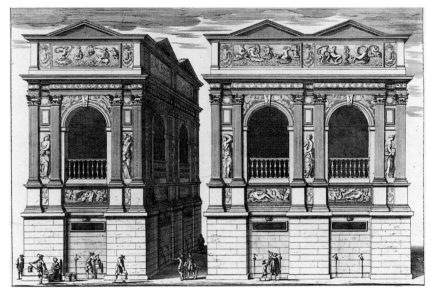

Fontaine des Innocents gave the people a glimpse of classical beauty before the ponderous structures of the Crown and aristocracy had risen above their footings.

## THE BURGESS HOUSE AND THE RENAISSANCE IDEAL

The people clearly liked classical design, which they associated with royal processions and celebrations, but the burgess house was very resistant to Renaissance influence. The average height probably increased in step with the population, but there were no major design changes in the sixteenth century apart from the occasional replacement of the gable by a pediment. Two facades of mid-sixteenth-century burgess houses later recorded by Lenoir carry carved friezes, and door and window pediments. The narrower house has

12 *Top*, elevation by Androuet du Cerceau of Lescot's courtyard front for the new Louvre.

13 *Above*, contemporary print of the two street elevations of the Fontaine des Innocents. The scale in relation to the human figures is greatly exaggerated.

a gable, and the other a pitched roof parallel to the facade, lit by pedimented dormers. Both have almost regular fenestration. There is nothing to suggest that the facades would conform to those of their neighbours, and both contemporary paintings and current survivals suggest that such houses would have been very much the exception in the sixteenth century.[34]

Traditional house construction methods were a big obstacle to Renaissance fashion. Timber-frame construction remained the norm in the sixteenth century, when it reached a peak of efficiency. Its visual results were unusual, and probably unique to Paris. The timber frame normally rested on a ground-floor circuit wall in heavy masonry, or on masonry piers. The main vertical timbers were angled inwards so that the facade leaned back towards the centre of the site. The ground floor, for its part, generally leaned outwards over the street (Fig. 14). Given that in many towns of northern Europe, timber-framed houses were jettied outwards to create extra room on the upper floors, the Paris practice is curious. In the absence of firm evidence, one can conjecture that royal efforts to prevent jettying had become successful some time in the later Middle Ages and that the carpenters had developed a much lighter frame now that it had to carry nothing more than a simple, clean facade. This interpretation conforms with the well-documented use of long, vertical beams, fashioned from the trunk of a single, very tall tree, to support the ceiling beams and other timbers up to the full height of the house. This method cut the amount of timber and carpentry to a minimum, but it appears likely that the use of rubble to fill the gaps between the timbers on the outer walls tended to pull these lighter frames apart (Fig. 15). The answer would have been to angle the front and back walls inwards, so that the weight of the walls would compress the horizontal beams and stabilise the whole.

The outward-leaning ground floor is even more difficult to explain. Clearly, the builders of backward-leaning houses sacrificed floor space. One solution was to jetty out the first floor above the street and lean back from there, but this was likely to run foul of the royal ban on jettying. The answer might therefore have been to lean the heavy ground-floor masonry outwards so that the project-

14 Façade with double lean in the Rue Cloche-Perce, probably dating from the sixteenth century.

15 Light timber framing in the Rue du Grenier-sur-l'Eau.

17

ing timber frame sprang, or appeared to spring, directly from the top of the masonry.

These building customs, widespread in the sixteenth century, produced bulbous facades which did not encourage the application of classical detailing. The timber frames of houses old and new could be rendered to provide a masonry-like surface, and this may have become a fashion as early as the sixteenth century. However, most burgess houses were too motley in their appearance to contribute to Renaissance street perspectives.

However, a trend towards order has been detected by Jean-Pierre Babelon, the leading authority on residential construction in early Paris. The building of adjacent houses to a common design became more frequent, and a greater taste for regularity is visible in the facades.[35] There may have been a movement towards wider houses, with a new type emerging around 1550. This had a wide, central bay flanked by two narrower bays. The central bay carried a modest gable or a pediment (Fig. 16).[36]

Two official initiatives were even more ambitious. In 1552 the Bureau de la Ville prepared a project for a row of houses between the Petit-Pont and the Hôtel-Dieu, on the island of the Cité. It had a continuous frontage of identical houses, each consisting of an arcade, two storeys and an attic roof. There were no gables; the roof was continuous and parallel to the street, as in some of Serlio's proposals. Moreover, the arcade contained classical features.[37] Then, in 1584, Henri III ordered the royal commissioners building a new street from the Pont-Neuf to the Pont Saint-Michel, on the Île de la Cité, to create building sites and to require the purchasers to build 'uniform houses according to the plans and estimates which they will receive'.[38] The results of both these projects are obscure, and any structures would have been swept away by Haussmann's clearances in the 1850s (see Chapter 6). It is clear, however, that the authorities wanted to build on the success of the Pont Notre-Dame by regularising other parts of the city.

Of course, the greatest potential for regularisation lay in the creation of new sections or districts as the city grew. The most recent estimate suggests that the population rose from 100,000 in 1500 to 130,000 at mid-century, with a sharp boost to 220,000 in 1600.[39] Early in the century, new districts grew up piecemeal, as they had in the Middle Ages.[40] The outer areas generated poor housing for the most part and there was no hope of careful layout here. However, much new land came from demolished *hôtels* and their gardens, vacated by their owners in their search for the most fashionable areas, and their abandonment of outdated styles and standards of comfort. Here there was a greater chance of an ordered *lotissement* (subdivision).

The royal family played a big part in this process as it moved out of the Marais, towards the Louvre. Using its unique powers, the Crown left a degree of order behind it. In 1543, for instance, François I sold five old *hôtels* in the Marais, including the rambling Hôtel Saint-Pol, which stood on an especially large site. The sale was governed by a royal edict, which allowed the cancellation of all the sub-leases agreed since the royal family had begun to vacate. The resulting Saint-Pol *lotissement* was given straight streets, ten metres (30 feet) in width. Large residential plots were laid out along the more secluded streets, while small plots lined the thoroughfares which were expected to be busiest. Here, the inclusion of a shop was envisaged.[41] In 1563, letters patent were published for the *lotissement* of the Hôtel des Tournelles. Jean de l'Orme, brother of Philibert, was to design a comprehensive scheme for streets and open spaces, including coherent street elevations for '*uniformes et semblables*' houses. The scheme was never started and no drawings have survived, but the intentions indicated progress towards the Renaissance ideal.[42]

The creation of new streets can sometimes obscure the day-to-day development of the old ones. The most important instrument of order was the *alignement*, or building line, which every structure was required to respect. The line was enforced from an obscure date in the Middle Ages by the Bureau de la Ville. In 1350 and 1388, the Crown intervened with ordinances protecting the thoroughfare from a variety of permanent and temporary intrusions.[43] An order of Henri II in 1554 requiring the demolition of houses which infringed the building line was very little applied, but it did suggest a growing royal concern for the achievement of the full potential width of the Paris streets at a time of increasing wheeled traffic.[44]

16 The house in the centre of this view, at 44–6, Rue François-Miron, probably dates from 1588. It was a town house of the Cistercian abbey of Ourscamp. The windows in the bays under the dormers were widened at a later date. The presence of a medieval, vaulted cellar indicates that at least one earlier house had stood on the site. The site was first developed by the abbey c. 1167.

A similar indication was provided by an ordinance of Charles IX in 1560, requiring owners to remove any projections over the thoroughfare when required to do so by the judges.[45] It was not, however, until the reign of Henri IV, at the end of the century, that the Crown made a concerted effort to regulate a city whose population had now passed its fourteenth-century peak.

HENRI IV AND HIS PLANS FOR A NEW PARIS

Henri IV (1589–1610) put Paris on the path of modernisation. Indeed, in a short reign he did more for the capital than any other French king, before or since. He combined regulation and royal projects in a single programme of improvements. His efforts in Paris were part of a wider attempt to create a national awareness in France after the Wars of Religion, and an efficient, impressive capital was essential to his objectives. His Italian queen, Marie de Medici, probably helped keep him in touch with Italian architecture, but his own interest in art and architecture would have been enough to make him sensitive to foreign developments.

Henri IV's experiments with piazzas too often divert attention from his city-wide regularisation programme. Regulations, and their enforcement by permanent officials, were the very foundation of his work. In 1600, he issued a royal order requiring owners to secure official confirmation of the building line before undertaking building or repairs. The order also banned all infringement of the line at ground level or in the form of projections.[46] In 1607, a fuller edict was issued, and the resulting creation of an administration appears to have established the *alignement* on a permanent basis.[47] The edict also sought to control some important aspects of building. The construction of timber houses was banned, including those with timber frames. Additions to existing facades which hung over the street, and new houses which projected structurally over the street, were also prohibited.[48]

The king's first big project was a large gallery building to link the Louvre to the Tuileries along the Seine frontage. Work started here in 1595, only a year after Paris had finally opened its gates to Henri as a Catholic convert. Three years later, the king ordered the completion of the Pont-Neuf, a project dating from 1578. In 1601, he was still giving priority to outstanding projects which had been delayed during the Wars of Religion. On 11 March 1601, for instance, he told the Bureau de la Ville that '. . . now that the country is at peace, regard must be paid to the embellishment of the kingdom, and in particular to finishing the projects begun by his predecessors, namely the Pont-Neuf and the [water supply] fountains'.[49] Within another three years, however, he had launched into a completely new venture of his own. In doing so, he created the tradition of the classical townscape in Paris.

## THE THREE PIAZZAS

The king's statement to the Bureau de la Ville linked beauty and utility in a way that was characteristic of him. A few years later he expressed this principle in his plans for three piazzas in the centre and east of the city, and a number of associated streets. They were all development projects, in that the sale of building sites was expected to recoup the initial investment, and all were intended to be commercial centres which would attract private capital. At the same time, they were to be designed by royal architects, with private owners required to follow the official elevations. Each piazza was intended to be an architectural entity, and there was to be no major divergence of style between the three of them.

In 1605 Henri announced his plans for a large piazza in the Marais. A royal silk manufactory was to be sited on the northern side and appeared to be intended as a workaday place. Then, in 1607, the king launched the Place Dauphine, a triangular piazza on the Île de la Cité, linked to the completed Pont-Neuf. In the same year, he approved a grander, more residential, scheme for the Marais piazza, now to be known as the Place Royale.[50] By 1610 he was working on a huge semi-circular piazza, with radiating streets, to the north of the Marais. This, the biggest project of all, was known as the Place de France.[51]

The Place Dauphine had the biggest commercial potential of the three. It was linked to the busy Pont-Neuf, completed in 1606, and was close to the Louvre and to the old palace on the Île de la Cité which still contained most of the royal administration. Henri IV entrusted the work to his minister, the Duc de Sully, Grand Voyer of France (Fig. 17). The architect was probably Claude de Chastillon (1547–1616), who had worked as a royal 'topographical engineer' since 1589.[52] The development lease was granted, in 1607, to a leading courtier, Achille de Harlay, first president of the Parlement de Paris.[53] The sale of sites was gradual, but not slow enough to undermine confidence.

The scheme extended much further east than the existing remains suggest. Much of the upper floors came to be taken up by furnished rooms, which were let to minor diplomats and provincials pursuing lawsuits in Paris. The arcades were filled with shops, workshops and restaurants catering for these prosperous transients, and the area soon became a place of fashionable resort.[54]

Commercial success enhanced the reputa-

17 The Place Dauphine project as seen by Claude de Chastillon, *c.* 1610.

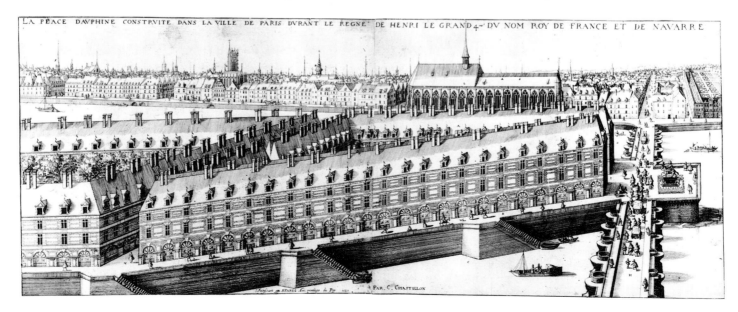

LA PLACE DAVPHINE CONSTRVITE DANS LA VILLE DE PARIS DVRANT LE REGNE DE HENRI LE GRAND 4ᵉ DV NOM ROY DE FRANCE ET DE NAVARRE

18 The Place Dauphine, west front, showing the only houses in approximately their original state.

tion of the visual qualities of the design. The distribution recalled the Pont Notre-Dame rows, with a commercial ground floor and two residential storeys, but the elevations were given an economical, Renaissance treatment (Fig. 18). A false arcade of round arches in rusticated masonry fronted the shops, their symmetry slightly distorted by narrow doorways. The upper floors were separated by horizontal masonry strips. Their identical, rectangular fenestration was arranged in bays above each arcade arch. A continuous roof with dormers replaced the gables of the Pont Notre-Dame. The facades were clad in brick, with stone dressings.

Like some of the *hôtels* of the period, the design combined the best Renaissance practice with French aristocratic traditions, very much in the manner of Serlio. The striking combination of brick and stone, for instance, was a French regional practice which made its Paris debut at the Hôtel de Nevers in 1582, and became fashionable thereafter.[55] Architectural historians have identified a variety of Italian influences, including Palladio and the piazza at Leghorn, apart from Serlio.[56] These are valid speculations, but the Place Dauphine has to be set in the context of Henri IV's determined campaign to unify the French nation around a modern capital city. Whatever the foreign contribution, the architecture of the piazza was intended to be seen as modern, French and Parisian.

The Place Royale was too remote to become a fashionable centre of commerce (Fig. 19). The solution here, after early indecision, was to emphasise fashionable residence by providing for a series of linked mansions behind a common facade. The large open space was reserved for parades and festivals. Sully, who had advised the move towards elegance as early as 1603, directed the project.[57] The king's letters patent of 1605 associated the needs of beauty, utility and recreation:

In the interests of the convenience and the ornament of our good town of Paris, we have decided to create a large square with buildings on four sides. The square will be appropriate to help the establishment of the silk industry which we want to attract to this kingdom. At the same time, it will serve as a promenade for the inhabitants of our town, who are very congested in their houses because of the multitudes of people who flood in from all sides. Moreover, on festival days, and on certain other occasions, great assemblies take place, for which such squares are very necessary.[58]

As at the Place Dauphine, the sales of sites envisaged shops on the ground floor, and the arcade was open, perhaps to allow spectators

19 Contemporary view of the completed Place Royale, with the equestrian statue of Louis XIII.

to shelter from rain (Fig. 20). The elevations were similar to those of the Place Dauphine, and may well have been the work of the same architect. However, the roof was different, with very tall, pitched roofs divided into hipped lengths of four bays. Large pavilions stood in the middle of each side. The proportions of the piazza match those proposed by Alberti, and the arcaded piazzas at Florence, Pienza and Vigevano must have been an inspiration.[59] On the other hand, the vertical effects were typically French and the result expressed a combination of tradition and modernity, like the Place Dauphine.

Little is known of the Place de France scheme, which was launched in 1609 but undermined by the king's death in 1610. Building lines were fixed for parts of the radiating streets but the architectural result was nil.[60] Plans and elevations were drawn up in 1609 by Jacques Alleaume and Claude de Chastillon, probably on the personal initiative of the king. The inspiration must have been the Piazza dell' Popolo in Rome. The Place de France was sited just inside the city to the north-east. Eight streets radiated from it towards the inner areas. They were named after French provinces, probably to symbolise

the union of Paris and the provinces, which official travellers were supposed to perceive on passing through the gates.

A drawing by one of the architects suggests that the style of the Place de France would have been similar to the other two piazzas (Fig. 21). Although nothing was built, the creation of building lines for sections of street, some of them in the following reign, suggests that attention was moving from piazzas to streets as a means of modernisation, particularly after Henri IV's big *alignement* edict of 1607. In 1607, for instance, the king had ordered Sully to require the owners of sites on the new street running south from the Pont-Neuf (Rue Dauphine) to adopt identical

20 The Place des Vosges (formerly Place Royale).

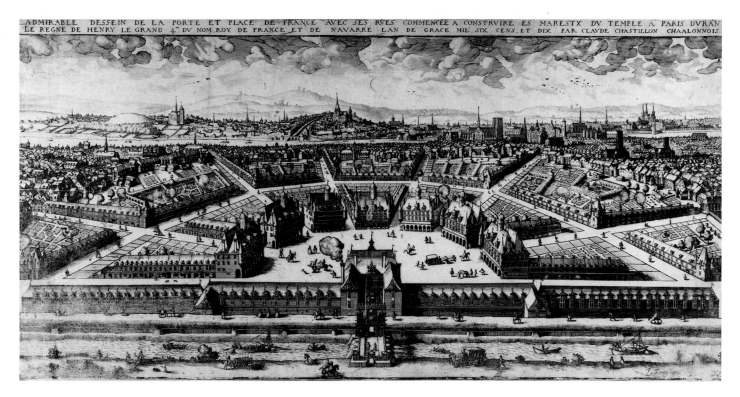

21 Claude de Chastillon's view of the Place de France project.

22 The Rue de Turenne, looking north towards the abortive Place de France.

facades, in order to provide '*un bel ornement*' at the end of the bridge.[61] This intervention had little effect, and was not repeated elsewhere, but building lines could at least determine the width and line of a new street, as at the Place de France.

The biggest achievement was the Rue de Turenne (Fig. 22). Historians have virtually ignored this puzzling echo of papal Rome, partly because its ramrod route had been fixed in the fifteenth century by a new sewer, and partly because its improvement was not begun until the reign of Louis XIII, when it was named after a minister rather than a province. As improved and developed by the mid-seventeenth century, it ran in a straight line from the Place de France to the Place Royale, and on through an angle to the Rue Saint-Antoine. If the seven other streets had been completed, the whole of the east of Paris would have been transformed, and its

modest destiny would never have come to pass. Even in its isolation, the Rue de Turenne suggests that, had he lived, Henri IV would be known today as the greatest early town planner. As it was, Henri gave Paris the pattern for three centuries of urban design. At last, the city had left the Middle Ages, and the way to a French urban classicism was open.

# 3    CREATING A FRENCH URBAN ARCHITECTURE, 1610–1715

## FROM ITALIAN RENAISSANCE TO FRENCH CLASSICISM

Despite the achievements of Henri IV and the leading *hôtel* architects, Renaissance architecture and planning had made only a fragmentary impact on Paris by the early 1600s (Fig. 23). French architects still faced the problem of creating an architecture that would be both classical and national, linking the Ancient world, Italian Renaissance theory and practice, and French taste and tradition.

One solution was to select ideal forms which could be used at any time, in a *classical* architecture which could outshine the Ancient world. This approach was encouraged by the rational cast of mind fostered by the Renaissance, and by the universal interest in the forms of Ancient architecture. Architects and scholars agreed that to identify persuasive proportions and a portfolio of design components would ensure true beauty, as in the Ancient world. At first, however, there was no agreement on what the proportions were.[1] The components, including columns, pilasters, capitals, lintels, pediments, porticos and niches, were easier to select, partly because they could be seen in position on the ancient ruins of Italy and southern France. Many undistinguished buildings relied on classical components, rather than proportions, to claim a classical identity.

However, there was a widespread feeling among French artists and thinkers that true beauty lay not just in regularity and proportion but in a unique quality of *grace*.[2] The arts and letters alike could share in the qualities of classicism. This aspiration transformed not just French architecture, but painting, literature, drama, music and all the other fields of creativity, during the seventeenth century. Creative artists looked beyond mere rules and the emulation of the past to a combination of harmony and originality which could guide and inspire a national cultural enterprise. Nothing like this French classicism had ever been seen before.

Underlying this extraordinary cultural phenomenon was France's position as the dominant country in seventeenth-century Europe, its Absolutist monarchy backed by a confident aristocracy and a compliant Church. Gradually, Italian classicism faded into the background. To the French, their art was classical, national and universal. Rather than stifling creativity, French classicism helped it to flourish. There were rules, but they held the arts together and provided the foundation for true invention.

The Crown used its own patronage to encourage classicism, just as François Ier and Henri IV had done during earlier stages of the Renaissance. A need was also felt, however, for formal, consultative and didactic

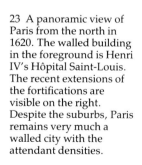

23  A panoramic view of Paris from the north in 1620. The walled building in the foreground is Henri IV's Hôpital Saint-Louis. The recent extensions of the fortifications are visible on the right. Despite the suburbs, Paris remains very much a walled city with the attendant densities.

institutions to create a national consensus among artists. The great royal academies, beginning with the Académie Française, created for Louis XIII by Richelieu in 1635, were unprecedented and, at first, unrivalled. The Académie Française was intended to establish the proper form of the French language. It was composed of a number of literary experts, appointed by the Crown, who met regularly and who were expected to produce some permanent record or product of their deliberations. The members soon decided to produce a dictionary and a grammar. The whole purpose of the exercise was to secure, under benevolent royal patronage, a French national orthodoxy which could be disseminated throughout the realm. It was foreseen that this creative process would reinforce the Crown's authority by providing a common French language for the diverse French provinces and the growing empire.

## THE ACADÉMIE ROYALE D'ARCHITECTURE

It took time to agree a basis for classicism in French architecture. Tradition was pervasive, and Italy was hard to ignore. Regionalism was a further complication in such a large country.

The Crown gave a strong lead, especially under Louis XIV (1643–1715). The mercantilism of Louis' minister, Colbert, provided a background for an expressive, national architecture, and the aristocracy followed the royal example. The foundation of academies continued. Mazarin founded the Académie Royale de Peinture et de Sculpture in 1648, and Colbert created several more academies from 1661. The Académie Royale d'Architecture, the last of the series, was founded in 1671, as an outgrowth of Colbert's Conseil des Bâtiments, which advised on royal buildings.[3] Some architects resented their tardy admission to the pantheon, but it resulted from an earlier assumption that architecture was an association of arts rather than an independent entity. The development of thinking on this point had nevertheless worked in the architects' favour, for by the time they were elevated to academic rank they had acquired a central role in all aspects of building design, including interior decoration.

The purpose of this new academy was practical, not scholarly; the eight members met once a week to study architectural problems. Their conclusions were disseminated through a formal record and publications. There was also a programme of lectures on two days each week, which was expected to generate 'a seminary, so to speak, of young architects'.[4] They soon became a full course of study, which by the early eighteenth century lasted two or three years.[5] They included, on Louis XIV's orders, an extensive scientific instruction, including subjects such as mathematics, geometry and hydraulics.[6] While attending these classes, students would normally learn the practical aspects of architecture by working in the studio of one of the academicians. This was the origin of the *atelier* system of instruction. Students who completed the programme successfully could obtain Crown employment.

From an early date, outstanding students were sent to Rome for lengthy study of the Ancient remains. This practice arose from the king's personal wish that prizes should be presented to the best students, with Rome as the ultimate reward. The king offered to pay the expenses of the Rome students, and he was able to lodge them in the Académie de France à Rome, founded in 1666 to promote the study of the arts at the very source of classical inspiration. As most of the Rome scholars later became academicians themselves, they were an important force in the retention of classical influence within French architecture.[7]

The academy's course had to embody clarity and authority. These qualities were visible as early as 1675 when the first director of the Académie d'Architecture, François Blondel, started to publish his lectures.[8] Such publication, which became normal in French higher education, not only helped students attending the academy course, but spread the academy's teaching throughout France and even abroad. At the same time, it tended to crystallise Blondel's teaching as a finite body of knowledge and to discourage debate among both students and professors. Blondel's text remained in wide use in the eighteenth century, and the academy course took it as a given.

Blondel was a great enthusiast for Ancient architecture, as he demonstrated in spectacular fashion with his Porte Saint-Denis in 1672 (Fig. 24). His teaching was rooted in the

24 The Porte Saint-Denis and the *grands boulevards*.

classical tradition as expounded by Vitruvius, but he showed great respect for the leading Italian theorists, Vignole, Palladio and Scamozzi. This admiration for Italian interpretations of the classical was common to the early French authorities, and Blondel made no attempt to belittle the Italian theoretical achievement. In his dedication to Louis XIV, however, Blondel expressed florid, national sentiments. Only with the splendour of Louis' reign had a start been made on effacing the crimes of the Barbarians, he averred. Developing the compliment, Blondel opined that Louis XIV had at long last given architects the chance to build monuments which could

rise above those of Ancient times. Their works would sustain the king's renown and perhaps even immortalise it. To sum up:

> And so will architecture, restored by the French, appear in all its brilliance and all its glory. It will fill your territories with so many magnificent buildings that the whole world will look on in wonder. In future, foreigners will come here to learn about the principles of architecture as well as to perfect their studies of the other virtues.[9]

Although this robust rhetoric must have been inspired in part by a sense of grievance that the elevation of architecture to academic status had been so long delayed, it would prove to have an extraordinary durability. It reflected a spirit of French architecture which would survive until the twentieth century and, in formal terms, until 1968. The utter confidence of Blondel and his successors consecrated the French interpretation of classical architecture. Alternatives were discouraged, and even variants were frowned on unless they sprang from within the academy via a consensual process. We have not seen the last of Blondelian rhetoric.

It must be stressed nonetheless that national rhetoric figured only in the introduction to Blondel's course. His lectures were solid, scientific expositions of the fundamentals of classical architecture. His main emphasis was on the orders, and their use in various types of colonnade and pediment. He treated elevations mainly in terms of arcades, storeys and bays, with arches, doors and windows discussed in turn. Vaults, ceilings and domes were not treated by Blondel, probably because they were studied by another professor elsewhere in the programme. Blondel's great expertise as a mathematician, in which he had tutored the Dauphin, clearly helped him establish exact proportions. The result was a system of related measurements, effortlessly producing complex forms within an infallible system of control. As presented in his book, Blondel's lectures formed a comprehensive and highly demanding course. Graduates must have felt that they had acquired an invaluable expertise, far superior to any architectural system which their own imaginations might have created. Professorial posturing alone could not have produced this result.

The academy thus accelerated the creation of a single, classical architecture in France. By the end of the seventeenth century that architecture was present in a multitude of new palaces, chateaux, mansions and churches. The many Crown commissions of the time played a big part in refining an architecture which was expected to meet royal demands above all. More striking, however, was the application of the new architecture to quite humble domestic buildings, especially in Paris. In all of this there was a national confidence which no other country enjoyed. It was to prove to be a self-renewing confidence.

## FROM ARCHITECTURAL PRINCIPLES TO THE ARCHITECTURE OF STONE

In Paris, the main French model for urban architecture, the second half of the seventeenth century saw impressive progress towards classical homogeneity. This was the product of a number of convergent factors.

First, a handful of key building types were distinguished and defined so closely that their architectural treatment tended to become more conventional than it had been as recently as the early seventeenth century. *Hôtels* and churches were the most numerous of these types. Second, the appropriate architecture for extensions of the Louvre was finally decided in the 1670s after a long period of wrangling. Third, architects became the normal designers of *hôtels*. Fourth, a growing proportion of architects were formally trained. Fifth, the burgess houses, which were still normally built by master masons rather than architects, remained sufficiently anonymous to complement classical buildings rather than clash with them. Finally, and perhaps most important, the aristocracy built so much in Paris, even after the royal departure to Versailles, that their tendency to follow royal taste, and their own love of mutual emulation, scattered classical architecture across the city. In many streets, two or more *hôtels* would be visible from any one point, producing a townscape of distinction and deference. Noble homes studded Florence and Venice in the same way, but only Paris was growing and only Paris had the new architecture of classical harmony.

The spread of classical architecture was not simply a function of genius, brilliance or even competence, however. With the academy course dealing with theory rather than practice, even qualified architects continued to lean heavily on engravings of influential designs, on visits to completed buildings in Paris and outside, and on personal contacts with leading members of the profession. Many architects were related by blood or marriage, and the resulting dynasties often led to artistic perpetuation or proliferation. The master masons were even more dependent on engravings and examples. The continuing standardisation of the *hôtel*, in particular, allowed the more workaday architects and master masons to follow recent and current design without mere copying, and without distorting the classical norm.

Towards the end of the century a growing number of texts made much use of engravings of recent architecture. Augustin Daviler, a titled architect, published his *Cours d'architecture* in 1710. His text was mainly a glossary of terms, and a collection of advice on the use of individual classical features such as niches. The value of all this was not evident, but contemporaries probably drew most guidance from his third volume, which contained a large number of plates drawn mainly from the work of French architects. The book was probably addressed to master masons, who would have found little use for theory. However, the spread of works of this type at a time when master masons were giving way to the architects suggests that they were playing a part in the design of *hôtels*.

By the end of the seventeenth century, therefore, the city's basic building types had moved a long way towards acquiring a conventional appearance and a standard architecture, which even moderate practitioners could reproduce. This was the key to the survival of classicism in a crowded and competitive city which might well have choked it.

THE PARISIAN CONTEXT

During the seventeenth century the population of Paris rose from about 220,000 to 510,000. By 1700 London had taken its place as the largest city in Europe but its population was still only slightly larger.[10] The resulting spread of building was accelerated from 1670, when Louis XIV demolished the entire defensive circuit.[11]

There was little change in the building forms fostered by past congestion, however. The tall burgess house continued to multiply, and the Hôtel de Beauvais and many other *hôtels* were built on constricted sites (Fig. 25). A number of new streets and street networks were laid out on the outskirts, some of them on a novel scale. Some were aristocratic districts, like the spacious Rue de Tournon approach to the Luxembourg palace in the south. Others were prompted by the plans

25 Elevation of the Hôtel de Beauvais during a royal parade, *c.* 1660.

for a new fortification circuit, under discussion in the 1620s and 1630s. In the northwest, where a reinforcement of the existing advanced earthworks created many hectares of building land, the resulting street pattern was close to a grid in places where modest structures were envisaged, notably in the triangle lying between the Rue Beauregard and the *grands boulevards*.[12]

Although most of the new sites were developed independently by their purchasers, the general effect was often one of space and organisation. Most striking of all was the division of the entire Île Saint-Louis into streets and building sites from 1614 to about 1645. Some of the city's most elegant new *hôtels*, such as Le Vau's Hôtel Lambert de Thorigny (1640), were built on the Seine frontage, while more modest houses fronted the inner streets. Similar effects were achieved when new streets were opened to serve *hôtels* in the aristocratic Faubourg Saint-Germain and Faubourg Saint-Honoré to the west. Most of the new streets opened during the century were straight, and up to ten metres broad, which allowed regular buildings to appear at their best.

In addition, the seventeenth century saw the emergence of two new types of thoroughfare. These were the boulevard and the avenue, both of them associated with the spacious outskirts of the city. The boulevard was a product of Louis XIV's demolition of the fortifications in the early 1670s. By this time the defences on the Right Bank were a

26 The mature *grands boulevards* promenade: the Boulevard des Capucines at the corner of the Rue de la Paix, painted by Robert Stanley, *c.* 1830.

modern, gunnery-related circuit with various stages of fortification using a lot of land. When they were dismantled, a crescent of open land was cleared from near the Tuileries palace in the west to the Arsenal in the east. Its depth varied, being greatest along the newer fortifications in the west, but there was a minimum depth of some hundred metres.

These northern fortifications had been a popular promenade for some time. They commanded a rural prospect, for they had been routed across higher ground, or had been banked up over depressions. Behind the defences proper lay a broad, well-drained *'boulevard'* (from the German *Bollwerk*), an elevated strip for lateral movements of men and equipment. This boulevard was linked by ramps to the city streets.

On the removal of the fortifications, the Crown decided to retain the promenade as a broad avenue, the *grands boulevards*. Strollers were attracted in even larger numbers, and the frontages were gradually developed. In the west, especially, the *grands boulevards* (Fig. 26) became a centre of fashion and the

aristocracy built mansions and pavilions there, such as the Pavillon de Hanovre of 1760. The bucolic atmosphere survived into the early nineteenth century, and the *grands boulevards* were a scene of architectural variety unique in Paris.

The avenue's parallel lines of trees gave it much in common with the boulevard, but it originated in the seventeenth century as a landscape architect's device linking town and country. Only with the spread of building did it become part of the urban scene.[13] The biggest was the avenue of the Champs-Elysées (Fig. 27), laid out from 1667 by the landscape architect Lenôtre as an approach to the west front of the Tuileries palace.[14] Meanwhile, on the Left Bank, the construction of the Invalides in an isolated position from 1671 prompted the creation of a tree-lined approach linking the main front northwards to the Seine, and three diverging avenues to the south (Figs 28, 29). The southern avenues were mainly symbolic, but their convergence on Hardouin-Mansart's great dome of 1708 created the most exciting perspective effect yet seen in Paris. Like the *grands boulevards*,

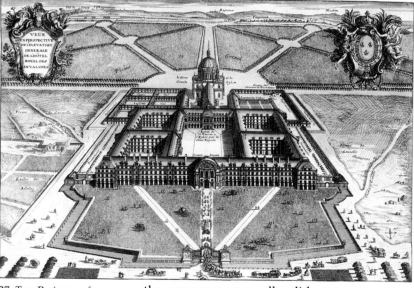

27 *Top*, Paris seen from the Champs-Elysées in 1741, by Crevenbroeck. Visible from the left are the avenue of the Champs-Elysées, the Tuileries, the Cours-la-Reine following the Seine, and the approach to the Invalides on the opposite bank. The transversal avenue in the foreground is probably the present Avenue Georges-V.

the avenues generally did not promote a homogeneous architecture, as the Champs-Elysées demonstrate to this day, but the perspectives were formed by the trees, not the buildings (Fig. 30).

As a permanent building site, the Louvre remained a constant source of debate. The Seine frontage gallery, under prolonged construction from 1594 by Jacques du Cerceau and L. Métezeau, was more coherent than Lescot's work, though the articulation of the facade still caused problems (Fig. 31). The courtyard frontages were extended by Lemercier and others in the early part of the century (Fig. 32), but the need to harmonise with Lescot's work probably contributed to these bland elevations. By the middle of the century, Italian architecture was again in favour at court and a move to a baroque style was in the offing. This was all part of the long search for an ideal, French architecture, but to contemporaries the picture looked confused.

When Colbert became Superintendent of Buildings in 1664 he was well placed to commission designs which would express his own strong concepts of a royal, Parisian architecture. Like some of his predecessors, he attached great importance to the Louvre as the epitome of the desired style. Widely accepted as the next task here was the construction of the eastern front of the Louvre, which faced a huddle of small houses and the church of Saint-Germain-l'Auxerrois.

Thanks to patronage by the influential Fouquet, and indirectly by Mazarin, the architect Louis le Vau had already had the

chance to draw up plans for the eastern front.[15] Colbert undermined Le Vau by consulting other architects, including Mansart, Bernini and other Italians.[16] None of the resulting proposals was acceptable to Colbert, however, while controversy mounted at the court as the competing architects sought support. Bernini's criticisms of French taste caused particular distress, but his own designs – both those completed in Rome, and the one completed in Paris after he arrived there in 1665 – found little favour, no doubt because of their extravagant, rococo character. When he returned to Rome in 1665 there was no sign of a solution.

In the following year Colbert required Le Vau and two other architects to produce a joint design. One of the newcomers, Claude Perrault, a classical enthusiast, proved to be the most persuasive. In 1667 a design was agreed for a simple, monumental facade dominated by porticos and a colonnade of giant columns (Fig. 33).[17] This diverged from the recent designs of Le Vau and also of Mansart, both of whom had envisaged huge features rising above the cornice.[18] Mansart's proposed dome echoed recent church designs in Paris, but Perrault's influence clearly came from imperial, not papal, Rome.

Perrault built the eastern, and then the southern, fronts of the Louvre between 1667

28 *Far left*, bird's-eye view of the Invalides from the north, showing the three radiating avenues to the south.

29 *Left centre*, aerial photograph of the Invalides from the south, c. 1980.

30 *Left below*, the three radiating avenues in their urbanised form, 1991.

31 *Below*, the original courtyard frontage of the new Louvre, showing Lescot's design to the left of the tower. The tower and the balancing frontage to the right are mainly the work of Lemercier.

32 *Top right*, central pavilion and frontages of the north courtyard façade of the new Louvre, by Lemercier.

33 *Right below*, engraving by Charpentier showing a version of Perrault's design for the east front of the Louvre.

and 1680. His elevations broke away from the awkward compartmentalism into which Lescot had drawn his successors. His taste for columns, porticos and pediments produced a powerful, classical effect on the east front, which was designed more to be viewed from outside than as a frame for interior rooms. A long colonnade was bounded by two pavilions, with a portico in the middle. The low roof was masked by a balustrade. This heroic statement showed for the first time in Paris what classical purism could achieve in the grand manner (Fig. 34). The scope for its application to aristocratic architecture was small, however. The setting back of the first and second floors behind a colonnade of paired columns involved the sacrifice of floor space and light, together with massive construction costs. What it provided above all was a stunning demonstration of the townscape potential of classicism, and a foretaste of the city of reason which an Absolutist Crown could create.

The southern facade, which faced towards the Seine, also used the giant order, but these rooms were meant to profit from the attractive prospect, and bas-relief pilasters were used instead of columns. The elevation was adjusted in consequence, but Perrault's successful articulation of a second, very long facade using classical principles reinforced the townscape potential of his work (Fig. 35).

The influence of the new design was, however, weakened by Louis XIV's decision in 1665 to build a new palace at Versailles. He chose Le Vau as his principal architect and the resulting free, ornate design made Perrault's classicism look cold and prim. Louis never showed much interest in the eastern front of the Louvre, which remained hemmed in by huddled houses.[19] The Versailles project undermined any ambitions

34 The central section of Perrault's east front of the Louvre.

35 Paris shaped by the Crown, at the end of the seventeenth century. The right bank of the Seine is dominated by the new Louvre courtyard and the Seine gallery running down to the Tuileries palace, near the Pont-Royal. The Pont-Neuf crosses to the Place Dauphine. The dome of the Collège des Quatre-Nations can be seen on the left.

which Colbert might have had to turn Paris into a new Rome. He went on to promote a number of isolated schemes, such as the triumphal arches of the 1670s, but his funds were limited and grandiose classical revivals were difficult for private builders and architects to emulate in residential projects. Colbert's weakness confirmed the aristocracy as the leading patrons of Paris architecture, and this meant that the *hôtel*, rather than the palace or the arch, would remain the leading expression of classicism.

## THE HÔTEL AS A PROTOTYPE OF CLASSICISM

The development of the Paris *hôtel* during the seventeenth century is one of the most brilliant episodes in the history of architecture. A dynamic amalgam of Renaissance, tradition and Mannerism was gradually replaced by a mature classicism. The process of change was an ordered one. No anarchic 'battle of the styles' took place, and the city was not disfigured by individualistic statements. Architects used a common syntax and vocabulary of design, expanded by their own efforts. What enhanced the achievement was the modest scale of most *hôtel* projects. Many were on small or inconvenient sites, with other buildings close by; many others involved the alteration or extension of older mansions, which was often the most difficult task of all.

During the seventeenth century, the Serlian plan of symmetrical courtyard and garden, separated by a house of rectangular plan, became the norm for nearly all the larger new *hôtels*. The mature form was present by the 1640s, thanks partly to the efforts of influential architects such as François Mansart, Pierre le Muet and Louis le Vau, whose clients included the Crown.[20] In very large *hôtels* a service courtyard was laid out beside the main one, usually with its own street access, and surrounded by stabling and stores (Fig. 36).[21]

Architecturally, the most important frontage was that of the main building, facing the courtyard. This was what visitors saw on arrival, however briefly. To enhance this approach the main building was slightly lifted and the entrance was approached by ornamental steps. The entrance was normally in the centre of the main building, but in the smaller *hôtel* it could be at a corner, in one of the wings. Every effort was made to create a rectangular, enclosed space in the courtyard by the identical design of the elevations of the flanking wings. Sometimes, where there was room for only one wing, a dummy frontage was provided on the other side, as at Le Muet's Hôtel de Saint-Aignan of 1645–50. This was, in effect, a reduced, urban version of the approach to a country chateau. However, while the main frontage of the chateau was normally visible from a distance, and designed to impress the local populace as well as visitors, the facade of the main body of the *hôtel* was usually masked by the con-

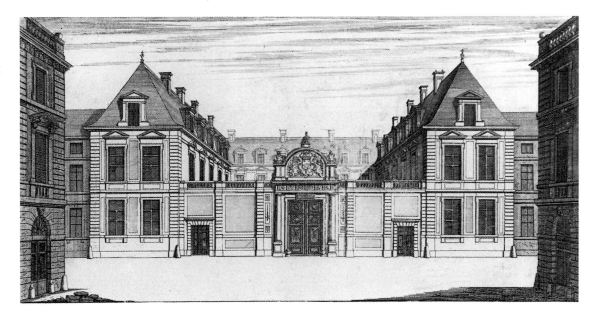

36 A classic *hôtel* street frontage: the Hôtel de Séguier, 1634. The *architecture d'accompagnement* framing the *hôtel* is clearly more wish than reality.

structions on the street frontage. The Serlian *hôtel* thus allowed the nobility to occupy an interior world of gentility within the teeming city, while their architects could build with confidence in both town and country.

Stone soon became the universal building material. The use of brick panels declined and after about 1660 they went completely out of fashion. By this time, it was generally accepted that classicism required a 'noble' material.[22] The use of stone ruled out polychromatic effects and generated a greater emphasis on stone-carving as a means of enlivening the facade. This was an important step towards the monochrome Paris of the nineteenth century.

The seventeenth-century *hôtel* was a challenge to the architect, mainly because high standards of symmetry were hard to achieve on all but the largest sites.[23] The old Mannerism would have emphasised distortions, but the restrained elevations of classicism diluted their effect. On the smaller sites the architect sought a formal intimacy using classical proportions which usually made the buildings and spaces look larger than they were. Restrained exterior treatment helped the architect to harmonise the frontages of the *hôtel*. Interior and exterior design schemes were closely linked. The same proportions were used and there was some continuity of motif, but the interiors were distinguished by rich, multi-coloured decorations and profuse carving. As the century wore on, a growing exterior simplicity was accompanied by more ornate interiors, as though some compensation were required for the exterior constraints. By 1700 these interior treatments verged on the rococo, but their basis in classicism was never lost.

The Hôtel de Sully (Fig. 37), built probably by Jacques Androuet du Cerceau for Henri IV's former minister in 1625, was a transitional design. With two floors and a dormer roof, it was a restrained but harmonious design, lacking classical features but based on the courtyard plan (Fig. 38). Similar proportions, though with more extensive rustication and a fortress-like treatment of the ground floor, were adopted by J. Thircot at his Hôtel Tubeuf (1635–42). Here and in other *hôtels* of the 1630s and 1640s, the pitched roof was retained, while in other cases the two main floors were topped by an attic, thus creating a tripartite division of the vertical lines of the

37 The street frontage of the Hôtel de Sully, recently restored, in 1969. (Photo: H.R. Walden).

facade. A compromise roof solution, the double-pitch (mansard) roof, was widely used from the 1640s, and its origins may have been even earlier.[24] Most roofs were partly masked by balustrades.

Progress towards a mature classicism by mid-century is reflected in the Hôtel de Saint-Aignan (Fig. 39).[25] This was a restricted and awkward site. The long, two-storey street frontage with pedimented dormers was clearly planned to supplement the limited floor space available on the site. It gave no hint of the spacious courtyard within. The awkward, northern corners of the site were crammed with rooms for daily living and a

38 The Hôtel de Sully courtyard.

tiny, secondary courtyard with a poky access, so that the greater part of the site could be given over to the ambitious courtyard (31 by 21 metres, 101 by 68 feet), a shallow garden, a first-floor gallery some 35 metres (110 feet) long, and a main building of limited dimensions. The significance of this design was that the architect and client attached such importance to the increasingly conventional Serlian plan and to the creation of classical facades in the courtyard and on the garden frontage that they sacrificed both floor space and convenience. With the Hôtel de Saint-Aignan, the classical *hôtel* was firmly established in Paris.

The giant order of Corinthian pilasters or columns, used to good effect in the courtyard facades of the Hôtel de Saint-Aignan, became common from the 1640s, especially in the courtyards.[26] Rusticated masonry became more usual, often in the form of vertical strips and surrounds for openings, as at the Hôtel Salé (Fig. 40). Arcades, using mainly round arches, were frequent. The round-arched

window, already present in the later six-teenth century, was reintroduced into the more correct classical facades of the mid-seventeenth. It mormally appeared on one floor only, to provide emphasis or variety, and it rarely undermined the coherence of the fenestration. Claude Perrault's Observatory of 1668–72 even used two levels of arched windows without explicit use of the orders, yet did not abandon the classical effect. Liberal Bruant's interior courts at the Invalides, built between 1671 and 1676, were dominated by huge, arched openings at both arcade and gallery levels (Fig. 41). Curved lines also appeared in the striking attached rotunda or bay at the Hôtel Lambert de Thorigny on the Île Saint-Louis. Some of

39 *Left*, the Hôtel de Saint-Aignan, street frontage.

40 *Top*, garden front of the Hôtel Salé, 1656, after restoration.

41 *Above*, main courtyard of the Invalides. The arcades were designed to allow veterans to stroll and rest in the shade, and their emphatic design reflects a central function of the building.

42 Courtyard front of the Hôtel de Soubise.

43 *Below left*, garden front of the Hôtel de Rohan.

44 *Below right*, courtyard front of the Hôtel de Rohan. Note the greater width of the garden front.

these features echoed the baroque style favoured by the Roman Catholic Church in its revival against Protestantism, but they did not overstep the bounds of classicism.

The departure of the court to Versailles restricted the building of aristocratic *hôtels* in Paris until the early 1700s. Smaller mansions now became the main area of innovation, with an emphasis on intimacy and even charm. Italianate features flourished in this climate. The best example was the house of the architect Liberal Bruant, built in the Marais in 1685, which reflected art rather than power and wealth in its modest, pedimented frontage de-formalised by a pattern of arched windows and niches. Lassurance's Hôtel de Charolais of 1700–4 was so relaxed in its use of arched openings that the classical

framework of its main elevation faded into the background.

The Versailles era was too short, however, to turn Paris into a city of modest charm. During the last years of Louis XIV's reign, court life at Versailles declined and the nobility turned back towards Paris. The building of large *hôtels* now resumed. Outstanding were the Hôtel de Soubise (1704–9) and the Hôtel de Rohan (1705–10) in the Marais, both by Delamair (Figs 42–4). Each combined impressive displays of columns and pilasters with arched arcades and other curved features. On these large sites, however, the traditional plan could be laid out without difficulty and the architect was at pains to push the overall effect of symmetry and order to a new degree of perfection. The designs were probably intended by the clients, the princely Rohan family, to reflect political stability and continuity, encouraging the architect to conjure up royal associations. The Hôtel de Soubise, especially, exploited its sweeping site in regal fashion (Fig. 45). No one who saw it could have doubted the thrall of classicism, and few could have detected any scope for improvement. With the Hôtel de Soubise and the Hôtel de Rohan, classical architecture had matured in Paris.

THE CHURCH, THE DOME AND THE BAROQUE

The church, like the *hôtel*, acquired a distinctive form under classicism. Church architects were content to limit themselves to classical

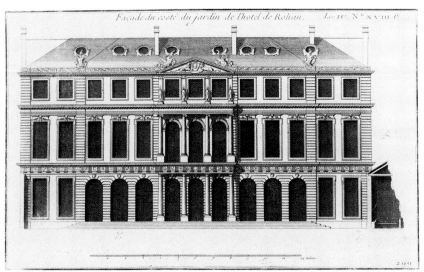

detailing until the early seventeenth century but they went on towards a complete design formula. This developed in the context of the understanding between the French Crown and the papacy by which the French Church was allowed to function as a national institution provided that the State defended its status.

The first step was to add massive, classical fronts to existing churches. As early as 1606 work started on a west front for the mainly Gothic church of Saint-Etienne-du-Mont (Fig. 46). By 1641, two more large fronts had been completed (Figs 47, 48). Although these designs were clumsy and pedestrian, their dimensions were impressive. Facing existing small open spaces or *parvis*, they made a bigger impact on the townscape than the *hôtels*.

From the 1630s the emphasis began to switch from alterations and additions to the building of new churches. Design conventions now became more coherent. Central to this religious classicisation was the acceptance of the dome as a quasi-essential feature of a modern church (Fig. 49). The inspiration came from Michelangelo's dome of St Peter's in Rome, but liturgical factors also played their part. During the Counter-Reformation it was agreed that the faithful should be brought closer to the altar and the pulpit. The space under the dome helped meet this need. Natural lighting could be enhanced by windows in the drum of the dome. At the same time, the nave was shortened and widened, and the chancel was greatly truncated and terminated by an apse. Fluted pilasters and Corinthian capitals separated

45 *Above*, panoramic view of the Hôtel de Soubise. The structures on the right are mainly service buildings of the *hôtel*. The size of the courtyard allowed the Hôtel de Soubise to figure as the Elysée palace in the film *Day of the Jackal*, a result which its creators would probably have taken as a compliment.

46 *Below left*, the new west front of the church of Saint-Etienne-du-Mont.

47 *Below right*, the new west front of the Eglise Saint-Gervais in a contemporary engraving.

straining of the Gothic church gave way to an effect of comfortable, relaxed strength both inside and outside the building.

This was formula architecture of astounding conformity. Wren went out of his way to vary his church designs in post-Fire London, but the parish authorities and religious communities of seventeenth- (and eighteenth-) century Paris bowed to a Roman ideal of conformity. The resulting dynasty of domes, particularly on the scholarly and abbatial Left Bank, created an Italianate skyline which loomed over the Gothic towers and spires of the inner city. The interiors, meanwhile, exposed the faithful to a lush form of classicism which recalled the ornate, baroque interior of the noble *hôtel*. Attendance at mass allowed the aristocratic household to renew its acquaintance with classicism, while the middle classes could taste an environment which they could not afford at home. At church, reality and aspiration were combined in a subtle and persuasive amalgam which strengthened the classical ideal from which both Church and State benefited.

The first product of the new thinking was François Mansart's transitional Sainte-Marie de la Visitation, completed in 1634. The domed church of the Sorbonne, built by Lemercier between 1635 and 1642, was the first mature product of the new, Roman

48 The west front of the Eglise Saint-Gervais.

49 A contemporary engraving of the west front of the church of Saint-Paul. The central dome is not visible in this illustration.

the bays. The triforium was abolished, allowing each nave arch to be repeated immediately above by a large window arch, pouring light into the nave and transepts through plain glazing. The smooth surfaces of the barrel or groin vaults were ideal for decoration with celestial scenes. The tense, upward

50 Bird's-eye view of the monastery of the Val-de-Grâce.

51 *Right above*, the Collège des Quatre-Nations in an engraving of 1670 by Silvestre. The incredible assembly of boats is probably intended to suggest a Venetian elegance and vitality.

52 *Right below*, aerial view of the Institut de France.

classicism. The years 1646–67 saw the construction of the royal monastery of the Val-de-Grâce, further to the south, with an ornate dome over the chapel which came closer to the baroque of papal Rome than any other major construction in Paris (Fig. 50). In this case, François Mansart's original plans were completed by Lemercier, Le Muet and Le Duc. Meanwhile, Le Vau and Liberal Bruant showed that the dome could be a very simple structure when they designed a sectional dome for the new Salpétrière hospital, built between 1660 and 1670. The eminent Jules Hardouin-Mansart's slender dome at the chapel of the Invalides was completed in 1706.

PUBLIC BUILDINGS IN THE VERSAILLES ERA

Secular public buildings were rare in Paris until the seventeenth century. This began to change under Louis XIV. The most important example was the Collège des Quatre-Nations (now Institut de France, or 'Institut Mazarin'). Built by Le Vau between 1663 and 1691 on the Left Bank of the Seine, opposite the Louvre, and financed by a bequest of Cardinal Mazarin, this extensive structure was arranged around interior courtyards, with two wings forming a hollow frontage on

either side of a domed chapel. The baroque style would have complemented Le Vau's proposals for the south front of the Louvre, opposite, had not Perrault's purer classicism been preferred.

The Collège provided a new variation on the formula for prestige spaces (Figs 51, 52),

39

with two-storey facades and a false arcade and a first floor with rectangular fenestration, linked by a giant order of engaged Corinthian pilasters. The two pavilions at the end of the wings sported massive hipped roofs with flat tops, equal in height to a third storey. Very much in the French tradition, they offset the strongly Roman character of the central church (Fig. 53).

The reign of Louis XIV also saw the creation of a structure which, from the very beginning, symbolised Parisian classicism. This was the triumphal arch which, after numerous fleeting appearances at royal parades since the sixteenth century, acquired a permanent form in the 1670s. When the fortifications were removed from 1670, all the old fortified gates were removed. After some discussion, the Crown commissioned the replacement of three of them by monumental structures. François Blondel was appointed to direct the work. Two were triumphal arches: the Porte Saint-Denis (Fig. 54), built by François Blondel in 1672 at the very begin-

ning of his directorship of the Académie d'Architecture, and the Porte Saint-Martin (Fig. 55), built in 1674 by his pupil, Pierre Bullet. The third arch was a fussy reconstruction of the Porte Saint-Antoine which satisfied no one.

It is clear that the arch programme was very important to the Crown and that the imperial symbolism was deliberate. Blondel was just the man for the task. As an enthusiast for Ancient Rome, he had long hoped for the chance to design a big Roman building. For him the triumphal arch was the acme of classical architecture, and Latin was the supreme language of power. His own account suggests that building the Porte Saint-Denis took him through an exciting reincarnation as an Ancient. He drew his inspiration from the greatest triumphal arches of Ancient Rome, and his Latin inscriptions converted Louis XIV's victories into imperial triumphs.[27] This dramatic authenticity reinforced Perrault's work at the Louvre and announced the neo-classicism of the follow-

53 View of the Institut showing a variety of concave spaces.

54 *Top*, the Porte Saint-Denis, looking north.

55 *Above*, the Porte Saint-Martin. The leaning house on the left, cleverly called 'Au-delà des limites', may date back to the later sixteenth century. It typifies the constructions which clustered outside the Paris gates from the Middle Ages.

ing century. The triumphal arch, meanwhile, was acclaimed by court and citizenry. It would reappear time after time in the design history of Paris, and as late as the 1980s.

THE REVIVAL OF THE PIAZZA

No new piazzas had been built in Paris since Henri IV's reign but the idea revived towards the end of Louis XIV's. Far more important than the mere creation of further piazzas was the transition from royal to private initiative which implied that market demand alone could prompt a piazza scheme. The two successful projects were speculative developments exploiting the piazza's established attractions as a residence for the rich. How-

ever, the promoters valued royal support and presented their efforts as a tribute to the rampant Absolutism of the day.

By the 1680s many towns were talking about celebrating Louis XIV's victories with an equestrian statue of the monarch. Ideally, the statue had to be located in a piazza to create the correct viewing distance and angle, as defined by Italian and French authorities. All this was easier said than done. However, in Paris the initiative was taken by a distinguished military commander, the Maréchal de la Feuillade. He had commissioned a statue of Louis XIV in 1681, and had given it to the king. He then decided to make a replica for display in Paris. It was completed in 1684, but De la Feuillade still had nowhere to erect it.

The solution was a property development scheme involving the Maréchal, a group of backers and the municipality. To create a circular piazza – the ideal location for a statue, according to the classicists – De la Feuillade bought an old mansion near the Halles, and agreed to combine part of its large garden with a number of properties which the municipality undertook to expropriate. The layout was entrusted to the leading Parisian architect of the day, Jules Hardouin-Mansart, who designed a piazza with a diameter of 39 metres (127 feet) and encircling facades in proportion. Completed in 1685, it was called the Place des Victoires (Fig. 56).[28]

The circular plan, as part of the elaborate tribute to the king, did not herald a new era in Parisian building layout. On the contrary, it was an impractical arrangement which devoured land and was difficult to integrate with nearby streets and sites. Much more important for Paris was Hardouin-Mansart's facade design. Its basic components – a false arcade, two full storeys and a double-pitch mansard roof lit by dormers – conformed to the formula adopted under Henri IV, but the composition and detailing were entirely classical. This reflected the progress towards French classicism under Louis XIV, and looked forward to the nineteenth-century street elevations of Haussmann.

The ground-floor arches were tall enough to include an entresol. This showed that the ground floor was planned for commercial use, the entresol having made its appearance gradually during the century as storage space and rough sleeping accommodation. The two

main storeys were linked by a giant order of Ionic pilasters, creating a palazzo effect. The upper floor was slightly the higher of the two. There was a tall, heavy cornice. Curiously, the elegance of the facade contrasted with the heavy treatment of the dormers with their alternating rectangular and arched windows, topped by segmental and semi-circular pediments. This was reminiscent of Mannerist practice in the sixteenth century.

The royal role in the Place des Victoires was tangential, and amounted to little more than the granting of approval to site a royal statue. Moreover, when the Crown lent its support in 1691 to a scheme to make the piazza completely circular by demolishing an older property, the main pressure came from members of the existing syndicate.[29]

The second piazza, the Place Vendôme (Fig. 57), arose from the purchase by Hardouin-Mansart and five financiers of a large *hôtel* and its gardens in the fashionable Saint-Honoré district. They divided their acquisition into small sites but were unable

to sell them. Their next plan was to interest the Crown in a complex of official buildings arranged around a piazza. With some encouragement, they started work on the piazza in 1685. Only the facades were constructed, the task being nearly complete in 1697.[30]

By this time, however, the piazza's failure to attract purchasers for the sites behind the facades led to a decision to plan a new piazza. In 1699 it was decided to build all four sides rather than three, as had been previously planned. The Crown offered the extra land required to the municipality, on condition that Hardouin-Mansart's new design was used.[31] The existing facades were demolished and the layout of the square was converted into an octagon by the insertion of five-bay diagonal sections at each corner, crowned by pediments. This was an elegant solution to the problem of the dark corner, used for the first time in Paris. There was an equestrian statue of Louis XIV in the middle of the square.

The design formula for the new elevation

56 The Place des Victoires.

was very similar to the Place des Victoires. The facade was composed of two full floors, linked by a giant order of pilasters, resting on a rusticated false arcade. Each side of the piazza was reinforced by a central portico, apparently of Palladian inspiration. The *piano nobile* was taller than the floor above. The pitched roof was very prominent, with overhanging eaves and tall, heavy dormers with large, ornate masonry surrounds and pediments. The steep angle of the roof pushed up to a ridge high enough to allow a second floor within the roof, lit by *oeils-de-boeuf* (circular or oval dormer windows). It was, however, the same height as the second floor below, the days of the towering, medieval roof being long in the past. The strong, horizontal lines of the overhanging eaves were echoed by a horizontal masonry projection above the arcade. Finally, the two main residential floors were given contrasting window treatments. The rectangular windows of the *piano nobile* were set in a decorative masonry surround, while the windows of the floor above were topped by a segmental arch and were contained in a more restrained surround.

The completion of these two piazzas between 1685 and the early 1700s was very influential. Many of the mansions on both piazzas were built by financiers, some of whom had been involved in the projects.[32] The tripartite distribution of false arcade, two floors and roof was widely adopted as

57 Aerial view of the Place Vendôme and its district.

a definitive resolution of the problem of associating narrow, urban houses in a bigger frame. The use of the classical orders on small houses gave great encouragement to architects trying to extend some of the distinction of the aristocratic *hôtel* to the houses of the middle classes. The closed arcade allowed owners to share in architectural fashion without losing part of their ground floor, while the entresol attracted valuable commercial tenants. All that was needed now was to extend the formula to the street.

CHANGES IN STREET ARCHITECTURE

It is easy to trace the development of the *hôtel* in the seventeenth century. Less clear is the evolution of the houses of the middle classes. Hardly any architectural drawings remain, and surviving houses have been subject to alteration. There are signs nevertheless that the classicisation of the *hôtels* prompted the emergence of a conforming architecture in nearby houses. This is known as *architecture d'accompagnement*.[33] It was foreshadowed by Pierre le Muet in his *Manière de bien bâtir pour toutes sortes de personnes*, published in 1647, with an augmented edition in 1663.

Le Muet was a royal servant, an *architecte ordinaire* who designed urban fortifications in Picardy. His book was dedicated to the king. Like his sixteenth-century forebears such as Serlio, he provided a series of model house designs. However, there was an introductory text on the principles of design. Le Muet stressed that houses should have '*une belle ordonnance*'. Essentially this meant symmetry. The components of an elevation, moving outwards from the centre of the facade, should be of dimensions equal to those of the equivalent component on the opposite side. These dimensions should be maintained at all heights of the building. Le Muet then went on to provide a series of designs for urban houses of varying types, on sites of increasing dimensions.

He began with a one-bay house on a tiny site, 12 feet wide and 21 to 25 feet deep, and gradually expanded as far as a four-bay house with *porte cochère*. Throughout, he maintained his principle of symmetry. Even the smallest house had an expensive elevation, with string courses and a semi-circular pediment with an *oeil-de-boeuf* to light the attic. He used steep pitched roofs (60 degrees approximately), parallel to the facade, and often included dormers topped by classical pediments. Prominent, tall chimneys on the street side were a striking feature. The detailing varied, but took the form of string courses or string enhancements around the window apertures. Some of the largest houses had windows surrounded by rusticated masonry, with pediments, and the eaves received an architectural treatment based on brackets or pendentives. The extremities of the facades were also often marked by tiers of rusticated masonry. In the largest houses the roof was hipped, separating it from the adjoining roofs as at the Place Royale.[34]

Le Muet's drawings implied that a single visual harmony could encompass a broad social hierarchy throughout the city. Indeed, he reinforced his argument in favour of a single principle of design by concluding the book with drawings for what was apparently a country chateau rather than an *hôtel*. However, by building outwards from the smallest one-bay unit, Le Muet produced a very repetitive effect, and by the time he reached the very expensive houses at the end, he seemed obliged to overload them with pretentious detail in order to distinguish them. In practice, architects must have designed just as often from the top down, modelling smaller houses on the more successful large ones. With Le Muet, however, the way to the disciplined street elevation was open.

The Crown remained interested in regularising street architecture, but the opportunities to do so were very rare. However, a unique possibility arose from the widening of the Rue de la Ferronnerie, near the Halles, where Henri IV had been assassinated in 1610. The king's carriage had been stationary in a traffic block caused by the narrow street, and there had been much talk at the time of widening it to prevent future tragedies. However, the idea was not carried out until the reign of Louis XIV, by which time the chapter of the church of Saint-Germain-l'Auxerrois was prepared to rebuild part of one side of the street as a speculation, allowing it to be widened to thirty feet. The Crown imposed the facade design by royal order in 1669, producing the earliest street ordinance in Paris, half a century after the first piazzas.[35]

The work was carried out between 1669 and 1677 by the church of Saint-Germain-l'Auxerrois, which was prepared to contribute part of the adjoining Innocents cemetery and to convert the remainder to a paved ossuary which would not scare health-conscious tenants away. This allowed the new construction to be planned as a long (fifty-two-bay) terrace along the widened street, with a simpler elevation facing the ossuary to the rear. There was a false arcade, including an entresol, three full floors and an attic floor (originally planned as a mansard roof). To hold this lengthy composition together, there was a central pavilion, with two terminating pavilions. Pairs of bays were separated by rusticated vertical tiers over the arcade arches.[36] This was the longest coordinated street facade in Paris (Fig. 58).

The design was imposed by a royal ordinance but it was clearly modified during construction. The result nevertheless showed that a private developer and the Crown could cooperate in a purely utilitarian scheme, and still generate an innovative design. In fact, complex ramifications of the deal extended beyond the immediate site, with the Crown securing from the developer a number of houses which it needed for the improvement of the Louvre.

It is very difficult to establish how far the houses built in Paris during the seventeenth century compare with contemporary architectural models, and the special, ordinanced facades. However, the workaday detail of Perelle's view of the Porte Saint-Denis from the north in 1674 inspires more confidence than most (Fig. 59). Two houses are shown just to the north of the arch, on the Rue du

58 New residential block in the widened Rue de la Ferronnerie.

LVDOVICO MAGNO.

59 Engraving by Perelle of the Porte Saint-Denis and nearby houses, looking south, in 1674.

Faubourg Saint-Denis. They look as though they were built or remodelled earlier in the seventeenth century.

They were three and four storeys high respectively, with dormer roofs. The dormer windows were very large, rose vertically from the frontage facades and had pediments. They thus appeared as an upward extension of the fenestration on the frontage, rather than as a projection from the sloping roofs. Both houses appear to be built of rubble with rusticated masonry corners and the familiar horizontal stone strips between the storeys. The larger house has an orthogonal pattern of vertical stone strips which emphasise the window bays on the upper floors. The roofs appear to be tiled, as was the norm in Paris by now, probably with lead sheeting replacing the lower courses and forming exaggerated flashings. A permanent, sloping awning juts out from above the ground floor to shelter clients of the booth-like shops. Flower pots stand on one window ledge. In the distance, inside the gate, a house of five storeys and a dormer roof is visible, suggesting higher densities in the old city.

The regular fenestration suggests that the random distributions of the Middle Ages have been completely supplanted. The houses have several bays and the roof is built parallel to the facade. The pedimented

dormers suggest that this was still one of the easiest ways of creating classical detail. In other respects the houses are vernacular in appearance, and the emphasis on verticality in one of them suggests that the idea of perspective had no currency as yet.

What then of the timber frame? Some historians have assumed that there was a movement away from timber construction after Henri IV's building regulations of 1607 and that Paris was largely transformed from a city of wood to one of stone or rubble during the seventeenth century, or even within fifty years.[37] Such a rate of renewal is out of the question. It is likely, however, that owners of houses with exposed timber frames covered them with a stucco rendering. This practice was ultimately enforced as a fire prevention measure in 1667 after the Fire of London had worried the Paris authorities. Many must have used the opportunity to mould fashionable detailing on to their walls and dormers. This change could have been very rapid, giving the impression of a general regularisation as well as of the demise of the timber frame.

It seems likely that few houses with timber frames were built after 1667. As a result, the leaning facade largely disappeared from new houses.[38] Some houses with masonry frames were built on the leaning principle, both before and after 1667, but the practice seems to have disappeared completely by the beginning of the eighteenth century. The generalisation of vertical facades made it easier to harmonise adjacent houses. At the same time, the generalisation of rendering over timber-framed houses or houses built of *moellons* (rubble, or ashlar) produced a progressive standardisation of facades. Whatever their dimensions and detailing, they were rendered in a stucco made of powdered local stone which did not look markedly different from facades built of dressed stone. Indeed, this stone-like effect was much valued. The use of stucco probably did more than anything else to make harmonious facades a realistic ideal.

This tendency was reinforced by the increasingly common alignment of the facades of *hôtels* with the burgess houses (Fig. 60). A growing number of *hôtels* had their main building constructed directly on the street frontage, echoing some of Le Muet's drawings.[39] The development of an *architecture d'accompagnement* in stucco allowed even modest houses to flank an *hôtel* in dressed stone.[40] This location, and this visual effect, normally boosted the rents of the houses. Harmonisation was even more likely to occur when *hôtel* owners developed adjacent sites as an investment or as accommodation for their clients.

Masonry construction, and verticality, made it easier to build balconies on the facades of burgess houses. Rare at first, they became a symbol of participation in urban life, as expressed in the street and its parades.[41] At first the example was set by the aristocracy, some of whom built balconies on their street facades, probably in place of the older turrets. A location over the *porte cochère* was much favoured, as at the Hôtel de Beauvais in 1655. Meanwhile, from the 1640s, wrought-iron staircases began to appear in *hôtels*. They soon spread to the houses of commoners and in the second half of the century iron was extensively used for balconies.[42]

At the same time, a movement towards the standardisation of roofs occurred. The double-pitch roof was later commonly named after Mansart, and known in English as the mansard, or gambrel, roof; by the middle of the seventeenth century it was becoming common after its obscure introduction in *hôtel* design earlier in the century.[43] Although

houses of all types could benefit from this roof form, it was almost certainly first developed in *hôtels*, because architects were especially eager here to lower the roof profile without reducing the potential volume of servants' and storage accommodation within it. It was therefore associated at first with broad frontages.

Meanwhile, the seventeenth century saw the gable go out of fashion in burgess houses. Not only were few new ones built, but existing gables began to be converted to pitched roofs rising from the street frontage, or to triangular or curved pediments of classical inspiration. Burgess houses in newly-developed streets tended to have broader frontages than in the older areas, up to three bays or more, and some of these used the mansard roof by the later part of the century. At any rate, multiple gable treatments were not attempted on these broader houses, and continuous roofs, parallel to the street, were the norm whether or not the mansard construction was used. Rectangular or oval dormers, the former sometimes with pediments, were a normal feature of these roofs. They usually stood directly above each bay, reinforcing the pattern of the facade fenestration.

Growing coherence at roof level was

60 The Hôtel de Beauvais, street frontage.

accompanied by a similar trend at ground level. Tall arcade arches, including an *entresol* (a low ceilinged floor, used mainly for storage, occupying the upper part of the space created by the tall arches), were very common in new building in the inner districts by mid-century.[44] They were also often used where *hôtels* stood on the street frontage, as at the Hôtel Lully, built in the Rue des Petits-Champs in 1674.[45] An early example, at the Hôtel de Beauvais in 1655, was intended purely to generate income, and the objective was probably the same at the Hôtel Lully. Clearly, street frontages had a highly persuasive commercial value and these tall, false arcades multiplied in the later seventeenth century and into the eighteenth.

Houses built for rental in mid-century were generally simple in design. In many cases, the only decoration was the indestructible Parisian horizontal strip which separated the floors. These strips reinforced the horizontal effect of the frontages if they were aligned. However, growing use was made, in all but the poorest houses, of rusticated vertical bands which were especially used to mark corners or property boundaries.[46] These 'refends' were widely used by the end of the century to suggest a masonry structure in cheap houses.

The more ornate and comfortable houses built for merchants, lawyers and other distinguished people used certain features pioneered in the *hôtels*. Around 1670 and 1680 we find the colossal order being used in some of these houses.[47] Curved and triangular pediments over doors and windows were common. In all these ways, therefore, the innovations of royal and aristocratic architecture were being extended to the middle classes by the end of the seventeenth century.

## FURTHER REGULATION OF PRIVATE BUILDING

As we have seen, the Fire of London in 1666 troubled the Paris authorities, who were responsible for an even larger, timber-framed city. Until this time, private building in Paris had probably been better regulated than in any other large city in northern Europe. However, London's post-Fire building regulations, with their emphasis on heights, street widths and materials, were probably the inspiration of the restrictions on projections and heights imposed in Paris during the next two years. In 1666 an ordinance of the Treasurers of France controlled the creation of projections, though this battle had of course been largely won much earlier.[48] In the following year Louis XIV's Bureau des Finances fixed a maximum height of 8 *toises* (15.6 metres) for the front walls of all new houses in Paris.[49] In normal circumstances this allowed a maximum of five floors, plus any accommodation in the roof.

The Bureau also required the exposed timbers of existing houses to be covered with plaster. New gables were banned, and roofs had to be aligned parallel to the street.[50] Assuming that the new regulations were enforced, they would have tended to produce a standardisation of ceiling heights and construction up to the full height permitted for the building. The result would have been greater visual continuity along the street.

In practice, the new height restrictions were either not enforced, or not enforced for very long, but the trend towards masonry construction and visual conformity was certainly encouraged after 1667. A century later, effective height restrictions would at last be enforced, but the basis for them was laid in the seventeenth century. The ordered Paris of the nineteenth century was already coming into being.

# THE EIGHTEENTH CENTURY: ARCHITECTURAL HARMONISATION AT THE CLOSE OF THE ANCIEN RÉGIME

## CLASSICISM REINFORCED

All the components of a classical architecture were present in Paris by 1715. Architects moved freely between city and country, between secular buildings and churches. The result was variety and stylistic development within an elegant framework respected by all. Classicism was, of course, an architecture of power, wealth and privilege, but few in France would have questioned the aesthetic result, whatever their station. As yet, however, the new architecture had not been applied to Paris on a scale sufficient to transform the city. That transformation would come much closer during the eighteenth century, with more ambitious piazzas and street networks, modernisation plans for the city as a whole, and a growing conformity of domestic architecture. The result was a classical frame of great strength and scope, within which a certain variety of design could be tolerated.

Behind the brilliant practice of French classicism lay a body of architectural theory unrivalled in Europe. The Académie Royale d'Architecture continued to provide a programme of lectures and it kept up standards, particularly in the design of public buildings, over which it maintained a general oversight. The idea that there was a French national manner of architecture, based on proportion, a very high standard of materials and execution, and on the correct use of classical features, was firmly established. Also firmly rooted by now was the belief that this mode of architecture was superior to practice outside France.

One strength of French classicism was its ability to incorporate stylistic variations without detracting from the overall aesthetic scheme. Paris passed through two important design phases during the eighteenth century. The first was the somewhat superficial rococo fashion in the first half of the century. Italian and German rococo influenced this episode, but the Parisian variant always had a lighter touch. The second was a more powerful movement which was partly a reaction against the self-indulgence of rococo, but which was also linked to the purism of the eighteenth-century Enlightenment. This was the striking neo-classical tendency which set its mark on public buildings and *hôtels* in the second half of the century and was applied with enthusiasm by the revolutionary, consular and imperial regimes until 1815. That this modernising movement should return to the principles of Ancient architecture reflected the timeless strength of French classicism.

Architecture was a frequent subject of publication. Books and engravings were almost always didactic in their purpose, and some were openly based on courses of lectures in the academy or in independent studios or schools. The century's most eminent and prolific author was Jacques-François Blondel, an energetic practitioner and teacher (who apparently was no relation of his great seventeenth-century namesake). His *Architecture française* was published in four volumes between 1752 and 1756.[1] It was followed by his nine-volume *Cours d'architecture* which appeared between 1771 and 1777. This included the lectures he had given in his own school of arts since 1750, and at the Académie Royale d'Architecture since 1756.[2]

The *Cours d'architecture* marked a move away from the orders and proportions which had preoccupied François Blondel a century before, towards the emulation of good examples from recent French architecture. Of course, François Blondel's great text could still be consulted and repetition of his teaching would have been otiose. Jacques-François Blondel chose to present a great array of building types and decorative features, echoing his massive survey of the French achievement in *Architecture française* and stressing the variety of external appearance that could be achieved within classical proportions (Figs 61–3). Interior treatments, and building science, completed the course.

Foreign architecture scarcely figured at all, but occasionally Italian examples were cited, and there was a striking reference to the elegant English 'Waux-halls'.[3]

Perhaps the most novel feature of Blondel's lectures was his interest in the houses of the middle classes. Here, Blondel made a strong call for proportion and simplicity. He wanted decoration to be reserved for palaces and *hôtels*.[4] He nevertheless hoped that a range of harmonious domestic styles could be developed for Paris, with each district having its own character. The ordinanced terrace of the 1670s in the Rue de la Ferronnerie showed what could be done, thought Blondel. Without this system, architects would be confused by the multiple uses of apartment buildings and would abandon all efforts to give each house its own character. Ultimately, thought Blondel, nondescript buildings would be erected throughout the city.[5] He recommended his pupils to 'imitate' the small number of facades which he had selected, together with others which they could visit in Paris, should they ever have to design an apartment house. This amounted to a statement of the *architecture d'accompagnement*, which sought to associate grandiose classicism and bourgeois anonymity in a harmonious scheme.[6]

*Architecture d'accompagnement* featured strongly in Charles-Antoine Jombert's *Architecture moderne*, a derivative manual of 1764, aimed at master masons.[7] His engravings of burgess houses progressed from the smallest

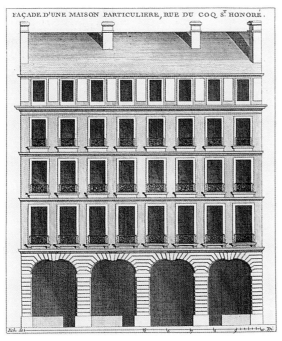

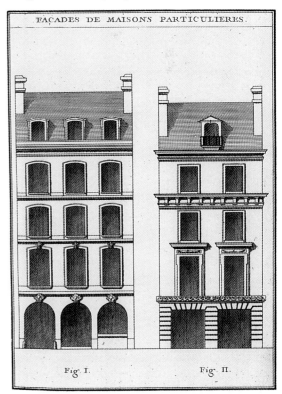

61, 62 and 63
Recommended elevations from Volume 3 of Blondel's *Cours d'architecture*. Fig. 61, designed by Franque, is an apartment house for the Celestine order of Paris, and probably dates from *c.* 1770. Close to the Louvre, it was the product of a development scheme in which the Crown participated. The facade was intended to fit its location. Fig. 62 shows two modest houses, the left-hand one built in 1719. Blondel praises both for their proportions. He clearly had no time for rococo. Blondel's taste for simple proportions in ordinary houses continues into Fig. 63.

sites to the largest in the manner of Serlio, and indeed they recalled Serlio in their simplicity. Horizontal bands were virtually the only decoration on the smallest, two-bay house. The next-largest added the vertical, rusticated bands known as *refends*, and variants of this decoration were carried through into the large, four-bay houses. Panels between the windows were frequently shown, suggesting that a stucco finish over rubble was assumed. Ground-floor arcades, and still less entresols, were infrequent, but ground-floor rustication appeared occasionally.[8]

The emergence of this design consensus was reinforced by a growing involvement of architects in urban planning. In the eighteenth century, Parisian classicism acquired a power to create the spatial compositions which had been glimpsed in the seventeenth century but had not been carried out on a large scale. Thoughts now turned to the planning of districts of Paris or even of the city as a whole.

In mid-century, urban planning began to figure prominently in the architectural literature. The leading authority was the Jesuit architectural theorist, the Abbé Laugier. He published an *Essai sur l'architecture* in 1755 which included a lengthy discussion on urban design.[9] Laugier stressed the link between the embellishment of a city through individual projects, and its functioning as a general entity. He had a broad perception of urban problems, including public health and traffic. Indeed, Laugier wanted to see the process of embellishment extended to entire cities. He deplored the narrow streets of central Paris and the lack of improvement work there during the previous thirty years. These practical considerations were also present in the later writings of Blondel and Patte, as was the idea that a general plan of improvement might be implemented gradually.[10] It will soon be seen how these ideas were applied.

THE EVOLUTION OF CLASSICAL PLANNING

By 1715 the triumph of classicism had launched the belief that Paris was one of the world's most beautiful cities. This was partly Sun King rhetoric, but the idea was reinforced during the eighteenth century. Isaac de Bourges, writing on the city's monuments

64 De Machy's painting of the isolation of the east front of the Louvre, 1764. This is one of a series of paintings by the artist showing the regularisation of Paris on classical lines in the wake of the Place Louis-XV project.

in the early eighteenth century, described Paris as 'currently one of the most beautiful [cities] . . . in the world'.[11] He identified symmetry and height as aesthetic virtues, and cited a number of examples including the widened Rue de la Ferronnerie and the Place Royale. He described the latter as 'not only the most regular and the most beautiful in Paris, but also in the whole world'.[12]

In reality, however, most of Paris remained a product of pre-classical times. The medieval core had been extended since the sixteenth century by mainly uncoordinated, straggling growth. Much of the periphery attracted a shifting, undisciplined population which was difficult to police, and which certainly did not engender an environment of classical regularity. Pursuing numerous precedents, the royal authorities tried to prevent uncontrolled growth in 1724, 1726, 1728 and 1765 by limiting the expansion of the city to a defined perimeter, but they had little effect.[13] Gradually, therefore, the authorities shifted their attention to the encouragement of development schemes which could provide a structure for new areas. Such schemes were especially numerous after 1770. The developers generally employed the best architects of the day, and the resulting design normally provided a persuasive example of urban regularisation which further strengthened the classical ideal.[14]

As regular districts were developed on the outskirts, interest grew in the regularisation of the inner city. A variety of plans was put forward, including new streets and piazzas, and the isolation of monuments (Fig. 64).[15]

The most influential isolation scheme was the gradual detachment of the Louvre from the old houses which encroached upon it, a process which began in 1758.[16] Some of the parishes joined in with schemes to achieve the partial isolation of churches by creating *parvis* outside their west doors. These schemes usually needed financial support from the municipality and the participation of private financiers and developers. Rapid completion was out of the question, but parish leadership often kept these projects in being long enough to secure their execution at a propitious time. The *parvis* of Notre-Dame was an early success, completed in 1757. Other projects took much longer or, like the *parvis* of Saint-Eustache, were only partially completed.

One of the biggest *parvis* projects was linked to the colossal parish church of Saint-Sulpice on the Left Bank. The church had been begun in the seventeenth century, and work was resumed in 1733 under J.-N. Servandoni. Progress on this massive task tended to draw attention to the fact that the church was hemmed in by older buildings. In 1752, Servandoni presented a plan for a large 'commercial piazza' in front of the great west portico (Figs 65–7). The piazza was gradually cleared but it was not completed until the 1830s. Although Servandoni's architectural scheme for the frontages was adopted in 1754, only one house, a simple, angular structure at no. 6, Place Saint-Sulpice, was built to his design.[17] The other buildings in the piazza nevertheless reflected Servandoni's concept, and the very lengthy execution confirmed the basic strength of this striking scheme of private regularisation.

65 *Below left*, the Place Saint-Sulpice project as presented in 1781. The site of Servandoni's model house is indicated towards the bottom of the plan.

66 *Bottom*, perspective engraving of the church and piazza of Saint-Sulpice, 1781.

67 *Below right*, Servandoni's model house of 1754.

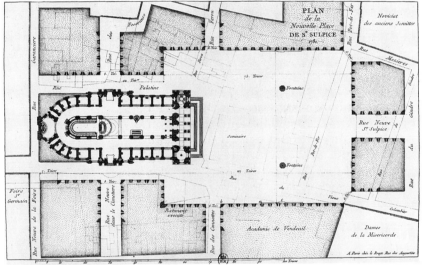

## THE PLAN OF CITY IMPROVEMENTS

From around the middle of the century, interest mounted in composite plans of local developments and improvement schemes for the whole city.[18] There was a new context of thought and action in which individuals were less willing to await royal guidance. This transition from a declining Absolutism to a creative Enlightenment marked much of French life in the last decades before the Revolution. The plans were the work of architects and they generally contained a strong element of embellishment, but practical objectives were often present, including hygiene.[19]

The first composite plan dates back to the reign of Louis XIV when François Blondel, on the king's orders, marked all the improvements currently authorised on a map of the city.[20] This was not a public gesture, however, and no debate ensued. In 1755, on the other hand, with a host of improvements under discussion, Marc-Antoine Laugier put forward the principles of an improvement plan in his *Essai sur l'architecture*. Laugier's method was to describe an ideal city, but he made clear that he had Paris primarily in mind.[21] In this account, he combined improvements which had been planned or carried out in Paris in the previous century and a half with some of the ideas currently under consideration.[22] Laugier's portrayal appeared as one chapter, 'The embellishment of towns', in what was otherwise a conventional text on architecture. In his urban vision, buildings were part of a total scheme or concept embracing the whole city and its surroundings. Although the idea of integrated design was not entirely new, Laugier directed Parisian architecture firmly towards the ideal of a universal harmony, the origins of which lay in the early Renaissance.

Travellers were to approach Laugier's city along broad, unobstructed avenues, lined by two or four rows of trees. The city was to be surrounded by numerous gates placed at equal intervals, with impressive architectural treatments in the form of triumphal arches.[23] Both these features recalled the improvements of Louis XIV's reign. Within the gates would lie a city of wide streets and commodious squares. The traveller would proceed into the city along one of a radiating network of rectilinear streets. Laugier compared this arrangement to the Piazza del Popolo in Rome, but it also recalled Henri IV's Place de France.

Throughout the city, building heights were to be fixed in relation to street widths, and Laugier made clear that he abhorred low buildings in wide streets.[24] At the same time, he felt that long streets with houses built to the same design were insipid.[25] His solution was to require each block to be built in a different style, allowing the character of the city neighbourhoods to change as one passed along the main streets. Facades in each block would be identical, but at each junction one would encounter a new treatment. There would be no excessive ornament on the facades. Colours could vary, but they would be harmonious.[26]

Pierre Patte, the architect and writer, took up some of Laugier's ideas when he published proposals for Paris improvements in 1767.[27] One of his major aims was to make new monuments visible from as far away as possible, but he was also interested in utilitarian concerns such as the removal of dilapidated housing.[28] He wanted the city of Paris to acquire slum areas, lay out new streets and sites, and allow private builders to develop them in accordance with a general architectural scheme.[29] He was careful to say that he did not favour a rigid street scheme on the lines of 'the cold symmetry of the cities of Japan and China'. Urban beauty did not repose on 'an assembly of houses laid out in a very regular fashion in squares or parallelograms'. The fundamental concern was that the approach to the houses should always be convenient. In architecture, Patte favoured variety: 'The traveller must not be able to take in everything at one glance. He must constantly be drawn by something new, varied, and agreeable, something which excites and intrigues him, and constantly arouses his curiosity'.[30]

Patte expanded these ideas in a major urban planning treatise with an emphasis on public safety, published in 1769.[31] He saw urban architecture in terms of functions, with the design of each building corresponding to its function. Echoing Laugier, he claimed that cities could be rebuilt gradually under regulation, as demolitions occurred. His proposals for ventilation, water distribution, decentralisation of cemeteries and sewerage indicated a keen appreciation of a city's practical needs from an engineering point of view. Altogether, he sought a pleasant environment and efficiency.[32] With Patte, architecture, planning and technology came together for the first time. The only weakness, perhaps, lay in his assumption that a regulated city could promote architectural variety. This was the beginning of a long story.

THE GREAT STEP FORWARD: THE PLACE
LOUIS-XV

The first half of the eighteenth century saw few important schemes of improvement or development in Paris. Partly to blame was the Crown's war expenditure. In mid-century, however, Paris acquired its most important design exemplar so far.

In 1748 the municipality decided to set up a statue in honour of Louis XV (Fig. 68). Such gestures were common throughout France after the Peace of Aix-la-Chapelle in that year had ended one of the century's frequent wars with England. A number of projects were drawn up by architects and speculators, all of them within the built-up area. The king, who was allowed to select the winning scheme, was reluctant to cause demolitions, and he offered a large, open site from the extensive royal estates to the west of the city.

This site was at the bottom of the Champs-Elysées, just to the west of the Tuileries gardens. It thus lay astride the great western avenue from the Louvre to the Etoile which had been landscaped under Louis XIV. A second competition now took place, and after many manoeuvres the distinguished architect Jacques-Ange Gabriel was placed in charge of an ambitious project for the statue and the surrounding piazza. The main significance of the final scheme, approved by the king in 1757, lay in the superimposition of a huge, open piazza on a seventeenth-century royal hunting avenue, and the creation of an ordinanced street running northwards out of the piazza at right-angles to the axis of the avenue, towards a large church (the Madeleine) which closed this shorter vista.[33]

The scheme itself surpassed all previous projects in Paris, but by partly urbanising the Champs-Elysées and linking the area west of the Tuileries gardens to the developing residential districts to the north-west of the Louvre, it also provided a framework for the whole of the western Right Bank. This area was further linked to the Faubourg Saint-Germain on the Left Bank by the Pont Louis-XVI in 1787–90. This elegant, classical bridge extended the axis of the Rue Royale to the south of the Place Louis-XV. The resulting twin growth areas for aristocratic *hôtels* created a combination of individual architectural elegance and a sweeping townscape on a scale previously unknown in the city and indeed anywhere in the world (Figs 69–73).

All the facades of the Place Louis-XV and the Rue Royale were the work of one architect, Gabriel, under royal approval. The piazza was an unusual challenge, because the maintenance of the open aspect in front of the Tuileries palace and gardens meant that only the northern frontage of the piazza could be developed. This frontage was split

68 Patte's composite plan of local proposals for an equestrian statue of Louis XV, including the royal proposal for a large, rectangular piazza to the west of the Tuileries gardens. Architectural interest in circular piazzas is evident.

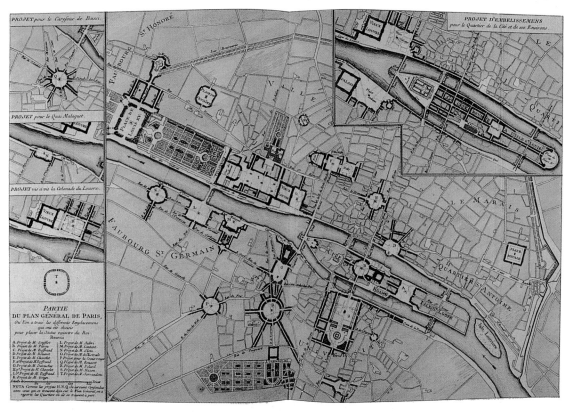

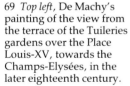

69 *Top left*, De Machy's painting of the view from the terrace of the Tuileries gardens over the Place Louis-XV, towards the Champs-Elysées, in the later eighteenth century.

70 *Below left*, the Place de la Concorde in its final form in the 1830s.

into two by the entrance of the Rue Royale from the north, so none of the intimate enclosure of earlier piazzas was possible. In 1753 Gabriel chose to build two large *hôtels* of three tall storeys, with frontages directly on the piazza, rather than two rows of smaller houses. The two extremities of each *hôtel* were marked by large pavilions with pediments and independent colonnades. A giant order of detached columns was used for the central facades, topped by a balustrade. The first and second floors were set back to make room for the colonnade. This solution met the need for a very strong statement on the north side of the square. It was comparable

to Perrault's eastern facade of the Louvre a century before. No more than Perrault's work, however, would it set an example for domestic architecture in Paris.

The construction of two large *hôtels* avoided the potential disagreements with private purchasers of sites which had plagued certain earlier piazza schemes. Even here, however, the facades were constructed first and some time elapsed before the rest of the sites were filled. Where adjoining streets were widened or realigned, the Crown tried to ensure architectural harmony. Royal letters patent of 1757 required the municipality to ensure that any new houses were closely supervised in order to ensure conformity.[34]

The treatment of the Rue Royale required stronger direction (Fig. 74). The Crown

imposed an architectural ordinance to Gabriel's design. The basic elevation was a development of the tradition of the Place Dauphine and the Place des Victoires, rather than a reflection of the elevations on the Place Louis-XV. However, the perspective solution had the effect of transferring the established piazza elevation to an important thoroughfare. This opened up the prospect of linking local improvements and extending the classical aesthetic across the city.

THE HOMES OF THE ARISTOCRACY

Publications and public schemes notwithstanding, most of the city's ablest architects still put their main efforts into building for aristocratic clients. *Hôtel* construction expanded in the eighteenth century and it continued to influence middle-class architecture, both directly and through the growing phenomenon of *architecture d'accompagnement* (Fig. 75).

The death of Louis XIV in 1715 ended the era of the permanent Versailles court. The nobility were able to spend more time in Paris, and *hôtel* building soon accelerated. New *hôtels* were especially concentrated in the Faubourg Saint-Germain on the Left Bank, but most districts in western Paris saw

goodly numbers of new *hôtels* during the century.

So central was *hôtel* design to Parisian output that it could not fail to reflect the century's baroque, rococo and neo-classical phases. Royal, official and public buildings, on the other hand, clung more closely to the national, classical style. Baroque was adopted for churches in particular, and rococo was mainly used for modest residences. The neo-classical was favoured above all by very large *hôtels* built from the 1760s. Meanwhile, the customary *hôtel* plan which had emerged by 1715 survived throughout the century. The efforts of the more innovative architects therefore never undermined classical *hôtel* architecture, nor were they intended to. The wealth and strength of their clients,

as a class, would alone have ensured this continuity.

Certain changes merit attention nevertheless. The mansard roof with dormer windows remained almost universal, but it was normally of modest dimensions and restrained design, and did not dominate the whole elevation as many mansard roofs had done in the seventeenth century. Towards the end of the century the trend towards pure classical detail meant that the roof was often reduced and masked by a masonry balustrade. The elegant *oeil-de-boeuf* was sometimes used in place of the bulkier dormer, and it often served to provide a distinctive feature on the facade itself.

A long frontage was still valued and, overall, the trend was towards wider frontages as building spread into less congested districts. The frontage was always composed of a number of bays of equal width. Windows with a segmental lintel were extensively used, normally for one of the storeys only, and topped by a decorative quoin, such as a classical head. Simpler, rectangular windows were used on other storeys to offset the segmental ones. Windows with full, semi-circular arches became less common as the eighteenth century wore on, but they were often a feature of the large, central entrance pavilions which formed part of many courtyard facades. Much use was made of ironwork balustrading in the window spaces, or on narrow balconies outside the *piano nobile*. Ironwork was particularly frequent in the entrance or flanking pavilions which occurred on the longer facades.

In the larger mansions, and especially towards the end of the century, porticos with four full columns in the Palladian manner were often used, especially for the main entrance on the courtyard side. The aim was usually to create a very strong central component for the facade, and to flank it by two symmetrical, but less prominent, wings. The width of the facade was stressed by horizontal masonry strips between the storeys, and a strong cornice. The longer the facade overall, the broader and more powerful the central pavilion or portico needed to be. Smaller pavilions were often used to terminate the facades. Rustication was very common here. The pavilions were often topped by classical pediments or raised roof structures. There was some carved decoration of the wall surfaces in the form of panels containing traditional compositions such as garlands and trophies.

Although most of these features had long been part of the classical repertoire, there was a growing tendency in the eighteenth century towards classical purism and an archaeological approach to the design of *hôtels*. Neo-classicism was the culmination of this trend rather than a sudden change of fashion. Greater use was made of the orders, and the overall treatment became more monumental and less domestic. By the 1770s some of the largest *hôtels* were taking on characteristics of the classical temple, palace or bath, with massive porticos, apses and blank walls emphasised by heavily rusticated masonry or large statues set in niches.

Interiors, on the other hand, were little affected by spartan, neo-classical tendencies (Fig. 76). On the contrary, interior design tended to become more ornate in the second half of the century. Architects saw no contradiction here, and were usually capable of designing in both modes. The carved wooden panels from the Hôtel d'Uzès, now at the Musée Carnavelet, provide an excellent example, for they are based on designs by

76 The Salon de la Princesse, on the first floor of the Hôtel de Soubise, by Germain Boffrand. This architect also designed the interior of the Hôtel de Rohan, creating striking contrasts with severe exteriors in both cases.

77 Intimate rococo treatment of the withdrawn, eastern frontage of the extended Palais-Royal by Fontaine, c. 1753.

78 *Below left*, north front of the extended Palais-Royal by Pierre Contant d'Ivry (left) and Fontaine (right), 1763. A return to classicism is visible here but the effect is nevertheless reminiscent of Le Vau's work at Versailles. The result is as much part of the royal tradition as of the Parisian classical tradition.

79 *Right*, *above*, a proposal by Peyre for the Hôtel de Condé.

80 *Right*, *below*, Ledoux's customs barrier at La Villette.

Ledoux, whose design for the exterior in 1768–9 is discussed below. Gilded trophies on white panels are separated by tree-like forms with leaves combined with man-made symbols such as harps, horns and quivers. Fireplaces and consoles are topped by arched mirrors. Interior design thus maintained an earlier tradition while the exteriors pursued a bold and experimental path. This dialogue provided a basis for both original invention and continuity.

Early hints of the coming neo-classical fashion are visible in the Hôtel d'Orrouer, built in 1731 by Charles and Pierre Boscry in the Rue de Grenelle.[35] This sober design stressed clean lines, functional structures and pure, classical components such as the Corinthian columns which supported the vaulted entrance canopy. Although the rococo style continued to develop (Fig. 77), with strains of the picturesque in some cases, the return to a classical purism was well under way by mid-century. The interior of the reconstructed Palais-Royal by Pierre Contant d'Ivry, completed in about 1765, gave it

strong encouragement (Fig. 78).[36] The prolific Claude-Nicolas Ledoux proposed a heavily classical design for the main facade of the Hôtel d'Uzès in the later 1760s, including a massive portico, the lintel of its heavy pediment supported by four Corinthian columns rising to the building's full height of two storeys. All the wall surfaces were pronouncedly rusticated.[37] Heavy, classical porticos and pavilions now became very popular (Figs 79, 80), though there was also a trend elsewhere towards light detailing of Greek inspiration, and simple, geometrical, structural forms adorned by simple cornices, niches and inlaid friezes. Etienne-Louis Boullée, who started to practise in the 1760s, was especially attracted by this mode of design.

By the 1780s a more romantic form of the classical was in fashion, for instance in the work of Pierre Rousseau at the Hôtel de Salm in 1782 (Fig. 81).[38] Here, a powerful Corinthian portico, an arched gateway and a rotunda, reinforced by colonnades, engaged columns, niches, large areas of plain wall and extensive rustication, created striking, simple forms in which freely interpreted classical features produced a very evocative and romantic effect. Claude-Nicolas Ledoux's Hôtel Thélusson, also built in 1782, used a similar style, though with less decoration and

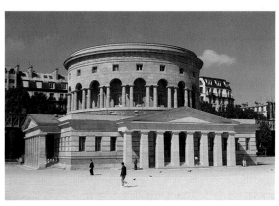

an even bigger ratio of wall area to window area.[39] The style was pushed to its extreme in Ledoux's municipal customs posts (*octroi*), built between 1784 and 1789. Here, a timeless symbolism and expressionism celebrated the gates of Paris and implied constant surveillance of goods passing by. This Newtonian, fantasy architecture had not had time, however, to influence domestic architecture before the Revolution suspended noble patronage.

THE ERA OF THE MONUMENT

If the mansions of the nobility continued to shun the street, the opposite was true of the growing regiment of public buildings which dotted the city. They were the essential complement to the open spaces which figured in the improvement plans. The spaces and the monuments interacted, each calling, as it were, for greater efforts from the other as their scale increased. The biggest achievements were made in the south, where the Church drew on its big reserves of land to finance huge churches and to promote residential building from the middle years of the century. The church of Saint-Sulpice and

later the church of Sainte-Geneviève crowned these titanic efforts.

Most secular buildings were more modest in their effect, but as the population of Paris rose to over half a million on the eve of the Revolution, building expanded over a widening range of public structures. Prominent were educational buildings, government departments, hospitals and theatres. The neo-classical style lent itself very well to public building, notably through the portico and the pediment. In many cases elegant or grandiose porticos, most of which were larger than the *hôtel* porticos of the day, were combined with a simpler exterior than most nobles would have tolerated in their main facades. They also helped to disguise the fact that these buildings filled their entire sites, or even whole blocks, with continuous frontages rising to a common height in order to maximise the accommodation provided. On large sites, ventilation and circulation were based on an internal courtyard, scarcely visible from the street. There was a precedent for buildings of this new type. This was the spacious, cellular complex of the Invalides, built in the late seventeenth century on a generous site on the Left Bank. Designed to house veterans, with all facilities on site, this

81 De Machy's painting of the Hôtel de Salm under construction, with the stonemasons' yard in the foreground. The masonry blocks were apparently still shaped on site, in contrast to the nineteenth century when they were prepared to order at the quarry.

82 *Above left*, the Ecole
Militaire.

83 *Below*, the Hôtel des
Monnaies.

84 *Right, above*, the Ecole
de Droit by Soufflot,
facing the massive portico
of his church of Sainte-
Geneviève.

85 *Right, below*, the Ecole
de Médecine. The severe
classicism here reflects the
scientific dedication of the
medical profession.

huge structure incorporated a continuous
exterior facade and a number of internal
courtyards. The portico of the chapel closed
the approach from the south, and the dome
dominated the planned vista from the north.

It was this combination of a simple and
even repetitive exterior, enclosing substantial
internal volumes, a portico to draw the eye
from medium distance, and (on a larger
building) a landmark dome or tower to dominate a distant view, that would influence
many of the public buildings of the eighteenth
century. It was influenced in its turn by the
great Salpétrière hospital, built outside the
city on the Left Bank by Liberal Bruant in
1670, and perhaps by abbeys such as the new
Val-de-Grâce of the 1640s and 1650s.

The Ecole Militaire by J.-A. Gabriel, dating
from 1752–7 and adjoining the Invalides, was
an early example of this new type of public
building (Fig. 82). Set at one end of a military
exercise field, the Champ-de-Mars, it used a
dome and portico set on a large, rectangular
building to dominate the open space and

to stand up to the impressive bulk of the
Invalides nearby. The design was unusually
eclectic, with superimposed porticos in the
Italian style as used in the Invalides chapel,
and a low, flat-sided dome with *oeils-de-boeuf*.
Even more strikingly representative of the
new style was the Hôtel des Monnaies (Fig.
83), the royal mint. This huge, severe, three-
storeyed building, built by Jacques-Denis
Antoine between 1768 and 1775, had a very
long facade arranged on either side of an
emphatic central arcade and portico. Its
status as a government building reinforces
its affinity to parts of Federal Triangle in
Washington DC and to Speer's chancellery in
Berlin.

However, administrative status was not
the sole qualification for a portico. The
Ecole de Droit (1770–83) and the Ecole de
Médecine (1779–86) both used them (Figs
84–5). The former, designed by Jacques-
Germain Soufflot as part of his ambitious
street-and-piazza approach to his church of
Sainte-Geneviève, made a strong statement
on a corner of the piazza facing the huge
portico of the church. Perhaps the most
striking of all was the Théâtre Français at the
Odéon, built in 1779–82 by Charles de Wailly
and Marie-Joseph Peyre on the site of the
Hôtel Condé, on land ceded by the Prince de

86 Rear elevation of the Odéon theatre.

87, 88 and 89 *Right and far right, above*, three stages in the development of the design for the west front of the church of Saint-Sulpice. The first two are the work of Servandoni while the third shows the towers designed by Chalgrin shortly before the Revolution.

Condé. Located on a semi-circular piazza at the head of a rising approach street, both planned by De Wailly, it was a simple, rectangular building with a broad, unpedimented, Doric portico. Horizontal rustication was extensively used to emphasise the simple strength of the whole structure. A major effort was made here to give Paris a national theatre worthy of its great classical playwrights, within a street scheme which itself had theatrical qualities (Fig. 86).[40] The Enlightenment implications of the whole enterprise were to be echoed in the early summer of 1968 when the theatre served as the home of the permanent political debates which enlivened the student and popular protests of that time.

Church architecture followed a similar path. The baroque style inherited from the previous century gave way to a classicism which could reach gigantic proportions. The massive western front of the church of Saint-Sulpice, which went through a number of changes during its construction between 1733 and 1777 by Servandoni and others, reflected this transition (Figs 87–91). Soufflot's huge, severely neo-classical church of Sainte-Geneviève (Fig. 92), built as a royal commission between 1755 and 1790, combined a giant Corinthian portico and a colonnaded dome (Fig. 93).

This convergence of secular and religious architecture provided a further reinforcement of Parisian classicism. At the same time, architects increasingly valued the relationship between the large public building and its attendant space. By the end of the century,

ÉLÉVATION DU PORTAIL DE ST SULPICE

*Composé et élevé par Servandoni, jusqu'au commencement des Tours, et les dites Tours, composées et élevées par le J.*
*Sᵉ Chalgrin Architecte du Roi Premier Architecte et Intendant des Bâtimens de Monsieur en 1782*

90 *Right*, the west front of the church of Saint-Sulpice as completed shortly before the Revolution. Chalgrin was unable to complete the reconstruction of Servandoni's right-hand tower to his own designs. Thanks to classical proportion, however, the difference in the dimensions of the two towers often passes unnoticed from below.

91 *Far right*, *top*, the entire project, seen from the air.

92 *Far right*, *centre*, Soufflot's project for the church of Sainte-Geneviève.

93 *Far right*, *below*, the Panthéon (formerly the church of Sainte-Geneviève) and the Rue Soufflot, seen from the air. The lower part of the Rue Soufflot was built by Haussmann, but the planning concept is Soufflot's. The scene exemplifies the ambitious role of the Church in developing the Left Bank in the eighteenth century.

approach streets were being seen as part of that space, as in Soufflot's titanic scheme. Most new *hôtels* still faced inwards, but the public building looked out on to the city. With the wave of public building from mid-century, the creation of a coherent, classical cityscape was well under way.

## THE HOUSES OF THE BUSINESS AND PROFESSIONAL CLASSES

Although Paris was no longer the largest city in Europe, it shared in the expanding economic climate of the eighteenth century. The presence of government, the courts and the aristocracy made it the national centre of the professions, and it was also by far the largest centre of business and finance in France. Its artisans specialised in high-quality production. The aggregate demand for housing from this productive population greatly increased during the century.

The result was extensive building for the middle classes both on the outskirts and in the centre. Voltaire was impressed by these numerous private houses which, far more than the *hôtels*, made Paris 'the most flourishing town in the world'.[41] The range of types was very wide. The richest could afford a large villa, akin to an *hôtel*, in or near the fashionable suburbs in the west and north-west. The least favoured would build or rebuild a house of several storeys on a small site in the Halles or another old commercial district, perhaps letting the upper floors as an additional source of income.

Whatever the size and location of the house, the owner and his architect endeavoured to add sufficient distinction to the facade to distinguish it from mere rental housing. This could even involve a move away from convention which the aristocracy would not have risked. In the 1720s and 1730s the more adventurous architects and decorators made some charming and even striking use of rococo in modest houses of this type.

Most of the houses built or remodelled for the middle classes were the work of architects rather than of master masons. Many were less distinguished than those who worked for the aristocracy, but their willing obedience to the norms of Parisian classicism produced work of quality in most cases.[42] A degree of conformity was inevitable, but it contributed to the harmonious streetscape which was emerging in many districts of the city.

The height of new houses tended to rise, especially in the centre.[43] There is even evidence that the practice of adding storeys to older houses, which was to flourish after the Restoration, was beginning in the later eighteenth century.[44] The rental house of nine storeys built in the Rue de Valois around 1780 was exceptional (Fig. 94), but six and even seven storeys became a common height for new houses in the centre, and even on the outskirts heights of up to four storeys were common. This trend was partly linked to the emergence of the apartment house, to which we shall return.

Large private developments combining apartments and commercial space, often arranged around an interior courtyard, became common in the enterprising atmosphere of the 1770s and the 1780s. The Palais-Royal (Fig. 95), developed as a centre of resort in the 1780s, was very influential, and it probably influenced the Cour Batave in the Rue Saint-Denis, a smaller scheme built in 1790. Both included arcaded shopping with commercial and residential space above. The architects of these larger buildings took the opportunity to design very long, coherent

94 Giant apartment house in the Rue de Valois, *c*. 1780.

facades, and so associated order with horizontality.[45] Like the rental houses of the time, their elevations were very spartan in most cases.[46]

In the early part of the century, false arcades remained common in burgess houses, as did entresols set in the arches of the arcades. One bay was normally filled by a double door which formed the entry to the house. *Portes cochères* were rare, because the clientele did not require them and the sites were usually too small to include a sufficiently large courtyard. Balconies, some of them continuous, often marked the *piano nobile*. Any full-height windows on the upper floors were protected by ironwork balustrades. Ironwork on the balconies and balustrades often used flowing scroll patterns. Windows with segmental lintels were very common, and in contrast to the *hôtels* they were frequently employed on all floors. The windows normally had a masonry frame, and the space above the lintel was often filled with decorative carving or panels, or a central carved head or bust.

The storeys were often separated by horizontal masonry or stucco bands according to the timeless Paris practice. In most cases, little or no effort was made in houses of four storeys to link the first and second floors architecturally, and to identify the third floor as the attic by interposing a cornice. The masonry cornice below the roof was nevertheless treated with care and restraint. The mansard roof and dormers were of restrained proportions and design.

An excellent example of such architecture is the Eynaud house, Rue de l'Arbre-Sec, built in 1717 by a future academician and royal architect, Pierre-François Godot. The overall effect is of a restrained, tasteful rococo, with the horizontal bands marking the storeys offset by the curves of the window lintels, the semi-circular arches of the arcade, the scrollwork on the balcony and balustrades, and the foliage decoration above the windows.[47] Even more pronounced was the rococo treatment of Martin Goupy's house for the Dubuisson family, built in 1736 at 29, rue de la Parcheminerie.[48] Here, the deep-set, arched windows were framed by luxuriant carving using natural forms, and gossamer-like ironwork on the balustrades.

The houses of the middle classes did not respond immediately to the neo-classical

95 Elevation of the interior court of the new Palais-Royal, 1784.

movement, but by the 1780s rococo detailing had disappeared even from the smaller houses and a spartan, geometrical style with skeletal classical components had taken its place. At the Cour d'Aligre in the Rue de Bailleul, for instance, a large rental house built in 1782 by Louis Bergevin and Michel Mellan, the six-storey building was adorned only by a heavily rusticated arcade and entresol, and a classical cornice below the attic floor.[49] Joseph Métivier's own house in the Boulevard Saint-Denis, built in 1789 and including rental accommodation, chose a different arrangement, but nevertheless provided very limited decoration distinguished mainly by a balcony at attic level, a rusticated first floor or entresol, and three weak pediments over windows at the *piano nobile*. With hindsight, this move towards a sparse, spartan style for rental housing threatened a departure from the Parisian classical tradition. The revolution of 1789, however, interrupted the trend and opened a period of building paralysis which launched a new era in the nineteenth century.

Building techniques did not develop sufficiently during the eighteenth century to promote changes in design.[50] The use of prefabrication in the preparation of decorative elements may have increased, allowing time and scaffolding to be spared, but all but the most basic, repetitive carving was still done on site. It is most unlikely that production constraints contributed to the reduction in decoration towards the end of the century, mainly because this design trend originated among the houses of the richest clients. The use of iron beams and structural reinforcement became more common, but it was always invisible except when used for emergency ties, and it had no effect on design.

The scale of development tended to increase in the second half of the century, with large buildings such as theatres and colleges, and private developments of some importance, in the central areas.[51] Architects, who had often shared in the promotion of buildings and development schemes early in the century, expanded their entrepreneurial role in the second half, and especially after 1780 when there was a visible atmosphere of speculation.[52] Architects were, therefore, close to the structure of demand and the machinery of development. They were also close to the building world, in which many of them had begun their careers as masons or other skilled craftsmen. Some were the sons of builders, entrepreneurs and developers. A growing minority of Paris architects, however, were formally trained at the Academy and had a more scholarly approach to building design. Many architects, accustomed to dealing with the rich, circulated in polite society and so were in intimate touch with aristocratic preferences. At the same time, royalty and aristocracy prided themselves on their architectural knowledge and taste, and often influenced the designs of their architects.

## THE RISE OF THE APARTMENT HOUSE

The origins of the Parisian apartment house are obscure. What is clear, however, is that a great surge in the building of apartment houses occurred after the middle of the eighteenth century. Growing densities in the central districts were the main stimulus.[53] They figured strongly in the large development schemes of the later eighteenth century, but they were also built singly. The apartment houses responded to a demand for convenient accommodation from single persons, small households and transients. They attracted tenants of some means rather than impoverished people.

The first half of the century had seen a continuation of the development of rental houses which had been visible in the later seventeenth century. Michel Gallet has published the original designs for two adjacent rental houses in the Rue de la Chanvrerie.[54] The architect is unknown, but the drawings date from the early eighteenth century. The houses are five storeys high, with a dormer roof. Storey and window heights decline gradually and almost imperceptibly from floor to floor, but the overall impression is of tall boxes with holes cut for windows. There are six rooms on each floor, but the interior plan suggests that no dwelling would exceed two rooms. The absence of the owner made a *piano nobile*, with its attendant architectural treatment, unnecessary. The only decoration is provided by the horizontal bands between the storeys.

Only slightly less spartan was the rental house built by H.-Q. Desbeufs in the Rue de la Monnaie in 1745.[55] Also consisting of five storeys and a mansard roof, its horizontal bands were supplemented by thin masonry surrounds for the windows. The first three residential floors and their windows were almost of equal height, but the fifth floor was much lower. Especially striking in its simplicity and uniformity was the long row of houses built in 1734 by the academician and royal architect Jacques Vinage, in the Place Baudoyer (Rue François-Miron) (Fig. 96). This site formed part of the development of the churchyard of Saint-Gervais. Tall, false arcades with entresols supported three low storeys and a mansard roof. Only the horizontal bands and the wrought-iron balustrades enlivened this facade. Not all rental houses were so simple, however. Some had facades enlivened by rustication, symbolic pavilions marking the centre of the facade, and carving and masonry surrounds around the windows. Indeed, they were

96 Rental housing and shops built in the Place Baudoyer by the Saint-Gervais parish in 1734 after the conversion of a graveyard into an ossuary.

cases identical facade designs were usual, producing streetscapes that might have been monumental had not the streets normally been both narrow and short. Examples of such developments with identical houses were the Rue d'Angiviller by Lenoir, and the Rue Mandar by Mandar (Fig. 97).[57]

THE GROWTH OF PUBLIC REGULATION

The architects' debate on planning and regularisation largely begged the question of execution. It was clear, however, that the *alignement* would play a key part in straightening and widening the streets. Hygienic considerations also now began to strengthen the case for wide and regular streets. In contrast to the seventeenth century, some progress was now made in enforcing building lines and so widening streets and junctions.[58]

Scattered evidence suggests that the existing building regulations were carefully enforced in the eighteenth century. They were, however, mainly the product of the seventeenth century, and towards the end of the eighteenth the need was felt for a review, particularly in view of the growing concern about health. Louis XVI, who came to the throne in 1774, showed great interest in the improvement of Paris. Although his finances were a serious restriction, he supported a number of efforts to regulate the existing city. In 1783 Edme Verniquet, a competent architect turned royal surveyor, was commissioned to prepare an accurate plan of the city as a basis for a review of the building lines, a task which was completed in 1791. Also in 1783, the royal authorities issued a new set of building regulations for Paris. This code, as modified in 1784, had little impact before the Revolution, but it would do more to shape nineteenth-century Paris than any later enactment.

little different from the individual houses of the day, though they perhaps lacked the opulence and the individualistic design of the latter.

The transition to the fully-fledged apartment house occurred in mid-century when a handful of very striking examples was built. Construction seems to have accelerated in the 1780s, by which time architects rather than property owners were often the promoters. Apartment houses clustered around the Palais-Royal on the Right Bank, almost certainly prompted by the huge commercial development there in the 1780s. Many more were built in the nearby Halles district.[56] There was another group on the Left Bank around the Rue de Seine. Rooms were generally small and ceilings low. Their utilitarian character justified their severe exterior appearance, but they were very solidly built in stone or with a stone frame, as befitted their size.

Some apartment houses were built as part of large development schemes involving the creation of entirely new streets. In these

The building code of 1783/4 was not the first attempt to fix maximum frontage heights for houses facing onto Paris streets. It was, however, the first to relate maximum height to street width. The maximum height for new buildings, including their roofs, was fixed at 60 feet (*pieds*) (18 metres) in 1783, and lower heights were prescribed for streets less than 30 feet (nine metres) wide.[59]

Unfortunately, almost nothing is known about the genesis of the new system. The

97 Private development of an entire street: the Rue Mandar, named after its promoter and architect.

65

royal and municipal authorities must have consulted, and there was clearly a link with plans for new *alignements* which would produce an official width for each street.[60] Architects and master masons must have influenced the result, particularly in the revisions of 1784. Behind the procedures, however, lay one massive threat: this was the rise of the giant apartment house since mid-century, and the underlying rise in building heights throughout the city.[61]

The preamble to the royal declaration of 1783 asserted that excessive building height threatened the salubrity of the atmosphere in a city as densely populated as Paris. It also threatened the safety of the population, especially by increasing the risk of major fires.[62] The main principle used was what would later come to be known as sunlighting. Maximum heights were determined by a line drawn at an angle of 67.5 degrees from the building line to the top of the house opposite. This compares with the angle of 45 degrees which became the norm in Europe in the second half of the nineteenth century, when health considerations were more demanding.

As early as 1765, a royal declaration had laid down a minimum width of 30 feet (9 metres) for new streets in the suburbs, and steps were taken to extend that principle to the creation of new streets in the older areas. It was therefore logical that the authorities should relate their maximum height to a street width of 30 feet. The new limit was considerably in excess of the maximum height of 15.6 metres laid down in 1667, but this had not been effectively enforced and any attempt to return to it would have been unrealistic.

The scheme was clarified in 1784 by letters patent, probably after representations from building interests.[63] Most important of all, a formula was found to embrace the various forms of accommodation and roofing above the cornice. The formula distinguished three main types of structure here, namely attics, mansards and roofs. The maximum height of the cornice was fixed at 54 feet (17 metres) in the 30-foot streets, including the cornices of attics and mansards built in place of attics. However, 10 additional feet (3 metres) were allowed for the roof in houses of normal depth. In houses of double depth, 15 feet (5 metres) were allowed for the roof. This gave an overall height, including the roof, of between 64 metres and 69 feet. Clearly, there was scope for interpretation, particularly of the terms 'mansard' and 'roof', but the 1784 changes cannot be interpreted as an attempt to reduce the overall heights authorised in 1783. On the other hand, the departure from the geometrical formula used in 1783 suggests that, on this occasion, the calculation was based on a conventional number of storeys (five or six).

These regulations were well thought out, and they were to be carefully enforced. Only the London Building Acts, which may have influenced them, were more developed. By requiring builders and owners to submit plans, they created the administrative machinery for the building permit which would do much to mould Parisian domestic architecture in the nineteenth century. Indeed, 1783/4 marks a turning point in the architectural history of Paris. From then on, mass domestic construction would be a prime concern of the authorities and also of the architects, whose task would become to produce the best results within the regulations. The shaping of nineteenth-century Paris begins in the 1780s.

# Revolution, Empire and Restoration: the Implications for Architecture, 1789–1852

The Crown, the aristocracy and the Church have played so big a part in our story so far that the collapse of the monarchy and feudalism, and the weakening of the Church, after 1789 might have been expected to create the opportunity for an architectural revolution. Moreover, the political instability which would last from the Revolution until the mid-nineteenth century might plausibly have generated a period of architectural instability which would have extinguished the legacy of the *ancien régime*.

History, however, has no place for 'mights'. The French Revolution was no architectural turning-point. None of the pre-1789 architectural legacy was discredited or even significantly questioned, and classical architecture continued in Paris without interruption. Until 1815, the neo-classical mode predominated. Thereafter, no single fashion had the upper hand but, in a period of restricted building, fidelity to classicism was unquestioned. The regularisation of Paris continued, largely on eighteenth-century lines.

Admittedly, a low building rate might have allowed time for reflection, with idle architects thinking afresh and looking abroad. They might have had time to notice the great surge of the European Romantic movement in literature and the arts from around 1820, and the growth of its French branch from around 1830. Romanticism, however, hardly impinged on Parisian architecture. It may have been the biggest design revolution of the century in England, Germany and the United States, but Paris 'saw no signal'. Once again, there are no 'mights'. But the Parisian faith in tradition needs explaining nevertheless.

## FROM REVOLUTION TO EMPIRE, 1789–1804

The Revolution was a disaster for Paris. The city's population dropped sharply in the 1790s and building came to a halt. Temporary structures and displays for the many republican festivals gave much employment to artists and architects. The resulting triumphal arches and backdrops appeared fantastic at first sight, but they were largely based on the neo-classical principles and forms of the 1770s and the 1780s. Reflecting above all the power of the State, they expressed continuity rather than discontinuity. All the post-royal regimes were of course interested in building more lasting monuments to their glory, but little was built on these lines. This was either because economic dislocation prevented the marshalling of funds, as was the case in the 1790s, or because so much investment was directed into military adventures, which was the inevitable result of Napoleon Bonaparte's approach to the government of France.

The near-paralysis of building in the 1790s helped the authorities to pursue the existing regularisation strategy by setting widening lines for many streets. Regularisation was also implicit in the work of the Commission des Artistes, a group of administrators and professionals set up in 1793. Its brief was to prepare a general improvement plan for Paris, but in practice its main task was to divide up the extensive Church and other lands confiscated by the State into building sites. The result was a number of largely unrelated proposals for new streets or local networks of streets. All were based on the rectilinear principle, with minimum street widths of thirty feet. Almost nothing had been done to execute these schemes by 1815, but they did have some effect on later building.

In one area alone did building flourish. The Revolution, which disrupted so much, inaugurated a golden age for the Paris theatre. Before 1789, theatres had been seen as potentially seditious and they were supervised by the Crown. In 1791 the assembly passed a law allowing anyone to set up and operate a

theatre. This freedom would come to an end
in 1807, but meanwhile theatrical shows
multiplied and a wave of new theatres were
built in Paris or converted from existing
premises.[1]

In Paris, progress from the fairground
booth to the permanent playhouse had taken
place in the seventeenth and eighteenth
centuries without making a clear mark on
the city or its architecture. Indeed, Parisian
theatre architecture has been judged inferior
to that of the provinces. The theatre of the
Tuileries, restored for the use of royal
companies in 1764, dated from a century
earlier. However, there had been a great leap
forward when three new theatres were built
between 1779 and 1783 – the Comédie-
Française, the Comédie Italienne and the
Théâtre des Italiens (Fig. 98).[2]

These impressive new theatres were built
in a sober, neo-classical style with elegant
and imposing porticos. The smaller, popular
theatres which already clustered on the
Boulevard du Temple were largely built in
a more relaxed classical style using round
arches and Serlian windows (with three
lights, the central one arched). The influence
of Italian theatre persisted here rather longer
than in the new, royal theatres, but the
effect was nevertheless one of elegance, even
where the buildings were quite small. A
number of these new theatres, of modest
dimensions or buried in popular districts,
were built in the 1790s, adding distinction
to the local scene and generally reinforcing
the classical character of the city. They also
associated classicism with popular entertainment for the first time in Paris.

THE INFLUENCE OF THE EMPIRE

Napoleon Bonaparte's interests were much
too broad to exclude the improvement of
Paris. He acknowledged the origins of his
power in the Revolution and he remained
faithful to Paris as his capital. His military
aspirations greatly surpassed those of his
royal predecessors, including even Louis
XIV, and during his victorious years Paris
became the capital of an immense empire and
associated territories. This implied far more
for Paris than had its status as the seat
of royal administration before 1789. Under
Napoleon I, it symbolised an international
modernising force.

Napoleon is cited as wanting to make Paris the most beautiful city in the world.[3] Similar aspirations had however been attributed to many of his predecessors, and during his short reign the emperor was heavily preoccupied in other ways.[4] Moreover, from the Empire onwards, practical considerations began to play a bigger part in planning.[5] Bonaparte was aware of these trends and often spoke of big civil schemes to transform Paris in the interests of public health, ·traffic flow and public facilities such as markets. At the same time, he was keen to build massive, symbolic monuments. His achievement, in such a brief reign, was considerable.[6] However, he did not change the face of the city, and the prolonged building depression meant that no predominant Empire style emerged. Most impressive of all were his plans for a giant imperial palace on the Chaillot hill, downstream from the city. This evoked Neronian memories, but nothing of it was built.

The emperor's tastes were strongly neo-classical, as befitted his imperial conception of France's role in Europe.[7] He placed great trust in his chosen architects and did not involve himself in the detail of their designs.[8] This allowed them to act as key arbiters of architectural taste and the result was, essentially, a continuation of pre-1789 classicism, with an emphasis on the neo-classical.

THE GREAT AXIAL VISION

The Empire's main achievement in Paris was the enhancement of the great cruciform perspective centred on the Place Louis-XV, now renamed Place de la Concorde. To the south, on the opposite side of the Seine, a large Roman portico was added to Palais Bourbon by Poyet in 1806–8 (Fig. 99). To the north, where the Rue Royale met the *grands boulevards*, the church of the Madeleine was begun in 1807 by Pierre Vignon (Fig. 100). The choice of this rectangular, Graeco-Roman temple with a peristyle of Corinthian columns was made by Napoleon himself. Vignon had been placed only third in the competition but the emperor judged the two winning designs to be too ecclesiastical.[9] Vignon's design, which was not completed until 1845, made a strong contrast with the two designs for churches on the site published by Pierre Contant d'Ivry and G.M. Couture before 1789. Napoleon also authorised the layout of the surrounding square, the Place de la Madeleine, in 1808.

Similar aspirations were expressed on an even larger scale by the Arc de Triomphe project, begun in 1806 and completed in 1836 (Fig. 101). It was the first important monumental arch in Paris since the 1670s. The arch was sited at the western summit of the

99 The portico of the Palais Bourbon (now the Chamber of Deputies) in a painting of 1870.

Champs-Elysées, and stood out on the horizon at the top of the Chaillot hill. With a length of over a mile, rising gently on an increasing gradient until its eventual disappearance into the clouds, the Champs-Elysées remained, as it had been since the seventeenth century, the most grandiose and potentially symbolic urban perspective in Europe. Napoleon's decision to mark the end of the vista with a great monument was very much in character, and the main uncertainty arose from the choice of scale and form that would be needed to impress the eye from as far away as the Tuileries. Napoleon required a simple grandeur similar to that of Blondel's Porte Saint-Denis of 1672.

The solution was to build the largest triumphal arch in history, to designs by J.A. Raymond and J.F.T. Chalgrin. The great size of the arch (50 metres high by 46 metres broad-162 feet by 150) was chosen because its elevated position would have diminished the impact of a smaller structure. The upper part was designed as an attic and heavily emphasised to prevent it from appearing to lean backwards or to fade into the clouds. Giant statuary and huge relief panels maintained the proportion. Although trees rather than buildings formed the perspective along the avenue, it provided a model which later

creators of Paris perspectives could not ignore.

The fourth arm of the perspective posed a unique problem. The view eastward from the Champs-Elysées was closed by the Tuileries. In the last few decades of the *ancien régime*, and in the 1790s, however, architects had proposed an eastward extension of the Champs-Elysées. A direct line was out of the question, but the great area of the Place de la Concorde allowed it to link two almost parallel east-west axes: that of the Champs-Elysées, and that of a new street running eastward from the north-eastern corner of the Place de la Concorde along the northern perimeter of the Tuileries gardens. By the later 1790s, when it was endorsed by the Commission des Artistes, the idea of this big, cross-city route had become virtually orthodox.

The problem then arose of monumental terminations for the new extension. At the western end, the lateral colonnade of a Gabriel *hôtel* modestly served this purpose, but the uncertain length of the eventual street precluded any decision on an eastern termination. In 1801 Napoleon authorised the first section of the new street, named the Rue de Rivoli, together with two new streets running north from the Tuileries gardens

100 The south front of the church of the Madeleine in a photograph *c.* 1900.

101 The Arc de Triomphe.

towards the Rue Saint-Honoré, the Rue de Castiglione (Fig. 102) and the Rue des Pyramides. These new streets produced a dense street network in an area of great potential for prestige building.

The architectural objective in the Rue de Rivoli, then, became not so much the creation of major monuments as the application of classical design principles along what was potentially a very long street and its tributaries. Admittedly, the first section of the Rue de Rivoli did not extend east of the Tuileries gardens, but it is clear that further extensions were envisaged. The resolution of this problem was the achievement of the emperor's favoured architects, Charles Percier and P.F.L. Fontaine. They provided a formula for continuous street architecture which, while based on *ancien régime* precedents, would shape nineteenth-century Paris. As such, the Rue de Rivoli was the most influential Parisian achievement in large-scale domestic architecture since the Place Dauphine (Figs 103–04).

Street width and facade height were the main variables. The architects chose a massive arcade, incorporating a set-back entresol, and added three full floors above, in contrast to the two floors which had previously been the tradition in Paris piazzas and the Rue Royale. A continuous balcony at the *piano nobile* provided the main perspective line. A second continuous balcony at the new, third floor reinforced the perspective and, together with the reduced height of the third floor, designated the extra floor as an attic. The roof began above the 'attic' floor, its dormers opening onto a third continuous balcony. As a result, only the second floor lacked a balcony, but the perspective here was reinforced by a standard masonry band. The effect of continuity and perspective was unrivalled anywhere in the world. The balconies may of course have been intended partly to generate spectacular elevated crowd participation in what was bound to become a cauldron of marching boots and waving banners, but individual balconies could have achieved as much.

102 The completed Rue de Castiglione in a painting by Canella.

103 Looking west along the first section of the Rue de Rivoli, begun in 1806. The photograph dates from about 1890.

104 Extension of the Rue de Rivoli ordinance to the east in the 1850s.

## OTHER NEW STREETS AND PUBLIC BUILDINGS

The Rue de Rivoli was slow to attract private capital. The government built the arches and vaults of the arcade, but the houses above were not completed until 1814. The difficulty arose from the trade depression, together with the established reluctance of owners to build to a government ordinance.[10] The sacrifice of a large part of the ground floor to an open arcade may also have caused concern, given that false arcades had become the norm since the seventeenth century and had formed part of the ordinance of the Rue Royale.

Similar efforts elsewhere were out of the question, and few other new streets were built in Napoleon's Paris. The Rue des Colonnes, notable for its arcades in an oriental manner, was a much smaller scheme (Fig. 105). Started in 1795 as a street scheme arising from a revolutionary confiscation, the colonnade was imposed by the national Domaines when the land was handed over to a private individual for development.[11] When the street was completed under the Empire it was welcomed as a contribution to the imperial aesthetic, albeit on a small scale.

In the absence of a big programme of new

105 *Top left*, the Rue des Colonnes.

106 *Below*, the Carrousel arch.

107 *Top right*, the Bourse in a photograph of *c.* 1905.

streets and squares (Fig. 104), the reshaping of imperial Paris depended largely on public buildings. Understandably enough, there were special efforts to make a striking, symbolic statement. The biggest of all, the Arc de Triomphe, was clearly a lengthy undertaking. In 1806, the year in which construction started, work also began on the triumphal arch of the Carrousel, designed by Percier and Fontaine (Fig. 106). This more modest design was completed in 1807. Like the Arc de Triomphe, the Carrousel arch stood on the Champs-Elysées axis, but in deference to the adjoining Tuileries palace it was a puny, even fussy, affair. It was certainly of Roman inspiration, respecting no doubt the two architects' earlier studies in Italy and Napoleon's taste for elaborate triumphs. The emperor did not, however, warm to the design.

Long rows of columns were a common feature of buildings aspiring to imperial significance. Archaeological research had now reached such a degree of achievement that the Greek or Roman pastiche became a strong temptation, especially at a time of new French involvement in Italy. The church of the Madeleine and the portico of the Palais Bourbon have been mentioned already. They were echoed by the Bourse, designed by A.T. Brongniart and started in 1808 (Fig. 107). It was a classical temple pastiche with a peristyle of columns, superficially similar to the Madeleine.

These scholarly, neo-classical creations were very effective townscape components. What they failed to do was promote a new mode of design which could be used more widely. Under the Empire this defect was scarcely visible, as so little domestic building took place (Fig. 108). Neo-classicism tended, however, to isolate the Empire within the long-term development of Parisian architecture.

THE NEW MONARCHIES, 1815–48

The Bourbon Restoration did not generate a total return to the styles of the *ancien régime*, but the absence of a design revolution between 1789 and 1815 permitted an easy return to a royal architecture. The revolution of 1830 which brought down Charles X replaced him with another king, albeit an Orleanist. Once again no major architectural transformation can be linked to the change of dynasty. As constitutional monarchs, these new kings lacked the resources of the Absolutist era and they were unable to function as leading architectural patrons. Meanwhile, industrialisation, which was beginning

to affect the development of architecture in Britain, had scarcely begun in France. The period from 1815 to 1848 thus marks a phase of continuity, particularly in public architecture. The most striking innovator was the Roman Catholic Church, which built a number of parish churches in a variety of styles from neo-classical to Gothic, with the occasional exercise in eclecticism. This independent tendency, which would flower under the Second Empire, nevertheless had little influence on secular building before 1848.

Without a clear lead from the State, business and an impoverished aristocracy, residential architecture failed to develop rapidly or on distinctive lines. The generally low rate of building was exacerbated by trade-cycle depressions such as that of the mid-1820s,[12] and there was an emphasis on peripheral, low-density development. New apartment houses were generally lower and smaller than those common in the later eighteenth century. A height of five storeys was normally the maximum in the centre, and four storeys elsewhere (Fig. 109). There was almost always a mansard roof with dormers. The building regulations of 1783/4 were partly responsible, but so was the general reduction of pressure on land and the decline in speculation. In 1829, during a serious building slump, an alliance of Parisian property interests tried to secure a relaxation of the building regulations in order to reduce construction costs and so stimulate building.[13] If the Ministry of the Interior had accepted their argument, smaller, flimsier buildings would have resulted, and the Parisian aesthetic would have been threatened. In practice, nothing came of the proposal, the authorities no doubt detecting a British-influenced deregulating tendency within the property alliance.

The most important novelty of the period was the covered commercial arcade, a cluster of them being built within some of the large sites in the busy north-west sector of the central area, on either side of the *grands boulevards*. These galleries were fashionable for a time, partly because street conditions in a pre-sidewalk era made covered shopping attractive.[14] The entrances from the street were usually monumental or they bore some striking motif, and the interiors used a great deal of glass and iron. There was often a

108 A rare example of the Italianate style favoured under the Empire for modest, domestic buildings. This is the Duphot riding stables, built when the Rue Duphot was laid out on confiscated Church land from 1807.

1828, when the architect, Dubois, built a massive apartment house at 9, boulevard Saint-Denis (now demolished). With eleven bays and a large interior courtyard, it had a false arcade topped by four full storeys, with two floors in the roof. There was a continuous balcony on the first floor, and masonry bands reinforced the horizontal emphasis. The whole construction echoed the Rue de Rivoli, and recalled some of the speculations of the 1780s on more central sites.[15] It also looked forward to the apartment blocks of Haussmann's era in the nineteenth century.

Most apartment houses were much smaller than this, and spartan and utilitarian in style, the product of practical considerations rather than architectural invention (Figs 110–11). In the outer districts they were often arranged around three sides of a courtyard, the fourth side being left open to the street, or closed by a lower building. The rooms were generally small and the ceilings were low. Materials were cheap and flimsily used, producing uneven floors and cracked ceilings when the structure slipped, as it usually did. The simple appearance of the facades was partly the result of the lack of features in relief. Balconies were occasionally present, at both

109 *Above*, apartment house at 10, Place de la Bourse, built in 1834 by A.J. Pellechet.

110 *Right, above*, houses in the Rue du Pont-Louis-Philippe, one of the few new streets of the July Monarchy, *c.* 1845.

111 *Right, below*, houses of the July Monarchy in the Rue du Château-d'Eau. On the right are flats and shops in the Porte Saint-Martin market, rebuilt in the late 1980s in a conforming style. City of Paris, standard-issue, imitation Second Empire gas lamp-standards light the fire station exit to the left.

gallery of shops or stores at first-floor level. Fireproof construction was a big feature of these arcades, and the interior aesthetic often combined elegance and intimacy. They looked back to some of the big commercial developments of the later eighteenth century, such as the Palais-Royal. They were not, however, associated with the creation of residential buildings. Their enclosed environments using glazed roofing were completely new, a product of the relative fall in the cost of iron and glass during the initial stages of French industrialisation. In one respect, however, this important innovation made almost no impact: on the street frontage, which was normally developed on separate lines, without reference to the arcade. Later, under the Second Empire, the creation of a new generation of comfortable streets, with wide sidewalks and awnings over the shop windows, would discourage the creation of further arcades.

The reduced level of property development meant that big combinations of apartments and commercial space were hard to find. Contemporary comment suggests that the most impressive example dates from

first-floor and attic levels, as at 104, rue de Richelieu.[16] The main external features, however, were the louvred, wooden shutters flanking the rows of windows on all the upper floors, which did not go out of fashion until the 1840s.

The lack of features in relief was partly due to an extension of the building regulations. Royal efforts to control projections dated, as we have seen, from the later Middle Ages. They had been extended in the eighteenth century, culminating in the royal declaration on streets and buildings of 1783 which, *inter alia*, had banned all projections from the facades of buildings facing the streets.[17] In practice this did not apply to balconies above a certain height, and balconies had been included in the Rue de Rivoli design. However, it may well have restricted the use of decorative elements, and in 1823 the Crown drew up special building regulations to clarify the position.

The royal declaration made clear that the principal consideration was the danger that, in a city of narrow streets with almost no pavements, tall carts could collide with projections and cause structural damage. Consequently, a maximum depth of 0.8 metres (31 inches) was allowed for balconies, and 0.22 metres (9 inches) for 'little' balconies (which presumably referred to window-

guards). Other, mainly decorative, projections were allowed only minimal dimensions. Corbelling was completely banned.[18] The ordinance of 1823 did not therefore liberate the architect from the restrictions implied in the text of 1783. However, the precision of the new code prevented all latitude, especially in decorative elements such as pilasters and pediments. The flat Parisian facade was thus relaunched into the nineteenth century from its origins under the *ancien régime*. It should be said, however, that the smooth facade was in fashion in the early 1820s throughout Europe, and there appears to have been no adverse comment in Paris at the time the new restrictions were published.

Most of the architects of modest homes were obscure, but Jean-Nicolas-Louis Durand is an exception. As a professor of architecture at the Ecole Polytechnique, he built a variety of small mansions and apartment houses, some of the latter being in the fashionable Madeleine area and in the Faubourg Poissonnière. He used a large version of the established *'décor économique'*. At 16, rue Lamartine, IX[e], for instance, he built a house of four storeys, the main feature of which was a modified Serlian window (Fig. 112). Ceilings and windows diminished in height towards the top of the building. There were no balconies, but there were

112 Durand's apartment house at 16, Rue Lamartine, dating from 1824. The modified Serlian windows echo the Empire fashion, which may have been reinforced by the example of Robert Adam during the Restoration phase of *'anglomanie'*.

simple window-guards. Elsewhere Durand favoured a simple treatment using Doric pillars and pilasters.[19] This taste for modest efficiency was reflected in his lectures.[20]

The Restoration period produced, more than any of its predecessors, a suburban alternative to the crowded central areas. The 1820s, in particular, were marked by peripheral land development schemes on a scale previously unknown. They were aimed mainly at modest purchasers such as small rentiers who would value an attractive environment at low cost at the same time as an additional investment which would appreciate as the city grew.

The largest schemes were the Batignolles development in the north-west, and (Beau) Grenelle, on the Left Bank of the Seine in the south-west. In both cases a comprehensive street pattern was planned, and public buildings were planned to attract purchasers of the sites. Little attempt was made however to control the design of the facades, it being envisaged that a low-density environment would emerge during a long-term construction process.

The creation of this new building land allowed the *hôtel* to escape the high land values of the inner city and to flourish here in a more modest form. Most of the new *hôtels* in the north-west faced on to the streets, with stables and service buildings at the bottom of the court.[21] The new developments were advertised as semi-rural, and owners and architects opted for an arcadian style. Little of this early building survives today, but it is important to note that, for a few decades, a suburban alternative to the multi-storey Parisian environment existed within easy reach of the old city. From around 1840, however, the pressures of urban growth and the increase in middle-class demand allowed the apartment house to become almost universal in these new areas.[22]

THE JULY MONARCHY

Louis-Philippe's interest in the embellishment of Paris had to be pursued with limited funds, at any rate in the 1830s. In two cases he took advantage of the existing potential of city sites by setting up the July Column on the Place de la Bastille, and by rearranging the Place de la Concorde, in 1836–40, around

113 The Sainte-Geneviève library.

a tall, Egyptian obelisk. Both these schemes reinforced the ideal of a central or focal monument dominating a large public space.

When the 1840s saw faster growth in France, thanks partly to the modernising policies of the government, building revived in Paris and the early railways strengthened interest in industrial construction methods. Henri Labrouste's design for the Sainte-Geneviève library (Fig. 113), built between 1844 and 1850 near the Sorbonne, and standing on Soufflot's great Panthéon (formerly the church of Sainte-Geneviève) piazza, made spectacular use of iron columns and roofing arches. Although iron roofing components had been used by Jacques Duban at the Ecole des Beaux-Arts in 1834, the method was still very rare, and Labrouste was regarded as a major innovator. No iron was visible, however, on the exterior, which was mainly notable for its long, two-storey facade with arched windows and heavy rustication.

This simple, indeed brutal, style was seen as appropriate to a purely functional building, and Labrouste, who was known as a brilliant product of the Ecole des Beaux-Arts, was spared criticism by his fellow architects. Also affecting the issue was the emergence of railway architecture since the early 1840s, which had made architectural opinion more accustomed to metal roofing within stone frontages, and facades with arched fenestration. Clearly, a new architecture was announcing itself in the 1840s, but too little building was taking place for it to challenge the classical French tradition which remained securely in place in 1848.

After about 1830, the Paris economy began to grow more rapidly and the building of apartment houses accelerated. In many streets in the outer districts, the sites used were wider than in the past, or distinct rows of apartment houses sprang up on adjacent sites. Their architects often welcomed this potential for regularity. The spacing of the window openings became regular, irrespective of the interior arrangement of the rooms. The facade of the individual house became a simple component, without individual character, and the buildings merged in long terraces.[23]

The Rue Rambuteau, a new street driven by the prefectoral authorities from the Halles to the Marais in the 1840s, was lined by apartment houses which, though they stood on very shallow sites, rose to a height of six storeys, plus a dormer roof. Nearly all the facades in the street were very spartan, with rows of identical window openings set almost flush with the facades. Aimed at modest, middle-class tenants, the apartments were notable for their small rooms, and the fenestration clearly related to the outside effect rather than to the interior arrangement. The ground floor contained shops but there was no entresol.

Under Louis-Philippe, some central districts saw the building of small apartment houses with a measure of carved decoration in a romantic style. The eastern *grands boulevards* are lined with many examples of this type (Fig. 114). Italianate arched windows are not uncommon and the whole facade appears relaxed and unassuming. There is use of Italian, French Renaissance or oriental detailing. An important corner site at the eastern end of the Rue Rambuteau (nos. 2 and 4), notwithstanding the simplicity of the rest of the street, was distinguished by richly carved window surrounds using foliage forms and carved grotesque heads in an emphatically medieval style.

Population growth accelerated in the 1840s when most of the new railways built termini in Paris. When the new Gare de l'Est was linked to the city centre by a wide, new street, the Boulevard de Strasbourg, from 1852, a large number of new apartment houses were built facing the thoroughfare and, in narrow courts, on extensive areas of

backland. Simple in style, their design was scarcely innovatory, but they provided a foretaste of a new Paris formed by apartment house districts organised around wide, straight thoroughfares.

The best guide to apartment house architecture under the July Monarchy is Victor Calliat's selection of 1850, complemented by Normand's three-volume depiction of modern Paris, published between 1843 and 1849.[24] Although Calliat set out to gather the most distinguished designs, most were very severe. They were enlivened mainly by engaged pilasters, some of them in the giant

114 Ornate facade at 38, Rue des Petits-Champs.

order. Window surrounds were generally rather thin. Some windows were equipped with classical pediments. Rusticated masonry made an occasional appearance, cladding the ground level up to the top of the entresol, or enhancing corners and ends of facades. Windows with full arches were extremely rare, in contrast to the Restoration period (though they were more prominent in Normand's selection). Niches were another Restoration feature which had faded away by 1830.

The *entresol*, on the other hand, remained almost universal, being associated with the *porte cochère* which was also present in almost all of Calliat's examples. Balconies gave signs of becoming more important. Short balconies of two bays or more were commonly used to emphasise the centres of facades. They were normally placed at *piano nobile* level and were combined with pilasters to create the effect of a central pavilion, two or three bays wide. In the 1840s, full-width balconies at *piano nobile* level become more common, but the emphasis on the centre of the facade was maintained. Meanwhile, many of the houses throughout the period incorporated a continuous metal balustrade at attic level where the facade was normally stepped back. This was usually of the same design as any lower balconies and reinforced the horizontal effect of wide facades.

Stylistically the predominant mode was a revived Louis XVI with a little of the Empire. The effect was very hidebound. Calliat included only one eccentric design, this being by Viollet-le-Duc, in the Rue de Berlin, built towards the end of the period. It used dressed stones to produce a strong masonry effect over the whole facade. The facade design was medieval in inspiration, and medieval string courses were used over the windows. This house was a complete departure from the norm, but the work of Viollet-le-Duc was unique in this period.

As was usual in the portrayal of apartment house designs, Calliat's elevations depicted one house at a time, as any neighbouring houses were almost always by different architects. However, when aligned in streets, these houses would have had enough horizontal elements to produce a harmonious effect, especially in view of the movement towards row development. Normand's selection of facades also showed a preference for long frontages, continuous balconies and symmetrical, continuous facade compositions capable of forming longer rows. Sober order, and decorative restraint, were clearly his preference.[25]

Modest though these developments were, they were enough to make the apartment house a subject of serious architectural interest for the first time in the 1840s. This new enthusiasm was reflected notably in the pages of César Daly's *Revue générale de l'architecture et des travaux publics*, founded in 1839 partly to encourage new techniques and design.[26] Victor Calliat's massive survey gave a similar impression. He saw the years 1830–50 as a fruitful period for the apartment house, with much design progress.[27]

*Hôtel* architecture evolved differently, moving towards a romantic miscellany of styles.[28] The construction of the main facade directly on the street frontage was now very common, and the adoption of neo-classical, Renaissance and Gothic styles generated a new variety in the streetscape. This new freedom of style reflected, to some degree, the emergence of a growing number of clients from the business and professional classes, and the decline of aristocratic building. Despite the Restoration, the old, pre-1789 royal court had disappeared. Many of the old nobility now came less frequently to Paris, and their *hôtels* deteriorated or were let as rooms or industrial premises. This was especially a feature of the Marais, where the city's oldest *hôtels* were clustered.

The new nobility engendered by the Empire, the Restoration and the July Monarchy were either firmly based on their estates, or too mobile to value an expensive residence in Paris. The new clients of the July Monarchy therefore had less interest in design continuity or conformity with their peers. Their architects, aware of the rise of the picturesque in Britain since the later eighteenth century, were tempted to engage in an architecture of individualism which also reflected the motives and values of their clients.

THE ECOLE DES BEAUX-ARTS

If building was depressed between the Revolution and the Second Empire, architectural education was re-established on a strong footing. This educational system was based on the Ecole des Beaux-Arts in Paris. During the nineteenth century it built up a reputation as the world's finest school of architecture. It would become a Mecca for student architects from abroad, and would extend the influence and example of French architecture throughout the globe. At the same time, the 'Beaux-Arts style', which would be widely acknowledged as the world's most complete and refined approach to building until as late as the First World War, became almost universal in France for public buildings and luxurious private buildings of all sorts.

The Académie Royale d'Architecture was dissolved in 1793 by the Convention, but its architectural teaching survived in a succession of forms until the new Ecole (Royale) des Beaux-Arts was set up in 1819.[29] The Ecole provided a full course in architecture.[30] The interim arrangements, which had emphasised neo-classical design, had not greatly disturbed the content of pre-1793 teaching.[31] From 1819, the architecture course at the Ecole des Beaux-Arts followed an ordered curriculum, the essence of which would survive until the dismantling of the school in 1968.[32] This curriculum was embodied in regulations in 1823. The range of subjects was broad, and the design work assigned to the students was useful and stimulating.[33] The theoretical element was especially strong. The components of study, and the examinations, competitions and projects, tended to increase in number and to become more precise as the century wore on. Practical training, as in the courses on building, was strongly emphasised.

There is no doubt that the Ecole provided a thorough architectural training which would remain unequalled anywhere in the world at least until the end of the century. The architecture of the Ecole nevertheless served the State, the aristocracy and the rich. Large public buildings were prominent among the design projects. In a course as thorough and academic as this, students were introduced to a variety of styles, but in the projects and competitions which measured their progress through the course, the contemporary variants of the French classical style were used almost universally.

The highlight of the programme was the annual Grand Prix de Rome (as it had come to be called by the mid-nineteenth century), the direct descendant of the eighteenth-century contest. This was a competition for designs for an important building, usually public in character, such as an embassy, a palace, a ministry or a luxurious resort hotel. Not only did the winner secure a further period of study of four or five years in Rome, much of it literally among the ruins, but he could aspire to an important public appointment or contract almost immediately on his return. Indeed, he could see his way forward, with considerable confidence, to a comfortable dotage as a doyen of the profession – in addition, with a good chance of being elected as one of the eight members of the architectural academy, which would make him in his turn a judge of Rome prize entries. Competition and continuity thus went together in the Prix de Rome.[34]

The most distinctive feature of the Ecole was the unit of practical study, the *atelier*.[35] These were studios of varying sizes to which students were normally attached. They were directed either by professors of the school or independent architects of distinction. Many were themselves winners of the Rome prize. Some twenty to thirty students worked in each atelier, usually in very cramped conditions. Here, they completed school assignments, prepared competition entries, and sometimes worked on commissions secured by the head of the atelier. Some ateliers were part of the Ecole and occupied space within the building or in houses nearby. Others were almost independent of the Ecole. By bringing together students at all stages of their development, and carrying through a variety of projects, the ateliers provided something approaching a practical experience. For most students the atelier was the main place of learning. Lectures at the Ecole, on the other hand, tended to be theoretical, didactic and often vague. They were, however, well attended, and apparently appreciated by the students.

Although the Ecole des Beaux-Arts provided a full and stimulating training for architects, its concentration on classical architecture and its French derivatives was too strong to ignore or avoid. Most graduates of the Ecole were aware of other styles and were able to design in them well enough, but they did not anticipate much opportunity to do so in their professional lives. Those able students who aspired to win the Prix de Rome or one of the minor prizes put their main effort into perfecting their mastery of classical design. Although broad concepts were valued by the judges, much emphasis was placed on detail in the later stages of the competition.

With the Prix de Rome setting the tone for much of the work of the Ecole, alternative approaches to design were generally seen as curiosities, or as standing outside the mainstream of French official architecture. Ecclesiastical design, while studied at the Ecole, was so regarded. So were industrial design and, to a lesser degree, colonial design.

Most of the students of the Ecole emerged with no more than a good education in architecture. No diploma was awarded until 1867, and few students registered for it even then. Many students had come from the provinces to study, nothing other than a purely technical training in architecture being available outside Paris. Some of these returned home, but there was a strong temptation to remain in Paris where public contracts, or opportunities to join the offices of successful contemporaries, could more easily present themselves. The architectural profession in Paris tended to be well stocked as a result, and by very able professionals.

Although no exact figures are available, it is clear that a large number of the less successful students became involved in apartment house design. Indeed, many became specialists, either independently or as members of larger practices. The effect of their work did not become clear until the Second Empire, when the building boom drew Herculean efforts from the profession, but two features were generally visible. These were, first, the normally impeccable quality of the designs, at any rate in the facade treatment (interior planning usually being a question of economics and the owner's letting strategy), and second, the use of a reduced and cheapened variant of the French classical style. The better Paris apartment house of the mid-century combined conformity and quality. This meant that a quality building could reinforce the harmonious quality of the townscape, while conformity could allow an average design to be lifted to a higher visual level.

## THE NEW WORKERS' PARIS: BUILDING IN THE EAST

After the Restoration, Paris began to generate or attract large-scale manufacturing. Little of it however set up within the city itself, preferring the suburbs outside the customs (*octroi*) wall, to the east, north and south. Here there grew up a different manner of building, an amalgam of rural and urban types. Gradually, there grew up a different townscape as well.

This new workers' city developed two main types of building. One was the two- or three-storey frontage building, often used partly for commerce and descended directly from the small-town, main-street buildings of the Île-de-France. Even single-storey buildings of this type were not uncommon, and they could also be found in courtyards behind the main house just as they could anywhere in northern France. The other was the 'workers' house' (*maison ouvrière*) of the industrial era, a simple construction in cheap materials, usually rising to no more than three or four storeys (Fig. 115). Such buildings lacked all decoration, except for the occasional string course when they were built of brick (after the railways made cheap brick available in the Paris area), but their main

115 This frequently-altered and extended rental house in the Rue de Bercy epitomises the workers' Paris of the nineteenth century.

distinguishing feature was the absence of a dormer roof. Instead, the top storey was topped by a pitched roof, often covered with zinc, and rising at a very slight angle. The lack of a dormer roof reflected, on the one hand, the absence of large numbers of servants and, on the other, the fact that there was no clash between building regulations and soaring heights. Also missing were balconies. Only the metal window-guards recalled the municipal city.

## ALTERNATIVE STYLES

The Gothic style was used for a number of new churches, notably the immense Sainte-Clothilde (1846–57) by F.C. Gau and Théodore Ballu.[36] The main influence here was English, but the style did not extend to domestic building, as it did across the Channel. Here, as in other examples of an outlandish architecture, what was permitted in large public buildings, not subject to building regulations, did not necessarily spread to domestic design. The Roman Catholic Church, in particular, felt the need to stand back from fashionable secular practice in order to make a more lasting statement. It could on occasion influence adjacent secular architecture, but it normally built in a world of its own.

The July Monarchy saw the first notable experiments in architectural polychromy. The central exponent was J.I. Hittorff, whose interest in Ancient architecture on the ground in Italy and Greece had led him to a number of classical precedents. He used polished blocks of lava at the church of Saint-Vincent-de-Paul when he took over the project in 1831, and he also used polychromy in his Cirque des Champs-Elysées (1839–41).[37] Polychromy was however more common inside buildings than outside, and the limited emulation of Hittorff's ideas merely emphasised the almost universally monochrome character of Parisian architecture. With all the timber frames now concealed, stucco renderings always mixed to resemble stone, and brick little used outside the east, a harmony of colour was maintained in Paris.

## THE ACHIEVEMENT OF THE EPOCH

The years between 1789 and 1852 mark something of a hiatus in the history of Parisian architecture and planning. They had the effect of maintaining the pre-1789, classical approach until industrial growth began in the 1840s. Architecture's confrontation with France's first Industrial Revolution did not therefore take place until mid-century, and especially during the Second Empire. Would changes now occur?

# 6    PARIS AS THE HUB OF FRENCH INDUSTRIALISATION: BUILDING A EUROPEAN CAPITAL UNDER THE SECOND EMPIRE, 1852–70

The transformation of Paris under the Second Empire is the biggest commonplace of urban history after the Great Fire of London. Looked at in another way, it was arguably the biggest urban renewal project the world has ever seen. It coincided with the first surge of French industrialisation, beginning in the 1840s and lasting until the Great Depression of the 1870s. It was a mixed-economy project, with public investment devoted mainly to the infrastructure, and private capital drawn in to create lettable space. The main emphasis was on streets, which were laid out in the periphery, or driven through the centre at the cost of thousands of demolitions. New streets and new buildings on this scale were bound to affect the appearance of Paris. If a radically new aesthetic had been chosen for the work, perhaps in deference to industrialism, the classical tradition might have been undermined. That the Second Empire did not adopt a radically new aesthetic is not a cause of surprise, for neither had Manchester and London since England's Industrial Revolution. Its new streets were wider and longer, and its buildings were a little taller and a lot bulkier. However, the principles perfected in Paris in the seventeenth and eighteenth centuries were adapted to the new scale. Classicism, far from being undermined, became a unifying force on a gigantic scale.

The basic building unit was the apartment house, which now acquired a standardised form and architectural treatment from one end of the city to the other. In the new arterial streets, more than just a terminal point was needed to create coherence; the frontages themselves had to follow a formula. The result was a city-wide visual unity which went far beyond anything achieved or even envisaged before 1848. The formula was not legally imposed in most cases, however. It represented a consensus of architects and clients. Participation, rather than direction, shaped the new Paris (Fig. 116).

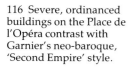

116 Severe, ordinanced buildings on the Place de l'Opéra contrast with Garnier's neo-baroque, 'Second Empire' style.

## ARCHITECTURE, INDUSTRIALISATION
## AND MODERNISATION

In 1850 Léonce Reynaud published the first volume of his weighty *Traité d'architecture*, Reynaud was a professor of architecture at the Ecole Polytechnique, the national school for military engineers. Architecture was taught there mainly to ensure that some at least of the corps of engineers could design a respectable school, hospital or customs post in some distant colony. His approach was down-to-earth, stressing construction and components rather than planning and aesthetics. Here, we might surmise, a modern architecture might be found. However, his introduction, which was almost certainly his introductory lecture in his Ecole course, set out an ideal of French classicism which would not have been out of place in a eulogy at the Ecole des Beaux-Arts. With the wheels of the French Industrial Revolution already turning, it is worth quoting at some length:

> . . . we have a very appropriate system of architecture, which responds utterly to the demands of our customs, our climate, our materials, and our taste. It is linked of course to Greece and Rome, but only in the same way as our literature and our civilisation are; like them it can draw valuable guidance from the world of the ancients but it does not look for absolute precepts there. It proved its independence and its strength by building the Louvre, that palace *sans pareil*, the chateau of Fontainebleau, the Tuileries, the chateaux of Anet and Blois, Versailles, the Hôtel de Ville of Paris, the *hôtels* of the Place de la Concorde, and so many other admirable monuments in which we should take pride. Men like Pierre Lescot, Jean Bullant, Philibert Delorme, Le Mercier, Mansard, and their successors, all of whom have contributed to the lustre of French Architecture, were definitely not humble copyists or sterile plagiarists, as some have dared to suggest. They proved themselves to be just as true, and just as virtuous, as our poets, our painters and our sculptors. Just as much as these, they conformed to the inspirations of our national genius. Art has not abandoned us in our buildings any more than it has in the other areas where it can manifest itself. Indeed, it may even have developed more freely there.[1]

This passage speaks for itself. So does Reynaud's inclusion of precisely the same text in the third edition of his book, in 1867. The completion of the railway network and the reconstruction of Paris had not changed his view of French architecture by one comma. For Reynaud, then, modernisation and industrialisation were not a threat to the French classical tradition, even when their physical impact was at its peak.

The Second Empire nevertheless posed new problems in Paris. The national strategy of economic development, and the improvement of communications, prompted rapid economic growth in the capital. Paris was the centre of the new railway network, and France's largest inland port. Manufacturing expanded, especially in hardware, engineering, precision instruments, luxury goods, fabrics and garments. New financial institutions and the growth of the Bourse boosted the city's role as the biggest money market in continental Europe. The professions expanded. So did the servant class. More troops were garrisoned in the city. With all this, the population nearly doubled between 1850 and 1870. The result was heavy pressure on accommodation, with soaring rents.

The French head of state between his election as president in 1848 and his capture at Sedan in 1870 was Louis-Napoléon Bonaparte, nephew of the first emperor. His progress towards personal rule as prince-president in 1851 and emperor from 1852 did nothing to weaken his modernising aspirations and he recognised the need to adapt Paris to the big changes of his day. The official strategy was to provide ordered space for a surge of new building by creating, directly or indirectly, a network of new streets. The new network had to open up the centre, the place of greatest congestion, but the costly new streets created there were linked to radials going out to link to new districts on the edge of the city where the bulk of residential construction would take place on cheap land.

In historical terms, Napoleon III had much in common with Henri IV. Paris had seen modernisers before, and would see them again. Architectural professors such as Reynaud clearly detected little change at the time. The changes of the Second Empire nevertheless brought Paris into the industrial era, and more quickly than any large city before it. There *were* implications for architecture and urban design, and we must now look more closely at them.

## HAUSSMANN'S IMPACT ON PARISIAN ARCHITECTURE

The search for these implications begins with Georges-Eugène Haussmann, who was appointed Prefect of the Seine in 1853. Since the 1790s the prefect had been the senior executive of central government power in Paris and its suburbs. Under the Second Empire the powers and influence of the prefect were reinforced. Not only was there no mayor, but the city council was selected by the prefect and its status was reduced to that of a municipal commission. Haussmann was well placed, therefore, to carry out the imperial modernisation programme.

Both emperor and prefect wanted the improvements, however practical, to enhance the aesthetic qualities of Paris. Both respected the French classical tradition. Neither had more than a general knowledge of art and architecture, but both had clear ideas about what they wanted. The emperor was interested in new building techniques, such as the use of wrought iron, and in practical design where this was appropriate. He wanted his buildings to be recognised as 'modern'. However, these aspirations rarely detached him from the classical style.

Napoleon III intervened in a number of projects, often stressing the need for 'modernity' in representative buildings. For the rebuilt Hôtel-Dieu, the city's main hospital, the emperor rejected the Gothic style which was at first mooted, and secured a simple, Italianate design with arched windows and rustication which Haussmann later described as 'absolutely modern', no doubt in tribute to its lack of decoration.[2] Its round arches also recalled the Bibliothèque Sainte-Geneviève and some of the railway architecture of the 1850s, in which full arches had come to the fore as an expression of practicality and day-to-day effort within the classical tradition. While a romanticist in some respects, the emperor disliked the Gothic style, and it was scarcely used at all in secular public buildings during the Second Empire.[3]

Haussmann, for his part, gave a higher priority to aesthetics, and he sometimes feared that his efforts to embellish Paris lacked the emperor's full support.[4] Striving to secure monumental structures to enhance the world's biggest system of urban perspectives, he was naturally faithful to classical design. Much more than the emperor, he was prepared to give precise instructions to architects on the size, planning and visual highlights of new public buildings. With much greater architectural patronage than the central government, Haussmann set a bigger mark on Parisian architecture than any of his contemporaries.

## THE NEW SCALE

If Haussmann remained faithful to tradition, how then did the new Paris differ from the old? The answer lies mainly in the much greater scale of the new developments. Haussmann's fidelity to the established objectives of perspective, symmetry and vista in a much bigger city helped produce an enhanced scale, but he also saw them as a means of imposing visual order on individual projects, many of which were themselves of unprecedented dimensions (Fig. 117).

The biggest enhancement of scale was in the length of the new streets. As the straight line was retained as a key organising component of the cityscape, rectilinear streets of unprecedented length abounded. The longest of all, the Rue Lafayette, was five

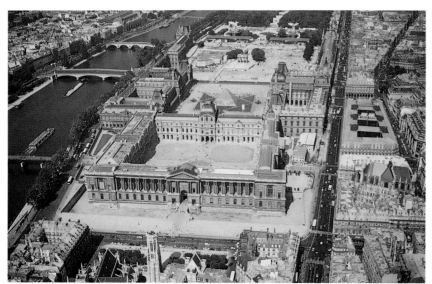

117 The Second Empire completes the work of the *ancien régime*: the Rue de Rivoli defines the northern boundary of an extended Louvre.

built up to the full height permitted, partly through the aesthetic encouragement of the city authorities, and partly owing to the influence of the very high land values and speculative effects engendered by the Haussmannic property boom (Fig. 120). The result was a common cornice line which reinforced the horizontal effect of the street perspective.

Haussmann was acutely aware of the need for powerful monumental terminations for his great new thoroughfares. At star and multiple junctions (Fig. 121), a central monument could terminate a number of streets, but in the radial street system required by a large, modern city this solution could not be universally secured. This meant that Haussmann continually sought to direct new streets towards existing monuments, but to provide specially constructed buildings where necessary (Fig. 122). As a result much of the new public architecture of Paris tended towards exaggerated volumes, striking outlines and emphatic detail.

Meanwhile, the facades of the apartment houses along the new streets carried minimal detail. Their horizontal lines were emphasised, and then harmonised by the intervention of city officials, to enhance the perspective effect. Standardisation and lack of decoration minimised building costs, and the effect was hailed as 'modern'. The owners also saw the standardised facade design of the day as a protection against fashion changes which might easily have

118 The north-south artery of the *grande croisée*: the Boulevard Saint-Michel looking north to the Boulevard de Sébastopol.

kilometres long.[5] Other very long streets, while not planned in a single straight line, were composed, like Roman roads, of a series of straight sections (Figs 118–19).

The new streets were also wider than most of their predecessors, for reasons of public order, public health and traffic engineering. Greater width tended to allow taller buildings on the frontages, especially when, in 1859, the first comprehensive building code since 1783/4 added some two and a half metres (eight feet) to the permitted height of facades on streets 20 metres (65 feet) or more wide. This increase of roughly one storey in the height of buildings on the new arterial streets did little to counteract the horizontal effect of development along the very long streets of the time. The new houses were generally

became less a barrier, and more a means of transition to a luxurious interior from which the outside observer was no longer excluded. Full arches were used increasingly, giving an elegant, softening impression. Roof lines and striking domes, towers and turrets were used in a manner which can only be described as picturesque, even within a classical mode which only a few years before would have excluded such effects. With Garnier himself describing his work as *'mise en scène'* and *'le confortable'*, a new design philosophy was definitely in being in the 1860s.[35]

Underlying some of these designs was an eclecticism or even exoticism which marked a new departure in the work of the Ecole. Emile Bénard, who won the Rome prize of 1867 with his design for an exhibition palace of fine arts, produced a classical building of such extraordinary exuberance that its effect was rococo or even picturesque. This result could be partly explained by Bénard's work on the new opera house as a member of Garnier's office.[36] However, both the competition programmes and the results suggested that the views of the academicians who normally set and judged the competition were changing in the light of the rapid evolution of taste in the Second Empire. Indeed, the great popularity of the Rome prize, which many students entered year after year, indicated a vital institution. It produced highly inventive solutions to programmes which were almost always both precise and challenging.

Whatever the defects of the Ecole, therefore, an able student normally acquired a first-rate design expertise which he could use to build, if he wished, in a variety of styles. His standards were always high, and his confidence in his profession was unbounded. It would be unfair to place the blame for any perceived defects of Parisian architecture in the period, and particularly of its conformism, primarily on the Ecole.

ALTERNATIVE ARCHITECTURAL TRAINING

The Ecole des Beaux-Arts was not the only source of architectural training. It was possible to train as an architect at the Ecole Polytechnique and at the Ecole des Ponts-et-Chaussées, the two important state institutions which trained, respectively, military and civil engineers. Courses in building and architecture were available at both, partly because French technical education was traditionally a rounded, comprehensive affair, owing to the early influence of the Academy, but partly also because the State allotted such a wide role to its engineers, both in France and in the colonies, that many of them were called on to design buildings or to plan settlements during their careers.[37] Léonce Reynaud, designer of the first Gare du Nord (1846) and both an architect and an engineer, taught architecture at both the Ecole des Ponts-et-Chaussées and the Ecole Polytechnique. Additionally, lectures in 'civil construction' were available at the Ecole Centrale des Arts et Manufactures as part of the civil engineering course and could be complemented by work in a private office.[38]

Some engineering students chose to specialise in construction. Their approach, and that of their teachers, lacked aesthetic finesse, but the design of a Paris apartment house would have been well within their capabilities. Indeed, at a time when there were no formal qualifications for architects, men emerging with a state engineering qualification could easily appear better qualified than the architects for certain building tasks. It was this sense of disadvantage among architects that had led to their creation of the Société Centrale des Architectes in 1843, at a time when engineers were securing many of the contracts for railway architecture.

Under the Second Empire, architects sensed that a broadening of architectural practice was taking place and this produced a number of changes in training. The most striking was the creation of a new school of architecture. This was the Ecole Centrale d'Architecture, founded in 1864 by Emile Trélat, an architect with a strong interest in public health and other practical aspects of architecture.[39] The new school's rigorous training programme, inspired by that of the Ecole Centrale des Arts et Manufactures, allowed the student to qualify much more quickly than elsewhere, while nevertheless passing through the essential atelier experience. It placed strong emphasis on architectural practice in an ambitious three-year programme, and it awarded a diploma. It remained small in comparison with the Ecole des Beaux-Arts, but met a need in the private building sector. A training of three years did not however suggest that the products of the new school could remain free of Parisian conformism. Meanwhile, Charles Garnier set up the Ecole Spéciale d'Architecture as an extension of his huge network of students working on the new opera house.[40]

Most aspiring architects however, so far as one may judge, received no formal training. As in Britain at this time, they were taken on as youths or very young men by an established practice. Gradually they graduated from menial tasks to a wide range of design functions which allowed some of them to practise independently. The majority never rose above a subordinate role, but nevertheless regarded themselves as architects. Emile Trélat estimated that three architects out of four learned their profession in this way.[41] Most of these men served in the ranks of apartment house design, and a combination of competence and conformism were the natural product of their experience.

DESIGN CONTINUITY IN A CHANGING PARIS

During the Second Empire, architectural production in Paris expanded to unprecedented levels. The training of architects expanded to produce a greater number of qualified men, and existing architects must have found themselves working up to the very limits of their time and inclination. Architects of moderate ability must have been promoted to work to which they could not possibly have aspired before the mid-1850s.

This situation might have produced big changes in Paris architecture. The leading architects might have introduced new styles, or foreign designs, arguably appropriate to a city in transformation. Mediocre designers might have botched their more simple tasks, turning the ubiquitous apartment house into a mere caricature of elegance and taste.

As we have seen in this chapter, the result was almost the opposite of this. At all levels, architects adapted the traditional, classical style of Parisian architecture to the new era. Their training certainly contributed to this generally harmonious evolution, but it took place on the foundation of an aesthetic scheme which Haussmann applied wholesale with the backing of the imperial authorities. The new street plan, which provided the spatial framework of the new architecture, had itself evolved from the great royal and imperial traditions since the seventeenth century. The three-dimensional design aesthetic applied to the new streets and squares from the early 1850s, through formal design ordinances and the persuasion of the *architectes-voyers*, was the direct descendant of the Place Dauphine and the Rue Royale.

Within this scheme, Parisian architects, with their classical training or experience, were aware of the design implications for individual buildings. The economic and technical changes of the era meant changes in their clientele and its motivations. By developing a 'modern' architecture within traditional norms, however, they could reassure their clients that their building would not, in a few years, be out of date or incongruous. Most of the influences therefore worked in favour of stylistic continuity. There would be no architectural revolution under the Second Empire. But the question was, would the creation of a mass of modern buildings in an essentially traditional style lead to the perpetuation of that style in Paris? Or would there be a reaction against it after the demise of the Second Empire?

104

# 7

# AFTER HAUSSMANN: A NEW PARIS IN AN ERA OF ALTERNATIVE ARCHITECTURES, 1870–1914

The Second Empire had shaped and reshaped Paris more energetically than any previous regime. Its aesthetic norms, however, were developments of an older, classical tradition. After 1870, under the Third Republic, the city grew more slowly, and the central government was less concerned to set its mark on Paris. Gradually, architectural variants, some of them originating outside France, began to appear. Ostentatious luxury, preservationism, anti-industrial craft values, internationalism and a new modernism were knocking on the door by the turn of the century. The apparently effortless pre-eminence of French classicism at last seemed to be under threat. Would the classical tradition, reshaped and reinforced by Haussmann, resist or absorb these forces? Or would it collapse, or be diluted?

## BUILDING AND ARCHITECTURE IN A PARIS WITHOUT HAUSSMANN

The resignation of Haussmann, defeat by Prussia, the collapse of the Second Empire and the chaos of the Commune halted public works and private building in the early 1870s. From mid-decade, however, the authorities resumed a programme of improvements based on new streets. Though carried out more slowly and intermittently, most of the work completed between the later 1870s and the First World War had been planned by Haussmann. In this way, the aesthetic potential of the Second Empire's street-building strategy was maintained until the early twentieth century.

Private building revived in the later 1870s, and in the early 1880s it reached a peak which surpassed the previous boom at the end of the Second Empire.[1] The general trend of building in Paris was downwards thereafter, as the supply of vacant land within the city boundaries dwindled and the rate of demolition remained lower than in Haussmann's time. However, there was no disastrous collapse for the building industry. After the accumulated demand of the early 1870s had been satisfied, and taking account of the fluctuations of the building cycle, some three thousand building permits for new buildings and extensions were being issued annually in the 1880s. By the early 1900s the building rate had sunk to around two thousand permits a year, but the growing volume of building outside the city boundary must have helped sustain employment among Parisian architects.

Most building in the suburbs lacked the distinction of western Paris, and we shall not pursue its characteristics here or elsewhere in this book. Those engaged in building and design in the city of Paris saw the suburbs as a distinct and largely inferior fringe belt with its own needs, its own government and its own design norms. However, even within the city the striking homogeneity of Haussmann's time was gradually undermined. This was partly because fewer new streets were built by the authorities and less effort was made to secure integrated facade designs. Although the *architectes-voyers* maintained their careful supervision of new plans, the authorities were unwilling for both financial and political reasons to pursue the imperial policy of visual order in new streets, at any rate after the early 1880s. At the same time, investment in public buildings, though fully in step with the requirements of a growing city, was no longer used to help construct the townscape to the same extent as in Haussmann's day. After 1870, Paris thus offered a greater freedom to the architect, much as it had done between 1815 and 1848 when the State played a modest role. It remains to be seen what use architects made of this freedom.

105

## ARCHITECTS AND ARCHITECTURE IN A REPUBLICAN FRANCE: THE ECOLE DES BEAUX-ARTS AT ITS PEAK

Despite its ostensibly democratic and progressive title, the Third Republic was designed to achieve stability. As a compromise between a wide range of interests and ideas, its values were conservative. Reaction and reform were alike discouraged, in the hope of allowing France to maintain the economic progress and social evolution which industrialisation seemed to offer, without eroding its traditional foundations.

Higher education, as the source of a professional elite which would be an important component of both stability and progress, was therefore spared the reforming attentions of the State after 1870. The Ecole des Beaux-Arts, having repulsed the reformers in the 1860s, was in no further danger of interference, and in consequence there could be no major change in the rest of the structure of architectural education in France. The main development came in 1903 when parliament, responding in part to the growing demand for places, voted to set up a number of Beaux-Arts schools in provincial cities. Created in 1905, these foundations reinforced the Beaux-Arts system, especially as their better students still sought to complete their training in Paris.

The result was the most brilliant period in the Ecole's history. Paris architecture, as before, reflected its *éclat*. No more than in the past did it foster a wide variety of styles. Instead, it focused on the elegant, luxurious variant of the French classical style which had emerged at the end of the Second Empire.[2] This variant had been launched by Charles Garnier's Opéra. Garnier's presence in Paris as a doyen until the end of the century, and the growing output of the dozens of Ecole students who had worked on the opera house, helped sustain the style, which offered infinite opportunities for massing and decoration. As an architecture of opulence which symbolised the *belle époque*, it supplied a multitude of jobs. If the Second Empire had been the age of the 'singing mason', a whole choir of architects was in full voice by the end of the century.[3]

The work of the Ecole was best reflected in the subjects of its prize competitions and in the winning entries. In line with the expected career destinations of the leading students, prestigious public buildings dominated these competitions, and especially the Rome prize. Little had changed in this since the early part of the century. There was, however, a change in the balance of the subjects towards utilitarian projects, and towards private-sector schemes. The selection of a number of hotels, spas and other leisure facilities reflected the increase in private consumption among the rich towards the end of the century and thereafter. There also appeared to be no constraints on construction techniques, with iron and glass extensively used to create warm, airy and light environments within the vaults and domes designed to shelter luxurious travel and healthy ease. This was no irrelevant, unreal or backward-looking architecture. It aptly served a rich, leisured, cultured and influential clientele.

The leading entries gave no hint of an approaching 'industrial' style, however. In 1874, Louis Duc, the veteran architect and specialist in iron, pointedly founded a special prize to encourage the invention of a new style of architecture. The 1876 subject, a railway station, was suitably utilitarian, but the winning entry, by Jean-Camille Formigé, was essentially classical (with eclectic touches), apart from the simple iron train shed.[4] In this and entries for other prizes, railway stations were invariably equipped with such a single-span iron structure, but ornamentation became more and more prominent as the years went by, while the station buildings used an eclectic classical style suggestive of holiday departures rather than daily business.

Towards the end of the century the subjects of the Rome prize leaned much more frequently towards the large buildings which the industrial era was increasingly able to create (Fig. 150). These did not, however, normally include factories and workers' housing. They reflected the leisured round of the upper classes, doing business in ornate banks, travelling in First Class and holidaying in their villas on the Côte d'Azur. Large state buildings and the homes of the aristocracy were now less frequent. There was more than a whiff of Nice in many of these entries, and Paris was less often the implicit setting than it had been in mid-century.

In 1891 the subject was a central railway station with a giant hotel. The winner, Henri Eustache, created a massive iron train shed with a huge narthex dominated by three giant entrance arches. The three arches, set within a powerful, monumental facade, recalled the central block of the Musée Galliéra (1878–1894) by Léon Ginain (Fig. 151), and thus maintained a link with the architecture of the late Second Empire.[5] Iron was used extensively, even in the narthex. The twin hotel buildings, standing away from the main station, were the height of classical conventionality, but the station frontage, with its massive round arches and flanking pylons, was strikingly brutal.[6] In 1900 the subject of the prize was a large thermal spa and casino. The winning entry, by Paul Bigot, was astonishingly eclectic, an amalgam of pleasure palaces through the ages.

The number of prizes multiplied at the Ecole towards the end of the century, many of them focusing on design problems associated with modernity. The Prix Godeboeuf, for instance, required students to propose treatments for engineering features such as bridges and lifts, and for electric lighting.[7] The entries, however, were essentially decorative, hiding the new technology rather than allowing it to express itself.

By the turn of the century the Ecole prize entries displayed an ornate exuberance which is often described as baroque, but to which we shall refer as the 'French luxury style' in deference to its national and international diffusion from the 1890s. The classical lines, proportions and features were always present, but more and more attention was given to costly effects and eclectic detailing. These projects and prizes were certainly an excellent training, but the lack of reference to cost constraints and the great prestige of these competitions meant that students tackled more modest schemes only as class or year exercises. The context of their training was a sunlit world of wealth and beauty which the First World War would transform for ever (Fig. 152).

## FRENCH ARCHITECTURE IN AN AGE OF INTERNATIONALISM

The pre-1914 world of elegance and leisure was increasingly an international world. The choice of the name 'Promenade des Anglais' for the fashionable seaside drive at Nice made the point nicely enough. The Ecole nevertheless clung to the idea of a French, national architecture, which was reinforced by the new wave of imperialism which affected most of Europe from the 1870s. Foreign students might attend the Ecole in growing numbers, including an important group of Americans by the turn of the century, but they were never allowed to feel that they had a distinct contribution to make to

150 *Top*, three entries for the Prix de Rome competition of 1902. The subject was a national printing works, the closest the jury came to an industrial subject before 1914. Only one entrant, Coutan, has chosen to make the machine shop a feature of his scheme when seen from the frontage. His stripped-classical treatment provides a rare example of the Beaux-Arts student struggling with industrial design.

151 The Musée Galliéra, its architecture intended to reflect the vitality of art.

152 *The architect*, an heroic painting by M.H. Magne, 1911. The architect, cane in hand, and formally dressed, directs a prestigious project, but his spotless gentleman's attire suggests that he does not intend to spend much time on site. The site foreman or master mason, in blue overalls, stoops to squint at a drawing which the architect nonchalantly dangles from one hand. The figure holding on to his homburg at the back is probably the contractor. The architect's top hat is clearly immune to the effects of the strong wind. The artist is probably a member of the Magne family of architects.

153  Aquarium poster at the exhibition of 1900.

154  Bird's-eye view of the 1900 exhibition.

155  Poster from the 1889 exhibition.

156  Main entrance to the exhibition of 1900.

the Ecole's work. They won few prizes except those created especially for them, and few practised in France. French students formed the overwhelming majority. Of the surviving alumni of the Ecole in 1895, 10 lived in Britain and 7 in Germany, whereas 939 lived in Paris or its two neighbouring *départements*. Even Belgium registered only 5 graduates of the Ecole.[8]

Meanwhile, the formal definition of French architecture remained unaltered from the Second Empire. In 1889, the respected Lucien Magne's short review of contemporary French architecture situated recent work in a very long tradition, with the customary self-satisfaction. For Magne, architecture was art, and French art was endowed with multiple virtues. The spirit of Magne's words dated back to the seventeenth century and his rhetoric at least to the first half of the nineteenth. Even more important however was his message, which pointed the architects of France towards a boundless future of achievement. Nowhere in this future, however, could an industrial challenge, or the needs of the masses, be discerned:

> To shine forth, as in the past, throughout the western world, French art must conserve and develop the qualities which are appropriate to its genius: clarity, sobriety and taste. It must not adapt to the exaggerations of other countries and other centuries.[9]

It is sometimes suggested that this self-conscious nationalism was leavened by the international exhibitions of which Paris became the world's leading host between 1867 and 1914 (Figs 153–6). Their impact on Parisian architecture and architects was, however, at best superficial and transient. The growing French Empire was strongly reflected in the many pastiche colonial buildings erected for the exhibitions, but a *flâneur* would have paced many a mile through the streets of Paris before he glimpsed a mansion or apartment block in an arabesque style.[10] Nor did the expanding role of Paris as the world's most important centre of international contact and exchange dilute the national character of its culture and environment. Parisians believed that foreigners respected the city's distinctively French qualities. International world there

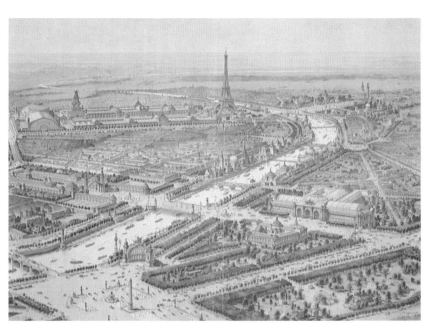

might be, but while London's Ritz Hotel could adopt a French style, the Langham could never be copied in Paris. Parisians were more inclined to see the exhibitions as the world coming to Paris, rather than as a chance to step out of the city's frame.

The physical arrangement of the Paris exhibitions evolved from the single, large hall of the 1855 exhibition to a motley collection of buildings. This arrangement reached its apotheosis in 1900. Many of these individualistic structures were constructed by exhibiting countries, and were usually the work of foreign architects. Most of those for general use were built by the City of Paris and all their architects were French. Nearly all the buildings were, in any case, removed after the exhibition. Variety and exoticism marked the 1889 exhibition, and even more that of 1900, but the transience of these events limited their influence on permanent architecture in Paris. The flimsy 'palace of the Bey of Tunis', built for the 1867 exhibition, was moved to the Parc Montsouris where it served for some time as an observatory, but it gradually mouldered away into oblivion and failed to influence even the residential streets nearby.[11]

The exhibitions, then, were no seedbed of architectural innovation. Only in decoration was Parisian practice influenced. Striking materials such as ceramics, and bright colours, may have been promoted by daring and experimental exposure at the exhibitions of 1878 and later, but even this is hard to establish.[12] M.-J. Dumont speculates that when the more solid bits of exhibition decor were auctioned off afterwards, some were added to the exteriors of Paris buildings, but it is hard to believe that this happened very often.[13]

A handful of the larger buildings were however built to serve more than one exhibition. They were commissioned by a state body, the Higher Commission for International Exhibitions. These favoured structures were all the work of French architects. Some were adventurous or innovative, such as the Galérie des Machines and the Eiffel tower, of 1889. Others, such as the Grand Palais and the Petit Palais, in 1900, were intended to make a sober contribution to a formal scene. Even a degree of permanence did not, however, greatly contribute to the broader influence of exhibition buildings. Like many of the other massive monuments of post-1850 Paris, they were treated as exceptions by local architects, tolerable as unique phenomena, but rarely examples to be emulated. The Higher Commission included a national and engineering representation which distanced itself to some degree from the Parisian architectural community. Viollet-le-Duc, for instance, was an influential member during the preparation of the 1878 exhibition. The resulting architectural decisions usually met the needs of the exhibitions, but they often puzzled or offended local architects, and this duality rarely prompted a constructive design dialogue.

## GREAT PUBLIC BUILDINGS AND THEIR INFLUENCE

The handful of surviving exhibition buildings joined a Parisian pantheon of public monuments which continued to expand after 1870, albeit more slowly than during the Second Empire. They were not entirely out of place there, for under the Third Republic, even more than under the Second Empire, public buildings were allowed to make individual statements within the townscape.

The Trocadéro (Fig. 157) provides a striking example of this tolerance. As an exhibition building, it could rank with the examples mentioned above, but it was always intended as a permanent structure and its position on the prominent Chaillot hill above the Seine gave it a very important visual status. The Trocadéro was built for the exhibition of 1878, which was intended to show how quickly France had recovered from the Franco-Prussian war. Preparation was hurried, and when the competition for the exhibition buildings was announced in 1876, only three weeks were allowed for the delivery of entries.[14] Gabriel Davioud won the contest for the Trocadéro. Trained at the Ecole des Beaux-Arts, Davioud had worked for the municipal parks department in Haussmann's time, and had specialised in the picturesque design which had been such a feature there.[15]

Davioud's design had a distinctly southern, not to say Moorish, flavour. Its curving wings and towers had something of the Giralda in Seville. It clearly reflected the international, carefree spirit of the exhibition rather than the disciplined environment of the host city, though the dominant image was probably one of French imperialism.

From the start, the Trocadéro attracted criticism. Viollet-le-Duc, as head of the competition jury, was a staunch defender of the design, but César Daly, from the eminence of his own journal, intoned against 'an amazing lack of a general conception, of a generating idea, and of an awareness of massing'.[16] The Trocadéro had no visible influence on Paris architecture between its inauguration in 1878 and its demolition to make way for the Palais de Chaillot at the 1937 exhibition. It remained an oddity throughout its existence.

157 The Trocadéro palace, built for the exhibition of 1878.

The Trocadéro had a contemporary, a large structure which stood on an even more prominent hill. This was the great basilica of the Sacré-Coeur at Montmartre. This structure, above all others in nineteenth-century Paris, was built to last. Its creators would have resented any comparison with the international exhibitions, but the result was as alien as the Trocadéro.

The Sacré-Coeur (Fig. 158) was a very unusual project from the start. During the war with Prussia a small group of influential churchgoers generated the idea of building an expiatory monument in Paris. This would draw attention to the sins and weaknesses which, from a devout viewpoint, had caused the French defeat. The Church took up the idea, and when a number of priests were murdered during the Commune of 1871 it began to see the monument as an expression of a moral condemnation of the sins of Paris.[17] It was also understood to be a protest against the self-indulgence of the Second Empire and, as the Archbishop of Paris made clear in 1872, it would be a challenge to other recent monuments which glorified vice and impiety, by which he may well have had Garnier's opera house in mind.[18]

It was clearly unlikely that the architectural product of all this invective would conform to Parisian traditions. Both political and ecclesiastical opinion quickly coalesced in favour of a site on the summit of the hill of Montmartre. It was associated with early Christian martyrs, and a lurid Communard murder in Montmartre had revived the link. However, the main advantage of the site was that the 'act of expiation' would be visible from most of Paris.

When the National Assembly authorised the project in 1873, the archbishop and his organising committee of clerics and conservative politicians moved quickly to organise a competition. The brief required a design for a basilica which would be imposing and consonant with Christian traditions. It also had to differ fundamentally from the vicious and impious architecture of the Second Empire.

There were seventy-eight entries for the competition in 1873. The predominant style was a somewhat emphatic neo-Romanesque. Completely alien to Paris, the style was associated with restoration work in churches and cathedrals in southern France, and it had been used there for a number of new churches. It probably reflected a sense of a return to fundamentals in a part of France which had not been implicated in the Commune, and had not been occupied by the Prussians. The winner was Paul Abadie, restorer of two cathedrals in southern

111

158 The basilica of the Sacré-Coeur under construction.

France.[19] He proposed a massive domed structure in white marble, in what he described as a 'Romano-Byzantine' style. Many of the other entries had also combined two or more styles in a manner appropriate to ecclesiastical pastiches but unheard-of in Paris.

Abadie's design had to be simple but the problem was to avoid crudity. The large, elevated site allowed great scope for symbolism but it also needed mass and silhouette. Extensive masonry surfaces were bound to result, and in a building intended to express guilt, atonement and good intentions, there was a case for leaving these surfaces bare and unadorned, and using a stone which would remain white like a sister's habit or veil. The result was widely derided as a monstrosity. Its impact was softened by leisurely construction, with consecration delayed until 1919, but Paris architects ignored the design rather than pilloried it. Consequently it is not surprising that the Sacré-Coeur had no influence on architecture in the city below, except in certain remote parish churches. Like the Trocadéro, its ungainly silhouette was tolerated, but no more.

THE ARCHITECTURE OF THE APARTMENT HOUSE

The brutal interruption of the war, the Commune and the subsequent building slump did nothing to weaken the design inertia of the apartment house which had built up during the Second Empire. Many building sites were deserted from 1870 to 1872 or even later, which meant that plans approved under the Second Empire were still being completed in the mid-1870s. From 1876 the city council, now democratically elected, agreed to finish a number of important streets which had been planned or partially built by Haussmann. Although architectural ordinances were no longer used, the persuasion of the *architectes-voyers* and a sense of common enterprise among the architects normally produced a design consensus which differed little from the Second Empire (Figs 159–60).

Official design policy was exemplified by the Avenue de l'Opéra (Fig. 161) when it was completed in 1877–8. Two short sections at each end of the avenue had been completed in the 1860s using an architectural ordinance similar to that of the Place de l'Opéra itself. Inferential evidence suggests that Haussmann would have continued this ordinance along the whole avenue. When the authorities decided to complete the avenue in time for the exhibition of 1878, much thought

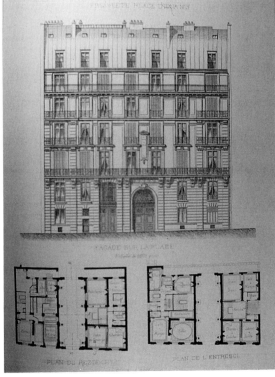

was given to the ordinance as a means of securing harmony and perspective in what was still conceived, as in Haussmann's time, as the most prestigious street in the city.

However, it was decided that the ordinance was too closely associated in the minds of owners and architects with the more dictatorial aspects of Haussmann's methods. As the street had to be built very quickly, and purchasers had to accept a deed of sale which required them to have their buildings ready by May 1878, it was feared that interference with detailed designs would threaten the whole enterprise. Instead, purchasers were simply required to build up to the full height permitted by the width of the thoroughfare, to include balconies, and to ensure that the main horizontal lines coincided with those of adjoining facades. This was similar to the formula used for many of the less important new streets built under the Second Empire, and it achieved an adequate perspective effect while allowing individual facade treatments and, in one case, a vertically integrated department store frontage.

The facades of the Avenue de l'Opéra were sober and restrained, but the architects, responding no doubt to the opportunity offered by a prestigious thoroughfare, moved towards a richer detailing which outshone Haussmann's ordinance on the Place de l'Opéra. This result was repeated in the other new streets of the later 1870s and early 1880s, such as the Boulevard Saint-Germain and the Boulevard Henri-IV, where the authorities

159 and 160 *Left*, apartment houses in Berlin and Paris, featured in the newly-founded *La Construction Moderne*, 2, 1886–7, plates 26 and 43. The emergence, and the divergence, of 'big-city styles' is emphasised here.

161 *Above*, the Avenue de l'Opéra, as completed in 1878. The buildings in the left and right foreground were built under the Second Empire according to an ordinance. The other buildings date from 1878 and were the product of a looser rein. (Photo: H.R. Walden).

had lesser aesthetic ambitions. In general, the result was one of continuity, but with a move towards a more ornate decoration.

It was not until the 1880s that novel design features became visible in Paris apartment houses (Fig. 162). Trends were complex and uneven at first, partly no doubt because of a lull in street building, which would have been an organising force. Many new houses were virtually unaffected, which meant that the spartan facades of Haussmann's day were still being built in the 1880s. By the later 1880s and the 1890s, however, a clear movement of change had become visible (Figs 163–6). First, apartment houses were tending to become taller. Secondly, the trend towards more richly decorated facades was producing not only carving of greater depth, but the concept of facade decoration as a single design, uniting and incorporating the greater part of the frontage.

Two further features ensued. One was

162 *Top left*, apartment house at 6, Rue Lentonnet, built in 1897 by J. Lombard in the claustrophobic district south of the Boulevard Rochechouart and west of the Gare du Nord. The two-bay, corbelled projection, occupying half of a more conventional frontage, may have been one of the experiments encouraged by the *architectes-voyers* in anticipation of the new building code.

163 *Below left*, house in the Rue Pavée, 1880s. It carries typical glass-and-metal 'bow windows' of the 'temporary' type grudgingly tolerated by the building regulations of 1882.

164 *Top right*, the first iron-framed house in Paris, built in the Rue de l'Aqueduc in 1878 by A. Lefèvre. This striking system, with muscular girders visible on the frontage, was not adopted in Paris. However, it seems likely that the house was built by a provincial engineering firm to demonstrate its prowess during the exhibition year, and that it was never expected to set a fashion in the capital.

165 *Below right*, house at 306, Rue Saint-Honoré built by A.J. Sellerier in 1892. The polychrome exterior may have been influenced by buildings at the exhibition of 1889.

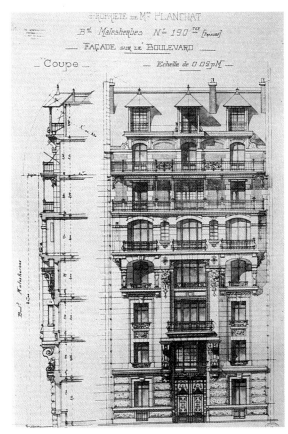

that upper storeys were increasingly emphasised, and the treatment of floors within the roof was integrated with the facades. Also, straight lines were abandoned in favour of curves. The curves came to dominate the decorative carving, and they also played a big part in structural design, especially in the roofs.

In addition there was more variety than there had been in the Second Empire and in the 1870s. The basic grid of floors and bays, now firmly established in Paris, was never questioned, but architects began to develop distinct treatments. The basic imperial type inspired by the Rue de Rivoli continued to be built until the end of the century, as in the young Charles Adelgeist's apartment house at 5, rue Franklin, in 1892.[20] The baroque, often in a very ornate and even romantic form, developed towards the end of the century for both villas and apartment houses, and figured prominently in the award of prizes in the municipal facades competition from 1898.[21] Louis-XIII brickwork panels became more common. Ironwork on balconies grew richer and more sinuous, echoing earlier baroque and rococo designs. Corner rotundas, which dated back to the

seventeenth century and had been built occasionally since 1789, became common, especially on the corners of commercial buildings, replacing the flat, cut-off corner treatments which had been the norm under the Second Empire (Fig. 167). The main influence here was Charles Garnier, who had built an elegant and prominent rotunda in the Boulevard Saint-Germain in the 1870s.[22] Above all, however, the Louis-XV style had made its mark by the turn of the century (Fig. 168).

These changes were reflected in, and encouraged by, changes in the building regulations. In 1880 the Prefect of the Seine started a review of the Second Empire building code. The review commission was staffed mainly by engineers and public health experts, and architects would later complain that it had neglected aesthetic matters.[23] The resulting changes, enacted in 1882 and 1884, did little more than tolerate greater depths and areas for projections from the facades, and higher roofs. At the time, however, the Paris architects welcomed the changes.[24]

166 Apartment house at 190 ter, Boulevard Malesherbes, whose permit was approved in 1898: an example of the top-heavy elevation which emerged in fashionable areas as a result of the use of elevators.

167 Corner rotunda, c. 1860s, in the Rue de Courcelles.

Facades and roofs were increasingly sculptured by corbelled treatments and projecting carving. The range of features in use was extended. The depth of decoration on the facades increased, and vertical additions in metalwork and glass, known as 'bow windows', were widely used to increase interior space and enhance exterior decoration. However, a combination of regulations and architectural practice tended to produce an enhancement of the upper storeys while leaving the ground floor, and one or more of the floors immediately above, more free from decorative accretions. Meanwhile, the traditional entresol had virtually disappeared by the end of the century owing to public health concerns, changes in shop layout and the decline of the very tall *porte cochère*.[25]

Underlying these changes was the further development of a high-density, residential 'West End', as educated Parisians came to call it. Increasingly solid and luxurious, the apartment house spread through most of the fashionable west, creating very high building densities right up to the city boundary and fortification zone which announced the beginning of the suburbs. The XVIe *arrondissement* was the main seat of this luxury densification but it extended into adjacent areas of the XVe and the XVIIe *arrondissements*, forming a great crescent around the west of the city. Much of this building was

redevelopment, with older mansions and villas demolished to make way for new streets and the rows of tall apartment blocks. The process of densification was at its height between the mid-1880s and the outbreak of the First World War. Developments towards the end of this period were to take full advantage of the greater heights which would be allowed, as we shall see, by the new building regulations of 1902.

The attraction of these habitats lay not so much in the external environment as in the apartment houses themselves. From the early 1880s, luxury apartment blocks of full height were normally equipped with lifts. Ceilings were high and rooms were large, in complete contrast to the pokey apartments to be found behind many attractive facades in other parts of the city. Window treatments were generous and, with larger rooms, they were more efficiently and attractively related to the interiors which they lit. Most rooms were linked by a spinal corridor system, allowing specific uses to be attributed to them, rather than being grouped in suites. The service staircase for use by servants and tradespeople, an innovation of the Second Empire, multiplied in the upper-class west. Service rooms were large and well equipped, allowing servants to be kept well out of the way except when needed.

Meanwhile, the range of urban equipment available became the most impressive in the world. The distribution of gas and electricity was developed using the most advanced techniques.[26] The telephone was available from 1879. The Post Office ran a unique pneumatic mail system, which allowed a letter to be delivered anywhere in Paris within an hour. In the concentrated, superbly equipped city which Paris had become by the end of the century, the attractions of the suburban villa as an escape from the city were by no means as clear as the American or British observer might have assumed. Instead, the modern apartment block, at any rate when located in a fashionable area, appeared to represent the acme of respectable living as indeed it came to do in an equally cramped Manhattan after the 1860s, where the Parisian apartment was the main model.[27]

168 Third prize-winner in the Paris facades competition of 1907, in the popular Louis-XV style.

The standardisation of apartment house architecture on geometrical lines that lasted from the early Second Empire until the 1880s was the main target of an unprecedented reaction which began in the 1890s. The origins of the challenge lay not in industrialism or the mass society, but in the artistic revival of the picturesque which began in the 1880s on a European scale, and which was largely a reaction *against* industrialism. Perhaps its single most important stimulus in Paris was the surge of interest in the buildings of the medieval city and those picturesque townscapes of the ancient core which had survived Haussmann. Meanwhile, architects began to react against the geometry and repetition of Second Empire Paris. The alternative which many of them favoured, the picturesque, was influenced to some degree by the Arts and Crafts movement in Britain and the Belgian Urban Art movement, but in essence it was a French and Parisian reaction to a period of conformity in which a vital, classical tradition had been reduced to a skeletal formula.

This trend was first expressed in the new *hôtels* which were still being built in the most opulent districts of western Paris. The majority were more modest than the huge *hôtels* of the Second Empire. They normally stood directly on the street frontage, and most were grouped in short streets or sections of street. Many of their owners and tenants worked in the world of the arts, and they required a distinctive design, which the architect nearly always supplied from an array of historicist styles. The result was a streetscape of contrasts which challenged the Haussmannic tradition.

The Rue Fortuny (XVII$^e$) was a striking example of this alternative. Opened in 1860 in a fashionable area north of the Parc Monceau, it was developed between about 1875 and the early 1890s. The typical owner was a successful man of letters or creative artist, such as Edmond Rostand or Sarah Bernhardt, though there were a number of industrialists and financiers as well. Nearly all the styles on display were French, but the striking, picturesque effect had much in common with similar streets in Brussels (Fig. 169).[28]

169 *Hôtel* in the Rue Fortuny by P.A. Gouny, 1890. The broad window hints at influence from Viollet-le-Duc.

In the 1880s this new taste for eclecticism and historicism began to affect the apartment house. At first, the styles used were mainly historic and French, but at the turn of the century a brief Art Nouveau craze allowed a revolutionary foreign style into the city.[29] The architectural debate over Art Nouveau and other, less alien styles took place within a broader context which influenced much artistic discussion: the idea of a single aesthetic system which would be guaranteed to produce beauty. This was of course the claim of the classicists, but the new system was seen as less a matter of rules and proportions than one of individual expression fired by a common spirit.[30] Meanwhile, the ideal of an efficient or functional aesthetic appropriate to an 'industrial age', or determined by modern technology, was virtually absent from the debate. 'Modernity' referred to a quality and style of life, and not to a present or future 'machine age'.

ART NOUVEAU

The boldest challenge to tradition, Art Nouveau, flourished so briefly in Paris that its revolutionary aspirations are often overlooked, but such a head-on encounter with

classicism was unprecedented there. Its supporters saw it as an integral system of design which offered a comprehensive alternative to classicism. Its aesthetic principles and philosophy were entirely different from those which had guided design in France since the seventeenth century. Above all, they were not even French, but the product of an international movement generated by the spread of industrialisation throughout Europe in the later nineteenth century. The episode had something in common with the Parisian rococo fad between the 1720s and the 1740s, and indeed the two styles had certain similar features. Rococo, however, was a development of classical architecture, and in Paris it harmonised well enough. Art Nouveau was presented by its Parisian supporters as the herald of a new century and a new culture, a deliberate challenge to tradition.

Art Nouveau began to attract serious attention in Paris from about 1895. In 1897 Max Doumic, the architect and writer, gave a lecture expressing both the need and the demand for a new architecture.[31] Like others before him, he spoke warmly of English domestic architecture and William Morris. The English contribution was however to him only a prelude, and Doumic reserved his main enthusiasm for Art Nouveau, which was mainly Belgian in its origins (Figs 170–1).

At first, Art Nouveau secured a foothold in Paris through art and interior design. It did not take root architecturally until the international exhibition of 1900, which created the usual demand for striking temporary buildings and street furniture. It was helped by the opening of the first Paris metro line in 1900. The occasion was deliberately planned to coincide with the exhibition and was presented as a symbol of Parisian modernity. The metro company commissioned Hector Guimard, a former professor of design turned architect, or 'architecte d'art' as he described himself,[32] to design a number of entrance canopies for the new line. Guimard built them in an expressionistic Art Nouveau style, using glass and iron (Fig. 172). The main influence seemed to come from Horta, in Belgium. So alien were the canopies to the Parisian design tradition that they could scarcely have been built other than in an exhibition year, and it was widely assumed that they would be as temporary as most of the other exhibition buildings.

Thanks mainly to Guimard, however, Art Nouveau was welcomed by the press and soon became symbolic of a daring Parisian modernity in that year. The implications of a new millennium, at a time of great optimism about the future of a world made by Europe, for once displaced the constant harping about French tradition. A self-conscious modernist

170 The Castel Béranger, 1898, by Guimard, who acted as both architect and developer. It was encouraged by the city authorities and was generally welcomed by Parisian architects.

171 Castel Béranger, main entrance. The masonry is not up to Parisian standards for a luxury apartment house.

119 *Left, below,* new streets built in Paris between 1850 and 1913. Almost all were planned by Haussmann, and the red streets had been completed by 1870.

120 *Right,* typical apartment house elevation of the 1850s. The slightly withdrawn attic floor, recalling the Rue de Rivoli design of 1806, was gradually replaced by the mansard roof, especially after the new building regulations of 1859 had created a formula for the roof treatment.

121 *Below,* the star junction of the Etoile, looking towards the Porte Maillot and the Défense, photographed from the air *c.* 1985.

122 *Far right, above,* the Boulevard Malesherbes and the church of Saint-Augustin, *c.* 1900.

123 *Far right, below,* apartment and hotel facades of the mid-1860s in the Rue Saint-Quentin, one hundred metres from the Gare du Nord. One architect designed most of the facades in this part of the street, producing a considerable effect of continuity.

devalued their investment in so rapidly changing a city (Fig. 123).

In the newer parts of Paris, the homogeneity of the facades was partly the product of the organisation of development. Enterprising architects, or the big development companies which flourished in association with the municipality, would purchase a large block of land, planning the street system and laying out individual plots. They would then set up one or more building companies to attract investment and to undertake the construction of the houses. A single drawing

office would prepare designs for all the land, sometimes introducing a degree of variety, but more often generating a large number of almost identical facades.[6] The authorities encouraged this process, being themselves legally unable to acquire and develop large areas of land on the periphery. The developers responded willingly to the authorities' views on the appropriate type of development, partly because it was in their financial interest to be absorbed into the broader planning strategy linked to the official street-building programme.

The minimal facade detail of the Haussmannic apartment house drew attention to an element of visual harmony which is often overlooked. This was the ubiquitous dressed limestone of mid-nineteenth-century Paris. Although the cheaper buildings did not use it, it set the pattern to such an extent that, as in the past, it was simulated in stucco finishes. By the early nineteenth century, local quarrying was in decline but the regional supply system, using water transport, allowed access to new sources of limestone, notably in the Oise. From the 1840s the railways extended the quarrying radius, and new types of stone became available.[7] During the Second Empire, improvements in quarrying and stone-cutting technology brought further economies. In the Second Empire, when little carving was done, the smooth, continuous stone facades of the apartment houses were acknowledged as a quality finish. This combination of quality and simplicity came to be seen as 'modern' and equated industrialism with the classical style.

## HAUSSMANN AND MUNICIPAL ARCHITECTURE

As soon as he took up office, Haussmann saw the need to enlarge and reinforce his architectural department, mainly with a view to designing the many municipal buildings which would be needed as the city spread. One of his earliest tasks was to establish a corps of architects working permanently for the city. This caused problems, because the established practice of recruiting independent architects for individual contracts was popular with the architects, who valued their freedom to undertake other work. Even when he was eventually able to create a corps of municipal architects, the system was undermined by some of the employees themselves and it did not survive Haussmann's resignation in 1870.[8]

However, for important projects Haussmann selected outstanding architects who would have been unlikely to accept employment as city architects – members of the Institute or Rome prize laureates, as Haussmann described them.[9] The result was that he achieved the very high standard of architecture in new public buildings that he desired. It was in recognition of this success that some of his friends persuaded him to seek membership of the Académie des Beaux-Arts, and his enthusiastic election bore witness to a wider respect in Parisian artistic circles for his architectural taste.[10]

Haussmann was not rigidly wedded to classical architecture, nor to the First Empire, which had some appeal in court circles. He wanted, however, to see strong relief on the facades of major buildings, which tended in consequence to stand out from domestic facades.[11] Although Haussmann admired the experiments in colour of J.I. Hittorff, who was one of his most valued architects, he did not see much place for polychromy on the outside of a structure. He preferred to admire the lines of a building without the distraction of colour.[12] His commitment to long, street perspectives led him to seek qualities of strength, mass and outline in the terminal buildings rather than obedience to classical norms of proportion. He was prepared to give clear instructions to these ends, even to very distinguished and experienced architects.

Like the emperor, he saw architecture as expressing change and modernity as well as national identity. He was prepared to back innovation and adventure as long as the result was distinctive and striking. He gave strong encouragement to Baltard's metal and glass design for the Halles after the outline design solution had been selected by Napoleon III, and he backed the experimental metal structure of Baltard's Eglise Saint-Augustin. He explained that to insert a capacious church into this narrow, triangular site required an adventurous design using new technology. It was also an experiment which, if successful, he expected to emulate on the other restricted sites generated by his new streets.[13]

Haussmann was therefore by no means a narrow and doctrinaire classicist. He was prepared for architecture to respond to the challenge of its site. As Haussmann probably created more awkward sites in seventeen years than the authorities had created in the whole of the preceding history of the city, he acted as an architectural innovator of some significance. Nevertheless, whatever the site and whatever the function, the resulting structures were almost always in the classical vein. Flexibility rather than creativity was the theme, and the result was a classical architecture for the industrial era rather than an industrial architecture.

## THE STANDARDISED APARTMENT BLOCK
## AS A PRODUCT OF INDUSTRIALISATION

Industrialisation and its attendant urbanisation always required the massive provision of new housing. In large cities the building process almost always generated standard types. In Paris, as in other capital cities, the main demand for new housing came from the middle class. Just as London developed the terraced house, in Paris it was the apartment block which came to house the majority of the middle classes under the Second Empire. We have seen that the origins of the Paris apartment house lay in the eighteenth century, but there was no precedent for the rigid design formula of the Second Empire version.

In earlier times, when the owner had often lived on the *piano nobile*, the character of the facade had been partly determined by the treatment of that floor, which was often related to the architect's view of the owner's preferences. Under the Second Empire the owner was less frequently in residence. Although the *piano nobile* remained the favoured residential floor, the facade treatment now tended to reflect a general sense of what the average tenant would consider appropriate. This meant that unusual or adventurous designs were not encouraged, and no floor was especially favoured.

Ceiling heights within the houses tended to converge, until their standardisation was reinforced by the minimum of 2.6 metres (8 feet) laid down by the new building regulations of 1859. The *piano nobile* often had the highest ceiling in the building but the other floors usually had a common height. The ubiquitous casement windows were mass-

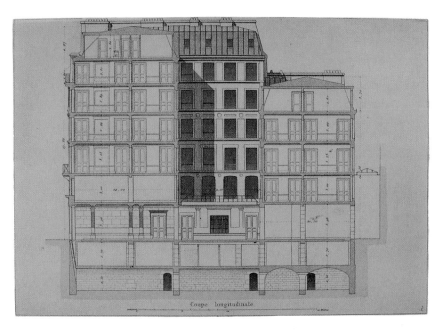

produced by joinery firms to common sizes determined largely by this ceiling height. Their regular arrangement in bays on the facades meant that they had no positive relation to the internal disposition of the rooms. The regulations of 1823 on projections, still in force after 1859, restricted the depth and surface dimensions of balconies and superficial decorations.

For all this, the apartment house still had to be individually designed. This work was almost always done by an architect, albeit a very obscure one in most cases. Official architectural ordinances affected only a tiny minority of new buildings. The authorities nevertheless tried to create sites of standard dimensions along the new streets. Most frontages ranged from 15 to 30 metres (49–98 feet), with the depth of the site varying from 20 to 40 metres (65–130 feet). The resulting rectangle of balanced proportions reflected a desire to maximise the frontage, and to avoid very deep sites, which would have included a large proportion of low-value land in the interior of the block (Figs 124–28). Under Haussmann the move away from the dimensions of the medieval burgage plot approached its conclusion.

The number of architects working in the city and the total amount of architectural work carried out were much greater during the Second Empire than at any previous time in the history of the city. However, the architects found themselves working as part of a building 'machine' which had not existed

124 and 125  Apartment house by Rolland in the Boulevard de Sébastopol, *c.* 1860.

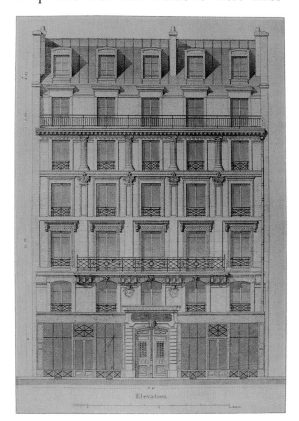

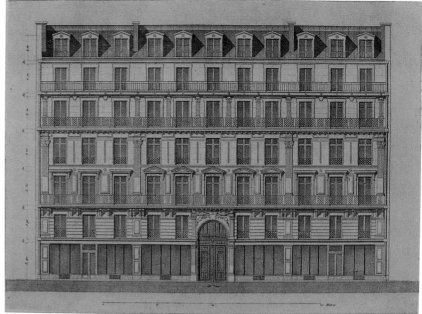

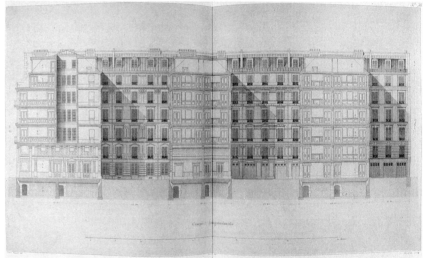

before the early 1850s. Their per capita output must have greatly increased, and some of them became closely associated with the big property companies that developed land on a large scale, especially in the west, or built new streets under contract to the prefectoral authorities. Others set up large practices employing junior architects, quantity surveyors and unqualified draughtsmen and artists, who handled detailing and other repetitive work.

Not only did apartment house design offer assured and lucrative employment: it also required only a limited technical and artistic competence. It was possible to leave formal training at an early stage, or to move to Paris from the provinces with only rudimentary qualifications. Arguably, this limited competence was reflected in the conformist facade of the Second Empire apartment house. On the other hand, many, indeed most, designers of apartment houses were probably not associated with a development company or a big practice, and worked for

the owners of individual sites. Even these, however, tended to specialise in apartment house construction and did not seek public contracts. Highly competent within their own sphere, they comprised an anonymous class of technicians whose products were marked by conformity and continuity.

Ironically, the most influential architects in the whole design process rarely or never built an apartment house themselves. These were the municipal *architectes-voyers*, qualified architects who supervised the issue of the building permit. They advised architects on how to harmonise the horizontal lines and fenestration of their facades, even along the entire length of a street, and offered advice on all aspects of design.[14] In some districts,

126 Party wall in the Rue des Francs-Bourgeois. The building dates from 1879 but the style is entirely that of the Second Empire.

127 and 128 Unusually large apartment house at 21, rue de la Chaussée-d'Antin by Paul Mesnard (the site is 80 × 32 metres – 260 × 104 feet). This very deep site lay on an older street and such dimensions were avoided as far as possible along Haussmann's new thoroughfares.

moreover, one or more influential buildings would be widely emulated, with the encouragement of the *architecte-voyer*, producing a degree of local uniformity.[15] In more mundane streets, mainly in the outer areas, Haussmann used *immeubles d'amorce* (starter buildings) to indicate the general lines on which building was expected to occur. These may have influenced the style of subsequent houses.[16]

## BUILDING REGULATIONS AND CHANGES IN FACADE DESIGN

It was appropriate that new building regulations should be drawn up for a city undergoing such a transformation, especially in the cholera era when public health preoccupied all Europe's cities. There had been no significant changes since 1783/4, apart from the ordinance of 1823 on projections. After the revolution of 1848 the provisional government under Cavaignac had fixed maximum facade heights relative to street widths, but the dimensions were almost exactly those of 1784. The only novelty was the roof profile, which was to lie within an angle of 45 degrees drawn from the cornice and a horizontal line 4.87 metres (16 feet) above the cornice. Except in streets of less than 15 metres (49 feet) wide, the angled line could be replaced by a quarter circle, permitting the bulbous roof with inset windows for which the Rue de Rivoli was noted.[17]

The decree of 26 March 1852 on Paris improvements referred to a future decree on building regulations, and this was published on 27 July 1859.[18] The height limits were those of 1784 and 1848, except that in streets 20 metres (65 feet) or more wide, facades were allowed to rise as high as 20 metres, provided that the number of floors beneath the cornice, including the entresol, did not exceed six. This formula produced a sunlighting angle of 45 degrees for the tallest buildings, reflecting the growing interest in public health, as did the minimum ceiling height of 2.6 metres (8 feet). The roof section was not to penetrate an angle of 45 degrees drawn from the cornice, or (on streets of 15 metres or more) a quarter circle with a radius not exceeding half the depth of the building. Up to two levels of dormers were permitted inside the roof.

The adoption of a new street-width norm of 20 metres reflected the spreading presence of Haussmann's arterial streets, nearly all of which were at least this wide. The reluctance to increase heights proportionately on narrower streets was clearly the result of public health considerations, especially as the tolerated sunlighting angle there was already much greater than 45 degrees. The inclusion of regulations covering courtyards and airshafts bore further witness to public health concerns, but in other respects the modifications appear to have had mainly economic and aesthetic objectives. The restriction to six storeys in the tallest buildings was ostensibly 'in view of the alignment and the harmony of the [principal] lines of the construction'. This meant that the windows, balconies and other horizontal lines of adjoining houses, if built to full height, would be continuous. The roof prescriptions seem to have had primarily aesthetic objectives. The upshot of the regulations of 1859, therefore, was that the basic dimensions and aesthetic of Parisian building were still those of 1783/4, except that in the major new streets an additional 2.45 metres (8 feet) – in practice the equivalent of one new storey – were permitted.

The regulations of 1859 did not in themselves contribute greatly to the evolution of facade design. The *entresols* became higher than in the past, often approaching the height of the ground floor. When there was no *entresol*, for instance because there was no *porte cochère*, or because the house stood in a purely residential side street, the *piano nobile* was nevertheless located at the level of the second floor. In effect, the *entresol* was being converted into a full first floor beneath the *piano nobile* (Fig. 129). This was partly a product of its status as a full floor in the eyes of the regulations.

With projections still restrained by the regulations of 1823, it was difficult to use major facade features to respond to increased heights. The use of the giant order of pilasters became common, however, to link the central floors on the facade. At first, the wider frontages were often given, as in the 1840s, a central pavilion composed of balconies, pilasters and brackets. This feature often stretched upwards from the balcony of the *piano nobile* to the balcony of the attic floor, which was frequently continuous. The ends

91

of the facades tended to be emphasised by pilasters or vertical rusticated bands. Windows usually had masonry surrounds, and there were often unadorned, rectangular panels between the windows. Sometimes the *piano nobile* balcony was continuous, as in the western section of the Rue de Rivoli. In the six-storey houses, there were generally three floors between the balcony of the *piano nobile* and the attic balcony, whereas there were two such floors in the five-storey houses.

The roof normally included one floor of accommodation. Its profile was usually of the mansard form and the lighting was by inset or dormer windows. More rarely, the roof was top-lit. On wide streets, there were often two floors in the roof, and here the upper floor was top-lit in most cases. The dormer roof sometimes had its own continuous balcony, above and set back from the attic floor balcony.

The most striking effect of Second Empire building was that the scale of the apartment house was markedly increased in comparison with that of the July Monarchy.[19] Greater height tended to obscure the proportions of the facade, and any effect of width had to be sustained by the neighbouring buildings. This required a sympathy of treatment, and

tended to divert the observer's attention from the house to the street frontage as a whole. In the new streets, and increasingly in the later years of the Second Empire, architects did little to emphasise individual bays. Bay succeeded bay, separated only by unobtrusive pilasters or strings. Almost always, each bay was topped by an identical dormer.[20] Continuous balconies at *piano nobile* and attic level reinforced the horizontal effect, after they had been revived by the early decision to extend the Rue de Rivoli using the original ordinance by Percier and Fontaine.

The extension of the Rue de Rivoli (Fig. 130) clearly provided an example to the architects of Paris, and it was intended to do so. The initial extension included arcades identical to those of the Empire, but owners' opposition led to their exclusion from the central and eastern sections of the new street. Calliat chose this modified design as his example of the Rue de Rivoli style; and rightly so, as no owner would freely commission arcades in an era of pavements and fabric awnings. The houses were very wide, and the horizontal effect was strengthened by a continuous balcony at the level of the *piano nobile*. Pilasters linked the *piano nobile* and the floor above. The idea of a central bay or group of bays was retained, but the width of the houses made them less evident, and anyone looking at a row of these buildings would have been almost unaware of their centralising effect. A second balcony at attic level, with dormers above, reinforced the horizontal impression by clamping the

129 Apartment house on the Rue de Turbigo by A. Huguet, 1868, showing the transition of the *entresol* as commercial space expands at the bottom of the building.

130 The extended Rue de Rivoli, looking west from outside the Louvre courtyard.

92

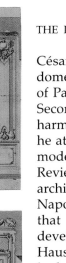

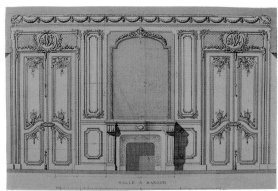

131 Salon of a house in the Rue Neuve des Mathurins, by Gastellier.

132 Dining room of a house in the Avenue des Champs-Elysées in the Louis-XIV style, by Victor Marié.

middle two floors between two black, metallic bands. Carved decoration was minimal, and it was clear that the visual impact was intended to be that of the street rather than the individual building. In such a scheme, powerful decoration would have been irrelevant and even detrimental. Interior design, however, was often more ornate (Figs 131–2).

The spartan appearance of the facades was softened by the trees that lined most of the wider streets. Under the Second Empire the number of trees growing in the streets of Paris increased from 50,466 to 95,577.[21] The official emphasis on the street also contributed to an unprecedented interest in street furniture. The furniture for new squares was carefully designed by the distinguished architect Gabriel Davioud, who also designed some for the new streets. In general, beauty and conformity in street furniture were now more valued than in the past, resulting in a tradition which has survived to the present day.[22] These virtual innovations, pursued with vigour by the authorities, further diverted attention from the design of the individual apartment house to the total effect that a street created.

César Daly, the leading commentator on domestic design, published a massive review of Parisian residential architecture under the Second Empire in 1864. He welcomed the harmonisation of building design, which he attributed to the atmosphere of concerted modernisation under the Second Empire. Reviewing numerous examples of Parisian architecture, and praising the influence of Napoleon III and Haussmann, he implied that a new urban architecture had been developed in Paris, in association with Haussmann's modernisation programme. It had escaped from traditional constraints created by the cramped form of the city, and was essentially a *modern* architecture. In other words, the homogeneity of the style reflected not conformity, but the validity of a design solution which all recognised.[23] Daly nevertheless noted that apartment houses tended to generate a particular type of architecture which distinguished them from single-family houses, because they had to appeal to a variety of tenants. The apartment house must not on the whole be distinguished by any too exceptional a feature. Its appearance must conform to almost every taste without leaning towards any one in particular.[24] Daly even implied that architects newly qualified (presumably at the Ecole des Beaux-Arts) struggled to adapt to the new modernism. Their heads full of the great architecture of the past, they found it hard to adopt the right frame of mind.

These judgments reflected not only Daly's long-standing advocacy of practical design, but his complete acceptance of the imperial claim to be the harbinger of modernity. His disparaging reference to architectural training was made in the context of the long-running debate over the reform of the Ecole des Beaux-Arts, which had set traditionalists against Viollet-le-Duc and other modernisers, supported by the emperor. Even Viollet-le-Duc, however, failed to set a clear mark on residential design in Paris. He designed four apartment houses between 1848 and 1865 in styles varying from a virile but restrained proto-medieval in 1848 (28, rue de Liège) to an 1865 example (23, rue Chauchat) which was almost indistinguishable from its conventional neighbours. This progression suggested that even the leading moderniser of the day found that the demands of standardisation and anonymity were stronger than his own interest in an industrial style.

As Daly himself accepted, most apartment house architecture was anonymous and repetitive, with the most striking changes occurring in the interiors, where the previous pattern of small rooms and cramped circulation was replaced by space and order. That Daly could designate such conventional building as 'modern' suggests that mass architecture in Paris was already the product of design inertia. Very remotely, this can be seen as a product of the industrialisation fostered by the Second Empire, and in that sense it was 'modern'. However, its spartan, regimented character would prompt a massive reaction after 1880, with the resulting florid architecture seen as 'modern' in its turn. This reaction will occupy much of the next chapter.

THE HOUSES OF THE RICH

The proliferation of the new apartment house by no means ruled out the construction of *hôtels* in Paris. On the contrary, the Second Empire was the last prolific period for the building of *hôtels* within the city boundaries. The new rich, who multiplied under Napoleon III, were keen to build their modern and luxurious mansions in Paris, as were the new imperial nobility. Most of them chose the fashionable districts sketched out by Haussmann's new street system between the Madeleine and the Etoile, and approached by the Boulevard Malesherbes (Figs 133–5). The architectural result was an inventive eclecticism within the classical vocabulary. In contrast to the apartment houses, costly decoration was emphasised. The early Renaissance and the baroque were favoured styles. No clear contemporary style emerged; on the contrary, there was an element of the pastiche, especially in buildings affecting the highly popular Renaissance manner, such as the Hôtel de la Paiva (Figs 136–7) and the Hôtel Dufayel (Fig. 138).[25]

The historicism of many of these designs paradoxically reflected the self-conscious novelty and 'modernity' of the new Empire, and the *nouveau riche* characteristics of many of the clientele. As in the design of apartment

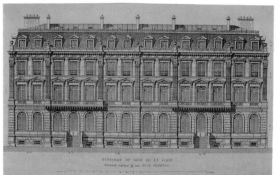

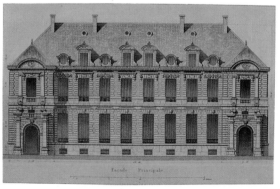

133 Mansion by Hittorff and Rohault de Fleury, Avenue de la Grande-Armée, one of a circle of ordinanced mansions on the Place de l'Etoile.

134 Side elevation of the Place de l'Etoile ordinance.

135 Mansion (1858) in the Louis-XIII style by Henri Labrouste, better known for his iron-and-glass library architecture, at 28, rue de Berry. The client was Louis Fould, a rich banker and collector. According to T. Vacquer, the design was inspired by the older buildings of the Bibliothèque Nationale, extended by the architect in the 1860s. The first Louis-XIII mansion in Paris, it was built of brick for archaeological authenticity.

houses, an era of economic change and social superficiality encouraged an architecture from the past. The *hôtel*, however, had to be an ornate expression of wealth or social aspirations. Zola's portrait of one such mansion and its Philistine occupants in *La curée*, though almost as overdrawn as a Daumier cartoon, creates a vivid picture of wealth accumulating in the greedy hands of non-Parisians as a result of crooked property deals, and squandered on the building of a tasteless mansion facing Haussmann's first

new park, the fashionable Parc Monceau. Zola's portrait was based on Emile Menier's *hôtel* on the Parc Monceau, built in the 1850s by Henri Parent (Fig. 139).

## BUILDING FOR THE NEW FUNCTIONS OF THE INDUSTRIAL ERA

Industrialisation brought to Paris a virtually new type of building: the structure needed for large-scale manufacturing, steam railways and high-volume commerce. These buildings started to appear in and around Paris in about 1840. Industrialisation did not however bring much mechanised manufacturing to the city of Paris. Even after the incorporation of the inner ring of suburbs in 1860, most large-scale industry was to be found outside the city in industrial suburbs such as Colombes, Courbevoie and Joinville. The architects of Paris were very remote from all this, both physically and conceptually. Industrial design was a matter for engineers, surveyors, builders or the industrialists themselves.

In practice, however, no such absolute exclusion was possible. First, certain important new constructions of an industrial character came to be required within the city of Paris as the result of the industrialisation process. The railway stations and the wholesale markets were the main examples. Second, many architects were aware of the potential results of the cheapening of industrial materials such as iron and glass, which economic progress was bringing about. Third, certain engineering techniques, such as the creation of broad spans using iron beams or vaults, were known to architects, who were not averse to using them in situations which did not detract from the quality of the total edifice. This did not necessarily mean, furthermore, that the materials or techniques would be disguised. It was necessary only to justify them by applying them to buildings which were openly associated with work. As we have seen, Labrouste made a daring and original use of both at the Sainte-Geneviève library in 1842. This precedent was generally respected by the architects of Paris, with Labrouste himself adapting this method to a more luxurious era in his

136 *Left*, *above*, Hôtel de la Paiva, 25, Avenue des Champs-Elysées.

137 *Left*, *centre*, garden front of the Hôtel de la Paiva. The rococo treatment contrasts with the eclectic, but more restrained, Champs-Elysées frontage.

138 *Left*, *below*, the Hôtel Dufayel, 76, Avenue des Champs-Elysées, in a Louis-XV style. As at the Hôtel de la Paiva, the front courtyard is bounded by dummy side facades applied to the walls of neighbouring buildings, but vehicular access is from the rear. The sinister effect of enclosure is especially marked here.

139 *Right*, the largest of the Parc Monceau mansions at 5, Avenue Van Dyck, home of the chocolate manufacturer Emile-Justin Menier. The architect was H. Parent, a specialist in neo-Gothic chateaux.

Bibliothèque Nationale reading room in the 1860s (Fig. 140).

The new mode of construction was strongly encouraged by the emperor's intervention in the scheme for the new central food markets. Beginning in 1852, the eminent architect Baltard had at first planned a cluster of large stone pavilions, utilitarian but offering limited space. The new emperor wanted to see a modern structure using industrial materials, and Baltard was asked to think again. Baltard came back with an extensive system of roofs and clerestories, all built of iron and glass, and offering maximum floor space and great flexibility. Completed in the mid-1850s, the new Halles were respected by Baltard's peers as a sublime statement of industrial efficiency. Their direct influence, however, did not extend beyond the design of the local market buildings which multiplied in a growing Paris under Haussmann. Like other large metal structures which would be built in Paris later, the Halles were treated as an isolated event which did not impinge on the Paris building tradition.

Rather more interesting from the latter point of view were the new railway termini. The early railway lines brought a new world of iron, speed and technological modernity to the very edge of traditional Paris. The early terminal stations, such as the Gare d'Orléans (1840) and the Gare du Nord (1846), used sober, arcaded, classical designs reflecting the horizontality of the trains and looking like orangeries or market buildings in the pre-Baltard style. Remote from the central areas of the city, they sought little more than a respectable and reassuring appearance and they were the work of the railway company architects and engineers rather than urban specialists from Paris.

It nevertheless became clear, with the completion of the terminal building of the Gare de l'Est in 1849 (Fig. 141), that a station had a double architectural potential which could reasonably attract the finest Paris architects. On the one hand, it offered the chance to create completely new spaces and circulation systems, using iron and glass in a more creative way than was normally possible

140 Labrouste's main reading room at the Bibliothèque Nationale.

96

in Parisian architecture. On the other, the station had an important monumental potential at the head of the approach streets from the inner districts.[26] Although the Boulevard de Strasbourg, the impressive link between the Gare de l'Est and the *grands boulevards*, would not be completed until the early 1850s, the station architect F.A. Duquesney was aware of the potential vista in front of the station. He chose to emphasise the semicircular vault of his train shed, which sprang above an arcaded frontage and was flanked by two three-storey pavilions, topped by a balustrade, in the formal style of railway offices of the day. At first the arch of the train shed was left daringly open to the street, allowing vapours to issue from it in a manner of which Etienne–Louis Boullée might have approved, but it was soon filled with radiating iron tracery and glass to form a striking wheel symbol.

Duquesney's successful combination of polite design in the Parisian tradition, and the sublime implications of steam and speed, had the makings of a new architecture for the city. Other architects, together with the railway companies and the authorities, took note. By the later 1850s, when many more

platforms were necessary at the terminal stations, a new phase of building and rebuilding began. In 1859, J.I. Hittorff, noted especially for his ordinanced villa designs around the Arc de Triomphe, and his striking amphitheatres (Fig. 142), replaced a more modest railway company architect in building the new Gare du Nord (Fig. 143). The invitation had come from the railway company chairman Baron James de Rothschild, who liked Hittorff's nearby neo-classical church of Saint-Vincent-de-Paul (1824–44). As so often in Paris, the fashionable architect showed that he could master the most technical of problems without any loss of architectural quality.[27] Hittorff planned a broad facade with a central pavilion, and two smaller pavilions at each end. The facade stood at an oblique angle to the new Boulevard de Magenta, but Haussmann supplied two short approach streets, and a modest street widening in front of the station.

The central pavilion was dominated by a large, glazed arch under a gable, similar in inspiration to the Gare de l'Est but defined by giant Ionic pilasters. The large gable, echoed by the gables on the end pavilions, reflected the wide pitched roof of Hittorff's simple but elegantly spacious train shed (Fig. 144). The frontage was also neo-classical in style, using doric pilasters in a very daring combination of orders. Huge statues, like those of the Gare de l'Est but much larger, stood on the facade. Like the Gare de l'Est, but on a much grander scale, the Gare du Nord combined a practical design for a railway station and the classical features of a self-conscious Parisian

141 *Left, above,* the Gare de l'Est shortly after its inauguration.

142 *Left, below,* Hittorff's Cirque de l'Impératrice on the Champs-Elysées, one of his two circular circus buildings in Paris.

143 *Above,* the frontage of Hittorff's Gare du Nord.

144 The 'cathedral' interior of the Gare du Nord.

public monument. At the same time, it dared to inject a strikingly new railway architecture into a conformist Parisian townscape.

Hittorff had been born in Cologne in 1792, and his architectural education and career in France were the result of frontier changes during and after the French wars. As one of the few German architects working in Paris in the nineteenth century, and one who remained in close contact with his homeland, he may have been more open to novelty than many of his contemporaries. He was certainly daring and versatile, as he demonstrated in his two circular entertainment buildings on the Champs-Elysées and at the Cirque d'Hiver.[28] It was however at the Gare du Nord, with its echoes of the Bibliothèque Sainte-Geneviève, that he presented his most persuasive version of a new architecture of practical modernism.

Although Hittorff complained about the lack of a monumental street access at the Gare du Nord, the problem was even more serious elsewhere. It arose from the early decisions by the companies to bring their lines into the city along the interstices between the radiating national roads. As the authorities were not normally prepared to build more than modest connections to the street network, the other companies' terminals did not stand at the head of great vistas and consequently they were less concerned about the monumental implications of their stations. The result could be a conforming Parisian facade architecture, virtually unrecognisable as a station, as at the Gare Saint-Lazare (Fig. 145), or a modest practicality, as at the Gare Montparnasse.[29] Following the early example of the Gare de l'Est, which bore a number of statues representing towns served by the company network, much use was made of heavy statuary representing towns or modern virtues.[30] Meanwhile, adjacent railway buildings such as hotels or offices were normally built in the official, classical style. Although the Second Empire undoubtedly saw the origins of a new, practical architecture associated with transport and industry, it had not made a strong impact by 1870. The department store, a

product of the Second Empire, was beginning to use tall bays in metal and glass by the late 1860s, as at the Belle Jardinière and the Magasins Réunis (now the Holiday Inn), but even here the rest of the exterior conformed to traditional qualities.[31] Educational buildings would not begin to adopt industrially-inspired design until the Third Republic. Hardly any large factories or plants were built inside the city boundaries. Viollet-le-Duc's advocacy of functional design won a number of admirers but virtually no emulators within Paris, and he continued himself to work mainly in conservation and the design of buildings in a free medieval, or academic Gothic, style.

THE PUBLIC BUILDING

More than any previous regime, the Second Empire sought to set its mark on Paris. Napoleon III acted quickly, aware that his empire was under constant political threat and unlikely to survive his death unless its institutions could be firmly rooted. Representative buildings were seen as one means of making imperial institutions look permanent. In some cases the government chose to complete previous achievements, as in its massive extension of the Louvre between 1853 and 1857. In others, it created something completely new, like the new opera house commissioned in 1861. Political objectives made it necessary for most public buildings to adopt an architecture which stressed continuity and associations with great reigns of the past, notably those of Louis XIV and Napoleon I. The need to attract royalist, Orleanist and republican, as well as imperialist, support justified a variety of styles, all of which could be designated 'modern' in the parlance of the time. Fine new public buildings could suggest that French modernisation was proceeding successfully, and that

an imperial regime could provide constant security and guidance.

The completion of the Louvre by Visconti and Lefuel drew heavily on the concepts of Lescot to produce towering, heavily decorated pavilions and wings. Like the original Louvre, however, it influenced little else, except that it encouraged rich, pastiche decoration. At the other extreme, the new opera house, started in 1861 and still incomplete in 1870, was by far the most novel and creative building of the Second Empire (Fig. 146). Indeed, its architect and many of its admirers saw in it a new, imperial style. The structure was the product of a competition in 1861, after a weak, commissioned design by Rohault de Fleury had aroused concern in government circles. It stood on a very large site created by Haussmann's street improvements. The winning architect, Charles Garnier, did not need to relate his design to any nearby building. On the contrary, he knew that the adjoining facades would be the subject of a submissive architectural ordinance. His solution for the new opera house was an exuberant neo-classical style with a persistent baroque character.

He used a closed arcade of arches at the entrance level and a Corinthian colonnade of paired columns above. The carved decoration was the most exotic ever seen in Paris, but the massing and volumes, inspired partly by the requirements of a huge, modern theatre, and of the vista up the Avenue de l'Opéra, supplemented by the architect's fantasies, were the main source of novelty. As a building of pleasure, frequented solely by the

145 The Gare Saint-Lazare in its second form.

146 The main frontage of Garnier's opera house in the formal setting provided by a square and ordinanced buildings.

rich, the opera house symbolised the life of the imperial elite, and it responded very well to the needs of this clientele (Figs 147–8).

This special role helps to explain why Garnier's opera house had little influence on public architecture in the 1860s. Most of the designs for public buildings in Paris during the Second Empire were restrained or severe. The Salle de Harlay at the Palais de Justice, built by Louis Duc between 1852 and 1869, was a simple neo-classical design.[32] Though very free in its use of classical components, it was a spartan, almost utilitarian composition. It won an imperial prize in 1869 for the best work of art produced in the Second Empire, but it recalled the 1840s, the time at which Duc had started work on the renovation and reconstruction of the older parts of the Palais de Justice (Fig. 149). Also very restrained, apart from the tall dome required by Haussmann to terminate the southern end of the Boulevard de Sébastopol, was Ballu's Tribunal de Commerce of 1865. Haussmann kept close supervision over most of these buildings, and announced himself generally happy with the results, but his main concern was to secure terminal points for his big streets.

CHURCHES

The contrast between secular and religious architecture was unusually pronounced under the Second Empire. Church architecture was varied and inventive, though some efforts to escape the classical style were lacking in taste. Many of the new churches stood on sites created by Haussmann's streetworks, and the municipal authorities' main concern was, as usual, to ensure that they functioned effectively as focal or terminal points. The ecclesiastical authorities were glad to take up the challenge, which gave

147 *Left*, the main staircase of the opera house as completed in the later 1870s.

148 *Top*, aerial view of the opera-house district, with a formal arrangement of streets and blocks without parallel in Paris.

149 *Above*, the west front of the Palais de Justice (Salle de Harlay), facing the Place Dauphine.

their churches a visual prominence which in the past they had often sought in vain. To fulfil their new, official role in the planned city, churches needed above all to make a strong vertical statement. The resulting domes, towers and spires, though sometimes overemphasised, were more adventurous than most of the city's new secular architecture. The styles used ranged from the utter pastiche, such as the flamboyant tower by Ballu which Haussmann used to regularise the frontage opposite the east front of the Louvre, to the eclectic, such as Baltard's domed church of Saint-Augustin, started in 1860, which combined a daring iron interior with curtain walls combining Byzantine and Renaissance features.

Eclecticism was not only a feature of some of the individual churches, but of the overall effect of the church-building programme. The aim was probably to suggest that the new churches were not associated with a period of secular history. They were to be linked with other periods of Christian history and, as in the past, with the spiritual glories of Rome. Eclecticism symbolised the eternity of Christianity. Churches thus made little or no effort to follow the conventions of Second Empire architecture. Even the neo-Gothic, which had made very little impact on France despite its great popularity in England after 1840, figured from time to time, as in Ballu's eclectic church of Saint-Ambroise, built between 1863 and 1869. At the same time, this free and inventive church architecture had little or no influence on secular design, even though most church architects also designed secular buildings.

ARCHITECTURAL TRAINING AND THE NEW PARIS

The persistence of a traditional, classical architecture in Second Empire Paris cannot be fully understood without reference to architectural education. The most influential and prestigious training was still that provided by the Ecole des Beaux-Arts. Enough has been said already to suggest that a national school which concentrated on training an elite of architects would teach an elite or official architecture. Political changes after 1789 had had little impact. But would the onset of industrialisation have any effect?

Although certain innovations, such as the new Halles, could be seen on the ground during the Second Empire, the architecture taught at the Ecole responded little to the new era of modernisation. The lectures were still mostly generalised and theoretical. The design projects were nearly all for grandiose public buildings. The classical style was encouraged, and great precision and scholarly accuracy were required in the execution. Cost limits were rarely mentioned, so most competition designs would have been very expensive to build. The idea of a client, whether public or private, who might lay down a budget or reject an expensive design, did not normally enter into the training.

The result, as demonstrated by competition entries at the Ecole, was largely a fantasy world of ambitious buildings, most of which could never have been built in real life. Ironically, what best kept them in touch with contemporary practicality was the classical style. Some ateliers encouraged work in alternative styles, such as the Gothic, for use in specialised buildings such as churches, but the classical style predominated in the competition entries. In practice it kept the fantasies of students and their masters within limits, though within a very expensive design mode requiring large quantities of dressed stone, heavy columns and lintels, extensive carving, and, in the interior, luxurious decoration and expensive flooring.

There was also an emphasis on theory, including not only classical proportions in the elevations, but geometrical arrangements of the floor plan which often had some symbolic or traditional value. Circles were often used for perimeters, and interlocked triangles often shaped the plans of components of a large building. As a rule, the exterior was expected to reflect the interior. This, however, often produced a grossly expensive exterior as symbolic decoration or unnecessary pavilions or roof treatments were brought into use in order to express different interior functions – interior functions which, in their turn, had to be emphasised by the distinctive arrangement and decoration of internal spaces.

The Second Empire nevertheless generated by far the strongest challenge to the organisation and practices of the Ecole that it was to encounter between 1819 and its dissolution in 1968. The challenge culminated in an imperial decree reforming the Ecole in 1863. Although most of the changes were soon reversed or undermined, the episode showed that there were forces within the Ecole, among both teachers and students, which favoured an alternative approach to architecture and its teaching. This approach was linked to a design philosophy which attached importance to efficient construction methods and a romantic aesthetic.

The new approach was associated most closely with the work and thinking of Eugène Viollet-le-Duc, an architect who had spent most of his career in the restoration of churches and other historic buildings, but who by the 1850s had built up a reputation as a writer on architectural theory and the history of architecture. At the request of some of the students, Viollet-le-Duc opened an atelier in 1856. His close links with the imperial court allowed him to secure a hearing for his ideas on the reform of the Ecole, and so it was that in 1863 the emperor issued a decree incorporating a thorough reform.

The reform's main effect was to transfer control of the Ecole from the Académie des Beaux-Arts to the government. Its professorial body was transformed and expanded, and the judgment of competitions was broadened. The most striking of the new professorial appointments was Viollet-le-Duc himself, but by this time a strong counter-movement had developed within the Ecole. Viollet-le-Duc's early lectures in 1864 were disrupted sufficiently for him to resign within two months of his first appearance. In his absence, the reform movement collapsed and gradually the changes were almost all reversed.

The reforms in themselves would not have established an alternative architecture within the Ecole. A much longer process of evolution would have been needed. However, their reversal definitely excluded the teaching of Viollet-le-Duc's approach, which might have brought the Ecole closer to the practical, cost-conscious architecture of commerce, medicine and education. It would also have promoted a greater acceptance of alternative styles, of which the Gothic was the most obvious. In the absence of these influences within the Ecole, architectural training there continued on the traditional lines centred on a classical approach. The failure of the

challenge of 1863 postponed a new challenge on a comparable scale for one hundred years.

The Second Empire nevertheless saw a development of designs and concepts which indicated a degree of evolution within the Ecole. The subjects of the Rome prize competition began to reflect the rapid economic and social developments of the period, and after 1863 there were notable changes. In 1866 contemporary realism made an unprecedented intrusion. The subject was 'a Parisian hôtel for a rich banker'. The problem was complicated by the site, which was amazingly irregular and which backed on to a public park to which it was expected to relate. A further complication was the inclusion of the bank within the site.[33] This brief called to mind the great mansions of the new breed of merchant and industrialist which had sprung up around Haussmann's first new park, the Parc Monceau. Although the scale of the winning designs was more that of a palace than of a mansion, the idea of designing for a man of commerce, and including his business premises, was very new.

The planning of the winning entries remained geometrical and symmetrical. However, the treatment of the elevations evolved from the ordered neo-classicism of the early decades after the Restoration into a more exuberant style which recalled the finest French architecture of the seventeenth century, or ventured into a modern reinterpretation of the Baroque. Charles Garnier's highly expressive design for the new opera house of 1861 was especially influential. It allowed many student architects to work for Garnier's office in the 1860s. Their clear enthusiasm for what they regarded as a new architecture representing the spirit of the age was transmitted to their work at the Ecole, and the opera house appears to have influenced numerous Rome prize entries for the rest of the decade.[34]

While remaining classical in proportion and composition, many of the entries moved towards elevations softened and enriched by multiple components and detailing, with carving extended to form large masonry units which interrupted or obscured the main structural lines. Polychromy became very popular, producing an effect of warmth and variable depth even within facades whose three-dimensional composition already offered beguiling relief effects. The facade

movement in the city, incorporating Art Nouveau, built up to a peak by 1900. It led on to the foundation, in 1902, of the Société du Nouveau Paris by a group of iconoclastic modernists composed mainly of artists and architects.[33] Its name implied a deliberate challenge to the city's main preservationist body, the municipally-backed Commission du Vieux Paris, founded in 1897. The new society sought to achieve a change in emphasis from the protection of the old to the creation of the new. Its first president was Frantz Jourdain, architect of an Art Nouveau symbol, the Samaritaine department store. Jourdain was a prominent critic of the Beaux-Arts style and an advocate of iron and other industrial materials.[34]

The society's propaganda campaign was almost unprecedented in Paris. To convert aesthetics into a mass issue was novel enough, but to promote modernity *per se*, and by implication to suggest that Paris had fallen behind the times, clashed with the normal assumption that Paris was in the vanguard. However, because Jourdain's campaign for modernity was linked artistically to Art Nouveau rather than to, say, functionalism or utilitarianism, it was undermined by the decline of Art Nouveau from around 1904.[35] The big turning-point came in that year, when Guimard's design for a striking metro

entrance in front of the Opéra was rejected by the city council and ultimately replaced by an unobtrusive stone balustrade in classical style.[36] The Société du Nouveau Paris campaigned against the decision, but in vain. Meanwhile, the completion in 1905 of Frantz Jourdain's towering new Samaritaine set off a mass reaction which centred on the two giant cupolas, seen by many as an insult to the Pont-Neuf and its historic environs. This 'scandale' would eventually lead to the decision by the owner, Cognacq, to demolish the cupolas under pressure from the city council in 1925.[37]

As early as 1905, then, Paris opinion had swung against Art Nouveau, which was widely condemned as an outlandish and ugly style, inimical to French and Parisian design traditions. Notwithstanding Guimard's initial claims that it was essentially French and did not mark a break with the past,[38] its opponents now made great use of the devastating accusation that it was 'foreign'. The Société du Nouveau Paris failed to incorporate alternative modernistic styles and it soon faded from the scene.

In the long term, Art Nouveau had very little influence on the city.[39] From it there did survive, on the other hand, a sentiment that 'art' had a bigger role to play in architecture than the classicism of the later nineteenth

172 Metro entrance by Guimard at the Bastille, probably dating from 1900.

century had allowed it. This new 'art', enhanced and applied since the 1890s, had achieved an essential Frenchness in its form and expression. It followed that, if Art Nouveau had been rejected as un-French, the new 'art' had the power to revive and prolong the city's established architectural traditions.[40] From this web of paradox emerged the new aesthetic which inspired the main changes in Paris between the turn of the century and the First World War.

THE NEW PARISIAN AESTHETIC

One of the weaknesses of Art Nouveau was that it had sprung from small-scale applications such as interior design and furniture. It never developed an approach to urban design as a whole. When its more striking architectural products ran foul of a brutal Parisian reaction in the early 1900s, it was unable to resist the charge that it was alien to the Parisian design tradition. The new Parisian aesthetic, on the other hand, was street-related from its very beginnings in the 1890s. It was not completely new, nor a foreign import, for it sprang partly from a local review of the Haussmannic aesthetic, which was still being extended as late as the 1890s as remaining streets from the Second Empire plan were still being built.

The idea of the 'tyranny of the straight line' had become a rallying cry among preservationists and a growing number of architects as early as the 1880s. It had won considerable respect by the early 1900s. Louis Bonnier, the most influential of the *architectes-voyers*, for instance, referred in 1902 to 'the lamentable, infinite perspective of the streets of modern Paris'.[41] M. Bouvard, the city director of works, spoke in similar terms when he was interviewed by a leading architectural journal in 1903.[42] This critique of the rectilinear street helped provide the basis for a new aesthetic and a new architecture.

The idea of an alternative aesthetic began to take shape in the later 1890s. The admirers of Art Nouveau contributed to the debate, but it also had the support of numerous apartment house architects who simply called for greater freedom to add decoration and variety to their facades. By 1901, this theme was prompting major publications. The fullest statement of the case for a radically

new street aesthetic was Gustave Kahn's *L'esthétique de la rue*, published in Paris in 1901.[43] He advocated a comprehensive 'street art' which extended beyond the buildings to all the street furniture.[44] He wanted all the buildings within a block to form a coherent design, with extensive use of polychromy.[45] His argument did not exclude the use of Art Nouveau, but he apparently did not wish to be associated with a single artistic tendency and he made no direct references to Art Nouveau or its creators. Instead, he wrote in much broader terms of replacing a defective nineteenth-century aesthetic, rather than modifying or extending it.[46] The most striking art would be in the street, for instance in the form of poster displays and other adventurous advertising. There was not a hint of the ideas of the Viennese aesthetic theorist Camillo Sitte in any of this, but Kahn hinted at Dutch and Belgian inspiration, including the work of Horta and others.[47]

The same year saw the publication of a comparable essay on 'public art' by Robert de Souza, an aristocrat with a strong interest in the quality of the urban environment. It was dedicated to André Hallays, the indefatigable Paris preservationist. De Souza's call for urban conservation was not new, but he based his argument on aesthetic rather than historical principles.[48] Following William Morris, De Souza linked beauty and utility, implying that aesthetics was a popular rather than an elite creation.[49] The Flemish and Walloon lead in 'public art' was acknowledged, and again there was no hint of stimulus from Austria or Germany.[50]

The debate over a new 'urban art' and a new aesthetic for Paris was conducted in somewhat imprecise terms. However, it was linked to a much more practical and directed discussion. This was the thorough review of the aesthetic aspects of the Paris building regulations which began in 1896 and culminated in 1902, though its results were contested until 1909. The tradition, potential and constraints of Parisian mass architecture emerge from this unique inquiry as from no other source.

## A NEW BASIS FOR APARTMENT HOUSE ARCHITECTURE: THE BUILDING REGULATIONS OF 1902

As calls for a more varied apartment house architecture multiplied in the 1890s, it became commonplace among the architects to blame the city building regulations. These were still essentially the controls of the Second Empire, for they had been only slightly relaxed in 1882 and 1884. Architects argued that without greater scope for projections, and for more varied rooflines and features, picturesque effects would be virtually impossible and a stark, repetitive streetscape would persist. They also often claimed that the Paris code prevented their following the best foreign practice.[51]

These complaints in themselves signalled a change since the mid-1880s, when the architectural community had accepted and even welcomed the regulations of 1882 and 1884.[52] To refer to foreign practice had been rare before 1890; now it implied a coming challenge to Parisian classicism. As L.C. Boileau, the architect of the innovative Bon Marché department store, described this mood a few years later:

> Creative artists and all men of taste were complaining about the lack of variety among the houses built on the new streets, and their lack of decorative significance. Some of our distinguished city councillors, while undertaking inquiries abroad, had been struck by certain picturesque features of houses at Brussels, London, Vienna, and in a few German towns. Back in Paris, they had urged that Parisian builders should be allowed the same freedoms as those enjoyed by foreign builders.[53]

In this new climate, the architects were beginning to take the lead in calling not only for a new architecture, but for building regulations which would permit and even foster it. In 1896, a new Prefect of the Seine would respond to their case. Justin de Selves was a brilliant administrator who was constantly aware of foreign example and who sought above all to modernise Paris. Responding to requests from his officials, he set up a commission to examine the building regulations immediately upon his appointment. Although its deliberations were limited

173 Louis Bonnier, a portrait probably dating from about 1900.

to projections to begin with, De Selves wanted from the very first to develop an aesthetic strategy for Paris in line with the leading architectural concepts of the day, and including municipal public works projects as well as private buildings.[54] The new commission, in contrast to those which had produced the regulations of 1882 and 1884, was composed almost entirely of architects, in response to the prefect's wish that aesthetics should be the main concern of the inquiry. Most were *architectes-voyers* or other municipal employees, but their sympathy with the private architects who sat on the commission, and with the broader community of Paris architects, was never in question. The debates immediately revealed a sympathy for 'the picturesque' and a belief in 'decoration' as a prime objective of architecture. At the same time, they were marked by considerable confusion. This confusion was resolved very largely by one man, the hitherto obscure *architecte-voyer* Louis Bonnier, who came to be accepted as the main ideologue of the new regulations during the course of the inquiry (Fig. 173).

Bonnier had an interest in Art Nouveau, having designed parts of Siegfried Bing's avant-garde Salon de l'Art Nouveau in the Rue de Provence in 1895.[55] He never referred to Art Nouveau in the commission debates, but he did not conceal a desire for greater

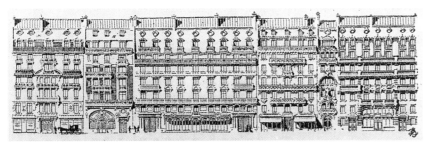

174, 175, 176 (*above*), 177 and 178 (*right, above*) Views and elevations drawn by Louis Bonnier in 1896 to show the results expected by the authorities from a liberalisation of the building regulations. They show: (1) a 20-metre street developed to the full extent allowed under the building regulations of 1882; (2) a street of 30 metres developed under the revised regulations; (3) a perspective view of the same street; (4) a 6-metre street under the existing regulations; (5) the same street redeveloped under the revised regulations.

licence which surpassed that of some of the other members. He averred that the changes in the building regulations in 1882 and 1884 had been the product mainly of public health considerations, which he wanted to offset by aesthetic ones: ' . . . for a nation, aesthetics is not a luxury but a need and a right just as hygiene is'.[56] This credo became a *leit-motiv* for Bonnier and was taken up by others.

In 1897, when Bonnier published some drawings showing the possible impact of revisions in the building regulations (Figs 174–8), it became clear that he favoured a radically new aesthetic for Paris, with varied facades bordering on fantasy in some cases, buildings set back from the streets to permit more greenery, strong colours on the walls and street surfaces, and a generally 'pic-

turesque' effect.[57] He had no objection to historical eclecticism – 'all the fantasies of ancient architecture' – if it added to picturesque effects.[58] There was not a hint of functionalism or modernism in what he proposed. It also became clear that the prefectoral administration, right up to the prefect himself, was broadly sympathetic both to the changes foreseen by Bonnier, and his vision of a picturesque, eclectic, historicist and individualistic Paris.

With opinion in the commission strongly in favour of larger and taller projections, De Selves extended the inquiry in 1897 to 'heights', which were inevitably affected by such increased dimensions. He set up a new commission for this purpose, but many of the members were the same, including Bonnier. The administration clearly assumed that only the heights and profiles of roofs would be considered, but discussions in the commission soon began to include facade heights as well. This reflected a widespread demand for freedom to build higher in the wider streets.

The most radical proposal generated by the new remit was for extra floors, additional to the maximum facade height, to be stepped back within an enlarged 'roof' profile. Theoretically, each set-back floor added to the width of the street and so permitted additional height, without disturbing the 45-degree sunlight angle which was now the Paris norm in all but the narrowest streets.[59] This formula was put forward by the Société Centrale des Architectes, the most influential national organisation of professionals, which had been studying the question since 1895. The society was formally represented on the inquiry, but Louis Bonnier had probably played a large part in its preparation. Other variants of the set-back formula were proposed by individuals, one of them, by Georges Debrie, involving a maximum facade height of 22 metres (71 feet) and an overall height rising in steps up to a maximum height of 30.5 metres (98 feet) on very deep sites.[60]

As the discussions proceeded, it became clear that the administration wanted to secure larger courtyards and spaces behind houses on public health grounds. Parisian practice prevented the authorities from reducing building rights embodied in existing regulations, so some compensation was seen to be necessary. Greater heights seemed to

offer an easy solution, so there remained only the question of how they would be achieved. Ultimately, the idea of a maximum facade height of 22 metres (72 feet) was dropped, but a formula was agreed allowing a greater volume in the roof. It owed something to Debrie's ideas, taking the form of an arc springing from the cornice with a radius equal to half the depth of the building, continued by a line at an angle of 45 degrees, up to the point where it intersected a horizontal line drawn from the top of the wall on the courtyard side, which was usually higher than the street facade.[61] In practice, it meant that an overall height of nearly 30 metres (98 feet) could be reached on large sites. The idea of a maximum number of floors under the cornice – which had been fixed at seven in 1884 – was dropped, against Bonnier's advice. In the narrower streets, extra height was allowed to owners who were prepared to build back from the building line, and in all streets even a withdrawal of part of the frontage from the building line earned the right to extra height. The intention of this concession was to break up the traditional continuous facades of Paris and promote greenery and the picturesque.

In October 1899 De Selves took the new regulations to the city council, which approved them with acclaim and without discussion.[62] Subsequent examination by state bodies was lengthy but no changes of substance were recommended, and the regulations came into force in August 1902 (Fig. 179). The new aesthetic could now move

179 Transitional houses in the Rue Lentonnet, 1896–7. The bays and *marquises* anticipate the building regulations of 1902, but other nearby architects did not use them. Discussions between the architect and the *architecte-voyer* probably account for the divergence in this case.

from vision to reality. But what reality would emerge, and how different from tradition would it be?

## THE NEW REGULATIONS AND THE PARISIAN TRADITION

The result of the regulations inquiry fell well short of its radical potential. The whole investigation was a largely local affair, with French provincial practice largely discounted as a mere derivation from Paris, or as regional aberration. References to foreign practice were few and generally condescending or disparaging. Louis Bonnier, who tried hard to encourage a broader awareness, prepared a dossier of regulations in other European cities, but little notice was taken of them in the discussions.[63] American experience was completely excluded, even Bonnier agreeing that American 'buildings' (skyscrapers) were too remote from Parisian practice to be of relevance.[64] Of course, precedent was very important in a city as large and densely built as Paris. Brutal changes in the building regulations could have upset the property market and prompted endless litigation. The fact remains nevertheless that most of the commission members viewed the matter in a purely local context, which suggested that the Parisian design tradition was as strong as ever.

Behind the deeper projections and taller roofs that were the main product of the 1902 regulations, there nevertheless lay a much bolder conception of a new Paris. The prophet of change was Louis Bonnier who, whatever the limitations of his colleagues, was constantly aware of foreign practice, and keen to promote the full exploitation of the new regulations with a view to creating an eclectic, international city on a massive scale. By 1902 it had already become clear that Bonnier had played the leading part in shaping the new rules. When he took on the task of explaining them to the Paris architectural community in a series of lectures at the Ecole des Beaux-Arts, he made constant reference to foreign practice.[65] His drawings of post-1902 street elevations, and his descriptions of painted firewalls and multicoloured sidewalks, with decorative street furniture, evoked a vision of an international city of consumption and leisure (Figs 180–1).

This was, of course, already the role of Paris, but Bonnier created its image almost from scratch, rather than as an extension of the existing city. This was a bold step, which had much in common with the ideas of Gustave Kahn. It came more easily, perhaps, to an architect who had designed extensively for the Paris exhibition of 1900.

Bonnier's ambitions overestimated both the artistic aspirations of Parisian property owners, and the tolerance of Parisian intel-

180 and 181 These two façades were entered for the municipal façades competition in 1899. The building in the modernised Louis-XV style by Georges Massa won a prize, but the house with the green ceramic bay was not honoured. Both, however, tried very hard. For a while, the façades competition certainly got architects to think about

beautifying their buildings, but this normally meant a Louis-XV decor rather than Art Nouveau.

182 *Below*, façades in the Avenue du Colonel-Bonnet, 1910. Such continuous overhangs, though permissible under the regulations, were regarded as an ugly abuse by the advocates of *façades mouvementées*.

lectuals, artists and conservative politicians. The new regulations were introduced during a building boom and by 1905 a large number of apartment houses conforming to them had been built. Most were in the central and western areas. Contemporaries were struck by their height, the top-heavy effect of the larger roofs and the taller projections, and the bulbous facades resulting from the use of wide, vertical bays rising from near the ground (Figs 182, 183). The volume of carved decoration, boosted by the new regulations

183 *Right*, post-1902 roof profiles opposite the Gare du Nord. The nearer example, on a shallow site, is an hotel dating from *c*. 1910. The massive party wall in the distance belongs to an office block dating from *c*. 1930, and standing on a deep site.

184 *Top right*, houses by Henri Rousset in the Place Alphonse-Deville, near the Hôtel Lutétia, 1911. The loggia and cupola treatment, merging the roof with the facade, is highly innovative. This is exactly what Bonnier had hoped the new regulations would encourage.

on projections, also aroused interest (Fig. 184). On the whole, however, the lack of variation in the rooflines disappointed informed observers, given that the reform advocates had promised some exciting displays of pinnacles, turrets and domes. Instead, the greater volume of usable space above cornices was usually filled with floor space, resulting in roofs looking like capsized men-of-war with gunports open, or the hanging gardens of Babylon. Few owners took advantage of the inducements for setbacks from the building line, and the unbroken street facade was maintained (Figs 185–6).

These disappointments would have been enough to reduce the morale of the reformers, but the regulations offended in a second, completely unexpected way. Some of the new buildings intruded on cherished views, most of which were classical perspectives created from the seventeenth century. The result was a powerful surge of reaction against the new architecture from about 1905. The claim that the new regulations had generated an insult to a number of national scenes and monuments was accompanied by the accusation that the resultant buildings themselves were vulgar, un-Parisian and, ultimately, un-French. The subsequent campaign for the reform of the regulations culminated in two debates in the Chamber of Deputies in 1908 and 1909, at the end of which the Ministry of the Interior undertook to reform the building code of 1902 to protect

the beauty of Paris.[66] There was also a long debate in the city council on 9 June 1909, centred mainly on tall buildings damaging traditional views, and ending with a resolution calling for a complete revision of the 1902 building code.

In practice, only a few slight changes were made to the code, to prevent certain 'abuses'. The State preferred to define protection zones around historic monuments and sites rather than review a building code which caused no problems over most of the city.[67] However, with a clear swing of opinion in favour of tradition, the climate was not propitious for a further liberalisation. The prefectoral authorities had set up a new review of the regulations as early as 1908, in response to early protests, and Bonnier again played a leading role.[68] This appears, however, to have been a holding manoeuvre, and no recommendations had been made by the time war broke out.

Meanwhile, the Commission on Monumental Perspectives, set up by the Ministry of Education and Fine Arts in 1909, became involved in the question of building regulations and reinforced the existing conservative influences on the Paris building code. Indeed, even Bonnier now began to evince a strong interest in the conservation of historic Paris and the protection of the city's beautiful perspectives.[69] Meanwhile, a new caution in the design of apartment blocks could be sensed, with a return to classical detailing on many buildings in the last years before the war (Fig. 187). At the same time, a modernist or functionalist style inspired by reinforced concrete began to emerge, though it was rarely adopted in the central areas and the West End (Figs 188, 189).

The enlarged dimensions of apartment buildings facing broad streets thus survived the reaction, but the whole episode of the 1902 building regulations merely projected the nineteenth-century apartment house, in a renewed form, into the twentieth century. Rare were the signs of an alternative residential architecture, even though the potential was clearly present (Fig. 190).

185 and 186 *Left, above,* post-1902 houses and roofs seen from the Eiffel tower.

187 *Left, below,* apartment house on the Quai d'Orsay by R. Bouvard, premiated in 1910. Clearly visible is the extra height in the roof made possible by the deep site and the open aspect onto the Seine.

188 *Right,* a commercial and residential block by P. Rigault, C. Duval and E. Gonse at 4–6, Rue aux Ours, 1909. The facade was featured in *L'Architecte* in December 1909.

189 *Below,* prize-winning apartment house in the Rue Scheffer by Herscher, *c.* 1913. The modernistic features in reinforced concrete were typical of the more workaday architecture of Paris just before the war.

190 *Far right,* artist's house in the Rue Cassini by Paul Huillard and Louis Suë, 1906. This neglected masterpiece draws on the best of European Art Nouveau and Jugendstil, with more than a hint of Charles Rennie Mackintosh. Country houses of a similar, individualistic style were built outside Paris in the early 1900s, for instance by Bonnier. This and other artists' houses in the Rue Cassini show what some Parisian architects could achieve when freed from the conformism of the apartment house. Huillard undertook this design in his very early thirties after studying at the Ecole des Beaux-Arts under Laloux.

## A NEW THEORY OF THE BEAUTY OF PARIS

While the authorities lay low, waiting for the storm of protest to blow itself out, the opposition generated a coherent case. This was based partly on a distinctly Parisian theory of aesthetics, and partly on the need for historic preservation, including the retention of districts notable for their townscape quality, and of the surroundings of outstanding buildings. More than in the past, the inherited streetscape was identified as worthy of interest and preservation.

This was, for instance, the assumption made by Emile Magne, the antiquarian, in his wide-ranging *L'esthétique des villes*, in 1908,[70] and by Charles Lortsch, lawyer and author of an influential book on the relation between the beauty of Paris and the law, published in 1913.[71] In his preface to Lortsch's book, André Hallays referred to 'the surprising ugliness and amazing incoherence of the Paris of today'.[72] The main object of this criticism was the 1902 building code and the resulting period of 'speculation' which had produced excessive height and bulk, and incoherent styles. However, Hallays detected a general deterioration under the influence of the international exhibitions and of growing speculation since the 1880s.[73]

For Lortsch, the beauty of Paris resided in the harmony of the relationship between its buildings and its streets and squares.[74] Beauty was necessary, claimed Lortsch, to the proper life of a people, and he ironically quoted Louis Bonnier's equation of aesthetics and hygiene as popular rights in support.[75] At the same time, as a lawyer Lortsch knew little about design. His main concern was to protect existing structures and scenes from intrusions by disproportionate buildings constructed under the 1902 code. In other words, he was not putting forward a formula for a new architectural style. However, the implication was that the dimensions and treatment of new buildings should conform to an older approach epitomising the essential beauty of Paris. This link between preservation and new building was potentially an important new influence on the development of architecture in Paris. Logically, the reaction concerned streets as well as buildings. While the rectilinear street of the classical tradition had been widely rejected by the theorists of the new century, the street itself was held up by many as the essential integrating element of the Parisian townscape. Charles Magny, a young jurist who wrote his doctoral thesis on the legal protection of the beauty of Paris, and who published it as a book very similar to that of Lortsch, remarked in 1911:

> It is the special appearance of the city which is under consideration. It is about its aesthetic appearance, the beauty of its perspectives. Besides, do not the streets of Paris have a distinct character and in some respects a special life?[76]

Perhaps the most influential expression of this new view of the parameters of Paris architecture was provided by the two debates in the Chamber of Deputies in 1908 and 1909. The main 'excesses' cited there were those affecting historic monuments and views, and the idea of a conflict between the national heritage and a combination of foreign art and selfish speculation was often implicit. On 11 November 1908 the Chamber carried a motion calling for the enforcement of all regulations affecting the beauty of Paris, the demolition of buildings which had been allowed to exceed the height limits, and the amendment of the 1902 code.[77]

Subsequent inaction by the authorities led to a new debate in 1909.[78] In this debate, Guillaume Chastenet, a senior Republican with an interest in fine arts, made a widely reported speech in which he put forward the idea of an urban aesthetic: ' . . . a great city is . . . a work of art. It is a collective and complex art it is true, but this makes it an even higher form of art.' Paris, he went on, is 'effectively the synthesis of our national life during eighteen centuries of our history'. In contrast, he referred to some of the new constructions near the Etoile as 'gratte-ciel'

(skyscrapers) and ' "buildings" à l'américaine'. This attack on foreign barbarism was followed by an assault on Parisian property owners, whose greed, he averred, underlay the 1902 building code. He stressed beauty, harmony, proportion, perspective and even eurhythm, as Parisian qualities. This was powerful rhetoric, but rhetoric which did little to encourage innovation.

THE TRIUMPH OF THE PARIS LUXURY STYLE

The rapid demise of Art Nouveau, and the conservative assault on the new building regulations, allowed a luxuriant and eclectic development of the Parisian classical tradition to continue as the dominant tendency in Parisian architecture between the mid-1890s and the First World War. Self-consciously artistic, it associated interiors and exteriors more closely than in the past, emphasising lush decoration throughout.

Stone-carving now reached its Parisian apogee. So luxuriant did it become that architects increasingly made it integral to the structure of their buildings, rather than applying it in panels or figures. The result was an ornate, even plastic, architecture in which there was no clear dividing line between the sculpture and the structure.[79] The combination of sensuality and, in many cases, pastiche styles idealising the classicism of the seventeenth and eighteenth centuries was well on the way by 1914 to producing a dream city – an urban version of Le Grand Meaulnes.

So rich and diffuse was the architecture of this period that no satisfactory selection of examples can be made. In what follows, railway termini, hotels, and department stores are emphasised, mainly because they required a combination of luxury and practicality which pushed their architects to the limits of their inventiveness, while remaining within the Parisian design tradition that these epic years had vindicated.

RAILWAY TERMINI

Two large railway termini were built at the turn of the century. Both companies had entirely practical objectives, but in the atmosphere created by the exhibition of 1900, they were aware of a strong obligation to enhance the cityscape. Both chose variants of the classical style. The Gare de Lyon, standing at the gateway to the East End, was more daring, using symbolism, the picturesque, expressionism and height, while the Gare d'Orsay, standing opposite the Louvre, managed to be suave and modest at the same time. The genesis of these two stations epitomises public architecture in Paris at the height of the *belle époque.*

The Compagnie d'Orléans announced its plans to bring an electrified line into the heart of Paris in 1894 and 1895. Immediately, a wave of concern and protest arose from the now very powerful Paris preservation movement.[80] The company made every effort to allay these fears. It had, in the first instance, approached the innovative municipal engineer-architect, Eugène Hénard, to act as consultant architect. His plans, however, soon caused embarrassment, notably because of his wish to use industrial materials on the Seine facade, opposite the Louvre. The company therefore held a restricted competition, stipulating the use of stone on the facades. Hénard declined to enter. Two new architects, Emile Bénard and Victor Laloux, were invited to take part, while a

third architect, Lucien Magne, was admitted after he had made his own approach to the company.[81]

The competition was supervised by a parliamentary committee which had been set up on the initiative of Emile Trélat. The committee's remit was to ensure that chaos did not result from the nearly simultaneous construction of the Gare d'Orsay and of a suburban terminal just to the west, the Gare des Invalides.[82]

All the entries were highly innovative internally, because of the underground tracks.[83] The exterior treatments, on the other hand, were thoroughly classical, with an arcaded Seine frontage common to nearly all the entries. The winner was Laloux, a Rome prize-winner who was noted for a large station which he had built at Tours. His Orsay entry was deemed to be the most successful in integrating the stone exterior and the metal vault in what he claimed to be a new architecture (Fig. 191). He was assigned the project, completing it in time for the exhibition of 1900.[84] The interior of the Gare d'Orsay recalled some of the big American union stations of the turn of the century (though it undoubtedly influenced them in its turn). Indeed, Laloux's atelier at the Ecole

191 Aerial view of the Gare d'Orsay, as slightly modified for use as a museum in the 1980s. The Louvre and the Tuileries gardens, which the new station sought to enhance, are visible at the top.

des Beaux-Arts attracted a total of ninety-seven American students over the years – far more than any other.[85]

Laloux clearly possessed an expertise and vision which stretched far beyond the normal bounds of Parisian design. The station exterior, however, offered little more than a restrained elegance (Fig. 192). This was Parisian tradition triumphant, and a model for everyone building in fashionable Paris.

The Gare de Lyon was a different story.[86] The problem here was to create, on an awkward site in a poor area, a station symbolising the role of the PLM (Paris-Lyon-Méditerranée company) as the main route to Lyon, Marseille, and their industrial and port regions, and also to the increasingly fashionable French Riviera.

The company had decided in 1891 to build an impressive facade, together with a luxury hotel nearby.[87] However, work did not start until 1895 because of site problems, and the station was not complete until 1902. The architect was Marius Toudoire, the PLM's company architect. The supple design, the

languorous sculpture springing directly from the walls and the colourful decoration recalled the architecture of luxury hotels and casinos on the Côte d'Azur. The point was rammed home by what must be the world's most palatial station restaurant in a lush neo-rococo. 'More decorative than utilitarian', was Paul Planat's pithy comment on the frontage building (Fig. 193).[88]

The drab industrial areas down the line were not reflected at all, except perhaps in the expressionistic clocktower which echoed recent provincial custom. The giant mural showing cameos of towns on the PLM network which ran the full length of the booking hall emphasised the historic towns and ignored the industrial features of the manufacturing centres. Industry's only appearance, though unintentionally, was in the claustrophobic iron train shed, clogged with dumpy columns and depressed by crude roof structures. In contrast to the Gare d'Orsay, there was no impressive integration of the station building and the train shed. This was partly, however, because the two wings of

192 Seine frontage of the Gare d'Orsay.

193 The Gare de Lyon.

the Gare de Lyon were so shallow that they were little more than screens for the platforms. As screens, however, with their hallucinatory clocktower dominating the main approaches, they might be seen as symbols of the fragile world of leisured luxury which the First World War would snatch away.

LUXURY HOTELS

Economic revival from the Great Depression in the mid-1890s boosted business travel, tourism and other international contacts, Paris, as the international centre *par excellence*, benefited more than any other city. One result was the construction of a number of large hotels from the late 1890s. This second generation of luxury hotels followed the first big era of hotel building under the Second Empire, when nearly all had been sited in the very centre of the city, or near the railway termini. This time, the promoters sought locations outside the centre, in the fashionable western districts, and their designs expressed luxury rather than practicality. Hotels now had to offer the same appearance, environment and comfort as private mansions and luxury apartments. For people who had left servants behind, they had to offer a full range of services. This normally required a very large building and, in consequence, the use of an entire block.

The years between 1895 and 1914 saw the construction of the Elysée-Palace, the Hôtel Astoria and the Hôtel Claridge, all in the upper Champs-Elysées district, the Hôtel d'Orsay, next to the new station, and the Hôtel Lutétia, on the Boulevard Raspail (Figs 194–5). All used the same elegant, comfortable neo-baroque style, as did apartment houses, especially after 1902. The resulting mutual influence tended to reinforce the common style of luxury which persisted until 1914 and discouraged quirky alternatives once Art Nouveau had been dismissed.

The Paris hotel style was admired to the point where French architects were commissioned to build hotels abroad. René Sergent, for instance, built the Savoy and Claridges in London, and the Grand Hotel in Rome.[89] Carving reached a degree of profusion which made this the classic period for French decorative sculpture.[90] Equally striking was the spread of sinuous forms, closely related to female bodies, and clinging

131

194 The Hôtel Lutétia.

Many histories of architecture have placed the Parisian department store at the leading edge of architectural progress. Their interiors fully justify this reputation. Between the 1860s and 1900 it had become normal for department stores to have an open, metal-framed interior with generous natural lighting, much of it from above. They shared this characteristic with exhibition halls, but in department stores the metal structure was unusually complex because of the need for several floors, linked by a central well and staircase. Paris, as the world's leading centre of fashion and luxury consumption, and of international exhibitions, was also the world leader in this area of innovative architecture.

The exterior treatment, however, moved in the opposite direction. The stark metal framing of the Halles was a product of the Second Empire. The sublime metal structure of the Galérie des Machines, built by Ferdinand Dutert for the 1889 exhibition and looking like a Zeppelin hall, was demolished in 1910. Meanwhile, new examples of open metal framing tended to be encased in masonry frontages and traditional rooflines. The design treatments varied, but by the end of the century these exteriors were being built in the same, luxurious variant of the Paris classical style as the leading railway stations, hotels, and apartment blocks.

The Grand Palais and the Petit Palais (Figs 196–7), built on sites of great townscape significance as permanent contributions to the exhibition of 1900, had neo-classical masonry exteriors, with lush, neo-baroque decoration.[91] At the department stores, glass and metal bays in the industrial style became universal from as early as the 1860s, but by the 1880s they were being framed by the decorative masonry piers and cornices of the Paris luxury style. The Au Printemps building of 1881, for instance, was a model of applied ornament, with bright colours and slim, coquettish cupolas.[92] The interiors of the lighting shafts became more and more ornate, and their neo-Rococo verged on the Art Nouveau by the later 1890s. The debacle of Jourdain's Samaritaine discouraged further experiments in metal exteriors, and other department stores continued to make a dignified use of masonry for the most part.

tendrils, which could appear anywhere on a building, inside or out. Apartment houses were decorated in a similar way, presenting a sybaritic image which, though appropriate to the Paris of the *belle époque*, was not conducive to the creation of a functional, industrial architecture. By 1914 the fashionable districts of Paris were beginning to look like a scene from *The Divine Comedy*, or a high-rise Bel-Air.

195 The Hôtel Claridge, Avenue des Champs-Elysées.

196 The Petit Palais, probably photographed *c.* 1900.

197 The Grand Palais, housing a display of sculpture.

main drive shaft running along the axis of the building, breadth was also sought. The main problem here was to secure natural lighting from windows in the lateral walls, and to reduce ceiling supports to a minimum to allow free use of the machinery. At first, mill architects used heavy wooden beams supported by wrought-iron columns. Wrought-iron beams were increasingly used in the nineteenth century but the expense was always a discouragement.

The resulting formula of a long, rectangular building lit from both sides, like an orangery or a real tennis court with several floors, was first adopted in France on a large scale with the building of the railways. It was not until the 1860s, however, that the advent of bulk steel resolved the problem of the beams, and from then onwards buildings of this type proliferated in Paris in situations where people or machines needed to work in a well-lit, open space. Machine-made bricks also became available from the 1850s, and by the 1870s they had become the normal cladding for industrial buildings.[93]

In Paris, however, the typical and most visible example was not so much the factory as the school. In visual terms this new building need not have clashed seriously with Parisian tradition. The bays were all of equal width and the windows, though very large, were identical. Economy normally dictated a pitched roof, but there was nothing new about this in Paris. Where the divergence emerged was in the vertical treatment of the window bays. Because the transoms which separated the windows had no structural significance, and were often of limited dimensions in order to maximise the area of glazing, they could be made of metal sheeting, ceramic or terra cotta, or formed cheaply and colourfully from brick. The result was often a vertical band of transoms and glazing, or continuous glazing, bounded by solid piers in masonry, metal, brick or tile.

Almost always, the uppermost window in the vertical bay was topped by a segmental arch, strongly emphasised in masonry or brick. Construction could rise as far as four storeys or more, but two or three storeys was the more common height. Even without a mixture of materials, polychrome treatment and the decorative tie-bar plates which became quite a fad, these buildings normally had a verticality and a rough vigour which

## AN ARCHITECTURE OF WORK: THE OTHER PARIS

While the Paris luxury style moulded the West End, a parallel architecture of work continued to develop, especially in the east. This was the functional, economical style which had continued to evolve from its mid-century origins. It was used for factories, large workshops, schools and training colleges, and hospitals.

Ever since the first large textile mills emerged in Britain in the 1770s, it had been normal to arrange powered production on several floors of a large building. Although the mills had a longitudinal plan, with the ran counter to the classicist norm. For this reason, they were rarely used in prestige areas, but elsewhere they were too useful to ignore.

Thanks partly to the approval of Viollet-le-Duc and his admirers, the new mode of design was adopted under Jules Ferry's national programme for the development of primary schools in 1879–83. Some three hundred primary schools were built in Paris between 1870 and 1914, many of them in the new style (Fig. 198).[94] Most of the structures were determined by the very careful design of the interior, directed by Ferry's regulations for school design in 1880.[95] By no means all reflected the influence of Viollet-le-Duc or used the rectangular plan, but pitched roofs, segmental arch windows, brick facing, polychromy, decorated tie-bar plates and banded brick and stonework, were very frequent. As government buildings, their style could not be questioned by the Paris authorities. A number of secondary schools used a variant of this style, such as the Lycée Lakanal at Sceaux, in the southern suburbs, designed by the proto-functionalist and member of Viollet-le-Duc's school, Anatole de Baudot, in 1885,[96] or the Lycée Buffon, built by Emile Vaudremer in 1887–9.[97]

Railway and industrial buildings used this mode of design, less obtrusively, until 1914.

It also spread to certain commercial buildings in the central areas from the 1880s. Many of these were devoted to textiles, garments, furniture and printing, and they often combined manufacture, storage, display and administration. The tops of the piers, level with the segmental arches or just below them, were often developed as a decorative feature, like symbolic capitals in coloured brick or tile. By 1914 buildings of this type had taken over whole streets, or sections thereof, in the northern districts of the centre.

The most striking example was the Rue Réaumur, driven in the late 1890s through an unfashionable area where quality residential building was unlikely. The authorities therefore encouraged the purchasers of sites to seek a high standard of commercial design (Figs 199–201). In several cases the results were striking developments of the industrial mode, with wide glass and metal facades flanked by heavily rusticated and decorated piers.[98] In large commercial and industrial buildings of this type, it was common to provide one or more residential floors above the industrial levels, and here a more traditional exterior was usually adopted. Such was the solution chosen by the architect Emile Leménil for a multiple factory/housing development, the Rue des Immeubles

198 *Left*, school in the Rue des Quatre-Fils by Chat, 1877.

199 *Right, above*, this large office block at the corner of the Place de la Bourse won a prize in the Rue Réaumur facades competition in 1898. Special permission for the unusual height was readily granted because the authorities wanted to encourage varied design in this commercial street.

200 *Right, below*, the office block at the corner of the Place de la Bourse (199) in 1991.

201 *Far right, above*, the Rue Réaumur looking east. Chedanne's innovative metal-fronted building (1904–5) is second on the left.

202 *Far right, below*, the Rue des Immeubles-Industriels, near the Place de la Nation, in the Faubourg Saint-Antoine, completed in 1873. This combination of centrally powered workshops and workers' homes allows the open bays of the industrial style and conventional tenement architecture to be combined in one building. The idea was developed by Leménil and the development company was Cail et Cie, which built a number of new streets and houses in eastern Paris from the later 1860s.

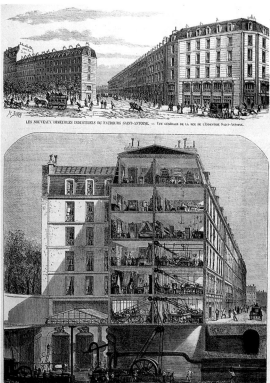

LES NOUVEAUX IMMEUBLES INDUSTRIELS DU FAUBOURG SAINT-ANTOINE. — VUE GÉNÉRALE DE LA RUE DE L'INDUSTRIE SAINT-ANTOINE.

Industriels (XI$^e$), in 1872–3 (Fig. 202), and subsequent divergence from this pattern was rare.[99] A dual solution was adopted by Paul-Adrien Gouny for his utilitarian railway offices of the Gare de l'Est in 1887 (Figs 203–4). The central post office, built in the Rue du Louvre, near the Halles, in the mid-1880s by the *grand patron* of a Beaux-Arts atelier, Julien Guadet (Fig. 205), used pillars, bays and an arcade with segmental arches to enclose a large interior hall and a complicated system of levels above, supported by arches

and metal beams. Although a pediment and certain other semi-classical features were used to disguise the industrial character of the architecture, the result was uneasy.[100] In 1893 the effect was exacerbated by Jean-Marie Boussard's amazingly ugly designs for the towering drum of the central telephone exchange, together with its neighbouring machine block, which were built at the corner of the Rue du Louvre and the Rue Jean-Jacques Rousseau.[101] Although Guadet's eminence helped spare him strong criticism, this ensemble cannot have helped the cause of rationalism as far as central Paris was concerned. Finally, the style influenced a small number of apartment houses (Fig. 206).

## PARISIAN ARCHITECTURE ON THE EVE OF THE FIRST WORLD WAR

Between 1870 and 1914 Parisian architects practised under a republican regime. For reasons partly beyond France's control, economic growth was slower than during the Second Empire, though there was some acceleration from the mid-1890s. This recovery did not generate a new architecture. Art Nouveau, which threatened to displace classicism for the first time since the sixteenth century, was rejected after a few years. Most architects clung to the Paris luxury style which had originally been inspired by Garnier's opera house and which reached its peak in around 1910.

205 *Left*, Guadet's central post office in the Rue du Louvre.

206 *Above*, in 1885, I. Suffit and O. Courtois Suffit built this apartment house at 134, rue du Faubourg-Poissonnière. The tie-bar plates suggest that a metal structure for the floors has been used. They, and the segmental arches under the gallery (permitted by the building regulations of 1882), suggest an allegiance to Viollet-le-Duc which cannot be expressed fully in an apartment building.

203 and 204 *Opposite, above,* two façades of a large office court built for the eastern railway company in 1887 by Paul-Adrien Gouny. The more restrained masonry frontage faces the Gare de l'Est. At the rear, on the workaday Rue du Faubourg-Saint-Denis, Gouny felt free to produce a virtuoso essay in the industrial style.

The failure of Art Nouveau confirmed that there was little scope for design alternatives. On the contrary, the work of Paris architects tended to reflect a general self-satisfaction and sense of comfort. This complacent attitude was largely justified by the status of Paris as one of the best laid out and best equipped capitals in the world, and perhaps the most elegant and civilised of all, thanks to its unrivalled role as an international centre and home of the aristocracy. Its architects were without doubt the best trained anywhere. Half the architects in France practised in Paris.[102] In the provinces, architects complained that they found it hard to resist the rising competition of the engineers, who were moving into building design. In Paris, however, the architects had no difficulty in maintaining their professional dominance and their design orthodoxy.[103] From a standpoint in the late twentieth century, this may sound like atrophy. Seen in the context of the time, Paris was the best-built city in the world.

Whether quality or complacency was the keynote, the First World War would change the context. Would the continuity of classicism survive, or would post-war disruptions create a new architecture?

# THE MODERNIST CHALLENGE, 1918–45

### THE FIRST WORLD WAR AS AN ARCHITECTURAL MILESTONE

The First World War altered the context of Parisian architecture. After 1918 the distribution of new building shifted towards the public sector. More new building took place in the suburbs, rather than in the city.[1] Luxury apartment construction slowed in the West End, especially in the 1930s. More modest building for the middle classes virtually faded away throughout the city.

All this meant less work for architects, at any rate within the city boundary. Some moved with enthusiasm into the public domain, developing striking new styles which they considered appropriate to the cheap but healthy housing of working people. Making much use of brick in varied colours, and elemental, semi-bucolic forms, these styles evoked an honest, artisanal simplicity which harked back to pre-1914 model housing designs such as the Rothschild estate.[2] Modernism played only a small part, and the resulting neo-vernacular was unsuited to the central districts of the city.

Other architects clung to their rich clientele. Though in much smaller numbers than before 1914, they built mansions and luxury apartment blocks in western Paris and in adjacent suburban areas such as Saint-Cloud, which qualified for quasi-Parisian status (Figs 207–8). That many of these buildings were constructed in new styles may cause surprise in view of the classical design inertia before 1914. The explanation may lie in the low building rate. Owners and architects were prepared to view each new building as a special case, and as potentially a major design statement which could readily adopt any of the fashionable styles that flourished, especially in the 1920s. These included Art Deco, neo-classicism, the Paris luxury style, and the distinctively French form of reduced neo-classicism using giant, square panels on lines inspired by Perret.[3] Modernism figured as well, often merging with the other styles in

the 1920s but coming to the fore in the 1930s. With only the wealthiest owners able to undertake new buildings, but consequently able to commission the most talented architects, the pre-1914 mass design phenomenon did not recur.

The result was an unprecedented diversity in Parisian architecture. The Ecole des Beaux-Arts, though still the major influence on training, no longer kept a tight grip on practice. Meanwhile, the war had opened up Paris to foreign architects, who for the first

207 and 208  Mansion at Neuilly-sur-Seine by Pussot and Lempereur, 1928. *La Construction Moderne* described it as being *'d'une note moderne très atténuée'*, with the client quoted as preferring a quality of solidity and stability.

time became a significant force in the history of French architecture. Was the traditional Parisian design consensus now under serious threat? Was the door being opened for modernism?

THE MODERNIST CHALLENGE

The development of architecture in the twentieth century has been marked above all by the self-styled 'Modern Movement'. This was intended to be a radically new approach to design, based on functionalism, 'industrial' materials, and a new aesthetic that valued simplicity, harmony and natural forms, and moved by objectives of social efficiency and even of social justice. Although its origins can be traced to the nineteenth century, it was boosted by the First World War and its aftermath. From this time onwards, it developed an aggressive ideology which denied a place to all other architectural schools. In 1928 modern architecture was confirmed as a world movement by the first of a long series of international congresses, the CIAM (Congrès Internationaux d'Architecture Moderne).

Pre-1914 Paris had been no fertile breeding ground for modernism of this sort. Rein-forced concrete, nevertheless, had been an important means of innovation. France acquired a world lead in this area in the later nineteenth century, thanks mainly to the prowess of its engineers, and Parisian architects, who were not averse to new materials in themselves, made growing use of concrete. A small group of specialists learned to build complete apartment blocks with it at the turn of the century. Early examples, including Hennébique's large apartment house in the Rue Danton in 1901, normally aped traditional styles, but Auguste Perret and other concrete specialists were already thinking about a more practical and rational concrete architecture. After a number of experiments with a concrete frame and slab system for apartment houses, Perret had the chance to build on a massive scale which Parisian opinion could not ignore.[4] Between 1911 and 1913 Auguste Perret was the architect of the Théâtre des Champs-Elysées (Fig. 209), a private project designed to represent the best in Parisian design and drawing on contributions from a number of innovative artists.[5] The strongly geometrical elevations, with the construction frame strongly emphasised, were a departure from the Parisian norm for prestigious public buildings, and even the large panels of Greek-inspired

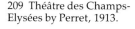

209 Théâtre des Champs-Elysées by Perret, 1913.

sculpture could not soften the strong but simple effect. On the other hand, there was the echo of a giant order of pilasters over the entrance and the facade had a strong stripped-classical flavour which Perret would reinforce in his later work.

Henri Sauvage was a specialist in reinforced concrete and had an interest in public health.[6] He took up the idea of stepped roofs, which was arousing some interest among Parisian architects by the later 1890s, and applied it to the entire facade. His main justification was sunlighting, but his total concept was much more grandiose. It involved the development of an entire block shaped like a narrow rectangle. The long frontages would be stepped back until they met at the summit of the building. The two short frontages would be developed with tall pavilions, while the hollow inner core of the block would be equipped for some public use which did not require natural light, such as a swimming pool.

In 1912 Sauvage was able to realise his vision in a co-ownership apartment house at 26, rue Vavin. The street was narrow but Sauvage achieved a height of 18 metres (58 feet) within the building regulations of 1902 by progressively setting back.[7] Sauvage went on after the war to develop the idea of a completely pyramidal form for apartment houses occupying the whole of very large blocks (Fig. 210).[8] Louis Bonnier had mixed feelings about the stepped facades, mainly because of the dark and frequently useless interior space, but even he came to see their value after the war. The idea sprang from a proposal made by Eugène-Georges Debrie, an architect member of the administrative sub-committee on heights, one of the contributors to the building code of 1902. Debrie argued that building should be controlled only where it did harm to others, and that in the interior a block might, under certain conditions, rise above the Parisian, street-related, norms. He had in mind a stepped structure ('un système de défilement'), which came to be known in official circles as 'un système de pyramide capable' (pyramidal envelope system).[9] The idea looked forward to the post-war 'city of towers' concept, where great heights would be permitted because of the large air volumes between the buildings.

Discussion of a modern, industrial architecture was accelerated from 1914 by the war with Germany. Paris was the main centre of the debate on the reconstruction of northern France and also of occupied Belgium. By no

210 Perspective of the Sauvage pyramid proposal, Salon d'Automne, 1928.

140

means all architects believed that this task would require a new architecture, but all accepted that planning and a mass housing programme would be needed. There was also much talk of creating a 'sanitary' environment throughout France as a tribute to the returning military, and the modernist proposals made a big feature of the French specialism of 'social hygiene'.[10]

The highlight of wartime discussions was an exhibition, held at Paris in 1916, under the title 'How can we rebuild our devastated towns?'. The work of the Modern Movement was not prominent here, with much interest among Belgian and French contributors in urban reconstruction on traditional lines. However, the event prompted modern architects to consider more fully their possible contribution after the war, and to recognise that in working for the masses – as they saw it – they could liberate themselves from the constraints of elite patronage.

One of the earliest radical statements was the book published by the respected survivor of the Viollet-le-Duc era, Anatole de Baudot, in 1916. He complained of the banal, mass-production appearance of most Paris apartment houses which made Paris so monotonous.[11] De Baudot wanted design to spring principally from materials, with polychromy where appropriate. He was an enthusiast for concrete, which he had used in his most important building, the church of Saint-Jean-de-Montmartre, built between 1894 and 1899. He wanted the architect to abandon all imitation of ancient forms. He saw the Ecole des Beaux-Arts as one of the obstacles to change. Overall, De Baudot admitted to being in search of a *rational* doctrine of architecture, on lines which anticipated Le Corbusier.[12]

Among the younger architects of this tendency were Auguste Perret, Robert Mallet-Stevens, André Lurçat and Roger-Henri Expert, who would later design the interiors of the *Normandie* liner. In 1917 they were joined by a young Swiss architect, Charles-Edouard Jeanneret, who soon adopted the soubriquet of Le Corbusier. The much-travelled Jeanneret chose to settle in Paris in order to take part in reconstruction work. He was the most able and versatile of them all, and also the greatest ideologue. With Le Corbusier, the old assumption that

French architecture had to be the work of Frenchmen was challenged.

Other foreigners took refuge in Paris from the effects of the First World War and later from the revolution in Russia. The young Armenian architect and minor member of the Modern Movement, Gabriel Guévrékian, a victim of Turkish persecution, brought his family to Paris and set up a practice there in 1921, after training in Vienna. He soon joined the Mallet-Stevens practice and designed a number of competent modern buildings.[13]

Many foreign students were still attracted by the Ecole des Beaux-Arts, but some of them joined in protests against its traditional programme. Foreigners joined the group of young students who tried to find a leading modern architect to direct a modernist atelier in 1923. Such breakaway initiatives were entirely within the tradition of the school, but so forthright a challenge to orthodoxy had not been seen since the era of Viollet-le-Duc in the 1860s. The group included several foreigners who would never practise in France, but Oscar Nitzchke, a student of German birth who had moved to Paris in 1920 and entered the Ecole in 1921, would make his career in the city.[14] Le Corbusier was approached but declined to involve himself in teaching. Perret, however, agreed to take on the task after Le Corbusier had recommended him. Perret's style was, of course, not unsympathetic to the French classical tradition and he may have helped to prevent a direct confrontation with modernism.

EARLY MODERNISM IN PARIS:
ROBERT MALLET-STEVENS

The pattern of architectural design in Paris was very fragmented after the war. Much modern design was eclectic or expressionistic, to the disappointment of Le Corbusier. One of Le Corbusier's biggest bugbears was Mallet-Stevens, who built much more in Paris and its region in the 1920s than the Swiss architect did, but who was lacking in system and principle. Mallet-Stevens, however, gave modernism a very respectable image, and history has not entirely borne out Le Corbusier's purist criticisms.[15]

In 1925–7 Robert Mallet-Stevens was

the architect-developer of a new street of apartment houses in the fashionable XVIᵉ *arrondissement*. This was the biggest scheme in modern architecture and planning which Paris had yet seen (Fig. 211). It was much larger than Le Corbusier's nearby Laroche-Jeanneret houses of 1923 (Fig. 212), and it attracted considerable attention in the press and Parisian society.

However, Mallet-Stevens never undertook another housing scheme of this type, and his approach to modern design was not widely emulated. Partly to blame was the absence of a powerful modernist design consensus in Paris in the 1920s. The war had weakened older conventions without removing them, and traditional aspirations could be detected in a number of new styles. Mallet-Stevens was no dilettante, but his training and career

epitomised the artistic approach to modern design shared by many of his contemporaries. He came from an artistic family background and began his architectural training in 1905 at the Ecole Spéciale d'Architecture, Emile Trélat's practical alternative to the Ecole des Beaux-Arts.[16] It was probably here that he acquired his interest in rational design and in the importance of public health.

Like other developing modernists of his day, he was in close touch with his equivalents outside France. He regarded Charles Rennie Mackintosh, for instance, as an inspiration. At first, however, he had to work mainly as an interior designer, and he did not receive an architectural commission until 1923.[17] By this time, Le Corbusier had become the main theorist of Paris modern architecture, and Mallet-Stevens's eclecticism and lack of system tended to peripheralise his architecture. When the Rue Mallet-Stevens was not emulated, he returned mainly to commissions for rich clients. By the 1930s he was working mainly in a style which is best described as Streamline Moderne.

## LE CORBUSIER'S STRUGGLE WITH THE PARISIAN TRADITION

A recent study of the Rue Mallet-Stevens has placed it within the Parisian tradition of architecture and planning.[18] An older Mallet-Stevens, one suspects, would have welcomed such a judgment. Ironically, Le Corbusier also associated his own work with Parisian tradition. This did not mean, however, that he wished to be *incorporated* in an older system. He liked to view his life in Paris as a struggle with a great city which could crush or ignore him, or lift him up to fame and influence.[19] One aspect of the struggle was what he saw as the city's resistance to his comprehensive ideals for urban architecture and planning. Far more than any other modern architect working in Paris between the wars, Le Corbusier developed a complete town planning system in which individual buildings were to be set. He devoted great efforts to its advocacy. Recognising the important position that Paris occupied in the world of architecture, he tried hard to secure commissions there, and he published or exhibited a number of theoretical schemes which, if implemented, would have replaced

211 House, Rue Mallet-Stevens, 1927.

212 The La Roche-Jeanneret houses by Le Corbusier, 1922. By building in the middle of a large block in an expanding district of the XVIᵉ *arrondissement* (and not far from the Rue Mallet-Stevens), Le Corbusier was able to achieve a compromise between urban and suburban building.

the city's traditional fabric by an environment of towers, slabs, open space and fast motor roads.

This advocacy work, together with the construction of several influential buildings, had made Le Corbusier the most complete representative of the Modern Movement in Paris by the end of the 1920s. However, even though he took French nationality, he never completely lost his initial outsider status. He increasingly resented what he regarded as the mindless resistance of Paris to his ideas, and he took pride in his growing international reputation. He became a leading member of the CIAM from their foundation in 1928, and he was the main author of the Athens Charter, the CIAM's town planning programme, in 1933.

Paradoxically, the Paris of which Le Corbusier desired to destroy so much was the inspiration for a large part of his vision of a new city. The high densities, vital social life and fine architecture in an ordered environment were Parisian qualities which he admired and wanted to perpetuate.[20] He persistently claimed that his Paris schemes were faithful to the classical ideals on which the city had been built since Louis XIV's time, and he often expressed amazement that this argument persuaded so few.

The first of his Paris-inspired city schemes

was exhibited in 1922 as 'A Contemporary City of Three Million Inhabitants' at the Salon d'Automne, a regular exhibition of all forms of art and design which had been created in 1903 by Frantz Jourdain during his strenuous modernising campaign. The population size of three million made it clear that this was intended to be an alternative Paris, but the proposal was flawed by the fact that the great majority of the assumed population were housed outside the central, high-rise city in mysterious 'garden cities' which did not form part of the scheme. In 1925 Le Corbusier made his point much more strongly when he exhibited a reconstruction proposal at the Exposition Internationale des Arts Décoratifs et Industriels Modernes (a Parisian effort to revive the city's pre-war tradition as an exhibition centre). This was the 'Plan Voisin' (Fig. 213), a project for the reconstruction of the whole of central Paris on the Right Bank with a grid of towers, 200 metres (625 feet) high, and lower residential slabs.

Although the Plan Voisin is best understood as a debating contribution, Le Corbusier was unhappy about the indifference or negative reaction that it provoked. In the later 1920s and 1930s he found himself busy with a number of contracts in Paris and its region, and with international consultancies and competition entries. However, he kept

213 Bird's-eye view of Le Corbusier's Plan Voisin proposal for central Paris, 1925.

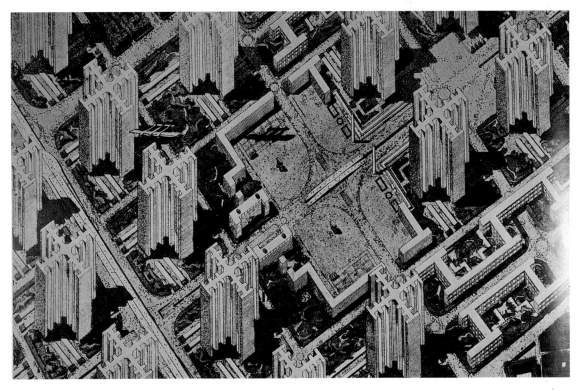

an eye on Parisian planning developments with a view to reviving interest in the 'Plan Voisin' grid. In the late 1930s, for instance, he tried hard to influence official plans for the reconstruction of slum areas and the fortification zone so that they could form part of an eventual rebuilding of the whole city according to his concepts.

Meanwhile, his work within the city was too scattered and disparate to establish a persuasive alternative to the traditional Parisian fabric. The international exhibition of 1925 had diffused Art Deco, a striking, elegant architecture based on applied art rather than modernism. Art Deco had no coherent design rationale and it was bound to cloy after a few years, but its early impact was devastating. As a geometrical expression of the pre-war luxury style it could draw on the talents of the pre-war generation of designers. Hector Guimard, for instance, switched to Art Deco in the 1920s. This continuity would continue into the 1930s when Art Deco merged into the Moderne style used in Paris for commercial buildings.

Only the Swiss residential house at the Cité Universitaire, completed in 1932 (Fig. 214), allowed Le Corbusier to build a tall, slab block on the piers which he considered essential to his landscape retention formula.[21] In 1932 he built another slab block as a Salvation Army night shelter, but this was less innovative owing to the requirements of the client.

Also in 1932, he built an apartment house in the Rue Nungesser-et-Coli, in the XVI<sup>e</sup> *arrondissement*. This was part of a big scheme of expensive apartment houses promoted by a development company which wanted to

encourage modern design. Sites were offered to a number of distinguished architects of the day, but all had to conform to the traditional street frontage layout. Le Corbusier's projecting facade clung to the building line, and the roof profile observed the standard limits of 1902. His first scheme had been turned down by the *architecte-voyer* because the ceilings were too low and because the projections took up too much of the facade.[22] For all this, Le Corbusier's building stood out from the others, but it exercised no influence elsewhere.

Although Le Corbusier's ideas for planning, mass housing, urban transport and commercial districts were all fully formulated by the mid-1930s, his apparent threat to traditional Paris and his exclusion from official schemes prevented him from placing a clear imprint on the city. At the Cité Universitaire, for instance, his successful Swiss building did not prevent the proliferation of students' residences which made up the biggest collection of pastiche buildings in Paris. One of the largest of them, A. Guéritte's Maison des Provinces de France (Fig. 215), built in 1934, sought to express the vitality of French regional styles in a lively, traditionalistic design which managed to refer to most of the available architectural qualities except modernity.[23]

Le Corbusier's inability to change the climate of opinion in the 1920s in no way reflected his own weaknesses. To a large extent it reflected the low-key character of the architectural debate in the decade. The volume of new building was too low to

214 Le Corbusier's Swiss student hostel at the Cité Universitaire, 1932.

215 The Maison des Provinces de France, a hostel for French students, by A. Guéritte, 1934.

generate mass design tendencies. The building regulations of 1902 were taken as a *ne plus ultra*, having already caused an outcry before the war. Above all, the traditional Paris aesthetic was not seriously questioned by the authorities or by the clients. When in 1929 Albert Guérard, a French professor living in the USA, published a widely read book on tendencies in Parisian architecture and planning, he typified this attitude:

> In reality, Paris is essentially a classical and a French city; that is its glory and its full extent. The point of perfection was reached round about the middle of the eighteenth century, after the excesses of rococo tenderness, and before the rigidities of ultra-classicism, which led it to perish from a kind of sclerosis of the arteries.[24]

From the early 1930s, however, Paris began to see a more coherent and persuasive modernism. It was by no means the dominant style, but its products were at last easy to recognise and they made a clear statement. The arrival of this powerful new modernism in 1930 and 1931 was reflected in two competitions at this time for an urban project of Haussmannic proportions. Though it would never be carried out owing to the economic disasters of the 1930s, the scheme allowed modern architecture for the first time to confront tradition on equal terms.

THE VOIE TRIOMPHALE: A TEST FOR MODERNISM

At the end of the war, the government decided to reinforce the great east-west axis by developing the western section, from the Etoile to the Défense, as a symbol of victory. This was to be known as the Triumphal Way (*Voie Triomphale*). A variety of plans were commissioned or encouraged, but they were more symbolic than practical, and very little was done to put all the rhetoric into effect. The debate continued nevertheless, in anticipation of economic circumstances which would allow the execution of an exciting project.[25]

The Triumphal Way was so long that architects favoured buildings of great size and height to create the necessary vistas. The greater part of the route lay outside the city of Paris, so some aesthetic licence could be anticipated. However, its whole length was visible from the Etoile, so a certain deference was needed to the Parisian scale.

The answer to this challenge was widely seen to be the monumental tower. Towers had been rejected before 1914 as appropriate only to American cities, but the surge of modern architecture in Europe since the war had won them a degree of respect, even in Paris. Le Corbusier's Plan Voisin was the most striking tower proposal of the period, but it was the debate on the Triumphal Way, where new building would not disturb the historic city, that allowed towers to be taken seriously. Auguste Perret began to publish tower proposals as soon as the Triumphal Way was announced; Henri Sauvage proposed ziggurats up to fifty metres high; and S.A. Laprade was also interested in towers.[26]

In 1930 a Parisian property developer, Léonard Rosenthal, privately organised a consultation for the study of the architectural treatment of a 'Place de la Victoire' at the Porte Maillot.[27] He invited twelve architects or partnerships to take part. One was a Russian, Viatcheslav Oltarjevski, who had worked in New York in the 1920s. The area of the consultation comprised the Porte Maillot itself and the adjoining Luna-Park, a fairground designated by the municipality's 1924 development plan for the fortifications. Rosenthal was seeking the lease of the Luna-Park at the time, but this involvement did not worry the interested parties, partly because Rosenthal was a helpful associate of the municipality in developments elsewhere.[28]

Rosenthal took care to invite roughly equal numbers of modernists and traditionalists. The task, as he defined it, was '. . . to add beauty, as the twentieth century understands it, to a unique heritage of splendour'.[29] Most of the entries fell into a modern category, which contained some quite striking proposals, and a neo-classical group, which for the most part showed a strong deference and sense of historical continuity.

The more modernistic entries placed a strong emphasis on height. Perret, Le Corbusier, Viret and Marmorat, Sauvage and Mallet-Stevens proposed very tall towers, most of them functioning as pylons marking the 'gateway'. A further common feature was a large square or park, dominated by the tower structures. The neo-classical entries had buildings of traditional height lining the main frontages of the square, and obelisks or monumental statuary marking the lines of perspective along the Etoile-Défense axis. The projects of Granet, Carlu, Labatut and Millochau, and the partnerships of Chappey, Julien and Duhayon, and Molinié, Nicod and Barbaud, were in this category. Much use was made of colonnades along the frontages, and several of these schemes recalled the Place de la Concorde. The modern and the classical combined in some entries, notably Perret's.

The models were submitted in April 1930. To the surprise of Le Corbusier, and no doubt of the other entrants, Rosenthal did not immediately display or publish the results. He told Le Corbusier that 'in present circumstances' there would be no point in publishing the projects, and Le Corbusier's above all. On the contrary, he claimed, time should be allowed to do its work, for no more than a few months, to facilitate the 'digestion' of the idea of the skyscraper which had emerged from the competition, and which deserved full consideration (rather than a peremptory dismissal). The Porte Maillot, Rosenthal believed, was the most suitable location in Paris for the demonstration of the skyscraper principle, so a small delay would do no harm.[30] In the end Rosenthal exhibited the projects at the Salon d'Automne in 1931, although the world financial crisis, which had probably been his main motive for the postponement, was no nearer resolution by that time.

Rosenthal announced the results in imaginative terms, referring–among many images–to a 'link between the Paris of yesterday and the Paris of tomorrow'. The results of the consultation were indeed completely new in Parisian architecture. They reflected a clear belief among some of the participants that a completely new environment could be created in Paris, albeit at the boundary between the city and the suburbs.

By late 1931, the authorities had decided to organise their own competition, mainly in response to pressure from a number of city councillors and the national societies of architects.[31] Entries were judged in the following year.[32] Only French architects were allowed to take part, indicating the official character of the competition.[33] It covered a larger area than the Rosenthal consultation, incorporating the whole of the road from the Etoile to the Défense. There were thirty-five entries, some of them by participants in the Rosenthal competition. These did not however include any of the radical modernists.[34]

Although the jury had forty-five members, it was left to Henri Prost, the senior government architect and principal authority on the planning of the Paris region, and Paul Lebret, chief architect of the City of Paris, to rank the entries. They used criteria which implied a moderate result. For instance, one of their initial assumptions was that the Arc de Triomphe should remain the main feature of the vista, and they therefore favoured designs of restrained height at the other main points along the perspective.[35] However, Prost and Lebret were more interested in the planning issues than in the architecture. They were especially concerned about traffic engineering at the Porte Maillot, which none of the entries had resolved, they claimed.[36]

Towers were less numerous among these entries than in the Rosenthal consultation, and a number of entrants proposed to site them at the very end of the Triumphal Way, at the Défense. Indeed, the Société Française des Urbanistes, consulted by the authorities, wanted to see the development of a monumental centre at the Défense rather than at the Porte Maillot, which would threaten the Etoile visually.[37] All the tower proposals were modernistic in style, however, there being no sign of American 'wedding cake' or historicist skyscraper influence. The predominant styles of the entries overall were either modernist (with an emphasis on monumental, symmetrical forms), or neo-classical, with an emphasis on the stripped classical. Virtually all exuded symmetry and perspective on a massive scale. However, with height discouraged, except at the Défense, the vista was a tedious one in most cases, very similar in its impact to the north-south axis which Albert Speer would design for Berlin from 1937. This resemblance was especially marked at the Porte Maillot, where buildings of standard height covered entire blocks. Some architects used pylons to enliven the view, reinforcing the neo-classical effect.

The fact that the second competition marked a reversion to classical tradition had no significance on the ground, because the authorities did nothing to implement the designs. French economic difficulties in the 1930s, when an overvalued franc restricted public expenditure, were the main reason for this lack of action. Instead, the authorities adopted a composite scheme for the Porte Maillot alone in 1934. The emphasis was on greenery, and implementation was seen as long-term.[38] The issue would revive after the war, but by this time the main centre of attention along the Triumphal Way would be the Défense. We shall return to this saga in the following chapter. However, the Triumphal Way's potential as a test-bed for large-scale modernism had not been realised by the outbreak of the war.

## DEVELOPMENTS IN NEO-CLASSICISM

Almost completely absent from both the Triumphal Way competitions was the Beaux-Arts luxury style of the pre-1914 years. However, the classical tradition was maintained by an extensive use of neo-classical design, in both its formal and stripped variants. This reflected a world-wide revival of neo-classicism in the 1930s. Most of the architecture was stripped-classical, largely abandoning conventional classical features and decoration but retaining the outlines and proportions. This was the classical in a cheaper version, also reflecting some of the simple, clean forms of the Modern Movement. Its greatest triumph came in 1937, when the City of Paris revived pre-war tradition and held an international exhibition. The stripped-classical style was adopted for many of the temporary structures and most of the permanent ones. The Palais de Chaillot (Fig. 216), which replaced the unloved and awkward Trocadéro, was a massive exercise in the neo-classical, as was the nearby Palais de Tokyo (Fig. 217).

Auguste Perret's movement towards the neo-classical in the 1930s symbolised the partial absorption of the modern by tradition (Fig. 218). His successes in concrete construction since the early 1900s had made him aware of the potential of concrete for producing simple lines, plain surfaces and classical proportions. By the 1930s his eminence could secure him important public commissions and he began to evolve. In this

way, Perret came to develop an architecture which, while distinctive and even idiosyncratic, conformed to the Paris inheritance by using neo-classical forms and details.[39] This adjustment by the doyen of the French modernists drew many progressive architects away from the pure doctrine of the Modern Movement towards a modern architecture of effect rather than principle.

The neo-classical style had a limited application, however. It was used almost exclusively for public buildings, usually of a monumental nature. It had little part to play in domestic design, where the range of stylistic choice had broadened since before the war, and it was not much used for commercial building. What had emerged instead during the last pre-war surge of

216 The Palais de Chaillot, 1937.

217 The Palais de Tokyo, 1937.

218 Perret apartment house and studio, Rue Raynouard, 1932.

which faced the challenge and opportunity of modernism over a longer period, and whose creators were more far-sighted than most.

VISIONARY ARCHITECTURE: CINEMAS AND CHURCHES

The building of cinemas and churches flourished between the wars. Demand for them was strong enough to ride over the economic fluctuations of the period and construction continued through the 1930s. Most were large enough to attract experienced architects who specialised in this area. Both building types were places of escape, of dreams or meditation. Both were prominent in the townscape. Here then was scope for the growth of new design traditions.

There had been a number of cinemas in Paris before 1914, but the purpose-built cinema did not come on the scene until just after the war. As a palace of fantasy, the cinema encouraged an exotic architecture which could look forward or back without serious artistic reproach. The church was also a home of visions and reflection, with a long-established tradition of independent architecture, where Parisian custom allowed the architect a greater degree of freedom than was tolerated in most secular construction.

commercial building, between 1928 and 1931, was a utilitarian style with modern overtones which conformed to no clear aesthetic pattern. Most structures of this type had reinforced concrete in common, but other features and tendencies are hard to discern. With the depression halting this development in the early 1930s, its significance for Parisian traditions is difficult to assess. Instead, we shall look at two building types

Throughout the inter-war period, both cinemas and churches made plentiful use of modern forms. Neither, however, made much impact on the central area. The Church struggled to serve the growing population in the suburbs. It built little inside the city boundary, and its effort here was limited to the outer ring of *arrondissements*. Its new Parisian churches were built for the most part in a modernistic style stressing simplicity and grandeur, or using historic forms executed by modern methods (Fig. 219). The maximum natural lighting was sought, and reinforced concrete was often used to reduce the volume of internal supports and increase the area of glazing. Interiors were simplified to improve acoustics. As in the past, church architecture was distinctive and even idiosyncratic, but its acceptance of modernistic techniques and forms suggests that modern architecture had an underlying strength in Paris that has often been disregarded.

Cinemas, as a new type of structure attracting a mass clientele, sprang up every-

where. The outer districts saw the building of most, however, because promoters, like bishops, sought to serve the main residential areas. In the centre, many cinemas were conversions of older premises, or small courtyard auditoria approached by cramped foyers created from a shop or *porte cochère*. Only on the Champs-Elysées, the *grands boulevards* and at Montparnasse were large, purpose-built cinemas constructed, and then only after the sound revolution of 1929–31 for the most part.

When large new cinemas were commissioned, the clients gave more detailed instructions to their architects than was customary in other buildings. Many of the design innovations were drawn from American or German experience. Gradually, certain Parisian architects began to specialise in cinemas and, rather like the church architects, they developed special styles and methods which set them apart. Large, striking frontages were the norm, usually on modernistic rather than picturesque or fantastic lines. Sizeable flat surfaces were favoured because they could be used for displays.[40]

In the early years after the war, cinema design attracted some very distinguished architects, many with modernistic interests. Henri Sauvage built the Cinéma-Belgrand (Gambetta-Palace, later Cinéma Gambetta) in the Avenue Gambetta, and the Cinéma Sèvres (Fig. 220) in the Rue de Sèvres. Both had simple exteriors with some light, superficial decoration, while the interiors were very stark, stressing the power of the concrete structure.[41] M.E. Vergnes, the main authority on cinema construction at this time, built a modernistic facade with decoration for the Splendid-Cinéma (Fig. 221), Avenue de la Motte-Picquet.[42]

In the later 1920s and 1930s new cinemas absorbed the Art Deco and Moderne styles, though, as we have seen, their locations were increasingly to be found in the suburbs. However, a few very large examples were built in the city centre in the 1930s, by which time the Moderne had taken over. The Gaumont-Palace, Boulevard Barbès-Rochechouart and the Grand Rex (Figs 222–3), Boulevard Poissonnière, with over three thousand seats each, were the largest cinemas ever built in Paris.

The Grand Rex, whose *grand boulevard* site made it the more fashionable of the two, was built in 1932 by Auguste Bluysen and an American cinema specialist, John Eberson.[43] Its exterior was formed from two giant, rectangular panels, with a layered, futuristic

219 *Far left, below,* church of Sainte-Odile, Porte Champerret, by Barge. Begun in 1935 and brought into use gradually, it was not consecrated until 1956. This modernistic reinterpretation of the neo-Byzantine typifies church architecture in the Paris area from 1920 to 1960. Even more than in the past, church architecture evolved in isolation from the rest of Parisian design.

220 *Above left,* the Cinéma Sèvres, by Sauvage.

221 *Above right,* the Splendid-Cinéma, Avenue de la Motte-Picquet, by Vergnes.

222 and 223 *Above*, the Rex cinema, 1932, photographed in 1992.

224 *Top right*, public housing at the Porte de Champerret by L. Plousey and H. Rencontre, 1924.

225 *Centre right*, public housing on former fortification land in the Boulevard Brune. The bold use of colour contrast is accompanied by a post-1902 roof line, arising from the decision to build up to full height.

226 *Below right*, public housing at the Cité du Combattant, Porte d'Italie. Densities are lower here, allowing the blocks to be arranged around a system of interior lanes.

tower over the corner of the site. Colossal, floodlit displays on the panels announced the huge interior theatre with its 3,300 seats and 'atmospheric' lighting, the first such lighting in Paris.[44] The luxury and grandeur of the Grand Rex (later, Rex) cinema brought the 'dream factory' to Paris in physical form, and as an architecture of effects it was as expressionistic as it was modern. The irony nevertheless is that by the 1930s hordes of Parisians regularly left their daily existence to gather in buildings, whether modern cinemas or the smaller number of modern churches, whose design heralded the future of modern architecture more effectively than did Le Corbusier's writings. Dreams and visions can look forward as well as back.

## RESIDENTIAL DESIGN AND THE 'PARIS SCHOOL'

The outer districts were a favoured location for new churches and cinemas partly because most of the new public housing was built there. Although public housing had been built in Paris before the war, neither its quantity nor its design had much impact on the city's architectural evolution. After 1918, however, France, like the other belligerent countries, chose to build public housing on a large scale.

Small sites could still be found within the city boundaries, but no large vacant areas were available for big housing schemes in 1918. The conversion of the fortifications to civil use, discussed at length before 1914 but not ratified by the City of Paris and the State until 1919, was therefore crucial to a municipal housing programme.[45] Before the war it had been widely assumed that the land would be used for open space and garden suburbs, but the post-war housing shortage was too urgent to allow this degree of indulgence.

The new approach was embodied in an outline project for the development of the fortifications and the 'zone', the encircling field of fire, which the prefect presented to the city council in 1924. While much of the land was given over to open space and other non-residential uses, and most of the 'zone' was still effectively in private hands, huge blocks of the fortifications area were allocated for the construction of housing subsidised under national legislation (HBM and HLM).[46] This decision was partly the product of the persistent municipal view that people gaining a living in Paris should also live there, in order to prevent a drain of the city's resources. An additional motive was the need to maximise income from the sale of the land on the fortifications in order to buy out the owners of the 'zone' and replan it at a later stage.[47] The implication was development at very high densities, and in practice the net density of much of this new housing was to be the highest in Paris.

As early as 1923 a number of large blocks at the Porte de Champerret and three other Paris 'gates' were made the subject of a competition for low-rent dwellings, to be built by the city's housing agency, the Régie Immobilière de la Ville de Paris.[48] The architectural profession took it very seriously and there were seventy-eight entries, some of them by the recognised Parisian leaders of the field (Fig. 224). Especially notable was the Groupe des Architectes Modernes, a consortium established after the war to apply a range of talents to new mass housing projects. It was directed by Frantz Jourdain with the support of Henri Sauvage and Hector Guimard, and its members included Alfred Agache, Jean-Marcel Auburtin, Louis Bonnier and Paul De Rutté.[49] The four winners were less well known, but the brief was so precise that originality and brilliance were not required. Indeed, the four winning designs had a great deal in common, and they did much to establish the pattern for subsequent housing schemes.

In 1924 the winning entries were incorporated into the municipal plan for the development of the fortifications.[50] The overall plan then became the main guide for individual schemes, and subsequent housing projects adopted the principal features of the competition winners. An additional objective was to mark the 'gates' of Paris by an appropriate architectural treatment on lines first advocated in Parisian planning circles before the war, and this helped to justify the monumental scale of the tenement blocks.[51]

The resulting bulky structures of seven storeys which gradually occupied large areas of the fortification strip were arranged around narrow courtyards or walkways. They fronted directly on to the main streets and open spaces which defined the sites. Large blocks were divided by narrow thoroughfares lined by facades as tall as the main frontages. This frighteningly intensive development was excused on the grounds that open space had been created nearby, but as architecture most of this housing looked back to a cramped Parisian past, rather than to the new era of sunlight and greenery which was emerging in Britain and Germany, and in the Paris suburbs (Figs 225–6). The simple treatment of the facades and the general use of brick evoked the rudimentary housing of eastern Paris, while the delineation of an attic floor and the use of the mansard roof and its variants suggested an attempt to caricature the apartment house of the west. In practice, modernism was kept at arm's length and some of the worst features

of the old Paris housing tradition were given a new lease of life. No wonder Le Corbusier constantly cited these buildings as an expression of official recidivism!

Private building, in complete contrast, was much more varied than before 1914 (Figs 227–8). The pre-1914 luxury style survived in a number of new apartment buildings erected after the war, but after 1925 it was largely replaced by the mannered and detail-conscious Art Deco style. By the later 1920s and early 1930s, however, the dominant style was a striking and elegant modernism which, while respecting the established form of the apartment house, replaced decoration by elemental forms such as angular bays and huge, geometrical windows. This geometrical modernism of plain surfaces also flourished in non-residential architecture in the early 1930s.

Michel Roux-Spitz made a big contribution to this innovative form of design.[52] He built more apartment houses in Paris between the wars than any other modern architect, and in this way he probably exercised a greater influence on the work of other modernising Paris architects than did any of his more celebrated contemporaries.[53] Roux-Spitz was an architect of great talent and impressive qualifications. He had completed the full course at the Ecole des Beaux-Arts, after early training at the Ecole Régionale d'Architecture in Lyon, and he was a government diplomat. This latter qualification was not uncommon among Paris architects after the war now that the diploma course was taken more seriously. More distinctive, however, was his status as one of a number of Rome prize winners who became involved in apartment house design after 1918, probably owing to the shortage of public commissions in the troubled 1920s.

Like some other architects of the period, Roux-Spitz became interested in developing a construction system which could be used efficiently on a variety of sites, and which at the same time could be aesthetically attractive within the modern mode. From his definitive establishment in Paris in 1924, Roux-Spitz perfected a simple, persuasively modern style for apartment houses using a concrete frame and a cladding of rectangular stone panels with very broad fenestration. The most striking feature was the vertical bay composed of a broad central window and two angled lights at each side. The bays normally rose from the first floor to the full height of the facade, while upper storeys were stepped back modestly within the permitted roof section. His style created a horizontal emphasis which had been lost in Paris since the Second Empire, while the quality of the cladding, in polished Hauteville stone,

227 Apartment house at 8, rue de la Mission-Marchande, by Jean Boucher and Paul Delaplanche, 1925. This is an economical version of the luxury style. Carving is virtually absent, with the architects relying on polychromy and striking or picturesque masonry components to produce an effect of affluent elegance.

228 Apartment house, Rue Huysmans, 1920. The corbelled loggia has the effect of pushing the *piano nobile* up to the top of the building.

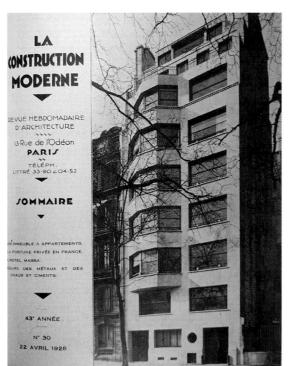

229 A typical Roux-Spitz facade, featured in a journal noted for its moderate preferences in architecture.

compensated for the absence of ornamentation. His first house, in the Rue Guynemer, undertaken in 1925–7, was heavily criticised for its repetitive facade, but he persisted, and had won wide respect and emulation by the end of the decade.[54] Indeed, he won the ultimate tribute in the form of virtual plagiarism by other architects (Fig. 229).

Roux-Spitz never won the respect of Le Corbusier and the other leading modernists, however. His essential opportunism became visible in the 1930s when, in a depressed building market, he moved towards what his biographer has described as 'sterile academicism', probably in response to the cautious preferences of his clients.[55] Always keen to contribute to the debates of the day, he began to attack some of the tenets of modernism, deriding in particular the idea that the structure must always be visible. During the Occupation he became an apologist for the traditionalist architecture of the 'new France'. In 1942 he helped found the semi-official journal, *L'Architecture Française*, as a docile advocate of Vichy ideas on architecture.

It was in an early article in this new journal that Roux-Spitz launched an idea which came to secure more attention than any of his buildings. His concept was a Parisian alternative to the Modern Movement, which Roux-Spitz claimed to discern in the 1930s

but which he linked to older traditions, and which he and others would project into the 1940s and 1950s. This was 'the Paris school' of architects, of which Roux-Spitz was proud to consider himself a member.[56] The school, as defined by Roux-Spitz, was composed of a variety of non-doctrinaire and non-iconoclastic modernists who worked within the 'Parisian' tradition of proportion and mathematical elegance, many of them inspired by reinforced concrete.[57] His biographer sees his career between about 1930 and 1950 as reflecting his search for a French architecture, embodying the 'eternal rules of eurhythmics'. This quest eventually led him into the academic tradition.[58]

Another commentator, viewing his career as a whole, sees him as a 'rationalising classicist'.[59] Although Roux-Spitz's Vichy involvement has tended to discredit his judgment, architectural historians have begun to see merit in the idea of a 'Paris school'. Once the experimental years of the early and mid-1920s were past, the extremes of modernism, neo-classicism and Art Deco tended to fade. Many new buildings had modernistic features or effects by 1930, but their scale and proportions gave them, in the words of Modern Movement commentators, Michèle Béhar and Manuelle Salama, 'une spécificité parisienne'.[60]

The 'Paris school' phenomenon did not make a spectacular mark on Paris because the volume of residential building between the wars was so small. A striking expression of it is the Rue Cognacq-Jay, part of a small district south of the Quai d'Orsay which was not developed until the end of the 1920s. The street was planned in 1928 on land belonging to Ernest Cognacq, the owner of the Samaritaine department store, who died in that year. This was intended to be a prestige development, and quality was expressed in a series of solid, almost threatening, masonry elevations. A typical design of 1929 by Michel Roux-Spitz at no. 22 (and no. 89, quai d'Orsay) stands out as undeniably modern, and there is a similar treatment close at hand by a more obscure practice.[61]

However, the prime site, a corner site at the western end (Fig. 230), is occupied by a scaly structure of 1930 by Léon Azéma, reminiscent of marine forms (nos. 24 and 26). Azéma was a government diplomat and

230 Apartment house by Azéma in the Rue Cognacq-Jay, 1930.

231 Commercial building in the Rue Beaubourg by Armand Néret, 1922–3. The overhang takes full advantage of the 1902 building regulations.

French economy, and it created a potential tension between the classical city of Paris, as enlarged by Haussmann, and the requirements of the 'second Industrial Revolution' of science and advanced technology.

There were, however, two big obstacles to a breakthrough by modern architecture in the business sector. First, the fluctuations of the French economy meant that very little new commercial building was done outside the period 1925 to 1931. Second, all new business structures had to observe the building regulations of 1902, which meant that most development stood on the street frontage with dimensions and proportions similar to those of apartment houses. As yet, no exclusive business district such as the City of London or Lower Manhattan had emerged in Paris, so even in the vicinity of the Bourse or the Banque de France, new commercial building tended to merge with older structures. Many commercial buildings incorporated residential floors in the roof for service tenants, as they had before the war. Within these limitations however, business clients did tend to encourage a move away from traditional architecture. The Rue Beaubourg, laid out before the war but not developed until the early 1920s, attracted little but commercial and industrial buildings, much as the Rue Réaumur had done (Figs 231–2). Some of the architects used a crude version of the pre-1914 apartment house

Rome prize winner, and his design was as idiosyncratic as anything built in Paris at that time. This was modern architecture, but it did not belong to any recognisable tendency except in its search for elemental forms. That Azéma went on to join the partnership that built the neo-classical Palais de Chaillot should cause no surprise.

Meanwhile, at no. 2, L. Plousey, another government diplomat, had built an apartment house in 1929 in an almost unmodified pre-1914 style. Most of the other houses were in an intermediate style using large masonry blocks with precise, almost self-conscious mitring, heavy stone balconies and stark window openings including, in one case, a row of round arches. The street as a whole suggests a group of fashionable architects and clients seeking a secure modernism in uncertain economic circumstances. As always, continuity and security went hand in hand in the design of the Paris apartment house, and it is here that the roots of the 'Paris school' are to be found.

COMMERCIAL ARCHITECTURE

After 1918 commercial architecture continued to develop its own character. This move away from the apartment-block style had been led by the department stores from the 1860s and by side-street wholesalers from the 1880s. It now extended to offices and to specialised manufacturing firms such as instrument makers and couturiers. This trend was a product of changes in the structure of the

piers separated by metal and glass bays. The stonework seemed to be in search of elemental forms, only mildly tempered by classicism. The roof was a tall, pyramidal affair of stone balconies and terraces. Although entirely within the building code of 1902, this festival of setbacks was clearly a test run for Sauvage's ideal of the pyramidal building. If the modern bowed to tradition at the Samaritaine (Fig. 233), it seemed ready to spring forth at the right moment.

The general run of commercial architecture in the 1920s was a motley affair (Fig. 234). A Perret-like style of square panels leavened by Art Deco detailing can be detected in many instances, but it was not until around 1929 that a fashionable modernist style of plain, white surfaces emerged with confidence. The change occurred with surprising speed, and

232 Transitional apartment house in the Rue Beaubourg by Le Guen and Briault, 1931.

233 The Seine frontage of the Samaritaine above the Pont-Neuf. The equestrian statue in the foreground is that of Henri IV, facing his Place Dauphine.

234 116 bis, avenue des Champs-Elysées, built by Jean Debouis in 1929. Built as a broadcasting centre, the facade is insistently modern, and recalls Dutch expressionism of the early 1920s. It had almost no influence elsewhere in Paris.

style, but others built on concrete frames, making full use of the projections permitted under the 1902 building code. Glazing was extensive in these cases and the results were boldly utilitarian.

The rebuilding of the Rue Beaubourg in a variety of utilitarian and hybrid styles did not however imply that the city authorities would have favoured such designs further west. On the contrary, they spent most of the 1920s harrying the Samaritaine department store. Ernest Cognacq was still pursuing his expansion policy, which required further floor space at the Pont-Neuf, and new warehousing on the fringes of the city centre. The authorities threatened to withhold building permits unless the Art Nouveau building of 1905 was bowdlerised. With Frantz Jourdain still working as chief architect, a compromise emerged whereby Jourdain removed the two towering cupolas and some of the more striking metalwork, and toned down what was left by new painting.

Meanwhile, a new building to complete the Seine frontage went up in 1926. An old associate, Henri Sauvage, worked with Jourdain on this project. The facades were based on the nineteenth-century department store compromise of elegant masonry

235 and 236 Striking corner structures in symmetrical positions at opposite ends of the Gare du Nord frontage. Both appear to be reconstructions of Second Empire buildings in about 1930. They may both have been hotels, as one of them is now. This exercise in modernistic *maquillage*, albeit on a small scale, suggests that modernism would soon have swept the board in Paris, had not the financial crisis of 1931 paralysed building for the rest of the decade.

hard surfaces suggesting luxury and solidity at a time of uncertainty. Brick, which did not produce the desired impression, was almost completely relegated to the public housing of the outskirts.[63] Fluted vertical piers, often curved in section, were very common, usually in buildings only remotely neo-classical in effect. Starkly rectangular fenestration, with simple or unobtrusive glazing bars, was widespread. The fussy triangular bays which had passed as modern architecture in the later 1920s faded away in the 1930s. Exterior, wind-down blinds became common, while balconies almost disappeared except on the set-back upper storeys. Unfortunately for the business sector, French deflationary policies put a brake on commercial building after 1932 and public housing again moved into the vanguard of modern architecture. Enough vitality had been shown, however, to suggest that even if Parisian architects had not taken up the International Style preached by the Modern Movement, they were creating a local modernism which retained the essence of Parisian traditions (Figs 235, 236).

WRITTEN IN STONE: THE BUILDING REGULATIONS

The Modern Movement ideal of verticality ran foul, as Le Corbusier constantly complained, of the city building regulations of 1902. The regulations would not have ruled out monumental or ornamental towers such as those mooted for the Porte Maillot, as exceptions could always be made 'in the interests of art and science'. However, such exceptions were rare, while the sustained effect of the regulations was to project the volume, mass, outline and dimensions of a tried and tested nineteenth-century habitat into the twentieth century.

When the war ended, the building regulations of 1902 remained under the review which parliamentary concern had prompted before 1914. The Commission des Perspectives Monumentales had a revised text ready in 1914, but it was shelved when war broke out. After 1918, pressure for reforms was undermined by the low volume of building and the consequent decline of preservationist concerns among the public. In 1923, however, the commission set up two sub-

by 1931 commercial buildings in a modern, or at any rate a Moderne, style had virtually replaced the muddle of the 1920s. Michel Roux-Spitz's suave Ford building on the Boulevard des Italiens in 1931 was very influential. Taking full visual advantage of a corner site, the architect expressed speed, technology and modernity, using strip windows and transoms, and stainless-steel columns with reinforced glass panels, fronting a double-height ground floor showroom.[62]

This horizontal emphasis was repeated in many other buildings in the early 1930s, with committees, one of which was asked to revise the 1902 code under the chairmanship of Louis Bonnier, who was now general inspector of the architectural and aesthetic services of the *département* of the Seine.

Bonnier's appointment indicated the importance of the task as seen by the authorities, but now that he was a very senior and versatile figure, he was seriously overworked in other areas. The work proceeded extremely slowly, and was at times apparently conducted largely as a personal interest of Bonnier. Nevertheless, it generated a number of ideas which were by no means unsympathetic to the proposals of the Modern Movement. Bonnier later made clear that the development of architectural ideas during and after the war had made it necessary to re-examine the regulations from scratch, which meant that the amendments proposed before 1914 were of no use.[64] His own thinking remained as flexible and constructive as ever, though always within the constraints of practicality and logic, an awareness of which was the hallmark of this impressive figure. For example, Bonnier developed the idea of the *'pyramide capable'* which had been put forward during the 1902 inquiry by Debrie. His growing interest in town planning, on which he lectured at the Institut Français d'Urbanisme after the war, made him more open to considerations of efficiency, health and movement within cities. He was clearly respected by the more radical architects of the day. However, Bonnier's sub-committee generally took the view that Paris, because of its great heritage and symbolic value, was a special case requiring a strong degree of continuity.[65] These circumstances help to explain why the sub-committee did not produce a definitive set of draft regulations until 1938.[66]

In their proportions and dimensions the new proposals conformed generally to the code of 1902. A new principle, the *'enveloppe générale'*, which dated back in Bonnier's thinking to the immediate aftermath of the 1902 decree, was used to prevent inner walls facing courtyards from rising substantially above the street facade and lifting roofs up to disproportionate heights. However, possible losses to owners were compensated by a 60-degree line rising from the tops of cornices up to a maximum height of 35 metres (114 feet). This would have produced, on very wide streets and facing open spaces, buildings with elevations composed of a vertical facade making up 57 per cent of the total height, and a series of stepped upper floors accounting for 43 per cent. This pyramid, or ziggurat, was closer to modernist opinion–and especially that of Henri Sauvage–than it was to Parisian tradition. However, once again war intervened. The authorities published further proposals in August 1942, but progress remained slow, and nothing more had been done by the time of the Liberation in 1944. In any case, there was no scope for ziggurats in the architectural climate fostered by the Vichy regime.

PARIS ARCHITECTURE DURING THE PÉTAIN REGIME

The French surrender in 1940 was partly justified by the Pétiniste argument that the French national heritage would in the long run be strong enough to demoralise and expel the invaders. Meanwhile, it should not be threatened or destroyed in a fruitless defensive campaign. The idea of 'heritage' included social institutions and values, but the physical environment also had an important place.[67] Paris, more than any other town or city, was seen as representing this fundamental strength of the French nation, and an early decision was made in May 1940 that it should not be defended. Churchill for his part wanted to see a street-by-street defence which would have provoked massive German air raids and a big reconstruction task after the war.[68] In the event, the Germans occupied the city without firing a shot.

Pétain's occupation agreement with Germany divided France into a northern occupied zone and a southern zone which would be free of German forces subject to certain conditions. The Pétain government made its home in the spa of Vichy in the southern zone. However, it had full authority in both zones and Paris remained under its administration. Indeed, a number of government departments remained in Paris and much routine administration was carried on from there. In 1942 the occupation of the southern zone, provoked by the Allied advance, prompted the government to move to Paris.

This explanation is necessary in order to

emphasise that Paris remained subject to French architectural and planning policies during the Occupation. In these respects the German occupiers had no authority there between 1940 and their departure in 1944. There were no Germanising planning programmes like those in Alsace and Lorraine, which in pursuit of timeless German ambitions were incorporated into the Reich.[69] Building was completely halted in Paris, but the planning and architectural debates could continue. In fact, the government was interested in planning and architecture as a means of defending and enhancing the urban heritage, and developing a new mode of design expressive of a renewed French society under Pétain. To this end, competitions were organised for architect prisoners of war in Germany (nearly all of whom, it emerged, were officers).[70]

The main initial task was seen to be the reconstruction of the war-damaged towns and villages. Thanks to the short campaign, these were few in number. Most were at river crossings and were both small and traditional in their fabric. The Vichy authorities generally favoured reconstruction on the old lines, with rationalisation carried out only where necessary. This approach conformed to a more general Vichy view that the urban environment should reflect traditional French values: something evoking an eighteenth-century market town, complete with square, arcades and pitched roofs, and built in local materials.

Paris was not directly affected by these concepts, but Parisian architects played a big part in drawing up the plans and participated in the somewhat disarticulated national debate on the new French architecture, which would have applied to Paris just as much as to other places. This architecture is not completely irrelevant to the history of Parisian design. First, it sprang from pre-war tendencies and was elaborated by architects with pre-war experience, and the same lines of continuity gave it a role after the Liberation. Secondly, the emergence of new architectural styles since the collapse of the modernist orthodoxy in the early 1970s has given a retrospective validity to Vichy design which to some extent allows it to take its place in Parisian architectural history.

Under Vichy much French architecture sought to reconcile two partially contradic-

tory objectives. On the one hand, it had to be 'modern' in the sense that it expressed a renewed national society. On the other hand, it had to embody the traditional virtues of French society, which had been lacking in 1940 and were needed now to rebuild France. The resulting debate, conducted for the most part in a climate of non-construction, produced a number of representative ideas, many of them associated with the fields of graphic and three-dimensional art, which were, of course, less restricted in their output. Among these ideas and images were physical vigour and health, neo-classicism, simple and expressionist monumentalism, thrifty functionalism, traditional craftsmanship and medievalising burgess housing on a small scale.[71]

It was principally in the devastated towns of 1940 that these could be put into effect, and Paris saw hardly any experiments in the new architecture between 1940 and 1944.[72] The Porte Maillot continued to prompt discussion, and there was some advocacy of a virile, monumental treatment on neo-classical lines which would show that Vichy had abandoned the effete classicism of the 1930s.[73] The competition entries of the prisoners of war, for their part, had in mind a scale and planning which suggested a close acquaintance with the plans for Berlin and other German cities under Speer's post-1937 programme.

German respect for French art, expressed in Paris by a number of Franco-German exhibitions and visits by German artists to their French colleagues, ensured that the German authorities were more tolerant of established French tendencies than they were in the countries which they administered directly. This meant that modernism, once purged of Jewish and other 'degenerate' contributions, could pursue its course. The most striking expression of this toleration was the inauguration in 1942 of the Museum of Modern Art in its new, neo-classical building at the Palais de Tokyo, a stripped-classical relic of the 1937 exhibition.[74] These artistic links can appear either touching or grotesque. But at least it can be said that the sincere German respect for French culture helped to ensure that Paris did not 'burn' in 1944. In this respect, if in no other, the Vichy resistance strategy had something to offer.

## BUILDING IN PARIS AFTER 1945

For ten years after the war, Paris continued to suffer the virtual moratorium on new building which had begun in the early 1930s. In the war-damaged towns, on the other hand, reconstruction was allowed to start. From them there emerged the typical modern city style of the era, Auguste Perret's monumental neo-classicism using large, rectangular concrete slabs. At Le Havre, he transformed an entire city centre in this way. In 1945 Le Donné published a book on the future of the architect which implied that the Perret style was the way forward.[75] Le Donné claimed that the goal was 'beauty', and that Perret could provide it. However, Perret had no chance to build in Paris after 1945, and the capital could do little to influence the provinces in its normal way.

The post-war paralysis of building in Paris created an even greater potential for change than the First World War had done. At the same time, it reinforced the image of Paris as an unchanging stage set. The huddled masses of the working-class centre and east continued to suffer, but for the more leisured observer Paris had become a world of instant nostalgia. How were these conflicts resolved?

# THE VITAL ENCOUNTER: MODERNITY VERSUS TRADITION IN POST-WAR PARIS

The need for national modernisation and renewal was widely felt in France after the Liberation. To this end, it wanted to share fully in the reconstruction of Europe, and ultimately in its integration. It was even prepared to countenance a reconciliation with Germany. Far more than in the past, France was willing to open itself to international influences and to countenance big social changes.

At first, however, the political parties resisted the constitutional reforms which could have led to more decisive government. Governments changed more frequently under the post-war Fourth Republic than they had in the last years of the derided Third. Fortunately, civil servants were able to maintain continuity of policy, especially in economic and territorial planning.

In the early 1950s the economy began to expand and, in the later 1950s and the 1960s, France moved into the spectacular final phase of its industrialisation which made it the wonder of Europe. In the early years, the public did not give much credit to the politicians. In 1958, however, a serious political crisis over the civil war in Algeria brought Charles de Gaulle back to power for the first time since 1946, when he had resigned as head of state after a bitter confrontation with the parties. De Gaulle took urgent action to promote further modernisation and soon acquired a directive role in most aspects of French life. His supporters liked to compare him with Louis XIV, but Napoleon III was a much closer parallel.

De Gaulle realised that attitudes had to change along with methods and institutions, and he was a determined moderniser. He sought the springs of progress, nevertheless, in national tradition. He was not in sympathy with the wave of Americanisation which had accompanied the revival of West Germany and other parts of Europe after the war. Of course, he trod a slippery path, assailed at every step by the traditional French political parties, and emphasising social differences which more cautious leaders had tried to disguise. His creation of the Fifth Republic in 1958 nevertheless expressed his determination to generate radical change even if he had to tear out some of the roots of an older France.

De Gaulle's 'second Industrial Revolution' produced a huge transfer of population from the country to town. A surge of urban building took place in the 1960s, mostly of cheap flats in the public sector. New factories and transport facilities burgeoned on the urban fringe, while the sleepy centres of picturesque provincial towns struggled with parking and traffic problems.

Paris was central to this 'urban revolution'. Before De Gaulle, the planners had aimed for a partial decentralisation of population and employment from Paris, on the lines adopted in Britain after the war. De Gaulle realised that French industrialisation would be retarded if industry were not allowed to locate freely in the Paris area. He also looked forward to the day when a very large and well-equipped Paris might become the formal capital of Europe, as it had effectively been in Bonaparte's time. He therefore ensured that the restrictions on the growth of the Paris agglomeration were removed, and that public investment was directed towards it. In many ways, therefore, the history of Paris under the Second Empire was repeated under the Fifth Republic.

The post-war recovery of the French economy did not at first have room for a building boom. With little war damage, French cities did not need to make up a housing deficiency comparable to that of Germany or even of Britain. There remained the problem of an ageing residential stock, but its treatment could be postponed.

Paris had an especially poor case for new housing investment. There had been some bombing in the suburbs but the Allies had ensured that only strategic installations were attacked. The status of Paris as an open city, established in 1940 to prevent damage by the German invaders, was in effect maintained by the German occupiers, who declined to defend it and who ignored Hitler's call for its complete destruction.

The first ten years after the Second World War were thus a dismal period in the architectural history of Paris. Almost nothing was built, and maintenance was neglected. Many of the stone facades, including the Louvre and other public buildings, were now completely blackened by smoke. Paintwork was in poor condition everywhere. Stucco finishes cracked, bubbled and lifted like dried mud. Slum districts deteriorated alarmingly, and the shanty communities of squatters on parts of the fortification zone grew to the point where they became a national scandal in the mid-1950s.

As a Parisian planning policy was progressively defined in the 1950s, it acquired a strong element of population and employment dispersal. Although this strategy was almost an international orthodoxy, in Paris it reflected a sense of defeatism among officials and politicians. Meanwhile, the municipal city came to be viewed as a 'crystallised' Paris where very little change would occur. This went hand in hand with the growth of the conservationist ideal, and with widespread support for a new type of *architecture d'accompagnement* which flourished in the inner districts when slum clearance and redevelopment at last got underway (Fig. 237).

The 1950s saw a gradual revival of commercial property values, but there was little building or rebuilding of office premises. The main office district, between the Gare Saint-Lazare and the Champs-Elysées, had been well equipped with office buildings since the turn of the century, and additional floor space could be provided by the conversion of residential buildings. Most of the structures in this area already filled the maximum volumes allowed by the building regulations, and redevelopment held little attraction.

Where new office building occurred, from the later 1950s, it adopted the traditional scale and frontage proportions. The office building at 37, rue de la Victoire, built by Balladur, Lebeigle and Tostevin, even had a modern version of the arcade, albeit in symbolic form. Facades were often curtain-wall exercises using glass and ceramic panels.[1] These maximised natural lighting at minimal cost, but architectural quality was largely incidental. This casual treatment was a departure from the Parisian norm, but public and official opinion tolerated or even welcomed these occasional signs of revival, especially as they were located in the most modern part of the city, well away from the historic core.

Building in the 1950s failed to provide a clear indication that modern architecture had replaced Parisian tradition. It was in these years, nevertheless, that a growing number of architects and planners, particularly among the young, began to envisage the solution to the problems of a seriously undercapitalised Paris in modernist terms. Much of the attraction of such solutions lay in the promise of a fresh start, a new efficiency, the creation of a modern city of air and light, and, ultimately, a new aesthetic. This implied radical reconstruction and dynamic outward growth, together with a new architecture.

237 The Jardins Saint-Paul, the result of slum clearance and redevelopment in Unhealthy Area no. 16, south-west of the Marais, in the later 1950s. Two restored *hôtels* appear to the right and left, separated by housing in a neutral style, a new version of the *architecture d'accompagnement*.

## THE RETURN OF THE MONUMENT

In the post-war years of building paralysis in Paris, a handful of exceptional, prestige schemes came to enjoy considerable architectural importance, rather like London's Festival of Britain site on the South Bank in 1951. As in the Festival of Britain, modern design was a strong feature of these buildings, and the architects, aware of their fortunate opportunity, ensured that quality was also present. These projects were the headquarters of the French broadcasting organisation, the ORTF, built between 1956 and 1963: the UNESCO headquarters, completed in 1958, and the exhibition hall at the Défense, completed in 1959. All these projects represented the city's traditional but still growing role as a centre of cultural diffusion, and all three were built in emphatically modern styles. There was a strong link here with the future of Paris, with the authorities seeking to encourage tertiary functions inside the city boundaries while manufacturing was gradually removed. The city's role, the future and modern design were thus linked explicitly for the first time in three buildings which monopolised public attention, in the absence of other significant building.

The UNESCO building (Fig. 238) did even more than this. As the largest building ever commissioned in Paris by an international body, it confirmed the continuity of the city's traditional international role. The authorities were already hoping that Paris would benefit both from increased economic cooperation in Europe and from the institutions of world cooperation established after the war under the aegis of the United States. The selection of Paris by the cultural arm of the United Nations seemed certain to strengthen the city's function of diffusion.

The design was a striking departure from Parisian norms. A Y-shaped plan produced three curving facades, eight storeys in height. The use of piers and the cell-like structure of the facades paid indirect tribute to Le Corbusier. At the same time, the building stressed horizontality and did not greatly exceed the city height norm. Its location in a remote area south of the Invalides prevented too glaring a contrast with tradition. Indeed, it won a measure of approval in Paris as a spark of modernity within an ageing city. With the UNESCO building, the future role

238 The UNESCO headquarters.

239 The 'Maison de la Radio'.

of Paris as a tertiary centre, and the ideas of internationalism and modern design, were combined as one concept.

The novelty of the scheme lay as much in the design team as in the architecture. The leading members were Marcel Breuer (USA), Bernard Zehrfuss (France), and the Italian engineer, Pier Luigi Nervi. Foreign architects had built in Paris before but not until this project had senior non-French practitioners been involved in a major public building. From the time of the UNESCO building onwards the authorities, together with Parisian opinion, could be more readily persuaded that certain projects – and particularly those with an international or educative function – might require the importation of skills from outside France.

The height issue, avoided at the UNESCO building, first arose with the Maison de l'ORTF (or 'Maison de la Radio' to the average Parisian) (Fig. 239). The concept had much in common with the UNESCO building, though it was the work of a French architect, H. Bernard. Completed in 1963, its

basic form was that of an electro-magnet, with a tower set inside a circular office block. The tower bore a simple, repetitive fenestration. The facades of the circular building had continuous, strip windows and an unadorned, white cladding. The circle was broken occasionally by pavilions clad in a dark colour.

This was a design for effect. Although the architecture was more International Style than Modern Movement, the building resembled the UNESCO headquarters in that it stood in a fashionable, open part of the city where it made a modern statement that was widely respected and admired. Its tower was permitted to breach the Parisian height regulations, with a height of 75 metres (245 feet). That this was a reduction from the architect's planned height of 100 metres (325 feet) shows how carefully the authorities weighed up the implications of height on this occasion. It also suggests, however, that the authorities, like those in London and some other European capitals, were beginning in the 1950s to believe that one or more tall secular buildings could enhance the beauty of a city, principally by enlivening the skyline. In this respect the Maison de la Radio was the thin end of a very thick wedge.

## ECONOMIC REVIVAL AND A NEW ROLE FOR PARIS UNDER THE FIFTH REPUBLIC

In 1958, the year in which the UNESCO building was completed, Charles de Gaulle resumed the government of France. By the early 1960s his policies of economic revival were clearly taking effect and migration to the cities was under way. This success had major implications for Paris.

Although De Gaulle inherited a fully-fledged decentralisation policy, he was not opposed in principle to the growth of Paris, which he saw as the main symbol of the vigour of the French nation. Indeed, he retained the hope, which had welled up in Paris and the government during the final stages of negotiation of the European Economic Community prior to 1957, that Paris might become, de facto or even de jure, the capital of Europe.[2] Although De Gaulle had no personal interest in urban planning, he was prepared to appoint energetic men who would be capable of questioning orthodox policies.

His most important appointment came in 1961 when Paul Delouvrier, a civil servant who had been proved a firm but creative negotiator in Algeria, was appointed to the new post of Delegate to the District of Paris. This awkward, hesitant title reflected the novelty of a form of regional planning in which a new 'district' was created to embrace the Seine département and the urbanised parts of the neighbouring départements of Seine-et-Marne and Seine-et-Oise. On paper, Delouvrier mainly enjoyed coordinating, rather than executive, powers. However, he had the backing of the president and the prime minister, and so enjoyed the full cooperation of the departmental prefects.

Delouvrier quickly built up his own planning staff and by 1963 he had published a strategic plan for the Paris region. Its most striking feature was the reversal of a large part of the decentralisation programme and a consequent big increase in the planned population of the conurbation and of the region.[3] It included plans to accommodate much of the increased population in 'new towns' on the edge of the built-up area.

In contrast to the New Towns planned for the London region after the war, it was assumed that nearly all the population of the 'new towns' would find work elsewhere in the Paris region, and principally within the conurbation. In consequence there would be big daily flows towards the industrial ring outside the city, and to the growing concentrations of tertiary employment in Paris itself and in its immediate western suburbs. Most of these journeys would however be short, as the 'new towns' were to be, in effect, extensions of the existing suburbs. Indeed, they filled up some of the spaces between the inter-war lotissements and the grands ensembles of the 1950s, to produce a more even spread of development across the conurbation. One of their functions was to provide services for suburban areas which had previously been deprived of them. The 'new towns' thus represented a strategic urban planning policy for the Paris conurbation rather than an attempt to create an alternative to it.

The new planning strategy had important implications for the city of Paris. A reduction in population was foreseen as housing standards improved, but a big increase in tertiary employment was envisaged. Drawing to some extent on previous Parisian thinking, Delouvrier decided to encourage office development near some of the big railway termini, sparing many railway commuters a further journey on the metro. He also accelerated plans for a regional express metro network (RER) linking the 'new towns', the existing suburbs, the city centre and some of the new office developments. In principle this policy would produce a happier population in both the 'new towns' and the suburbs but, aware of the disastrous reputation of the grands ensembles in their early years, Delouvrier decided that the 'new towns' should be given concerted planning and architectural attention. In practice, this would mean that the main town planning effort in the Paris region would initially be devoted to creating the 'new towns'.

These developments beyond the city boundary did not at first arouse much interest or concern among Parisians, most of whom had no great respect for the suburbs or their residents. However, the 'new towns' and related schemes were of course not so much isolated projects as expressions of a new regionalism. Sooner or later, the city would recognise the implications of the new planning policy: an increase in office employment and a reduction in manufacturing jobs, a decline in the working-class population, an increase in the middle-class population, an increase in property values, especially near the nodes of the new regional transport system, and the chance to make rapid progress on the redevelopment of the eastern slums. In short, the more successful the new regional strategy, the more the city of Paris would benefit in terms of prosperity and modernisation. The new policy could be seen as a challenge to Paris, but it was one that the city could scarcely fail to take up.

The effects of the policy were indeed far-reaching. In the early 1960s a rapid transition occurred from the 'crystallised' Paris of the post-war years, set within a region which it had virtually ignored, to a hub of growth and change in the fastest-growing capital region in Europe. Regional planning led to regional government. By the end of the decade a prefect presided over the Paris region while the city of Paris had its own prefect.

These changes were welcomed in what was clearly a prospering city. Politically, however, they had more subtle implications. With Paris now defined as a self-governing municipal unit rather than a component of the *département* of the Seine, both the city council and the electorate grew in self-conscious civic patriotism. The Prefect of Paris, inferior in status and influence to the regional prefect, showed some sympathy to the council. The case for appointing a mayor of Paris, with some of its *sans-culotte* overtones, was heard again. At the same time, some of the more disruptive implications of the city's position at the core of an expanding region began to arouse concern. It was here that architecture became an issue.

In the stimulating climate of the late 1950s and the 1960s, the city authorities were prepared to consider new action to secure a healthy building rate and to encourage creative architecture. To this end, they launched a review of the venerable building regulations of 1902. Their aim was partly to incorporate architectural concepts and planning techniques which had become orthodox since 1945 in London and other European capitals. Indeed, Paris now began, almost for the first time, to look seriously at foreign practice. More visible at the time, however, was the local influence of an elderly Le Corbusier, whose unremitting modernising campaign since 1918 was now vindicated. Just as the world's leading classical architects had once been Paris residents, so Paris could now claim the world's greatest modern architect. After decades of neglect in his adoptive city, Le Corbusier could bask in an almost uncritical respect.

The new perspective on building regulations developed against the background of a more vigorous and directive approach to the planning of Paris after the war. The Vichy regime's urban planning law of 15 June 1943 had initiated a long-term review of Parisian planning which led to the approval of parts of a *Plan directeur d'aménagement* in 1950. In 1959 various additions and amendments were included in a comprehensive *Plan d'urbanisme directeur*, which was applied progressively over the following years until the plan was formally approved in 1967.

The first important change affecting building form was made in 1959, when a system of use zoning, building regulations and plot ratios (site area in relation to area of floor space) was approved by the city council, as part of the *Plan d'urbanisme directeur*.[4] Zoning had been first mooted in 1950 but had not been fully introduced in practice. Its association with plot ratios was novel. The plot ratio had been developed in London after the Second World War, and had spread to most of the western world in the 1950s. It could be used to secure greater open space and lower density within a site, while conceding extra height. Louis Bonnier's committee on the building regulations had been moving in this direction between the wars, while architectural and planning opinion in the 1950s had begun to associate height with a desired modernity and greater visual variety. The implications for the traditional townscape, especially in the historic core, were little considered. Instead, the revival of building throughout the city after years of paralysis was a major aim.

Six use zones were defined for the city, each with its own plot ratio.[5] The plot ratio varied between 1:3 in residential zones and 1:3.5 in business zones.[6] Additionally, a number of protected zones were defined to incorporate areas of historic interest or beauty. Here, all new buildings and modifications of existing buildings were subject to special controls.

On 26 October 1959 the city council met to discuss the *Plan d'urbanisme directeur*.[7] It heard an address from the Prefect of the Seine Jean Benedetti, who pulled out all the stops to claim that this was an historic moment for Paris and indeed all those foreign cities which awaited its decision with bated breath. He painted a picture of a dynamic, commercial capital of the future, retaining all the forms of its historic and aesthetic prestige but continuing to decentralise population and employment into both the suburbs and the provinces.[8] The average residential plot ratio of 1:3, as the city council was told later, was intended to permit the retention of the present population level of the city.[9]

In the lengthy debate which followed, little attention was paid to the volume and character of the new building which might result from the plan, though the zoning system was much discussed. The plot ratio was presented as modest, being well below the existing average of much of western Paris, and the council's tolerance allowed rapid progress to be made on a code of new building regulations.

The new regulations resolved some of the problems of 1902 by tolerating greater heights and volumes within entire blocks, subject to the constraints of the plot ratio. Building sections were determined by maximum heights and envelopes applicable to entire blocks, and governing the rear portions as well as the street facades.[10]

The new building code came into effective use in 1961, though it was not formally approved until 1967, when it formed part of

240 Results of the building regulations of 1961/7. An apartment house on a deep site in the narrow Rue du Père-Corentin achieves height by stepping back. The rear facade, facing a large interior space, is vertical.

the Paris *Plan d'urbanisme directeur*.[11] While building heights generally remained proportional to the depth of open space in front of buildings, considerably greater heights were allowed than in the past. Together with the plot ratio, they encouraged owners to draw their buildings back from the building line. Greater heights could also be achieved by setting back the upper storeys to an extent which could no longer be described as a terraced roof (Fig. 240).

Access to sunlight was the main criterion, and if the section of a building could be maintained within a line drawn at 45 degrees from the opposite side of the street, its height was normally immaterial up to a zonal maximum.[12] This maximum overall height was fixed at 37 metres (120 feet) in the outer *arrondissements*, in line with a city council decision of 1950, and 31 metres (101 feet) in inner Paris, in deference to its historic value. The latter height did not greatly exceed the maxima permissible under the 1902 regulations, but the height permitted in the outer *arrondissements*, where most of the redevelopment of sub-standard housing would occur, was a radical departure from the Parisian norm (Fig. 241). Even greater heights, furthermore, could be permitted where appropriate. The general intention

241 Redevelopment in south-eastern Paris seen from the Cité Morland, a municipal office block in the Marais, in 1986. The Cité Morland, which dated from the early 1960s, itself infringed the height regulations in the central area, and was one of the second-rank eyesores of Delouvrier's early years.

was, however, to prevent undue heights, especially in the central area.[13]

These regulations have to be understood in the context of the city plan, which envisaged the eventual demolition of two out of three Paris blocks and provided special planning regulations for the redevelopment of such blocks in their entirety.[14] Here, as in the suburbs, great latitude had to be allowed with a view to creating a completely new townscape in the long term. The impact on the older, historic part of the city (*arrondissements* I-XII) was expected to be more restrained. As the official report on the plan stated, '. . . the introduction of these new rules is tempered by tradition and there is no danger that it will provoke violent discontinuities . . .'.[15] These new policies of building control, formally approved in 1960 and 1961 but already effective in most cases a few years earlier, were to provide the charter for the biggest transformation of the Paris townscape since the Second Empire. Welcomed at first as a quick route to modernisation, their effects would generate a powerful reaction by the early 1970s.

However, their novelty did not lie only in greater heights and volumes, and their encouragement of Modern Movement planning. They also recognised, for the first time, a distinction between two zones in Paris.

In an inner, central and historic, zone lying within the old customs wall of 1780 (now replaced by the *boulevards des fermiers-généraux*), the relaxations of the old controls of 1902 were modest. Here, it was recognised that major changes might disturb a fully developed area containing countless historic buildings and much-loved scenes and vistas. In the outer areas of the city, which contained the fashionable, residential west but also much larger areas of working-class and lower middle-class housing, more generous regulations, and a greater encouragement to modernist layout and architecture, could be permitted. The poorer districts here contained much slum housing and they were badly equipped in all respects. With some big municipal reconstruction schemes already planned, private redevelopment had to be encouraged as far as possible, to prevent a drain to the inner suburbs where a greater freedom was available to architects and builders.

BUILDING UNDER THE NEW REGULATIONS

The new building regulations coincided with the early stages of a great surge in building in the city. The residential sector was entering a period of transformation as De Gaulle's government gnawed away at the city's venerable rent controls, and slum clearance started in earnest. Commercial building was now propelled by a speculative drive which had been largely absent in the 1950s.

Architects, as in other European cities, responded to the demands of builders and owners by making flexible use of an economical style which was both functional and visually modernistic, though in a largely repetitive way. The repetition arose from the use of heavily standardised units and cost-cutting on materials. It was sustained by the widespread use of reinforced concrete which had long been a French speciality. Rectangular concrete panels attached to a concrete frame were the cheapest way of building large structures. Surface treatment of these exterior panels was difficult and rare. A coloured paint surface was sometimes applied to blocks of flats in the outer ring but there seemed to be a consensus that the monochrome character of traditional Paris should be maintained by the untreated concrete. Office blocks made wide use of the glass and ceramic curtain wall from around 1950, normally on a concrete frame.[16] Most of this economical architecture, now known to the purists of the Modern Movement as the International Style, was however sited in the outer *arrondissements*, where despite its height and bulk it arguably did not impinge on the historic areas.

A milestone had nevertheless been reached. For the first time since the sixteenth century, the architecture of the centre had ceased to penetrate the outskirts. On the contrary, the reverse was beginning to threaten, as developers and the construction industry converted to the new style. A rapid transition was made in the outer ring from the bleak workers' tenement house and courtyard to the towers and slabs of the public and co-operative housing sector. In contrast to the flats erected on the fortifications in the 1920s, this new building made no reference to the housing forms of the centre. This spatial dichotomy was unique in the history of Paris.

THE IMPACT OF MODERN ARCHITECTURE

During the 1960s modern architecture made a striking impact on Paris, including the centre. For the first time in decades, private redevelopment became noticeable in the centre and the West End, encouraged by the enhanced tertiary and luxury residential functions conferred by the new regional strategy and the city plan. The new building regulations encouraged such redevelopment, even in the centre (Fig. 242).

The fresh modernist enthusiasm was reflected in the handbook by I. Schein, *Paris construit*, which was first published in 1961 but had to be updated, with many new buildings, in 1970. Schein was a strong supporter of the Modern Movement and the books exuded confidence in its Parisian potential. Not only did he identify a number of buildings as outstanding exemplars of modern architecture, but he pointed out that the work of several great modern architects, such as Le Corbusier, had been conceived for Paris, thus implying that Paris had engendered or inspired some of the best work of the Modern Movement.[17]

This 'victory' of modern architecture was accompanied by a denigration of the old, and especially of the training of the Ecole des Beaux-Arts. Maurice Besset, for instance, wrote: 'The system of values defining the Beaux-Arts spirit, composed of vulgar pretension and rhetorical artifice, imprisons architects in a philistine condition from which few have the taste or resources to escape.'[18] A similar questioning of tradition, it should be said, arose within the Ecole, with the first serious critical debates taking place in 1955.[19] The competence of French architects in modern design was questioned nevertheless. Sir Richard Rogers recalls that when he and Renzo Piano won the competition for the Pompidou Centre in 1971, the French chairman of the jury advised him not to employ French architects in their project team because their standards were so low.[20]

Besset went on to argue that the modern was an architecture of the people whose introduction in Paris had been delayed by a stifling of debate by conservative forces. Decisions had been taken behind closed doors, and the French public had remained largely indifferent to architecture. This association of modern design with democracy was a feature of the 1960s.[21] There was, however, more than one set of closed doors. Le Corbusier's eminence and Parisian residence had built up a large body of admirers and supporters who for many years had had little chance to apply

242 Redevelopment in the business district. This is the Agence France-Presse building, which replaced a number of Second Empire structures on the Place de la Bourse in the early 1980s. Great care has been taken in inserting a very large building into a nineteenth-century scene.

his principles in Paris. When the Modern Movement quickly gained ground in the 1950s and early 1960s, these disciples emerged. They found themselves to be a group of architects and planners ranging from the most recent graduates to senior figures who had first been inspired by Le Corbusier's brilliance as early as the 1920s. This army of adherents was able to achieve, in just a few years, an architectural revolution such as Paris had not known since the Renaissance.

### THE TOWER: THE ULTIMATE CHALLENGE TO TRADITIONAL PARIS

The new climate allowed the tower to rise to the top of the agenda for the first time since the Porte Maillot competitions in 1930 and 1931. It was a symbol of modernity which appealed in particular to De Gaulle's prime minister, Georges Pompidou. When Pompidou became president himself in 1970 he was able to give free rein to his taste for modernistic symbolism.

Pompidou's efforts to modernise Paris were energetic and even brutal. Unlike De Gaulle, he involved himself directly in design decisions, fortified by his own expertise as an art collector. He was prepared to embrace towers, motorways and expressways, and large-scale urban renewal.[22] Although he rarely expressed his views in public, preferring to allow the city and regional authorities to represent Parisian policies, he was not afraid to speak out when called to task over his own influence. He especially valued the tower as the vanguard of a new aesthetic and a potent symbol of change. He was prepared to call for the rejection of 'an outmoded aesthetic'.[23] So strong was Pompidou's motivation that he might have prolonged the modernist approach had not a cruel illness taken his life in 1974.

The tower first entered Paris in the 1950s, with the Maison de la Radio. At the same time, a clutch of them was planned at the Défense office complex. The Défense, however, lay outside the city and little interest was shown in the very slow development of the site. Within the city, the tower made its entry in a much more brutal way. The new Gaullist regime of 1958, eager to stimulate both building and property values in Paris, saw the existing regulations and the associated administrative mentality as a hard, restricting shell which needed to be broken open. With a general revision of the building and planning regulations already under study, the government felt that something even more dramatic was needed to produce changes quickly. Very tall towers, it was felt, were the answer, and here Pompidou played a crucial part.

The first tower to be completed under De Gaulle was part of a hotel and exhibition complex close to the Porte Maillot, by G. Gallet. This descendant of the competition entries of the early 1930s was completed in 1968 and was not a product of the new regime.[24] The scheme attracted little interest, partly because it stood so close to the city boundary, and partly because of its distinctly cheap appearance. The hotel tower was sited away from the Etoile-Défense axis to avoid intruding on the perspective.

The second tower, known as the Tour Montparnasse, was a bigger challenge in every way (Figs 243–4). It was very tall (210 metres–680 feet) and bulky, closer to the city centre, and sited on a hill facing Montmartre, with its basilica of the Sacré-Coeur, across the historic core. The project sprang from a post-war decision to rationalise the Montparnasse and Maine railway stations, but when building began in 1958 it had mighty government

backing and the strongest encouragement to build high.

The scheme progressed slowly, mainly because of the need to relocate railway facilities within a very crowded site. The new station was bounded by massive slab blocks, completed in 1964, but an unprecedented publicity campaign ensured that Parisians were waiting eagerly for the tower, on which work started in 1969 and finished in 1973.[25]

The *société d'économie mixte* responsible for the entire project secured a strong American involvement in the construction. The developers, the consulting architects and the consulting engineers were all American, but the architectural design was the work of four French architects. There were no closed

244 The Tour Montparnasse benefits from a lush foreground in a redeveloped Montparnasse, 1991.

243 Aerial photograph of the Montparnasse redevelopment scheme, *c.* 1974.

doors here, the idea of a tower of 200 metres having been approved by the city council, and the whole project was publicised by the authorities as a symbol of the city's belated entry into the modern world. By the time the tower was completed in 1973, public opinion had swung against tall buildings. During its planning and construction, however, it was an inspiration to all who looked forward to a new Paris, and senior figures hinted that it would be followed by many more tall towers throughout the city.

## FRENCH MODERNISM: A FLAWED ACHIEVEMENT

By the early 1970s it appeared that modern architecture had at last made a break through in Paris. There had been no equivalent break-through since the sixteenth century. There seemed to be no respectable alternative to the Modern Movement. Its powerful theories had driven out all rivals, just as the architecture of the Renaissance had done.

In the event, any rejoicings would have been premature. As we shall see, Machine Age architecture came under heavy attack in the 1970s. Much of this episode revolved around specific buildings and the concept of intrusion. However, French modernism had a fundamental weakness which would have been an Achilles heel in any context. With their national confidence in reinforced concrete, and faced with an opportunity which exceeded their capacities, French architects relied rather more than their foreign counterparts on the repetitive use of standard components. The results will be apparent to anyone looking through the compilation of highlights of French modernism by Maurice Besset, published in 1967. This tedious parade of untreated concrete, bleak symmetry and constant repetition, represents the emergence of a world of modern architecture which lacks many of the qualities of the old while retaining some of its defects, such as obsessive symmetry, and conformity (Figs 245–6).[26] It seems that so few architects could handle the new architecture that they depended on formulas and peer emulation, just as their traditional predecessors had been accused of doing. In any event, the Modern Movement had not replaced an outdated architecture as it claimed to have done. Defective execution by architects of moderate ability made it as prone to challenge as any other style.

## THE MODERNIST PARADOX: DEFEAT FROM THE JAWS OF VICTORY?

The Parisian version of the Modern Movement was backed by a complex theory which drew heavily on Le Corbusier. Not only did it correspond to the industrial era, it was also the heir of the Parisian classical tradition. Its supporters therefore saw no reason why it should not replace the city's traditional architecture to general approval.

Most of the public were however unaware of these claimed associations. They were struck instead by a verticality which, even to

245 The Avenue d'Ivry, in the Italie redevelopment area, in 1986.

246 The Italie redevelopment area in 1990.

the untrained eye, conflicted with the city's established horizontal design plane. Moreover, almost all the redevelopment projects seemed to involve the loss of treasured scenes. In comparison with the old, much of the new architecture looked repetitive and indeed cheap, even in the city centre. Huge screens of curtain walling broken only by vertical ribbing – Mondrian without the coloured squares – suggested that the nondescript International Style, and not the Modern Movement, had taken over the city despite the presence of Le Corbusier. In practice the towers were outnumbered by the slabs, but the towers aroused the greater concern because, however distant they were, they often intruded on 'traditional views and perspectives'.

By the later 1960s modern architecture was coming into conflict with a very broad Parisian consensus on the proper appearance of a unique and cherished city. This consensus ran from the vocal *clochard* on his subway exhaust vent to the city councillor and opportunist deputy, via the city's older middle-class residents and its numerous conservationist intellectuals. It also included a number of architects, most of them at the end or the beginning of their careers. This conflict, and its resolution, is the subject of the rest of this chapter.

THE NEW CLIMATE

The context of this architectural debate was not simply Parisian, however. In 1973 the massive OPEC oil increases perturbed the western economies. France was badly affected. The building rate fell and public investment was held back. In 1974 a Gaullist president was replaced by a liberal, and the big public projects were placed under review.

A second contextual element affected Paris from the mid-1970s. This was the new world fashion for 'post-industrial' architecture. The United States and Spain were at first the main founts of this new approach. An earlier France might have remained isolated from a style based on fantasy, indiscipline and expressionism, just as a similar phenomenon, Art Nouveau, had once been rejected. However, Paris, and France, had opened the door to foreign influence and foreign architects during the rapid importa-

tion of modern architecture in the 1960s. Then, in the immediate aftermath of the events of 1968, architectural education had been opened up by the division of the Ecole des Beaux-Arts into eight teaching units ('*unités pédagogiques*') scattered through the Paris area, with a number located in the suburbs, each with its own expertise and interests. It was assumed at the time that the Modern Movement would be the main beneficiary of the reform, but the new freedom allowed much post-industrial design work to be done. Meanwhile, exposure to foreign influence was increased, and much of the students' post-industrial design reflected the freedom, individualism and even anarchy for which the students had struggled in 1968.

The third climatic change was the greater respect for traditional Paris which had emerged under the Fifth Republic. Modernisation and change, however welcome they had been after forty years or more of stagnation, soon generated a reaction in favour of the defence of the old and the familiar. Just as greater funds were available for new building, so they could be applied to conservation work and the creation of a greater public awareness of the value of the past. This effort extended, for the first time, to ostensibly mundane townscapes such as those of the nineteenth century. The public were encouraged to value, in the absence of the architectural or historical distinction previously associated with 'monuments', the qualities of harmony and representativeness present in 'ensembles' and townscapes. This had the effect of making almost the whole of the centre and west of the city into a valued and respected inheritance, where almost any new development was likely to be seen as an intrusion. In addition, the forms, proportions and treatments which now acquired enhanced value in their historic manifestations tended to secure respect from young architects as appropriate to the requirements of Paris. Even the study of modern architecture shifted from creative, new work to pioneers such as Perret who had tried to work within a French tradition. Growing respect for the past therefore worked to spare Paris some of the less disciplined essays in post-industrial architecture such as multiplied in North America. Conservationists and designers alike were once again agreed that the presence of Paris was a privilege which imposed both a duty and a discipline. The old was to be preserved as far as possible, and the new was to respect the old.

## THE ARCHITECTURAL 'SCANDALES'

Important though the changes in the architectural climate were, contemporaries were more aware of a series of battles fought against a few big, modern schemes. These battles were directed against projects which were already in execution, and little could be done to halt or alter them. Subsequent decisions, however, were greatly affected.

All the campaigns were waged as traditional French 'scandales', with the exposure of massive public incompetence or malfeasance by a wide-awake media and citizenry. Parisians had a taste for these things and, once launched, they could build up a big momentum. The most important targets were the Montparnasse tower, the towers of the Défense and the reconstruction of the Halles district.

## THE MONTPARNASSE TOWER

As we have seen, the Montparnasse tower was completed in 1973 after a lengthy period in which it had been presented by the authorities and the media as the herald of a new architectural era in Paris. Instead, it became the first big 'scandale'.

The architects of the tower had taken great care to soften its chunky profile with a sinuous, indented plan. The elevations were wrapped around the body of the building using an unobtrusive curtain-wall system. Vertical and horizontal strips in contrasting colours were employed to emphasise height and to mark the approach to the upper section of the building, which was given a slightly tapered effect by a number of subtle features.

In comparison with New York's bulky PanAm building, whose architects had faced similar problems a few years earlier, the Montparnasse tower was an effective and considerate design. Its bulk could not, however, be readily disguised (Fig. 247). The slow but inexorable ascent of the steelwork of the Montparnasse tower from the end of the 1960s generated a grim fascination in Paris, much as the rise of Centre Point's modular concrete structure to an unexpected height had horrified many Londoners in the early 1960s.

Even before the tower's thoughtful and sensitive exterior was fully applied, its bulk had turned most Parisian opinion against it. Opinions about the design might have differed, but in 1971 the media began to pillory

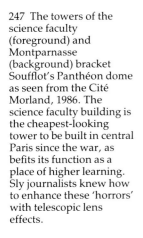

247 The towers of the science faculty (foreground) and Montparnasse (background) bracket Soufflot's Panthéon dome as seen from the Cité Morland, 1986. The science faculty building is the cheapest-looking tower to be built in central Paris since the war, as befits its function as a place of higher learning. Sly journalists knew how to enhance these 'horrors' with telescopic lens effects.

the tower's intrusion into a number of familiar Paris views. By 1973 a wide consensus of opinion had grown up that modern buildings should not exceed the traditional scale of the city, at any rate in the central areas.

The media now switched their attention from modernisation to earlier mistakes in the design process. It transpired that, during the very complex consultations for so important a building, the government's Commission des Sites had given its somewhat reluctant approval for a tower of 154 metres (500 feet) in 1965. It had been encouraged by André Malraux, Minister of Culture, a fervent supporter of De Gaulle and the advocate of a combination of the best of old and new architecture in Paris. Its height was then increased by a further 30 metres (98 feet) without reference to the commission. The city council had approved the project with rather less reluctance, accepting it as a means of regenerating a stagnant area and ignoring misgivings by its cultural affairs committee. Claims were made, however, that the council had not been fully informed and that it had been pressured by the authorities.

*The Défense office complex*

As the Montparnasse tower's bulky mass levered its way into the southern Paris sky, an even greater cause of discontent was emerging over the western skyline: the Défense office complex.[27] This exhibition and office centre, designated in 1950, was the descendant of pre-war plans for the Triumphal Way. Sited outside the city, its development lay within the remit of a variety of authorities and private interests. Plans for a large exhibition hall were drawn up by a private consortium from 1951, while the idea of an office centre originated in 1951 and culminated in a decision by the authorities in 1956. The prime mover at this stage was the central government, which set up a public agency, the Etablissement Public d'Aménagement de la Défense (EPAD), to develop office space in 1958.

The designated redevelopment area covered over a thousand hectares on both sides of the axis of the Avenue de Neuilly, but its core, the office district, was located on a pedestrian deck spanning the avenue over a distance of one kilometre from near the Seine as far as the exhibition hall, at the original star junction of the Défense. This rectangular

concourse, with several levels of underground services, prompted a neo-classical design solution in the first instance, with two aligned rows of towers of equal height, rising above buildings of traditional height arranged to create more intimate and enclosed spaces at ground level. However, the changing requirements of what was seen as a purely commercial project produced frequent amendment. The final plan, including twenty office blocks of twenty-five storeys, was approved in 1964. As architecture it attracted little attention at the time, partly because the expensive infrastructure, which was the responsibility of the State, contrasted with the sketchy, spartan and mundane treatment of the buildings, most of which were intended to attract private investment.[28]

In any case, none of this had much bearing on the centre of Paris. What brought matters to a head was the rapid implementation of the new growth policy for the capital which emerged in the *schéma directeur* of 1963. The Défense was designated as one of a number of out-of-town tertiary centres lying between the urban core and the suburbs. Situated on an axis between the city's financial and shopping district, and the prosperous western suburbs, the Défense was to take full advantage of its potential. Although success did not follow immediately, efforts were made to attract big companies to build their own premises at the Défense.

In the late 1960s the companies began to press for the right to build wider and taller towers, while the Minister of Equipment, Alain Chalandon, wanted to encourage much heavier private investment on the site. The EPAD began to make concessions in 1968. In 1969 the EPAD was reorganised to take full advantage of the developing property boom, and to generate an increased income to cover the very high costs of the infrastructure, which had risen because of the provisions necessary to sustain the post-1963 role of the Défense office centre. Then, in the wake of the reorganisation of EPAD, the area was replanned to include double the office space and double the number of jobs.[29]

This increase in scale had to be achieved mainly by greater heights, as the ground area available was largely determined by the deck. The actual heights permitted depended partly on the inclinations of the owning companies, and the original plan for constant-height towers was abandoned. The tallest tower was that of the Groupement d'Assurances Nationales, the GAN building, at 200 metres (650 feet).

No thought was given to the possible impact of these tall buildings on the great axis of the Triumphal Way. It was expected, of course, that they would be visible to an observer looking north-west from the Etoile down the Avenue de la Grande-Armée, but this section of the great vista had never been highly valued. What caused the outcry was the appearance of Défense towers within and around the Arc de Triomphe when seen from as far away as the Tuileries gardens (Fig. 248).

Like those who have heard the first cuckoo in spring, many are those who claim to have been the first to detect the intrusion. Perhaps the most attractive claim is that of Valéry Giscard d'Estaing, who was among the first to notice the dark bulk of the GAN tower when he left his car at the Ministry of Finance in the Louvre one day in early 1972.

By May the GAN tower was a frequent topic of conversation in Paris.[30] A variety of phantasmagoria enlivened the issue; weather conditions and time of day affected the appearance of the towers, as did the exact spot from which they were viewed. Telephoto pictures were used on television and in the press to exaggerate the towers and diminish the Arc de Triomphe, which seemed to be at the mercy of devouring Behemoths.

Most disturbing of all was the gradual increase in the height of the silhouettes. The features of the Montparnasse tower had been well publicised, including its height, but wild rumours circulated about the intended heights of the Défense towers, and many believed that the project was somehow out of control. This all made a powerful potion of complaint. On 1 September 1972 Giscard d'Estaing wrote to Pierre Messmer, the prime minister, calling for height reductions at the Défense, in order to contain the damage before the towers were completed. Within a few weeks the prime minister, in consulta-

248  The Défense district in 1989, looking out of the city towards the Grande Arche.

tion with President Pompidou, decided that there should be no intervention and that the towers should rise to their full height.[31]

Messmer defended the decision on financial grounds, but he also argued that every period should make its own contribution to the architecture of Paris. It was clear, however, that behind his words lay the thinking of the president. Although the decision to proceed with the Défense as planned marked a victory for modernism, the whole episode did more than any other to discredit the official advocacy of modern architecture. Pompidou, like his predecessor, had been reluctant to broadcast his views on Paris, but by 1972 the Défense was an issue of policy at the highest level, and the president – who had very clear views on the future of Paris and its architecture – agreed to give a personal interview to *Le Monde*. The interview was published on 17 October 1972.

Since the beginning of the Fifth Republic all formal interviews with presidents had been official statements in sheep's clothing. *Le Monde* was used to this deferential role and its readership was well aware that the president would talk about what he wished rather than answer the questions that a journalist might normally ask. This explains why the interview began with the interviewer drawing attention to Pompidou's great attachment to questions of art, architecture and town planning. The president went on to say that he never imposed his ideas in these matters, but that he did intervene 'when an enterprise is national in character in terms of its objective or its size – such as the Défense'. The creation of a large business district housing the headquarters of large companies was part of the effort to make France a great economic power and Paris a large business centre.

This evocation of the national interest, implicit in Paris regional planning since the time of Delouvrier, was always risky where the Parisian identity was at stake. Certainly, the Défense was ambiguous, lying as it did outside the municipal city, but Pompidou had made an awkward start. Nor was there much improvement when he went on to discuss one of the major complaints, that planning and building regulations had been waived at the Défense to achieve greater heights. Waivers of regulations had been inevitable, the president maintained, because

the building regulations were so restrictive. Indeed, there were too many regulations, he went on. This argument might have been appropriate to the suburbs, but here again the president seemed to ignore the general sense of an uncontrolled attack on Paris from the outside.

Turning from matters of legality and opportunity to the aesthetics of the affair, the president drew deeply on his inheritance as a French head of state and conjured up the classical ideal of the perspective and the monumental termination. In this case he had in mind the perspective north-westwards from the Etoile to the cluster of towers at the Défense. The Défense was also a chance to carry out an important project of modern architecture, he claimed. If neither of these arguments gave much support to the interviewer's initial claim that the president attached much importance to questions of art and architecture, he put himself beyond the pale when he said that he favoured 'a forest of towers' as a backdrop for the Arc de Triomphe when seen from the Champs-Elysées. 'There is nothing worse than five or six towers trying and failing to hide themselves.' Pompidou went on to suggest ending the perspective at the Défense with a giant statue or fountain which would be visible through the Arc de Triomphe. Although this idea was to culminate in the 1980s with the 'cube', later known as the Grande Arche de la Défense, it raised major doubts in 1972 about the president's taste, especially in relation to Parisian tradition.

The interviewer now allowed the president to dilate on architecture in general. He was opposed, he said, to the idea of nationalism in architecture. Modern architecture was international. In a revealing aside, the president claimed that *he* had 'found' one of the eventual architects of the Maine-Montparnasse complex in Chicago – an extraordinary indication, this, of the extent of Pompidou's involvement in architectural detail.[32] Detail, however, was clearly not on the interview agenda for Pompidou. Modern architecture meant towers, he averred. The French, and particularly the Parisian, opposition to height was retrograde. French artistic taste was conservative, especially among the elite, and that was why he was working hard to change it. 'I repeat, there is no modern architecture in cities without towers.' And with this, attention turned to the president's views on art, which took up roughly half the interview.[33]

The president's views were clear enough, but their crudity offered no scope for further debate or refinement. The overall momentum of the anti-tower movement was now at its height, and with President Pompidou at the beginning of a fatal illness, the future of modern architecture in Paris hung in the balance.[34]

### The Halles redevelopment scheme

The third important episode was a redevelopment scheme in the medieval heart of the city. It arose from the decision, finalised in 1963, to remove the central wholesale markets to a suburban site at Rungis. This move had been under discussion for a number of years, but the eventual decision was made in the context of the new regional growth strategy, and the authorities saw it not simply as a local measure of decongestion and decentralisation but as the key to the transformation of the oldest part of central Paris, in the context of the enlarged urban region.

It was clear to the authorities that the departure of the Halles, while removing the most dynamic and prosperous functions of the district, would leave behind a collection of more marginal activities, and a partially transient, low-income population. These features were inconsonant with the area's potential for high-rent functions as the core of a great city. The authorities therefore built up a strategy for the Halles based on the high-density reconstruction of the area of the old market pavilions, the creation of underground levels for shopping, parking, and the central Paris interchange of the new regional express underground railway (RER), the demolition of additional areas of old buildings just outside the perimeter of the Halles, and the gradual redevelopment of the rest of the district by private capital. Just to the east, across the Boulevard de Sébastopol, the authorities planned to carry out the redevelopment of the notorious Îlot I, which had been designated as the worst slum area in Paris before the First World War. These ambitious plans were boosted in the post-1958 climate, and Delouvrier promoted them with enthusiasm. In the climate of the early 1960s, it is not surprising that the rebuilding envisaged should have been modernistic, not

to say futuristic. Both the authorities and educated Paris opinion sensed a serious stagnation in central Paris as the business centre moved to the west and north-west. The Halles scheme provided an ideal opportunity to make a modernistic statement in the old heart of the city, and to attract additional redevelopment capital into nearby streets.

The plans for the Halles gradually alerted a minority of Paris conservationists and intellectuals. Although the district was generally in a poor condition, its fabric was of great historical interest. Nor did its narrow streets and tall houses lack in picturesque qualities. What it did lack, however, was the collection of fine *hôtels* which could be found just to the east, in the Marais. Indeed, at first there seemed to be little chance that the Halles district could secure the same respect from the authorities and even from the conservation movement as did the Marais. This pessimistic assessment was actually reinforced by the revival of interest in the Marais which began in the early 1960s, and which was based on a cultural and social elitism which did not seem capable of transfer to more workaday parts of the city.

The Halles, however, had something that the Marais did not – ambitious public plans for redevelopment. These alone were capable of making the existing environment look preferable. The whole episode would demonstrate that the obstacles to an architectural revolution in Paris lay just as much in the city's physical legacy as in any defects of modern architecture. Although the Halles redevelopment plans were both varied and obscure, by 1966 a clear presumption had been established that the scheme would be dominated by the creation of office space at high densities, with some very tall buildings. The area to be demolished around the market perimeter would be extensive and its treatment would largely conform to that of the Halles site itself. The whole would be dominated by a 'world trade centre' which would both make the old core of the city a prestige office district and express in business terms the international function which was generally seen to be Paris's main virtue.

It was in 1966 that serious opposition to the Halles redevelopment scheme was first expressed, when the preservationist and historical societies first won the ear of politicians and the media. The city council debated the issue at its spring session in 1966, when the loss of low-rent housing and space for artisanal trades became a concern of the Left. The council nevertheless agreed the compulsory purchase of 35.4 hectares at this time.[35]

In 1967, the authorities attempted to defuse the gathering conflict of views by inviting six architects to present projects for an area of 15 hectares which would be acquired within five years. The brief implied modernity but the normal ceiling height of 27 metres (88 feet) was fixed for all the new buildings. This was not a competition so much as an attempt to identify a solution which could secure consensus support. Most of the submissions were modernistic or even futuristic, their authors seeking to make a striking contrast with an area of traditional Paris which appeared to typify the worst of the city's slum problem. Only one entry, by Claude Charpentier, a specialist in preservation, stressed the retention of the existing environment. At the time it caused some amusement, because it demolished almost nothing apart from the Halles buildings themselves, which it replaced with a park.

When the prefect presented these schemes to the city council in 1968, he dismissed Charpentier's as too conservative.[36] However, he made an important concession, accepting that central area redevelopment needed to respect the scale, spirit and pattern of the urban tissue.[37] As a sop to the council's objections, he asked two architects whose projects had combined modernity with a degree of modesty, Hoym de Marien and Jean Faugeron, to modify their plans by including more open space and conforming to the *schéma directeur* strategy for central Paris.[38]

Before the authorities had had the chance to bring forward modified plans, the student-related events of the summer of 1968 had created a completely new climate. If the political effects of the student 'revolution' were largely superficial, the physical environment passed into the hands of the public in a more permanent way. Just as young people now strolled on the grass in the public parks, so the Halles and their district were appropriated by the younger intelligentsia as a popular legacy. The market buildings were used for displays and happenings, with the more aware student and local political leaders claiming that they had a permanent popular festival to outshine the elitist Festival du Marais which took place annually to the east. Baron Jacques de Sacy, veteran leader of the national preservation movement, produced a historical and architectural guide to the district which boosted popular appreciation of its value. Appropriately, De Sacy's aristocratic title did not appear on the title page.[39] These products secured respect for the Halles district as a centre of popular culture which did indeed have much in common with the Marais.

The market buildings remained standing until 1971, three years after the market traders had left. So strong was the momentum of conservation by this time, that a vigorous campaign was fought to retain Baltard's market buildings as a monument to the city's working history and as a permanent venue for spontaneous activities. The campaign failed to secure its object, which would have greatly complicated the building of the RER station, but it suggested that the once modest claims of the conservationists could now extend to almost anything in central Paris.

Action was, however, accelerated by progress on the express metro line. From 1971 onlookers used to the claustrophobic atmosphere of central Paris gazed in amazement as excavators on the old market site gradually opened up 'le grand trou', ranked by the media as the largest urban hole in the world. This took a very long time to dig and to line with the necessary concrete walls. Once the station had been built at the bottom of the hole, the rest had to be filled up with a variety of concrete levels and shafts. It was possible for a while to postpone decisions about what should be put on the top, but by 1974 the time for a decision was fast approaching. It was now, in April 1974, that President Pompidou died. His successor, Valéry Giscard d'Estaing, was a political centrist with a respect for traditional French values and balanced budgets. His involvement in the Défense affair had marked him out as an incipient conservationist, and from his early months in power he strove to modify a number of Paris projects. At the Halles, he halted work on the world trade centre, which occupied only part of the site of the market buildings and which had been presented as the inoffensive remnant of the sweeping schemes of previous years. He also insisted on the landscaping of the whole of the market site to form a park. The demolition of adjacent blocks of houses was completely halted.

It was nevertheless left to the prefectoral authorities to prepare detailed schemes, and in April 1975 the matter was back before the city council. Three weeks of debate produced a compromise, with the large park by the Catalan architect Ricardo Bofill, favoured by the president, rejected by the councillors. Bofill was asked to reach a compromise with an architectural group led by Bernard de La Tour d'Auvergne, which wanted to build on part of the site. De La Tour d'Auvergne was quoted as saying that he deplored Bofill's constant reference to the past rather than to the present.[40]

Despite such differences, the cooperation produced sketch designs which were approved by Giscard d'Estaing in July 1976. The park was now reduced to seven-tenths of the redevelopment area, allowing the eastern part, which lay over the RER station, to accommodate a multi-level underground shopping centre (the Forum).[41] The remaining plans were more fluid, but there was a clear movement towards more modest structures and conformist styles. At the same time, Bofill's new park was more formal, less dominated by romantic foliage, than in his previous versions.

The problem still remained of converting the sketch designs into reality on what was now seen to be the most complex urban redevelopment site in the world. In February 1979 the authorities presented their new 'final project'. At that time, only the RER station and the Forum had been built. Nothing existed above ground. This was seen as a last opportunity for the protesters, and in April 1979 the Syndicat de l'Architecture de l'Île de France launched an 'international consultation' to generate new ideas. It set up the Association pour la Consultation Internationale pour l'Aménagement du Quartier des Halles for this purpose. By linking the redevelopment site to the whole of the district it defined a zone of intervention which would clearly tend to emphasise conservation. It also maintained that considerations of architecture should be uppermost in so important and complex a scheme. A public architectural debate would replace the technocratic and secret processes which had so far dictated the fate of the Halles.

The brief, published in 1979, was strongly historical in emphasis, a major objective being to secure architectural solutions which would allow a last chance in Paris for a district to be rebuilt in a manner 'worthy of its past'.[42] A long section discussed the history of the area, and Baltard's market buildings, though demolished, were stressed as an important feature of the traditional Halles environment.[43] A total of six hundred 'counter-projects' were received from a variety of countries, most of them postmodern or historicist in style. The exhibition of the entries marked a further step towards the democratisation of planning and architecture. Moreover, in common with other Paris projects, the Halles question was now internationalised. The distinguished jury included eight foreigners out of sixteen (though to these must be added a number – probably four – of representatives of local pressure groups).

Even within the Association there was little hope that the exhibition would deflect the authorities from their own project. The final version was announced by the city's new mayor in January 1980. In addition to the Forum, there were some shops on the street frontages at the eastern end of the markets site. To the north of the Halles perimeter, further shops and apartments were planned. To the south, a large office complex would be built on the site of some blocks of old housing. An underground road system, and underground parking, would cover those parts of the site which were not needed for the RER station.

This modest scheme reflected the power of the opposition generated since 1976. The architectural team of De La Tour d'Auvergne had sought to avoid brutal intrusions into the traditional fabric. The Forum was largely underground, the commercial buildings on the frontages were low and followed the building lines. The new buildings outside the market site were only slightly larger than traditional dimensions, and traditional features such as mansard roofs and dormer windows were included.

Few were satisfied by the result, which

was forced and self-conscious, attempting ultra-modern treatments in small-scale situations, and softening larger structures by simplified traditional elements (Figs 249–52). The design solution, nevertheless, represented the defeat of modern architecture's aspirations to exist independently of the physical context in which it found itself. Only underground was it allowed self-expression, for instance in the 'new town' architecture of the Forum whose architects, Vasconi and Pencréac'h, had designed the commercial centre at Cergy Pontoise.[44] At any rate, the Halles controversy was now over, the final solution providing a good example of the compromise architecture generated by the 1970s.

THE POMPIDOU CENTRE

The cases discussed so far have shown the creation of an informal Parisian defence against the excesses of modern architecture. In one important case, however, the defence failed to form and the result rivalled the basilica of the Sacré-Coeur and the Eiffel tower in its indifference to Parisian norms. While the Halles dispute dragged on and on, half a mile to the east a related project moved rapidly from conception to completion. The main architectural product, the Pompidou Centre of the Arts, was one of the most daring urban cultural projects in the world, a unique design statement comparable to the Sydney opera house.[45] Its scale and design were completely out of touch with Parisian practice. Its architects, Richard Rogers and Renzo Piano, were Italian-born British and Italian respectively. Their huge design team was staffed almost completely by foreigners. As the most extraordinary episode in the entire history of Paris architecture, the Pompidou centre merits careful review.

Redevelopment of the unhealthy area no. 1 (Îlot I) was a logical extension of the gradual progress on the Halles scheme to the west. The immediate stimulus, however, was the election of President Pompidou in 1969. The new president wanted to emphasise culture. As an art lover, he decided in December 1969

249 *Below*, the Forum and harmonising buildings to the north, 1986.

250 *Right, top*, the park, the Forum and the sixteenth-century church of Saint-Eustache early on a rainy summer morning in 1991.

251 *Right, centre*, the maturing park, and harmonising buildings to the south of the Halles, in 1991.

252 *Right, below*, above-ground section of the Forum and harmonising housing to the north, on the Rue Rambuteau. (Photo: J. Diefendorf).

to create a cultural centre which would have a popular rather than an elitist character. As no suitable sites were yet available in the Halles, he was attracted by the idea of using the large site which had been cleared in the Îlot I in the 1930s to build a museum of contemporary art in all its forms. He envisaged a large structure, to be linked to the Halles by a pedestrian axis serving other cultural buildings. Above all, he wanted the design of the building to express its era.[46]

The authorities welcomed the president's intervention at this unproductive stage in the Halles affair, even though the site was officially designated for a public library and new housing. They took up his proposal with enthusiasm, allowing Pompidou to remain in the background, as he preferred to do in such cases. However, he retained an interest in the design, and he was behind the great international competition which the authorities launched in 1971.

This was the first international competition ever held in Paris.[47] As such, it reflected the post-1968 sentiment – which went up to presidential level – that French architecture had been restrained by the Beaux-Arts training system and that the best modern architects were likely to be found abroad. There were 681 entries, a total uncannily similar to that of the unofficial Halles competition later on. The Pompidou centre competition was not, however, a mere consultation. It was required to produce a single winning design, with the ultimate selection or endorsement to be made personally by the president.

All of this was a new experience for Paris, and from the start the selection system showed signs of overload. The large number of entries alone complicated the choice. The 'sure judgment of French taste' was no longer much use, and a momentum developed which escaped the age-old controls and constraints which had protected aesthetic traditions in the historic core. The competition jury was central to this effect.

Logically, the jury was strongly international. Selected by civil servants on lines laid down by the president, it contained only one French architect. More surprisingly, however, practising architects were not allowed a dominant presence, at least in numbers. The jury consisted of four directors of large museums, and one French professor. Oscar Niemeyer, the architect of Brasilia, and Philip

Johnson, the pioneer American modern architect who was on the verge of becoming the pioneer American post-modernist, were the only outstanding architects on the panel. Emile Alliaud was the lone French architect. The French engineer, Jean Prouvé, was made chairman. Notably absent was anyone who would have appreciated the architectural context of one of the oldest districts in Paris.

The work of the jury appears to have been dominated by Philip Johnson. With more architects, a broader architectural consensus might have emerged, but the result seems to have been far more an international exercise in idealistic modernism than an attempt to cater for Parisian needs, at any rate once the museum directors had had their say.

The winning design, by Renzo Piano and Richard Rogers, was nothing if not modern. There was no attempt here to merge with the city as even the creators of the Montparnasse tower had tried to do, in their way. The architects saw it as an 'activity container', mixing a number of cultural forms and attracting swarms of people, from foreign tourists to local residents. It was very much an anarchic, post-1968, 'happening' arena. Much of the interior felt like permanent accommodation for student sit-ins. There were echoes of some of the more utilitarian

parts of the Architectural Association School of Architecture, where Rogers had qualified (Figs 253–4).

Outside, the centre looked like the middle section of the hull of a beached *Queen Mary*, with the bow and the stern sheered off and all the superstructure and exterior plating removed. This possibly unconscious imagery was reinforced by the nautical ventilation tubes which were a big feature of the back of the building. The exterior was a trellis of metal columns and pipes, supporting a glazed curtain. It was 166 metres (540 feet) long, 42 metres (136 feet) high and 60 metres (195 feet) deep. The total floor area was 110,000 square metres (1,150,000 sq. ft.), the size of a giant department store.[48] Perhaps the Galérie des Machines was the nearest precedent, but it had stood well outside the city centre in an exhibition area. The crushing impact of Rogers' inflated, self-conscious, bombastic, posturing building on the centre of the city was completely new. The requirement of the brief that entries should be 'perfectly integrated into the urban environment' was completely ignored. Instead, the design seemed to reflect a number of unresolved debates within British and American modernism in the 1960s.[49] In fact, there is evidence that the president was dis-

253  The Pompidou centre, west front, in 1986.

182

turbed by the winning design but endorsed it because of the near-unanimity of the jury.[50]

Piano and Rogers were urged to build quickly and, after excavation work started in 1972, the centre was soon powering its way into the sky, a constant source of amazement to onlookers and the national television audience. In view of the continuing disagreements over the scale and type of development at the Halles, a massive public and professional outcry might have been expected over the Pompidou centre. The Left was fended off with promises of caviar for the general, but there were no concessions at all for aesthetes, artists, historians and other guardians of the beauty of Paris, apart from a reduction in the planned height of the structure on the insistence of the Paris authorities.[51]

An outcry indeed occurred, but it was never enough to threaten the project or to force changes. President Giscard d'Estaing considered halting the project in August 1974, just after he came to power. Only the substructure had been built at that time. However, he contented himself with budget cuts and minor modifications.[52] Like large, non-conforming public buildings before it, the Pompidou centre secured a grudging toleration. A clear decision had been made, and by a president of France, and this contrast to the muddle at the Halles was welcomed by many Parisians.

One thing could be predicted. Whatever respect or obloquy the building would eventually secure, there would never be another Pompidou centre. Nor did the work of its foreign creators influence any other architecture in Paris. Piano and Rogers came and went; they left a big mark, but they left only one. When the slum streets to the north of the Pompidou centre were demolished to make way, this time, for housing, they were gradually replaced between 1970 and 1983 by a curious mixture of sinister, medievalised apartment buildings and alleys in the Ridley Scott style which bore no relation whatever to the work of Piano and Rogers. The objective here was to recreate 'a true Parisian quarter'.[53] Older houses facing the Pompidou centre were carefully restored as though to delimit an alien form.

This development of a contrasting frame for the work of Piano and Rogers was not simply a reaction against the 'Pompidoléum', however. It was part of a massive swing of architectural opinion. For, by the time the Pompidou centre was completed in 1977, Paris had turned against the Modern Movement and all its works.

254 Aerial photograph of the Pompidou centre, 1983. Sensitive insertion into an historic district is not one of the features of this concept.

255 The impact of more generous building regulations in outer Paris: post-1961 redevelopment along the Avenue du Général-Leclerc, photographed in 1986.

## THE RETURN TO TRADITION AND THE CONSERVATION OF THE PAST

The Paris media aimed their main criticism at big towers. However, the early 1970s saw growing criticism of private redevelopment under the post-1960 building and planning regulations. Boosted by economic growth and the dismantling of rent controls, developers were at last able to plan the assembly of sites within which greater heights and efficient layouts could become possible (Fig. 255).

In the outer areas such projects caused little concern. In the centre, however, the demolitions attacked buildings dating from before the Second Empire for the most part, later structures being still in good condition and making efficient use of their sites. These destructions soon began to cause resentment among the populace. It proved to be very difficult to demolish any older building in the central areas without damaging some historic or treasured scene, especially as so little had changed there since 1931. The media could make good copy of many of these minor projects, and by the early 1970s the value of the traditional Paris street, in addition to that of individual buildings, was being touted.

The *plan d'urbanisme directeur* of 1967, which codified the new regulations, had been published too soon after Delouvrier's regional *schéma directeur* of 1963 to absorb its full implications for the city of Paris. In the early 1970s, however, an awareness of the city's changing role began to impinge on the

city council and its officials. In June 1973 a major debate took place in the city council on the future of Paris. It centred on an unexpected report published, on state initiative, by the DATAR (Délégation à l'Aménagement du Territoire et à l'Action Régionale) and the prefecture of the Paris region. The report detected a 'decline of Paris' in its international role and attacked previous policies which had contributed to that decline. It emphasised the 'international vocation of Paris' in cultural, economic, social and political terms.[54]

Many city councillors expressed wry surprise that the preparation of the report had remained a secret until shortly before the debate, and that the Paris authorities had been scarcely consulted on the question of the international character of the city. Instead, the authors had used a Delphic technique, consulting large numbers of mainly foreign experts. The result of their questionnaire was that London stood out clearly as the leading international centre of culture. Whereas thirty-five experts had voted for London, only nine had voted for Paris, and five of these were French.[55] The report went on to aver that the expulsion of the elderly and those with low incomes from the centre of Paris was socially harmful, while the policies favouring business had not succeeded in attracting large numbers of foreign banks and multi-national companies.

Although the councillors were far from unanimous over this diagnosis and its causes, a certain unease was present in a number of speeches. A powerful speech by Pierre Lépine expressed the basic concern. He maintained that Paris no longer stimulated artistic activity nor attracted foreigners as much as in the past because its recent planning policies had favoured offices rather than artists' studios. They had sterilised the heart of a Paris which once had been the stimulus of the cultural life of the whole of France. In short, Paris had decided to neglect the essential quality of life which had once been its pride. It had given up something both unique and precious in pursuit of an American mirage.[56]

Unusual though this episode was, particularly in respect of the unexpected state intervention in the city's affairs which many resented, it helped create a political climate favourable to the post-Delouvrier evolution of the city's planning policies. The measured speech by the Prefect of Paris maintained that the report, and the city's developing policies, had similar perspectives. He especially emphasised policies affecting the planning of the environment and building regulations which would soon come before the council.[57]

All this was a prelude to the land use plan for Paris, published in 1974 within the context of the new, regional planning strategy of 1965, and the Paris structure plan of 1968.[58] The plan accepted the regional strategy, under which all population growth would occur outside the Paris boundaries and employment growth would be halted within the city, with new office space concentrated in densely developed office districts near major railway termini. This greatly reduced the need for the private creation of additional floor space within the city boundaries. The redevelopment of the east would proceed, but poor housing in the older areas of the centre could be entrusted to private modernisation processes which would retain its historic character.

The land use plan of 1974 combined careful zoning and sensitive building regulations. The regulations were the product of a working party composed of city councillors and representatives of state and city departments, closely advised by the APUR (Atelier Parisien de l'Urbanisme) under its director, Pierre-Yves Ligen.[59] The APUR was a semi-independent study team which the City of Paris had recently set up to present its policies to the public, and to develop new planning concepts. It had carried out research designed to identify the essential differences between the Paris of the 1902 regulations and the development fostered by the modernistic building code and the zoning and plot ratios of 1961. The APUR took the increasingly fashionable view that all new development should create continuity and harmony with the inherited fabric.[60] The street, the site and the block should all be respected, even on the outskirts of the city. The importance of established heights, and building lines, was emphasised.

This stance reflected the world-wide interest in conservation which emerged in the early 1970s, and which, especially after the oil crisis of 1973, had called into question the single-minded race for economic growth and modernisation which had arguably dehumanised many large cities in Europe. It also represented an extension of concern from giant projects like the Montaparnasse tower to domestic buildings and the streetscape, both of which were the victims of an insidious modernisation which Ligen and his colleagues were able to quantify.

The working party agreed that it was important to preserve the image of Paris. To do this, it was necessary to '. . . protect prestigious or picturesque perspectives, and to maintain the appearance of interesting streets'.[61] The creation of the building line in 1607 was identified as the first, essential step towards the creation of the traditional Parisian environment which was now the goal of the planners:

> It is the beginning of the classical period in which the French conception of urban art will take shape, as the mark of order, clarity and sobriety. In the seventeenth and eighteenth centuries Paris will acquire that nobility and grandeur which are universally acknowledged.[62]

The Second Empire townscape was not viewed in such an ecstatic light, but its qualities of utility and its good physical condition were stressed.

To protect these inherited qualities, a maximum overall height of 25 metres (83 feet) was fixed for the centre, compared to heights of 31 metres (100 feet) and of 37 metres (120 feet) in various districts of the outskirts, which were retained from the 1967 plan. The height ceiling in the central area was very close to that created by the building regulations of 1783/4, and several zones with even lower maxima were designated, such as Montmartre. The plot ratios were reduced throughout the city, restricting the total potential floor space which Paris could provide, depressing land values and discouraging redevelopment. The frontage heights of new buildings throughout the city were normally limited to the width of the street plus two or four metres (six or twelve feet), according to the zone.[63] The design treatment of individual facades was subject to official control, in order to secure harmony with neighbouring frontages.[64] Model profiles were used to secure the traditional building forms, and construction at the building line was again normally required. Ambitious widening lines which threatened the traditional appearance of older streets were revised in order to maintain the existing frontages. Taken as a whole, the new controls reproduced 'the forms consecrated by the regulations of the last three hundred years which have shaped the traditional cityscape of the capital'.[65]

The proposals went through a series of careful debates in which the councillors' concern and involvement contrasted with their complacency and indifference in the later 1950s.[66] Finally, the land use plan was approved by the city council on 19 December 1974, and introduced in 1975. It was a resounding triumph for the traditional Paris aesthetic, and more precisely for Ligen and his APUR, who had been allowed to advocate a policy which drew more on the views of the Left Bank intellectual and the well-heeled conservationist than on those of building and business interests.

Private architects were generally on Ligen's side. With modern architecture largely associated with big public projects, most had no direct commitment to it, and the quality of much of this work did not impress them. From 1975, architects not only respected the new dimensions and prescriptions, as they were of course obliged to do, but they developed modest, conforming treatments which allowed many of them to merge with their older surroundings. This was the very antithesis of the Modern Movement which had dominated the pages of *Paris-Projet* as late as 1973. The Parisian public was, however, clearly content with the new approach. Even the developers said little against it, partly because economic deceleration was undermining the property market and making the leasing of empty buildings the main priority.

In the later 1980s there would be a partial move back towards freer regulations, Mayor Chirac having sensed that building and redevelopment were being discouraged. The regulations were revised in 1989 in consequence, but the changes were for the most part small adjustments. By this time, Parisian architecture had responded to the new framework by creating a new Parisian mode of design. In its combination of modernism and tradition, it recalled Roux-Spitz's concept of a 'Paris school' which guided apartment house design between the wars.

## THE NEW TRADITION

The rejection of the urban ideology of the Modern Movement, though widely welcomed, did not in itself solve the problem of designing new buildings and environments for a city which, though growing more slowly than had been expected in the 1960s, still needed to adapt to its regional role. Meanwhile, the redevelopment programme in the east was still incomplete. These problems were resolved in time, however. The architectural commentators Michèle Béhard and Manuelle Salama detect a broadening of the architectural debate in France around 1975. Paris was an important contributor to this new climate, and Béhard and Salama identify the development of 'a new urban architecture' there. It was partly the product, they thought, of a reorientation of Paris towards the east, and of a shift away from offices and towards housing and public buildings.

> This architecture runs counter to the planning of the 1960s. Its basic theme is the restructuring of the city, and its reunification through the care taken by architectural practices to share in the traditions of the city. The new Plan d'occupation des sols, completed in 1974, is significant in this respect in that it marks a return to the building line and to the traditional maximum dimensions.

The result was a renaissance in Parisian architecture, and in France as a whole, they claimed.[67] This is a fair judgment, for from our viewpoint in the early 1990s it looks as though the brutal clash between modernism and tradition was resolved during a creative and even exciting period beginning in the later 1970s and still underway. In practice, once the doctrinaire eruption of the Modern Movement had been repulsed, modernism contributed to a further development of the Parisian tradition just as each succeeding classical variant had done since the seventeenth century (Fig. 256).

The genesis of this 'new urban architecture' was complex. It sprang partly from a new appreciation of the urban habitat, stressing tradition and a human scale. In 1980, for instance, Michel Jean Bertrand's comprehensive study of urban architecture, published in a prestigious architectural series and drawing

256 Parisian neo-modern: a new apartment house on the Quai de la Loire, 1986. (Photo: J. Diefendorf).

257 Modest apartment house in the Rue Amelot, built in the early 1980s.

258 Apartment house in the Rue Mathis, 1985, by Buffi. The 'hollow' facade, very popular in the early 1980s, was intended to integrate the private space of the flats with the public space of the street, thus overcoming the possible alienating effects of the official return to frontage development.

mainly on Parisian examples, stressed the organic relationship between urban buildings, their sites and urban history.[68] He presented the city as a collection of habitats and, although he did not rule out modern development where appropriate, he clearly aimed to provide a series of implicit guidelines for new building within a conservation strategy. This approach to new design was backed by a new surge of conservationism as the happy effects of early restoration projects in the Marais became visible. In effect, traditional Paris would determine the future, as it had during the classical era.

Many architects now took considerable care to link their buildings to adjacent, older structures. This could lead to a subdued, new *architecture d'accompagnement* (Fig. 257), or to a self-conscious or pretentious intellectual effort to link a non-conforming design to the local habitat or to the community in general, for instance by symbolism. J.-P. Buffi's apartment house of 1982 in the Rue Mathis is an example of the latter (Fig. 258).[69] An even bigger exercise in integrative symbolism was the brick-built block of flats at the Porte de Pantin (Fig. 259) by the partially reconstructed Modern Movement prophet Paul Chemetov, now returned to favour, which was completed in 1981.[70] Chemetov chose to use nearly a million red bricks to link Paris to the proletarian suburbs by saluting the 'red belt' from within the city boundary.[71] He was presumably not responsible for the capitalist signs and advertising which festooned the city frontage by 1991.

Chemetov's love of bathetic gesture was not typical, however. Even on the outer fringes of the city, most designers of large-scale social housing sought above all to achieve integration, variety and a human scale.[72] 'Contextualisme' was a popular concept.[73] Although the step from the new conformism to out-and-out pastiche might have seemed easy, it was hardly ever taken. Parisian architects remained for the most part modernists at heart, and public buildings were greatly influenced by Jacques Chirac, the city's first mayor since time immemorial, who was elected in 1980. Chirac was an admirer of modern architecture, and he soon launched a series of competitions for schools and other municipal buildings.[74]

The result was a humane, varied architecture which is best described as 'neo-modern',

259 Chemetov's transitional block at the Porte de Pantin, 1981. The use of red brick on this scale recalls a strong tradition in Italian modernism since the 1920s.

260 Schools and flats for the City of Paris at 158–62, avenue Jean-Jaurès, 1985. The architect is Georges Pencréac'h, author of the Forum. He has adapted to the more conformist style of frontage development now in favour, using holes in the same way as Buffi, giving a result more neo-modern than post-modern.

and which had a common character throughout the city (Fig. 260). Although it was intended to be decorative, and displayed a light touch and, almost for the first time in Parisian modernism, a sense of humour, it did not draw to any great extent on the American post-modernism which was becoming fashionable at the time. Admittedly, Spanish architects such as Ricardo Bofill, who built in an ecstatic post-modernist style, were invited to work in the Paris conurbation, but they and French post-modernist architects were mostly relegated to the 'new towns', where they tried to make social housing look special. The Paris authorities did not wish to see large-scale architecture moving from gigantic and brutal modernism to another jarring style, however anti-modern and humane it claimed to be. Certain arguably

post-modernist features appeared in new, municipal buildings but these were mainly the product of the eclecticism which the neo-modern could tolerate.

By the early 1980s the authorities were beginning to take pride in their new, official architecture. In 1982, when the estates department of the City of Paris published a review of municipal architecture since 1977, Jacques Bardet, the architectural commentator, summed up the mood in his introduction:

> . . . the bureaucratic application of abstract, universal rules has made way for a willingness to take the particular character of each individual case into account, in terms of scale, location, surroundings and, ultimately, impact on the homogeneity of the district.[75]

In 1985, Jean-Michel Hoyet could still write in his preface to a survey of contemporary Parisian architecture:

> It is no longer the time for big urban reconstruction projects which remodel the very structure of the city. Indeed, on the rare occasions when such opportunities have presented themselves, they have been wasted. The Halles bear gloomy witness to this fact. In the French capital today, the key interventions are made on a district scale, and in this way they link up with the very essence of the organisation of the Parisian fabric.[76]

Although the spread of neo-modern design allowed some very striking facades to appear among the older houses of the city, the architectural impact of the later 1970s and the 1980s has to be set in the context of the revitalisation of the existing fabric. A move towards conversion and refurbishment, especially in the creation of new business premises, set in from around 1975, with developers and owners now stressing the traditional character and integrity of their premises. The removal of rent controls and the spread of co-ownership among the older buildings encouraged a big improvement of the residential stock, partly accompanied by gentrification (Figs 261–2). This revival extended even to some very degraded houses in the older districts, so the historic fabric of Paris received a new lease of life which postponed the threat of redevelopment. For the most part, therefore, the neo-modern,

*Pour construire l'avenir,
il faut savoir aussi rebâtir le passé.*

RENOVATEUR - INVESTISSEUR IMMOBILIER.

261 and 262 Property advertisements aimed at rich or business clients in 1991. The emphasis on rehabilitation reflects the building slump, Paris planning policies since the early 1960s, and a general respect for a reassuring past.

which was already a humane and unassuming style, sensitively used by Paris architects, was absorbed by an older Paris which was now in a better condition than for many decades. This happy compromise must be the envy of most of the world's great cities.

As the 1980s wore on, there was a growing emphasis on 'inserting' even large new buildings sensitively into established districts.[77] The largest, and in some ways the most representative, of these schemes was the new opera house of the Bastille which, despite its more distant origins, was a Mitterrand *grand projet*. The *grands projets*, however, require their own treatment.

## THE PARIS OF THE GRANDS PROJETS

The rejection of the more threatening aspects of modern architecture in the mid-1970s had implications for large public projects as well as for private buildings in ordinary streets. Immediately on his election to the presidency in 1974, Giscard d'Estaing reviewed the existing big schemes, especially with respect to towers. In some cases it was too late to make changes, but the president came down firmly against further tower projects, at any rate in central Paris.

Giscard d'Estaing's understanding of the beauty of Paris was clearly close to that of the conservationist and traditionalist interests which had been forming ranks since the late 1960s. However, he also distrusted the acquisitive, materialistic values which had been encouraged under De Gaulle and Pompidou. As a moderate, he wanted to reinforce the traditional French values of probity, thrift and generosity. Giscard d'Estaing's modest regime not surprisingly failed to generate new public projects which could have represented the alternative philosophy which the president offered to the French people. In fact, he failed to set his mark on France in a very difficult economic period. He served only one term, and in the presidential election of 1981 he was replaced by the long-running anti-Gaullist François Mitterrand, the Socialist leader.

After the failure of his early experiments in redistributive socialism, President Mitterrand adopted a practical stance based on achieving both economic efficiency for France, and a popular respect secured by rising living standards and world admiration for an independent French foreign policy. Although he was often accused by trade unionists and other Socialist and Communist politicians of pursuing bourgeois and contradictory policies, he was well in step with world political trends in the 1980s. By the middle of the decade his formula was working well and he came to be associated with the French spirit of the age, much like De Gaulle in the 1960s.

Mitterrand's attitude towards Paris improvements was complex. His socialist allegiance made him more favourable to public investment than Giscard had been. He attached great value to the city's cultural role, which he wanted to promote, not at the expense of commercial development, but alongside it. He believed that culture could enhance the life of the masses, particularly at a time when further redistribution of income and wealth was hard to envisage. Like a number of previous heads of state, he wanted to leave his personal mark on Paris, and his socialism did not prevent his identifying with the classic presidential mentors such as Louis XIV. Finally, he wanted to promote the international functions of the city so that it could become the effective capital of Europe as the integration of the European Community proceeded.

Mitterrand very quickly started work on what became known as his 'grands projets'. These were a number of new, existing or modified schemes which were scheduled for accelerated execution under the personal patronage of the president.[78] Several months of discussions and studies involving leading figures from the government and the municipality, and direct consultations between the president and the Gaullist mayor of Paris, Jacques Chirac, led to the announcement in March 1982 of eight major architectural and town planning schemes.[79] To these was effectively added the scheme for a museum of the nineteenth century in the old Gare d'Orsay, which dated from 1977. Gradually, other projects of architecture and urban reconstruction came to be associated with the 'grand projet' programme, producing a very impressive portfolio effort distributed mainly through central and eastern Paris, and at the Défense.

President Mitterrand played a personal part in the 'grands projets' which recalled the two Bonapartes. He had a general preference for modern design, but he did not attempt to impose a personal style, or to encourage a consensus style representing his era or his philosophy. In the design turmoil of the postmodernist 1980s he was, of course, wise not to do so. Instead, he sought to attract the best architects from France and abroad, sometimes through international competitions and sometimes by personal approaches. His free use of foreign architects caused a degree of concern among the Parisian intelligentsia, but his personal involvement clearly kept a closer control over them than in Pompidou's day.[80]

The new projects were so varied in location and function that each could usefully be allowed to generate its own architecture. Competitions were so frequent that two thousand architectural teams were estimated to be working world-wide on Parisian projects in the later 1980s.[81] At one extreme, the Tête-Défense project, well outside the city, permitted a gigantic, modernist symbolism of an almost outlandish character. At the other, the renewal of the hill of Sainte-Geneviève, perhaps the most picturesque district of the Latin Quarter, involved the renovation and conversion of existing buildings, and pedestrianisation, rather than extensive new building.

The competitors, and especially the foreigners, showed a much greater awareness of the Parisian context than they had during the iconoclastic years of the Halles and Beaubourg contests. Slick and jokey post-modernism and domineering, intrusive modernism rarely figured in the designs of these years. Instead, the 'neo-modernism' of glass, colour, space, light and elegant materials came to the fore, much as it did in the municipal projects and social housing built under Chirac's influence.

The new approach could be detected early on in a project which Mitterrand inherited from a notorious 'scandale' of the 1970s. The expensive reversal of plans for a meat market and abattoir at La Villette allowed the creation there of a huge cultural centre emphasising science, technology and music. After an international competition, a French architect, Bernard Tschumi, directed the project between 1982 and 1989. The generous,

canalside site, well away from the central areas, gave Tschumi free rein to create a formal but humane modernism based on the rectangular tradition of the exhibition hall. This elegant monumentalism, despite its dimensions, prompted a gigantic, modernistic architecture which managed to achieve an elegant environment which welcomed rather than threatened (Figs 263–4). Finally, the geometrical layout and the horizontal emphasis of the facades showed a respect for Parisian classicism which would emerge in other 'grands projets'.[82]

The year 1982 also saw what was claimed to be the resolution of the aesthetic problem of the Défense, within a presidential 'grand projet'. The development of the Défense had gone forward ever since the 'scandale' of 1972 which had exposed its aesthetic limitations. By the early 1980s the towers on the deck housed thousands of workers. The space below contained an important communications centre, including a major station on the express metro (RER), a massive bus terminus, and a commercial centre serving the office

263 Part of the Cité des Sciences, photographed in 1991.

workers and an extensive district of public and co-ownership housing nearby. The quality of the architecture nevertheless remained for the most part very poor. Glass and metal facades, some of them mirrored, were repetitive and monotonous, and various architectural sculptures at ground level merely reinforced the impression of an off-the-peg environment.

To counteract the weaknesses of the commercial scheme, the EPAD launched an international competition in 1982 for a building to occupy the outlying position, at the end of the deck, known as the Tête Défense. It was even more international than the norm, the brief being drawn up with the help of the International Union of Architects. One aim of the competition was to fill the arch of the Arc de Triomphe as seen from the Tuileries, in belated fulfilment of Pompidou's ambition, but most of the brief stressed communications technology and the chance to bring to life 'a modern district that expresses the functionalist tendencies of the 1960s'.

The competition was won by a Danish architect, the late Johan Otto von Spreckelsen, with a simple, open cube implying a further extension of the Triumphal Way to the west.[83] Building took place between 1985 and 1989. It was not accorded *'grand projet'* status at first because of the low standing of the Défense, but as it approached completion, public opinion swung in its favour and the authorities started to make a great fuss of it.[84] They even stopped calling it 'the cube' and hailed it as the Arch of the Défense (Fig. 265).

Popular admiration for this daring but banal structure (two office slabs with a lid on) strengthened the reviving modernist case in the later 1980s. However, as had always been intended, it made no impact on the historic areas of the city.

Some of Mitterrand's more imaginative schemes could provoke ribaldry in the popular press, which enjoyed more freedom than the mainly State-controlled television channels. Indeed, in 1986 the start of work on the Chinese-American architect I.M. Pei's glass pyramid design for the new museum entrance in the outer Louvre courtyard produced one of the most striking Paris headlines since 'J'accuse': 'Who does he think he is, Rameses II?.'[85] This wit was soon trumped by other newspapers with their constant use of the nickname 'Mitterramsès'.

265 The arch of the Défense, soon after its completion, in 1991.

These jokes tended to belittle Mitterrand's serious commitment to modernism. Trusting in his own artistic judgment, he came out in open support for the modern. There was not enough of it in Paris, he averred, and he intended his 'grands projets' to make up the deficit. Interviewed in 1984, he said that he especially liked pure form. He cited the 'cube' at the Défense and the pyramid at the Louvre, which had just been approved: 'Basically, I think I have rather classical tastes and I am attracted by pure, geometrical shapes.'[86] The key to Mitterrand's architecture was scale, location, form, efficiency and visual integration. The strength of the pyramid project rested herein. The president's allusion to classicism clearly reflected his knowledge of the neo-classical, geometrical projects of Ledoux and Boullée in the later eighteenth century. It also drew on the success of another, more obscure pyramid in the developing Bercy business district. This was the huge indoor sports hall of Paris-Bercy, built between 1980 and 1984 by Michel Andrault and Pierre Parat (Fig. 266). Its visible parts were designed as a pyramid and the playing area and seating were set into the ground deliberately to reduce its bulk. Only 30 metres (98 feet) high, its slopes were covered with grass to suggest integration with the surrounding park.[87]

The more famous pyramid at the Louvre by I.M. Pei was even more modest and retiring (Fig. 267). Built between 1984 and 1988, its dimensions were restricted and it was sheathed in glass, according to its architect, partly so that it would not blot out the view of the older facades around it. It had a very practical function as the canopy of a new, combined entrance to the Louvre museums. It nevertheless became a *cause célèbre* or '*scandale*' of unique proportions.

The trouble started in 1984, when the Pei design went before the Commission Supérieure des Monuments Historiques, which had the power to pronounce on all new schemes near national monuments. The plans were a complete surprise because, for once, there had been no competition and Pei, approached unofficially by a senior civil servant after a Delphic consultation of museum directors, had prepared his scheme in secret.[88] Although the votes of the civil servants gave it a majority in the commission, the independent members briefed the media with rare venom, having already, it is said, reduced Pei to tears during the meeting.[89] *Le Figaro* happily took up its familiar role as defender of the Parisian heritage. The resulting controversy passed through a number of lively stages until *Le Figaro* threw in the towel on the completion of the pyramid in 1988,

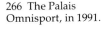

266 The Palais Omnisport, in 1991.

either to curry favour with the newly re-elected president or because the public rather liked the finished building.[90]

Although the controversy had at times looked like setting back the cause of modern architecture in Paris to where it had been under Giscard d'Estaing, so many condemnatory arguments were brought to bear that the result was often grotesque and embarrassing for Pei's many opponents. One cohort of critics claimed that the pyramid was a modernist insult to the city's heritage, while a completely different group asserted that it was poor modern architecture. The fact that the adjacent Louvre facades were no older than the Second Empire, and had not previously won much admiration in architectural textbooks, did not help the conservationist case.[91]

Nor did the understandable but atavistic efforts to caricature I.M. Pei as a monstrous or naive intruder carry as big a punch as they might have done before 1950. At full blast in the early months of its campaign, *Le Figaro* quoted a senior civil servant in state buildings as saying: 'I am surprised that they have brought in a Chinese architect from America to handle the development of the historic core of the capital of France.'[92] Pei's origins were confusing, however. Some critics seemed uncertain whether Pei's work was essentially 'chinoiserie' or 'Disney'. This did not stop some of them from railing not only against Pei but against the monstrous regiment of foreign architects which had descended on Paris since the day a victorious Richard Rogers and his pirate band had

swarmed on to a ministerial *bâteau-mouche* in jeans and tee-shirts to unaccustomed cries of 'Vivent les Anglais!' What these traditionalists did not realise, apparently, was that nearly every foreign architect who won a contract employed dozens of local assistants. Much as Garnier's use of an army of Beaux-Arts students in his Opéra atelier had spread his style world-wide, the great foreigners had recruited an army of Parisian apprentices who now had a career interest in modern design.

The core opposition to Pei and his works therefore came mainly from artistic conservatives such as the senior preservationist author, Yvan Christ. These people were poor judges of modern architecture. One suspects, moreover, that many Parisians did not place a high value on the Louvre extension and its courtyard, which magnified the defects of the original Perrault concept without generating compensating qualities.

Ultimately, perhaps, it was the approval of Jacques Chirac, the Gaullist mayor of Paris, that protected the Pei scheme. Chirac valued the *grands projets* and did not want the president to lose his enthusiasm for what were entirely utilitarian schemes. When Chirac was appointed prime minister for two eventful years in 1986, he did nothing to question these projects. The pyramid progressed more smoothly than did the Défense arch and some of the other schemes between 1986 and 1988, and when it was completed in the latter year the media quickly swung in its support. Their main theme now was the happy marriage of old and new, which had of course been Pei's objective all along.

Some of the other *grands projets*, such as the Institute of the Arab World, were completely unobtrusive in both design and dimensions.[93] Pascaline Cuvelier, writing in the ark of the Modern Movement, *L'Architecture d'Aujourd'hui*, in 1984, complained that modernity had been renounced, but she seemed unable to recognise that ethnic traditions were compatible with the neo-modern architecture now emerging in Paris.[94] However, the neo-modern was to be put to its sternest test with the new opera house of the Bastille.

267 The Louvre and the completed pyramid, in 1989.

The new opera house of the Bastille was one of the list of 'presidential' projects announced in 1982. It sprang from a ministerial review of Paris music facilities in 1981.[95] The Bastille site was not universally favoured by the authorities and the public but the choice seems to have reflected the ambition of a Socialist president to bring culture to the east.[96] It was intended to foster a mass interest in opera rather than to compete with the existing opera house in the West End.[97]

The presidential *'mission'* (task force) appointed by Mitterrand to direct the work was strongly in favour of holding an international exhibition to generate the design and the chief architect. The president had in any case implied a competition in his announcement of 9 March 1982. The lack of specialist opera-house architects precluded a closed consultation, and wide interest had already been aroused in the architectural world.[98]

To prevent errors and misunderstandings, a very detailed brief was published in December 1982. The jury had twenty members, and represented both a variety of architectural tendencies and the world of music. As in the other *grands projets*, the jury had to present a shortlist of entries to the president for his final choice. Care was taken to ensure that a single architectural tendency would not dominate the list and so narrow the president's choice.[99] Half the jury were French and there were no women members. The non-French members were, with two exceptions, of European origin. Clearly, some of the lessons of the Pompidou centre competition had been well learned.

The competition attracted numerous foreign entries among a huge total of 787. The winner was an independent Canadian architect, Carlos Ott, who was selected by the president from a shortlist of six. With so many foreign entries in an anonymous contest, the chances of selecting a non-French architect were clearly very high, but the days of maverick winners were long gone and Ott's solution belonged to a very numerous tendency among the entries. This group sought to combine modernism with insertion into the street network and building pattern, together with a strong presence on the Place de la Bastille, notwithstanding the cramped, tapering, angled site.[100] The planning elements of the brief, which advised *insertion* into what could claim in some respects to be a historic area, were largely the contribution of Pierre-Yves Ligen and the Atelier Parisien de l'Urbanisme, and Ligen had gone on to serve on the jury.[101] Ligen was a strong supporter of Ott's project in the final stages, and Jacques Chirac also favoured it.[102] Ott himself said that he had always approached the project as 'urban design', and as architecture for everyman (Figs 268–9).[103]

Following the implications of the brief and the long, irregular site, partially hemmed in by older buildings, Ott created a linear collection of linked buildings which, despite their massive scale, paid tribute to the irregular environment of the Faubourg Saint-Antoine. He retained (though not in his original submission) the facade of an eighteenth-century house which framed the main entrance, and rebuilt the entire interior and roof. The glass and ceramic sheathing which clad the auditorium building on the Place de la Bastille was certainly not in keeping with the other frontage buildings, but these were so disparate, and so widely dispersed around the *place*, that no integration was possible. Instead, Ott gave the whole exterior surface, including the glass, a light green hue which matched the weathered copper of the Colonne de Juillet. This effect, which varied according to the light, produced a constantly changing relationship between the two great popular symbols of what had long been the most disappointing urban space in Paris.

268 Planned insertion of Ott's opera house into the Bastille district.

195

The main entrance was a problem on such an awkward site, but Ott's solution was no worse than most of the others which adopted his interpretation of the brief. The simple bulk of the auditorium with its curved lines and black entrance gantry recalled the stern of a docked car ferry, and many Parisian critics regretted what they saw as a lack of monumentality. The aim of the design, however, was to suggest that opera was an experience of quality which ordinary people could enjoy without paying for frills and pretentiousness. The total effect, including the elegant, Japanese-inspired interior, the emphasis on simple, durable materials of quality, and the succession of workshops, offices and practice suites behind the auditorium, conveyed that point very well. Indeed, Christian Dupavillon, former assistant of the Minister of Culture, Jack Lang, wrote in *Monuments Historiques* in 1984 that the new opera house, contrasting with the insular monumentality of Garnier's building of 1861, could be seen as inaugurating a new generation of urban monuments.[104] Derided though it currently is, Ott's opera

house may yet come to be seen as the achievement of the age, the epitome of a Parisian, neo-modern architecture.

EPILOGUE: HOPES, DOUBTS AND COMPROMISES

The mayor of Paris, Jacques Chirac, always presented himself as the stout defender of Parisian interests. The city's subdued role within the regional growth strategy was so much at variance with historical tradition that Chirac was bound to question it. One of the ways in which he did so was to order the preparation of a new land use plan to stimulate development, notably of offices. On 25 November 1985 the city council approved Chirac's proposal for the preparation of a new plan, to be ready in two and a half years. Chirac described the 1974 plan as a '*carcan*' (iron collar) which had stifled the building of offices and luxury apartments. Since the 1960s the office building rate had dropped by 75 per cent, and that of luxury flats by 90 per cent. The target was to raise the plot ratio back to 3.5 throughout Paris.

269 Ott vindicated: a glimpse of a new monumental architecture for historic Paris.

Chirac even wanted to amend the laws of 1917 and 1930 on the protection of historic sites and monuments.[105] Little came of these efforts, however, partly because Paris could not be allowed to divert from the regional strategy.

As a firm advocate of new building in Paris, Chirac was no rigid conservationist or pasticheur. In the later 1980s, Paris moved away from the caution of the 1970s towards a more energetic form of redevelopment. This was the result, as the APUR perceived it, of competition between the world's major cities and a 'raising of the stakes'. On the other hand, the mayor valued the Parisian environment and sought to recreate it in new schemes. When, in June 1990, the city council approved a redevelopment plan for 'Seine rive gauche', a riverside strip of 130 hectares running south-east from the Gare d'Austerlitz, Chirac introduced it to the public as a human scheme which would enhance the city's heritage:

> Paris is changing. Every day, its extraordinary architectural heritage of new monuments [sic] is enriched. New building sites are opened up. In this great transformation of our day, Paris has a duty to preserve its essential [quality]. Paris is the most human of the great capitals, and this is what distinguishes it from the world's other great cities. I hope that for a long time to come the man in the street will be able to say, like George Sand: 'I know no other city where it is more pleasant to stroll about with one's dreams.' To preserve a certain quality of life is an absolute priority. This is why I wanted the 'Seine rive gauche' project, with its residential blocks on the Seine frontage, to give priority to conviviality.'[106]

This emphasis on humanity, harmony, the city's traditional qualities and participation in a renewed, balanced region and a nascent Europe ran through the whole of Chirac's statement. An alliance of 'tradition and modernism' was how he summed it up.[107] The rhetoric took on a life of its own at times, but the objective was clear enough, and was confirmed by the plans and drawings published by the APUR.[108] Equally significant was the decision to proceed with the reconstruction of an area which had long been one of the most remote in the city, a forgotten zone of river wharves and railway yards, the most neglected part of a neglected XIIIe *arrondissement*. This strip of unknown Paris was now to be incorporated into the city of tradition and modernity. A new university and national library, together with artists' studios, no less, would combine with commercial offices and new housing to produce an 'extension of the Latin Quarter'.[109] Apart from the four one hundred-metre (325 feet) towers of the new national library, no high-rise construction was planned – a strong contrast, this, to the modernist Front-de-Seine scheme for luxury housing and prestige offices in the 1960s. Instead, 'Seine rive gauche' was to become part of the ultra-successful tertiary and quaternary Paris set in a human environment, designated by the authorities as the model of the city's future in a prosperous and integrated Europe.

Much was made of the sector's location within Paris, yet in contact with the suburbs. Although the character of the buildings was merely outlined, to concede as much initiative as possible to private interests bidding for sites, overall densities were fixed at 'Parisian' rather than suburban levels to counteract the decentralising tendencies affecting most large cities. As François Grether, of the APUR, summed it up: '"Seine rive gauche" must offer contemporary solutions which can act as markers, but they must also extend and renew the long-run logic of the development of Paris.'[110] The implications of this formula for design and architecture were that a fabric of traditional mass and scale would be created, whatever the detail of the designs adopted. The four towers of the national library were an exception, but the building fell into the 'unique and unrepeatable' public monument category which allowed it special latitude and would, in theory, spare it criticism.

As a special project, the library allowed the winner of the design competition in 1989, Dominique Perrault, to make an independent statement.[111] The four towers were a practical response to the problems of housing millions of books on a restricted site. They could have been housed underground, as at London's new British Library, but Perrault preferred a landmark approach which, in view of the remote location of the district, conformed to the strategy for integrating the area into central Paris. Perrault's glass towers, like

270 Modernist icons. This dazzling fresco in the Rue Dussoubs was painted on an exposed party wall in 1987. Called *'la ville imaginaire'*, it was commissioned by the City of Paris, and shows exemplary buildings by Parisian rationalists and modernists since the eighteenth century. Visible in the foreground is the Sauvage pyramid project. This fresco reflects the revival of interest in modern architecture at the Hôtel de Ville in the early 1980s. The only graffiti, in 1991, was *'Sortir des villes.'*

271 Chemetov rampant: the Finance Ministry from its least flattering angle.

most of the winning entries, were modernistic. Ironically, however, in an international field of over two hundred entries, towers were few and far between and Perrault's solution of a low podium, depressed inner court and free-standing towers at the corners was unique and among the boldest to be submitted:[112]

So I proposed to construct upwards [Perrault was quoted as saying]. Constructing upwards offers particular virtues, particular qualities. It allows the building to create a place for itself on the city skyline. . . . The towers will show you where to find the library, they will make it a landmark.[113]

This was, of course, the rhetoric of the 1960s, but it was tempered in practice by the proposed glass casing of the towers which, here as at Pei's pyramid, was a symbol of modesty as well as of modernism.

Indeed, this combination of modesty, modernism and culture, more than in any other new building of its day, marked the readmission of modern architecture into the Parisian canon (Fig. 270). That the young architect of the library should be the namesake of a leading architect of the Grand Siècle was a happy coincidence. More important, the design philosophy of the new modernism could now be seen to incorporate the Bastille opera house, and Henri Gaudin's Paris archives building (1990), on the very edge of the city at the Porte des Lilas.[114] It also embraced earlier designs such as many of the smaller municipal buildings completed in the 1980s.

In contrast, Paul Chemetov's new Finance Ministry headquarters at Bercy recalled some of the domineering and inhuman modernism of the 1960s (Fig. 271). A competition in 1982/3 brought Chemetov back to full favour but apart from the huge, internal atria which were much admired, the building was a classic 'Ministry of Fear' leavened only by enlarged versions of classical Paris forms and proportions. The use of squares and rectangles in numerous dimensions echoed Ott's work at the opera house and suggested a link with Richard Neutra's humanist style, but the endless walkways over a congested spine road with parallel slabs and towers recalled some of the modernist concepts of the 1920s which Le Corbusier had ridiculed.[115] It also had echoes of London's post-war 'street of the future', London Wall, whose success alone had ensured that it was never repeated.

While Parisian public architecture succeeded in reintegrating modernism in the 1980s, particularly in the form of its distinctive neo-modernist approach, post-modernism continued to be kept at arm's length (Figs 272–3). With post-modernism in chronic decline by 1990,[116] there seemed to be little further danger of its appearance in the historic parts of the city. In this perspective, a restrained modernism appeared to be no longer a threat to traditional Paris, at any rate now that sensitive planning excluded it from historic areas and views in the old core (Fig. 274).

In the later 1980s and early 1990s, the pages of the leading modernist journal, *L'Architecture d'Aujourd'hui*, reflected an openness to, and respect for, international architecture which epitomised the incorporation of French architecture, and French architects, into a world debate. Strong links with the worlds of culture, art and social science were visible. Here, as in Paris itself, a combination of originality and maturity could be seen. It looked as though tradition and modernity were at last being reconciled in the world's most creative city.

Any study of history eventually encounters a present which proves intractable to historical analysis. To predict the future would be foolhardy. What this book has suggested, nevertheless, is the immense strength of heritage and tradition in Parisian architecture. The modernist challenge of the 1960s, so indifferent to Parisian forms, was beaten off, yet modernism lives on outside the protected historic areas in a more sensitive, or neo-modern, form. Meanwhile, Paris never adopted the extremes of postmodernism essayed in the 'new towns', or in the United States. The importance of scale, location and surface treatment now seem well understood in Paris. As our era itself recedes into history, it will doubtless take its place within the continuum which this book has sought to discern and explain. Whatever the period, the architect or the style, we can reasonably expect that nearly all we and our descendants see in Paris will be, above everything, *Parisian* architecture.

272 *Top*, hotel complex at Bercy, recently completed when photographed in 1991: international architecture in a remote district of the city.

274 *Left*, a touch of colour against a historic monochrome, at the corner of the Rue des Ecouffes and the Rue du Roi-de-Sicile. Colour contrasts are a strong feature of Parisian neo-modern, but in the historic areas they are required to adopt a modest role.

273 *Centre*, an elegant example of Parisian conforming neo-modern residential design, *c.* 1990, on the Avenue Jean-Jaurès.

# 10 CONTINUITY IN PARIS ARCHITECTURE: THE DYNAMICS OF A UNIQUE PHENOMENON

We have travelled through nearly two thousand years in the architectural history of what, many would say, is the most beautiful city in the world. We have looked especially carefully at the five hundred years since the Renaissance. This latter part of the story has been distinguished above all by continuity, with a persistent respect for the classical principles of design restored by the Renaissance, or at least for a Parisian building tradition based on customary forms, proportions and materials. So far, however, no general explanation has been attempted.

The fabric of a city is the product of demand. At least four-fifths of that fabric is residential, the product of a basic demand for shelter. The market mechanisms of building were complex even in the Middle Ages, and their products were increasingly regulated by authority, but they ensured that nearly all urban building responded to real needs, and did not exceed the resources available to satisfy those needs. In this sense city building proceeded on rational lines even in primitive times, and the resulting forms reflected the society of the city.

All developed urban land needed to be accessible to pedestrians and, where possible, to wheeled vehicles. The resulting network of thoroughfares marked out islands of land, or street blocks, on which building could occur. From as early as the Middle Ages, the streets were usually in the public domain, partly because they could not bear a rent. A potential conflict was created in this way between the public street and the private land of the blocks. The private sites tended to infringe on the streets, reducing them in some cases to narrow alleys, and accentuating the curves, angles and projections inherited from their original establishment. Even the rectilinear streets laid out in Roman times suffered later from these distortions.

The area of the street was coveted by the owners or tenants of individual properties because the street frontage was the most valuable part of the site. Medieval town creation proceeded in most cases through the creation of urban plots by a landowner in return for rent. These plots, known to historians as 'burgage plots' because their burgess tenants were allowed a non-servile tenure, were the product of the demands of urban trade within a low-level economy. Because the street or the marketplace were the main locus of trade, competition for street frontage space was acute. The landowners therefore offered sites with very narrow frontages, often permitting a structure of no more than one or two bays. Behind, where the land was much less valuable, they offered considerable depth, usually creating a large area for cultivation. Clearly, the great depth was a function of the narrow frontage. This site layout contrasted with the planned cities of ancient Rome, with their gridiron streets and compact blocks divided into sites of nearly square proportions.

The contrast between the crowded street frontage and the remote depths of the burgage plots was accentuated as the towns grew and their trading activity expanded until the fourteenth century. Cultivation of the inner areas became less crucial, but competition for space on the street frontage increased. The result was taller building, jettying of upper storeys over the street, and encroachment on the street at times of reconstruction, for instance after the fires which were so common in medieval towns. The resulting frontages threatened to enclose or choke the street, undermining the trading function of the town and creating a threat to public order.

Urban authorities began to react to this threat as early as the later Middle Ages, beginning in northern Italy. Concern increased in the sixteenth century when, with population rising again, much rebuilding was undertaken throughout Europe in more robust materials. In Paris, by far the largest city in Europe, building congestion was at a peak. It was faced, however, by the French Crown assisted by a puppet, semi-municipal administration. With the Paris street system legally the property of the Crown, powerful intervention was possible. A series of royal edicts, which we should not assume to have been ineffective, culminated in Henri IV's regulations of 1607 which allowed the systematic definition and defence of building lines. This and later enactments would permit the regularisation of the Paris street while retaining the continuous frontage of buildings. This corridor, straightened and provided with a regular width, would become an essential component of the Paris cityscape.

In medieval northern Europe, most towns were largely composed of narrow, burgage plots, but in Paris the site layout was complicated by the numerous residences of the royal family and the aristocracy. These were built on larger, wider sites, and they were often arranged around interior courtyards. Much the same was true of monastic buildings, which were also very common in Paris. Only the smallest of these buildings focused on a single, narrow street frontage like those of the burgess houses. They were partially or completely surrounded by their own walls, often occupying entire street blocks. However spacious their interior buildings and courts, their exterior limits often had at least the appearance of fortification. With no interest in the street as a place of meeting or exchange, they were oriented inwards, towards the centre of their sites. By the end of the Middle Ages these buildings, though more common in some districts than others, formed part of a dual townscape in which clusters of burgess houses were interspersed by the fortified frontages of the elite, with more comfortable residential buildings often visible behind.

The townscape of medieval Paris thus expressed a second conflict, between the spacious homes of the unproductive royalty, aristocracy and priesthood on the one hand, and the huddled houses of the trading and artisanal classes on the other. As the city grew, and aristocratic building moved to new areas of fashion, some of the older sites of the elite were redeveloped with burgage plots. The reverse, however, was rarely the case,

and older districts like the Halles became more densely constructed. Even in the Halles, however, burgess houses and *hôtels* still mingled, and by the sixteenth century there was no sense of a single coherent, architectural treatment other than the general impression of enclosure created by the street. There was as yet no Parisian architecture, no unified aesthetic, no clear style standing out from other large, medieval cities. Nor were there specialised architects, distinct from the masons and master masons who built most secular buildings. Only the churches drew on the services of architects, but their designs stood out from the rest of the city more sharply than any other building type.

It was in the sixteenth century, however, that Paris began to move towards the classical design model which has become its hallmark (Figs 275, 276). It was a time of economic renewal for Europe after the disruptions of the fourteenth and fifteenth centuries. Trade was boosted by the American discoveries and growing bullion imports through Spain. Wheeled vehicles probably multiplied in the streets. The activities of royal government increased and its administration was largely located in Paris, notwithstanding the intermittent royal interest in provincial residence along the Loire, and at Fontainebleau. The city thus became a growing centre of administrators, lawyers and other professionals. The university expanded, while the Church resisted the rise of Protestantism and took part in the costly work of the Counter-Reformation.

The resulting building boom coincided with the main impact of the Renaissance in northern Europe. From the early sixteenth century a completely new architecture, derived from that of the Ancient world and developed in Italy since the later fifteenth century, was available in France. By the later part of the century it had acquired an urban design dimension. This expansion was possible because theorists, practitioners and clients saw classical design as a comprehensive system within which designed objects from a brooch at one extreme to an entire city at the other could conform to common design principles. This revolutionary aspiration was unprecedented in human history, but once implanted into the European psyche it could emerge once again, as it would for instance in the Modern Movement in architecture in the

early twentieth century, when the Bauhaus in Germany and Le Corbusier and his school in Paris created comprehensive design systems for the industrial age.

Completely new systems are always expensive to introduce and in Paris only the Crown, the aristocracy and the Church could commission examples of the new design. New palaces, mansions and churches, or extensions of these, were the main result. Not until the beginning of the seventeenth century did Henri IV, the most important modernising king in the history of Paris, extend the system to the common people by commissioning piazzas and planning symmetrical, perspective streets. Their harmonious frontages could not only embellish the dwellings of the middle classes, but they could also transform the townscape rather than merely interrupt, dominate or contrast with the medieval vernacular as Renaissance *hôtels* tended to do. Moreover, this potential was progressive and cumulative, because the essence of classical design principles was that they did not change either through time or through space.

The building of piazzas and streets depended at first on a massive royal commitment. After the assassination of Henri IV in 1610 the Crown withdrew from the more expensive aspects of Parisian improvement. By now, however, the aristocracy had fully adopted the classical style, and during the seventeenth century new *hôtels* multiplied throughout the city, but especially in the newly fashionable *faubourgs* of Saint-Germain and Saint-Honoré. In response to royal and noble demand for buildings in the classical style, the architectural profession had expanded, and from the early seventeenth century the new mansions were built by men describing themselves as architects rather than by master masons. More closely in touch with Italian classicism, yet aware of French traditions and of royal interest in a national style, they jointly created a distinct appearance for aristocratic residence which was both classical and Parisian.

The seventeenth century saw the emergence of a group of prolific Paris architects whose work was widely respected and emulated by others. The archetype was François Mansart (1598–1666), who built a wide range of buildings including mansions and churches and whose style was both personal yet acceptable to many of his peers. Many of his solutions to design and structural problems were adopted by others. From 1673 the drive and coherence of the classical style were reinforced by the royal creation of an academy of architecture which trained and advised architects. Although the main intention was to help royal architects to design in the classical mode while maintaining a French identity, the academy, which predictably was located in Paris, was a meeting-point and information exchange from which the corps of Paris *hôtel* architects probably benefited more than any other group.

By the end of the seventeenth century the accumulating mansions and churches in the classical style were numerous enough to give the impression of a new city of the elite growing up inside the old one. The aristocratic clients clearly provided a brief for the architect in general terms, for instance by specifying the size of major rooms, but there is little sign that that they tried to determine stylistic features. Of course, in classical archi-

tecture they did not need to. The key was the initial choice of architect.

However impressive and coherent the new mansion architecture, its influence was spreading only gradually to the buildings of the middle classes by the end of the seventeenth century. There was some progress in piazza development, and Henri IV's regulations on building lines of 1607, together with a permanent body of inspectors, provided a basis for cumulative efforts to regularise the building frontages. Far more important, however, than public controls was the growth of a fashionable design mode for the facades of burgess houses and the smaller mansions. This has come to be known as *architecture d'accompagnement*, a simple style designed to set off the more striking features of adjacent *hôtels*. Horizontal ribs often separated the storeys, and the architects tried to align them from house to house. The dimensions of openings varied little, and when they were clad in stucco, as in most cases, the plasterers added ground limestone to the mixture to produce

275 and 276  The timeless classical tradition in Parisian care: De Machy's portrayal of the foundation stone ceremony of the Eglise Sainte-Geneviève in 1755, for which a full-size painting of the portico was erected on a scaffolding; and a painting of the Rue Royale frontage of the Madeleine in 1991, hiding an unsightly restoration project.

a masonry-like appearance which merged with nearby stone structures.

By the eighteenth century this modest treatment had spread to ordinary houses even at locations where there were no mansions or churches to emulate. Timber framing, already in decline in the seventeenth century, was now very rare, and new frontages increasingly conformed to the masonry-like norm. With gables now banned on new houses, most facades were rectangular in outline, and their multiplication along the street tended to produce a strip aesthetic which pointed towards the cellular urban palazzo effect which had begun to emerge in terraced houses on the aristocratic estates of the West End of London, and in the Palladian spa of Bath.

Crude though many of these facades were, they echoed some of the basic components of the classical style. Their designers, whether architects or masons, clearly had no wish to break away from convention in a city which was still dominated by the aristocracy. Many professionals were clients of the aristocracy and lived in houses built or purchased by the aristocracy near their mansions. The Church also built or owned many residential properties, and encouraged a similar conformism. By the middle of the eighteenth century, however, conformism was being further reinforced by a new factor, mass demand.

So crowded was Paris, and so poor the bulk of its people, that most households had been accustomed to live in one, or at the most two, rooms since the Middle Ages. Nothing changed in this in the eighteenth century, and by 1750 speculators were building specially designed apartment houses for single-person and other small households from the middle classes. This was a competitive part of the rental sector, and construction costs were minimised. Facades were austere, and the entrances were almost invisible. The early examples were successful, and apartment houses expanded as a proportion of new Paris building. The austerity, simplicity and homogeneity were rarely questioned because in large rental houses any individualistic or exotic design was likely to discourage tenants. The owners of apartment houses were unwilling to commission divergences from the norm and the resulting pattern would not greatly change until the twentieth century.

The success of the apartment house spread a simplified version of the classical aesthetic to the very limits of Paris during the nineteenth century. Rigid building regulations in 1783/4, 1823 and 1859 produced a further standardisation of design, and Haussmann's improvement programme created a new street-and-plot framework based self-consciously on Renaissance principles of urban design. Mass building in the 1850s and 1860s produced a basic apartment house type which altered only slowly after 1870. The majority of Parisian architects worked on hordes of the world's most repetitive yet elegant apartment houses, while the cleverest graduates of the Ecole des Beaux-Arts, in almost continuous existence since 1673, developed a classical monumental style for a Second Empire which looked backwards as well as forwards. Classicism thus came to cover the full range, from Garnier's opera house to the anonymous apartment house on a new sidestreet. It was not by chance that this universal, almost unstoppable, design momentum was based on classical principles, for classicism had sought universal application ever since the Renaissance. At any rate, few questioned the result during the Second Empire.

By the later nineteenth century the Parisian classical design system was so firmly implanted that alternatives had little chance to establish themselves. Advocates of the Gothic made little headway in mid-century. No clear 'battle of the styles' ever took place, except in the sense that hôtel architects played with historic variants of the French classical style from around 1850. Art Nouveau was too startling a challenge, and it burned itself out in less than ten years. The distinctively French 'railway' or 'industrial' style, encouraged by Viollet-le-Duc, was restricted to commercial buildings and sidestreets. Even the picturesque variants encouraged by the City of Paris itself in 1902 flourished only briefly, while a great deal of hindsight is needed to detect any rise of modernism before 1914.

It is clear that industrialism had reinforced rather than undermined the Parisian classical design system. No obvious evolution towards modernism can be perceived in Paris, and its emergence after 1914 is difficult to explain except in terms of the unprecedented effects of the First World War and the emergence of an international community of architecture. The arrival of foreign architects as refugees or as contributors to the reconstruction programme, and the resulting closer links with German modernism, helped create a new climate. So did the great decline in the production of private apartment blocks, which allowed the varied preferences of villa owners and their architects to generate an entertaining 'battle of the styles' in the 1920s. Meanwhile, with most mass housing built in the public sector, much of it outside Paris, architects began to create an artisanal style which developed into a striking modernism in the Paris 'garden cities' of the 1930s. Private apartment houses, too, adopted modernistic styles in the 1930s, while Art Deco and the curious expressionist or picturesque modernism of the 1920s faded away. However, so little was built in the 1930s during the French defence of an overvalued franc, followed by rearmament, that clear trends were hard to discern. In any case, many of the modernists, from Le Corbusier to Roux-Spitz, declared their allegiance to Parisian aesthetic traditions, and neo-classicism was becoming a favoured style for public buildings in the later 1930s.

After the Second World War the massive European reconstruction task again brought modern architecture to the fore as the most efficient means of rapid construction. Refugee architects from Germany had helped boost modernism in the USA, Europe's main source of repair funds. In Paris, no building had been done since 1940, and Vichy advocacy of a historicist-classicist-popular architecture had been completely discredited, despite its links with the past. Consequently, when building began again in the mid-1950s in the form of housing estates and prestige buildings such as the UNESCO headquarters, modernism was widely welcomed as a sign of better times, and a better-equipped environment, to come. In any case, most of these new buildings were outside the centre of Paris, or in the suburbs, and they did not involve demolition. Architectural training programmes, even at the Ecole des Beaux-Arts, began to take account of modern design and construction methods, and specialists in reinforced concrete and prefabrication began to practise in Paris in greater numbers. When De Gaulle began his efforts to modernise France in 1958, a variety of new forms and methods was encouraged and it appeared that the classical tradition had at last ceded its place to the modern.

In the event, this clear prospect was clouded by the reaction of a Parisian public wedded to a classical townscape and familiar, vernacular scenes. The central, regional and local authorities, driven by a national programme of change, had gone out of their way to commission or tolerate a number of large, modern buildings, together with a new building code. From the end of the 1960s, the Montparnasse tower, followed by the Défense towers, became architectural *scandales* whose impact the government could not ignore. With a change of president in 1974 a massive reaction took place in favour of tradition. In a world climate of anti-modernism linked to the oil crisis of the mid-1970s, Paris became once again a paragon of architectural virtue, while shortage of credit produced a return to repairs and refurbishment throughout the building stock.

Although this was a welcome respite to many, the building slump could not be allowed to persist, and an economic recovery from the early 1980s boosted construction investment and revived the architectural issue. Fortuitously, Mayor Chirac and President Mitterrand, despite their political differences, had an interest in good, modern architecture. Both recognised, however, that modern buildings needed to be of a high quality, varied in appearance, and conforming in scale, colour and treatment to traditional Paris. Chirac's programme of municipal buildings, and the presidential *grands projets*, were carefully thought out in this respect. Using many of the able and versatile architects produced by the Ecole des Beaux-Arts since its reform in 1968, they generated a 'neo-modern' form of architecture which could be confidently set in the historic environment of the city. Meanwhile, out-and-out 'post-modernism' was largely limited to the new towns, and pastiche was rarely essayed. So this architectural history of a city ends with modernism firmly established in Paris, yet without disturbing the context of a unique, classical tradition. Now, as in the past, Paris creates its own architecture.

The classical tradition has been at the heart of this architectural history of Paris (Figs 275–6). It has been sustained above all by public buildings. The Crown adopted it in the sixteenth century as a style of power and wealth imported from the most advanced region of Europe, Italy. In the seventeenth century Louis XIV emphasised its national and imperial character, and deference to Italy was dropped. An Absolutist monarchy required a deferential and conformist court, and the nobles were happy to build their Parisian and provincial homes in the royal style. Colbert's Academy of Architecture maintained the identity of the national style with the participation of the architects. From the 1670s, royal, aristocratic and public buildings all conformed to the classical tradition yet rigidity was avoided. Disciplined as it was, the tradition was broad and flexible enough to incorporate stylistic variants such as the baroque, the rococo and the neoclassical.

The survival of the classical tradition after 1789 was mainly due to the continuity of the French State. Although the aristocracy survived the Revolution they were no longer rich enough to build on the old scale. The succession of insecure regimes which stretched from the 1790s to 1870 also lacked funds, but they represented the national identity of France. They made sure that all public building and design held to the classical tradition. Even Napoleon III, who pushed forward the industrialisation of France in partial emulation of the British Industrial Revolution, encouraged the classical style. Anything else might have further exposed the weakness of rulers whose knell had tolled back in 1789.

If state architecture was to some degree a theatrical set after 1789, how did the middle classes respond? Industrial buildings began to make their way towards a new utilitarianism from about 1840, but there were few of these in Paris. Residential buildings, having evolved as an *architecture d'accompagnement* before 1789 in deference to a royal and noble townscape, continued to conform in the nineteenth century. They no longer deferred to any great extent to the houses of the rich and powerful, for these were less in evidence. What now came to the fore was the apartment house, developed from around 1750 for single tenants and small families, but multiplying in the growing Paris of the 1800s as the standard home of the middle classes. Increasingly regulated by the authorities on public health grounds, apartment houses developed a conformist architecture to promote easy letting to a variety of tenants. Architects, underemployed in the absence of noble patronage, switched to apartment houses and gave them all the elegance they could within the classical mode. They knew that houses could be grouped in palazzi and they had the skills to produce this effect. The classical townscape of massed apartment houses reached its apogee under the Second Empire. Paris, capital of the French Industrial Revolution, achieved a sixteenth-century ideal.

This extraordinary achievement established the industrial version of the classical ideal on a very firm basis. Commercial architecture, mainly in the form of department stores and wholesalers, showed signs of independence after 1870, but it was not until the 1920s that a self-conscious, didactic 'Modern Movement in architecture' made its appearance in Paris, on paper as well as in reality. The Modern Movement was an attempt to replace both Renaissance design and industrial squalor by an architecture of the Machine Age. Parisian classicism resisted, incorporating many 'modern' architects into a compromise apartment house architecture which valued its roots. Modern architecture did not break through until the 1960s when the State promoted it. This was a decisive intervention. Just as François Ier, Henri IV and Louis XIV had transformed Paris by promoting classical architecture, De Gaulle and Pompidou encouraged the Modern Movement. Their goal was one of modernisation, just like that of their royal predecessors.

With the State again active in Parisian architecture for the first time since the Second Empire, modern buildings began to change the city. One thing was different, however. France was now a democracy and in the 1970s a swing of opinion against Gaullism coincided with the growth of opposition to new, modern architecture in Paris. From 1974, residential building reverted to a more conformist style, self-effacing or modern in a more harmonious way. Public building, from the early 1980s, sought a modernism capable of complementing the Parisian tradition. So our story ends, as it began in the sixteenth century, with the intervention of the State. Yet whereas the first initiative swept medieval Paris aside, the second has ultimately deferred to classical Paris.

# Notes

PREFACE

1 Introductory text in D. Leborgne (ed.), *Les Champs-Elysées et leur quartier*, Paris: Délégation à l'Action Artistique de la Ville de Paris, 1988, p. 5.

CHAPTER ONE: ARCHITECTURE AND THE CAPITAL CITY

1 Among the important exceptions to this generalisation are: D. Olsen, *The City as a Work of Art: London, Paris, Vienna*, New Haven and London: Yale University Press, 1986; M. Girouard, *Cities and People: A Social and Architectural History*, New Haven and London: Yale University Press, 1985; M. Girouard, *The English Town*, New Haven and London: Yale University Press, 1990; A. Clifton-Taylor, *Six English Towns*, London: BBC Publications, 1978; A. King (ed.), *Buildings and Society: Essays on the Social Development of the Built Environment*, London: Routledge and Kegan Paul, 1980; E. Relph, *The Modern Urban Landscape*, Beckenham: Croom Helm, 1987. Among the specifically Parisian studies dealing with the whole townscape, and with architectural genesis, are A. Chastel, F. Boudon *et al.*, *Système de l'architecture urbaine: le quartier des Halles à Paris*, Paris: Editions du CNRS, 1977; B. Rouleau, *Villages et faubourgs de l'ancien Paris: histoire d'un espace urbain*, Paris: Seuil, 1985.
2 See e.g. A. Clifton-Taylor, *Six English Towns*, and its sequel, *Six More English Towns*, London: BBC, 1981.
3 See e.g. E. Relph, *The Modern Urban Landscape*, Beckenham: Croom Helm, 1987.

CHAPTER TWO: PARIS AT THE DAWN OF THE RENAISSANCE

1 The best survey of the physical form and architecture of Lutetia, including the latest archaeological evidence, is *Lutèce: Paris de César à Clovis*, Paris: Musée Carnavalet, 1985.
2 For a recent summary of the history of pre-Renaissance Paris, see M. le Clère (ed.), *Paris de la préhistoire à nos jours*, Saint-Jean-d'Angély: Editions Bordessoules, 1985, pp. 188–221.
3 S. Roux, 'La construction courante à Paris, du milieu du XIVe siècle à la fin du XVe siècle', in *La construction au moyen âge: histoire et archéologie*, Paris: Les Belles Lettres, 1973, pp. 176–7.
4 P. and M.-L. Biver, *Abbayes, monastères et couvents de Paris des origines à la fin du XVIIIe siècle*, Paris: Editions d'Histoire et d'Art, 1970.
5 D. Thomson, *Renaissance Paris: Architecture and Growth, 1475–1600*, London: Zwemmer, 1984, pp. 64–7.
6 *Ibid.*, pp. 39–43.
7 See J. Favier, *Paris au XVe siècle, 1380–1500*, Paris: Hachette, 1974, pp. 13–51.
8 Histoire Générale de Paris, *Registres des délibérations du Bureau de la Ville de Paris, 1499–1614*, Paris: Imprimerie Nationale, 1883–, vol. 1, p. 1, 25 October 1499.
9 J.-P. Babelon, *Paris au XVIe siècle*, Paris: Hachette, 1986, p. 111.
10 Histoire générale de Paris, *Registres des délibérations*, vol. 1, pp. 5–6, 23 November 1499.
11 Babelon, *Paris*, p. 116.
12 P. Lavedan, *Histoire de l'urbanisme*, Paris: Henri Laurens, 1959, vol. 2, p. 139.
13 See examples in Babelon, *Paris*, pp. 333–41; A. Chastel, F. Boudon *et al.*, *Système de l'architecture urbaine: le quartier des Halles à Paris*, Paris: Editions du CNRS, 1977, p. 361.
14 J.-M. Pérouse de Montclos, *Histoire de l'architecture française de la Renaissance à la Révolution*, Paris: Mengès, 1989, p. 80.
15 D. Thomson, *Renaissance Paris: Architecture and Growth, 1475–1600*, London: Zwemmer, 1984, pp. 105–12.
16 Pérouse de Montclos, *Histoire*, p. 81.
17 See S. Serlio, 'Sesto libro'. The originals are held by the Avery Library of Columbia University, New York City.
18 M.N. Rosenfeld, *Sebastiano Serlio on Domestic Architecture*, Cambridge, Mass.: MIT Press, 1978, p. 11.
19 *Ibid.*, p. 12.
20 See J. Androuet du Cerceau, *Livre d'architecture*, Paris: B. Prévost, 1559.
21 See e.g. Thomson, *Renaissance Paris*, p. 18.
22 *Ibid.*, pp. 64–7.
23 *Ibid.*, especially pp. 18, 129–36, 192–3.
24 D. Thomson (introduction), in J. Androuet du Cerceau, *Les plus excellents bastiments de France*, Paris: Sand et Conti, 1988, p. 10.
25 D. Thomson, *Renaissance Paris: Architecture and Growth, 1475–1600*, London: Zwemmer, 1984, especially pp. 18, 192–3.
26 R. Coope, *Salomon de Brosse and the Development of the Classical Style in French Architecture from 1565 to 1630*, London: A. Zwemmer, 1972, pp. 56–7.
27 Thomson, *Renaissance Paris*, pp. 20–1.
28 *Ibid.*, pp. 129–32.
29 *Ibid.*, especially pp. 192–3.
30 *Ibid.*, pp. 36–7.
31 See *La Bibliothèque Historique de la Ville de Paris*, Paris: Bibliothèque Historique de la Ville de Paris, 1969.
32 J.-M. Pérouse de Montclos, *Histoire de l'architecture française de la Renaissance à la Révolution*, Paris: Mengès, 1989, p. 101.
33 D. Thomson, *Renaissance Paris: Architecture and Growth, 1475–1600*, London: Zwemmer, 1984, p. 77–9.
34 *Ibid.*, pp. 102–3.
35 J.-P. Babelon, *Paris au XVIe siècle*, Paris: Hachette, 1986, p. 116.
36 J.-P. Babelon, *Les relevés d'architecture du quartier des Halles avant les destructions de 1852–1854*, Paris: Gazette des Beaux-Arts, n.d., p. 26.
37 Thomson, *Renaissance Paris*, p. 74.
38 Archives Nationales, Z 1 Ï 1065, fol. 90 V°.
39 J. de Vries, *European Urbanization, 1500–1800*, London:

Methuen, 1984, p. 275.

40 P. Lavedan, *Histoire de l'urbanisme*, Paris: Henri Laurens, 1959, vol. 2, p. 146.

41 D. Thomson, *Renaissance Paris: Architecture and Growth, 1475–1600*, London: Zwemmer, 1984, pp. 31–2.

42 *Ibid.*, p. 35.

43 J.-L. Harouel, 'La tradition du règlement', in F. Laisney and X. Malverti (eds.), *La ville régulière, II: formes urbaines et règlements*, Paris: Ecole d'Architecture de Paris Belleville, 1990, p. 3.

44 *Paris-Projet*, 13/14, 1975, p. 27.

45 Bullet, *Architecture pratique*, Paris, Hémissant, 1762, p. 515.

46 *Manuel des lois du bâtiment élaboré par la Société Centrale des Architectes*, Paris: Morel, 1863, pp. 1–4.

47 *Ibid.*, pp. 3–8.

48 J.-P. Babelon, *Demeures parisiennes sous Henri IV et Louis XIII*, Paris: Le Temps, 1965, pp. 51–2; P. Léon, 'Maisons et rues de Paris', in *Revue de Paris*, juillet-août 1910, pp. 848–9.

49 O. Ranum, *Les Parisiens du XVIIe siècle*, Paris: Armand Colin, 1973, pp. 61–2.

50 H. Ballon, *The Paris of Henri IV: Architecture and Urbanisme*, Cambridge, Mass.: MIT Press, 1991, pp. 57–68.

51 Ranum, *Les Parisiens*, pp. 92–3.

52 J. de Brunhoff, *La Place Dauphine et l'Île de la Cité*, Paris: La Manufacture, 1987, p. 58.

53 De Brunhoff, *La Place Dauphine*, pp. 25, 63, 67.

54 *Ibid.*, 25.

55 D. Thomson, *Renaissance Paris: Architecture and Growth, 1475–1600*, London: Zwemmer, 1984, p. 142.

56 See e.g. M. Girouard, *Cities and People: A Social and Architectural History*, New Haven and London: Yale University Press, 1985, p. 172.

57 Duc de Sully, *Oeconomies royales*, ch. 124, cited in J.-P. Babelon, 'Histoire de l'architecture domestique à Paris', Ecole Pratique des Hautes Etudes, IVe Section, in *Annuaire, 1975/1976*, Paris: 1976, p. 706.

58 A. Deville and E. Hochereau (eds.), *Recueil des lettres patentes . . . concernant les voies publiques*, Paris: Imprimerie Nouvelle, 1886, p. 1.

59 *Ibid.*, p. 707.

60 P. Lavedan, *Histoire de l'urbanisme*, Paris: Henri Laurens, 1959, vol. 2, pp. 344–5.

61 O. Ranum, *Les Parisiens du XVIIe siècle*, Paris: Armand Colin, 1973, pp. 92–3.

## CHAPTER THREE: CREATING A FRENCH URBAN ARCHITECTURE, 1610–1715

1 W. Herrmann, *Laugier and Eighteenth Century French Theory*, London: A. Zwemmer, 1962, p. 37.

2 *Ibid.*, pp. 64–6.

3 D. Egbert, *The Beaux-Arts Tradition in French Architecture*, Princeton: Princeton University Press, 1980, p. 20.

4 F. Blondel, 'Préface', in Cours d'architecture enseigné dans l'Académie Royale d'Architecture, Paris: Lambert Roulland, 1675, vol. 1; Egbert, *The Beaux-Arts Tradition*, p. xxi.

5 R. Chafee, 'The teaching of architecture at the Ecole des Beaux-Arts', in A. Drexler (ed.), *The Architecture of the Ecole des Beaux-Arts*, New York: Museum of Modern Art, 1977, p. 61.

6 Blondel, 'Préface', in Cours d'architecture, vol. 1.

7 See P. Pinon and F. Amprimoz, *Les envois de Rome (1778–1968): architecture et archéologie*, Rome: Ecole

Française de Rome, 1988.

8 Blondel, *Cours d'architecture*.

9 *Ibid.*, 'Au roy', n.p.

10 J. de Vries, *European Urbanization, 1500–1800*, London: Methuen, 1984, pp. 270–5.

11 L. Bernard, *The Emerging City: Paris in the Age of Louis XIV*, Durham, N.C.: Duke University Press, 1970, p. 7.

12 J. Nagle, 'La ville de l'absolutisme triomphant', in L. Bergeron (ed.), *Paris, genèse d'un paysage*, Paris: Picard, 1989, pp. 119–24.

13 M. Girouard, *Cities and People: A Social and Architectural History*, New Haven and London: Yale University Press, 1985, p. 178.

14 D. Leborgne (ed.), *Les Champs-Elysées et leur quartier*, Paris: Délégation à l'Action Artistique de la Ville de Paris, 1988, pp. 13–14.

15 O. Ranum, *Les Parisiens du XVIIe siècle*, Paris: Armand Colin, 1973, p. 265.

16 *Ibid.*, pp. 265–6; A. Braham and P. Smith, *François Mansart*, London: Zwemmer, 1973, vol. 2, p. 476.

17 Ranum, *Les Parisiens*, pp. 265–6.

18 Braham and Smith, *Mansart*, vol. 2, pp. 477, 480–517, 535–9.

19 Ranum, *Les Parisiens*, p. 267.

20 M. le Moël, *L'architecture privée à Paris au Grand Siècle*, Paris: Commission des Travaux Historiques de la Ville de Paris, 1990, p. 102; Braham and Smith, *Mansart*, vol. 1, pp. 31–8.

21 Le Moël, *L'architecture privée*, pp. 102–3.

22 B. Marrey and M.-J. Dumont, *La brique à Paris*, Paris: Picard, 1991, pp. 32–3.

23 A. Braham and P. Smith, *François Mansart*, London: Zwemmer, 1973, vol. 1, p. 32.

24 Le Moël, *L'architecture privée*, p. 102.

25 *Ibid.*, pp. 104–13.

26 *Ibid.*, p. 104.

27 F. Blondel, *Cours d'architecture enseigné dans l'Académie Royale d'Architecture*, Paris: author, 1683, vol. 2, 4th part, pp. 610, 618.

28 A. Deville and E. Hochereau, *Recueil des lettres patentes . . . concernant les voies publiques*, Paris: Imprimerie Nouvelle, 1886, pp. 10–11.

29 *Ibid.*, 11.

30 P. Lavedan, *Histoire de l'urbanisme*, Paris: Henri Laurens, 1959, vol. 2, pp. 295–6.

31 M. le Moël, *L'architecture privée à Paris au Grand Siècle*, Paris: Commission des Travaux Historiques de la Ville de Paris, 1990, p. 36; Deville and Hochereau, *Recueil*, pp. 14–16.

32 Le Moël, *L'architecture privée*, p. 59.

33 P. Francastel, 'Paris et la création urbaine en Europe au XVIIe siècle', in Francastel (ed.), *L'urbanisme de Paris et l'Europe, 1600–1680*, Paris: Klincksieck, 1969, p. 19.

34 See P. le Muet, *Manière de bien bâtir pour toutes sortes de personnes*, Paris: Iean du Puis, 1663.

35 P. Gresset, *L'écart du système: critique des relations entre les figurations et discours instaurateurs du bâtir à l'âge classique (1665–1720)*, Paris: publisher not stated, 1977, pp. 101–2, 107; A. Deville and E. Hochereau, *Recueil des lettres patentes . . . concernant les voies publiques*, Paris: lmprimerie Nouvelle, 1886, p. 6.

36 G. Dethan, *Paris au temps de Louis XV, 1660–1715*, Paris: Hachette, 1990. p. 398.

37 For instance Francastel, 'Paris et la création urbaine', p. 28.

38 J. P. Babelon, *Demeures parisiennes sous Henri IV et Louis XIII*, Paris: Le Temps, 1965, pp. 141–2.

39 Le Moël, *L'architecture privée à Paris au Grand Siècle*, Paris: Commission des Travaux Historiques de la Ville de Paris, 1990, pp. 83, 86.

40 P. Francastel, 'Paris et la création urbaine en Europe au XVIIe siècle', in Francastel (ed.), *L'urbanisme de Paris et l'Europe, 1600–1680*, Paris: Klincksieck, 1969, p. 31.

41 *Ibid.*, pp. 83, 86.

42 Le Moël, *L'architecture privée*, p. 97.

43 *Ibid.*, p. 67.

44 *Ibid.*

45 *Ibid.*, pp. 77, 80.

46 *Ibid.*, p. 71.

47 *Ibid.*, p. 74.

48 F. Laisney, *Règle et règlement: la question du règlement dans l'évolution de l'urbanisme parisien, 1600–1902*, Paris: author, n.d. [1988?], p. 7.

49 L. Bonnier, *Les règlements de voirie*, Paris: Charles Schmid, 1903, p. 5.

50 *Manuel des lois du bâtiment, élaboré par la Société Centrale des Architectes*, Paris: Morel, 1863, p. 8.

CHAPTER FOUR: THE EIGHTEENTH CENTURY: ARCHITECTURAL HARMONISATION AT THE CLOSE OF THE *ANCIEN RÉGIME*

1 J.-F. Blondel, *Architecture française*, Paris: Jombert, 1752–6; see also D. Thomson, *Renaissance Paris: Architecture and Growth, 1475–1600*, London: Zwemmer, 1984, pp. 181–2.

2 J. F. Blondel, *Cours d'architecture ou traité de la décoration, distribution et construction des bâtiments*, Paris: Desaint, 1771–7, vol. 5, pp. v–vi.

3 *Ibid.*, vol. 2, pp. 289–93.

4 *Ibid.*, pp. 233–43.

5 *Ibid.*, vol. 3, p. 458.

6 *Ibid.*, vol. 5, pp. vi–ix.

7 C.-A. Jombert, *Architecture moderne*, Paris: author, 1764.

8 *Ibid.*, vol. 2, plates.

9 W. Herrmann, *Laugier and Eighteenth Century French Theory*, London: A. Zwemmer, 1962, p. 134.

10 F. Monclús Fraga, 'Teorias arquitectonicas y discurso urbanistico: de las operaciones de "embellecimiento" a la reforma global de la ciudad en el siglo XVIII', in *Ciudad y Territorio*, 79 (1), 1989, pp. 26–30.

11 I. de Bourges (ed. V. Dufour), *Description des monuments de Paris*, Paris: A. Quantin, 1878, p. 9.

12 *Ibid.*, pp. 58, 74.

13 M. Gallet, *Paris Domestic Architecture of the 18th Century*, London: Barrie and Jenkins, 1972, p. 1; Lavedan, *Histoire de l'urbanisme*, vol. 2, Paris: Henri Laurens, 1959, p. 338.

14 L. Bergeron (ed.), *Paris: genèse d'un paysage*, Paris: Picard, 1989, p. 186.

15 *Ibid.*, pp. 156 ff.

16 *Ibid.*, pp. 161–2.

17 *Ibid.*, p. 163.

18 W. Herrmann, *Laugier and Eighteenth Century French Theory*, London: A. Zwemmer, 1962, pp. 134–6.

19 See P. Lavedan, *Nouvelle histoire de Paris: histoire de l'urbanisme à Paris*, Paris: Hachette, 1975, pp. 301–23; Bergeron, *Paris: genèse d'un paysage*, p. 176.

20 F. Blondel, *Cours d'architecture enseigné dans l'Académie Royale d'Architecture*, Paris: author, 1683, vol. 2, p. 604.

21 M.-A. Laugier, *Essai sur l'architecture [1755]. Observations sur l'architecture [1765]*, Brussels: Pierre Mardaga, 1979, pp. 209–10.

22 Herrmann, *Laugier*, pp. 136–9.

23 Laugier, *Essai*, p. 214.

24 *Ibid.*, p. 227.

25 *Ibid.*, p. 228.

26 *Ibid.*, p. 229.

27 P. Patte, *Monumens érigés en France à la gloire de Louis XV*, Paris: Rozet, 1767, pp. 212–19.

28 *Ibid.*, pp. 213–14.

29 *Ibid.*, p. 223.

30 *Ibid.*, p. 222.

31 P. Patte, *Mémoires sur les objets les plus importans de l'architecture*, Paris: Rozet, 1769.

32 *Ibid.*, pp. 2–4.

33 See P. Lavedan, *Histoire de l'urbanisme*, Paris: Henri Laurens, 1959, vol. 2, p. 313; A. Deville and E. Hochereau, *Recueil des lettres patentes . . . concernant les voies publiques*, Paris: Imprimerie Nouvelle, 1886, pp. 29–30.

34 Deville and Hochereau, *Recueilp.* p. 30.

35 M. Gallet, *Paris Domestic Architecture of the 18th Century*, London: Barrie and Jenkins, 1972, plates 64–6.

36 *Ibid.*, plates 99–100.

37 *Ibid.*, plate 115.

38 *Ibid.*, plates 153–7.

39 *Ibid.*, plates 158–61.

40 *Théâtre de l'Odéon, 1782–1982*, Paris: Délégation à l'Action Artistique de la Ville de Paris, 1983, p. 3.

41 Quoted in Gallet, *Paris Domestic Architecture*, p. 63.

42 See the painstaking and impressive register of architects in Gallet, *Paris Domestic Architecture*, pp. 139–88.

43 Roche, *Le peuple de Paris*, Paris: Aubier-Montaigne, 1981, pp. 101–3.

44 *Ibid.*, p. 116.

45 See M. Gallet, *Paris Domestic Architecture of the 18th Century*, London: Barrie and Jenkins, 1972, pp. 66–7.

46 *Ibid.*, pp. 67–8.

47 *Ibid.*, plate 11.

48 *Ibid.*, plate 47, p. 163.

49 *Ibid.*, p. 135.

50 Gallet, *Paris Domestic Architecture*, pp. 15–16.

51 L. Bergeron (ed.), *Paris: genèse d'un paysage*, Paris: Picard, 1989, pp. 179–80.

52 Gallet, *Paris Domestic Architecture*, pp. 18–19.

53 See e.g. F. Loyer, *Paris XIXe siècle: l'immeuble et la rue*, Paris: Hazan, 1987, pp. 7–9.

54 M. Gallet, *Paris Domestic Architecture of the 18th Century*, London: Barrie and Jenkins, 1972, plate 48.

55 *Ibid.*, plate 51.

56 F. Boudon, 'Tissu urbain et architecture: l'analyse parcellaire comme base de l'histoire architecturale', in *Annales E.S.C.*, 30 (2), 1975, p. 780.

57 Bergeron, *Paris: genèse d'un paysage*, p. 180.

58 J.-L. Harouel, 'Les fonctions de l'alignement dans l'organisme urbain', in *Dix-huitième siècle*, 9, 1977, pp. 135–9.

59 The texts are published in A. Deville and E. Hochereau (eds.), *Recueil des lettres patentes . . . concernant les voies publiques*, Paris: Imprimerie Nouvelle, 1886, *1er supplément*, p. 38 and *2ème supplément*, p. 69.

60 J. Pronteau, *Edme Verniquet, 1727–1804*, Paris: Commission des Travaux Historiques, Ville de Paris, 1986, p. 313.

61 Roche, *Le peuple de Paris*, p. 104.

62 Pronteau, *Verniquet*, pp. 312–13.

63 *Ibid.*, p. 314.

## CHAPTER FIVE: REVOLUTION, EMPIRE AND RESTORATION: THE IMPLICATIONS FOR ARCHITECTURE, 1789–1852

1 G. Radicchio and M. Sajous D'Oria, *Les théâtres de Paris pendant la Révolution*, Bari: Elemond, 1990, pp. 7, 14–19.
2 *Ibid.*, pp. 14, 16.
3 M. Guerrini, *Napoleon and Paris: Thirty Years of History*, London: Cassell, 1970, p. 60.
4 P. Lavedan, *Histoire de l'urbanisme*, Paris: Henri Laurens, 1952, vol. 3, p. 102.
5 *Ibid.*, p. 7. See also B. Ratcliffe, 'Cities and environmental decline: elites and the sewage problem in Paris', in *Planning Perspectives*, 5 (1), 1990, pp. 189–222.
6 See M. Biver, *Le Paris de Napoléon*, Paris: Plon, 1963.
7 P. Lavedan, *Nouvelle histoire de Paris: histoire de l'urbanisme à Paris*, Paris: Hachette, 1975, p. 330.
8 Guerrini, *Napoleon and Paris*, pp. 61–2.
9 H. Hitchcock, *Architecture: dix-neuvième et vingtième siècles*, Brussels: Pierre Mardaga, 1981, pp. 34–5.
10 Lavedan, *Nouvelle histoire de Paris*, p. 339.
11 *Ibid.*, p. 333; M. Taxil, *Recueil d'actes administratifs et de conventions relatifs aux servitudes spéciales d'architecture . . .* , Paris: Imprimerie Nouvelle, 1905, pp. 11–12.
12 See the report of Louis Daubanton in *Recherches statistiques sur la Ville de Paris et le Département de la Seine*, Paris, Imprimerie Royale, 1829.
13 *Mémoire adressé par une réunion de propriétaires, architectes et constructeurs de la Ville de Paris à MM. les membres de la Commission d'enquête instituée par . . . le Ministre de l'Intérieur en date du 7 juillet 1828*, Paris: Renard, 1829, pp. 25–47.
14 F. Bédarida and A. Sutcliffe, 'The street in the structure and life of the city: reflections on nineteenth-century London and Paris', in B. Stave (ed.), *Modern Industrial Cities: History, Policy and Survival*, Beverly Hills: Sage Publications, 1981, pp. 21–38.
15 A. Normand, *Paris moderne*, Paris: Normand *ainé*, 1843–9, vol. 1, plate 93.
16 *Ibid.*, plate 8.
17 J. Harouel, 'La tradition du règlement', in F. Laisney and X. Malverti (eds.), *La ville régulière, II: formes urbaines et règlements*, Paris: Ecole d'Architecture de Paris Belleville, 1990, p. 6.
18 L. Bonnier, *Les règlements de voirie*, Paris: Charles Schmid, 1903, p. 6.
19 W. Szambien, *Jean-Nicolas-Louis Durand, 1760–1834: de l'imitation à la norme*, Paris: Picard, 1984, pp. 117, 301.
20 See J. Durand, *Précis des leçons d'architecture*, Paris: author, 1802–1821.
21 L. Bergeron (ed.), *Paris: genèse d'un paysage*, Paris: Picard, 1989, p. 206.
22 M. Dennis, *Court and Garden: From the French Hotel to the City of Modern Architecture*, Cambridge, Mass.: MIT, 1986, p. 182.
23 F. Loyer, *Paris XIXe siècle: l'immeuble et la rue*, Paris: Hazan, 1987, pp. 15–17.
24 V. Calliat, *Parallèle des maisons de Paris construites depuis 1830 jusqu'à nos jours*, Paris: Bance, 1850; A. Normand, *Paris moderne*, Paris: Normand *ainé*, 1843–9.
25 See Normand, *Paris moderne*.
26 See Dennis, *Court and Garden*, p. 182.
27 V. Calliat, *Parallèle des maisons de Paris construites depuis 1850 jusqu'à nos jours*, Paris: Morel, 1864.
28 *Le Parisien chez lui au XIXe siècle, 1814–1914*, Paris: Archives Nationales, 1976, p. 44.
29 R. Chafee, 'The teaching of architecture at the Ecole des Beaux-Arts', in A. Drexler (ed.), *The Architecture of the Ecole des Beaux-Arts*, New York: Museum of Modern Art, 1977, pp. 65–82.
30 *Ibid.*, pp. 61, 79–97.
31 *Ibid.*, pp. 71–7.
32 *Ibid.*, p. 79.
33 *Ibid.*, pp. 82–3.
34 D. Egbert, *The Beaux-Arts Tradition in French Architecture*, Princeton: Princeton University Press, 1980, p. 4.
35 See R. Chafee, 'The teaching of architecture', p. 88 ff.
36 H. Hitchcock, *Architecture: dix-neuvième et vingtième siècles*, Brussels: Pierre Mardaga, 1981, pp. 166–7.
37 *Ibid.*, p. 76.

## CHAPTER SIX: PARIS AS THE HUB OF FRENCH INDUSTRIALISATION: BUILDING A EUROPEAN CAPITAL UNDER THE SECOND EMPIRE, 1852–70

1 L. Reynaud, *Traité d'architecture*, Paris: Dunod, 1851, vol. 1, pp. vi–vii.
2 G.-E. Haussmann, *Mémoires*, Paris: Guy Durier, 1979 (new edn), vol. 2, p. 271.
3 *Ibid.*
4 A. Sutcliffe, *The Autumn of Central Paris: The Defeat of Town Planning, 1850–1970*, London: Edward Arnold, 1970, p. 180.
5 P. Lavedan, *Histoire de l'urbanisme*, Paris: Henri Laurens, 1952, vol. 3, p. 108.
6 Ex inf. Maxine Copeland.
7 F. Goy-Truffaut, *Paris façade*, Paris: Hazan, 1989, p. 96.
8 Haussmann, *Mémoires*, vol. 2, pp. 223–4.
9 *Ibid.*, pp. 224–5.
10 *Ibid.*, p. 234.
11 *Ibid.*
12 *Ibid.*, pp. 238–9.
13 *Ibid.*, pp. 230–2.
14 F. Loyer, *Paris XIXe siècle: l'immeuble et l'espace urbain*, Paris: Atelier Parisien d'Urbanisme, n.d. [1981], vol. 1, *Objet et méthode*, pp. 52–4.
15 *Ibid.*
16 *Ibid.*, p. 25.
17 *Le Parisien chez lui au XIXe siècle, 1814–1914*. Paris: Archives Nationales, 1976, 62.
18 Text in M. Jourdan, *Recueil de règlements concernant le service des alignements et des logements insalubres dans la Ville de Paris*, Paris: Imprimerie Chaix, 1887, pp. 34–7.
19 See V. Calliat, *Parallèle des maisons de Paris construites depuis 1850 jusqu'à nos jours*, Paris: Morel, 1864.
20 See the house by Rolland, Rue de la Cossonnerie, *ibid.*, plate 87.
21 P. Lavedan, *Histoire de l'urbanisme*, Paris: Henri Laurens, 1952, vol. 3, p. 418.
22 *Paris, la rue: le mobilier urbain du Second Empire à nos jours . . .* , Paris: Société des Amis de la Bibliothèque historique, 1976, p. 8.
23 C. Daly, *L'architecture privée au XIXe siècle sous Napoléon III: nouvelles maisons de Paris et des environs*, Paris: Morel, 1864, vol. 1, p. 2.
24 *Ibid.*, pp. 16–17.
25 D. Leborgne (ed.), *Les Champs-Elysées et leur quartier*, Paris: Délégation à l'Action Artistique de la Ville de Paris, 1988, pp. 75–85.
26 K. Bowie, *Les grandes gares parisiennes au XIXe siècle*,

Paris: Délégation à l'Action Artistique de la Ville de Paris, n.d., pp. 32–8, 43.

27 *Ibid.*, p. 104.

28 See *Hittorff: un architecte du XIXe*, Paris: Musée Carnavalet, 1986.

29 Bowie, *Les grandes gares*, pp. 54–65, 88–92.

30 *Ibid.*, pp. 76–9.

31 B. Marrey, *Les grands magasins des origines à 1939*, Paris: Picard, 1979, pp. 40–1.

32 A. Drexler (ed.), *The Architecture of the Ecole des Beaux-Arts*, New York: Museum of Modern Art, 1977, pp. 428–9.

33 D. van Zanten, 'Architectural composition at the Ecole des Beaux-Arts: from Charles Percier to Charles Garnier', *ibid.*, pp. 232–9.

34 *Ibid.*, pp. 251–88.

35 *Ibid.*, p. 278.

36 *Ibid.*, pp. 240–1.

37 See e.g. X. Malverti and A. Picard, 'Algeria: military genius and civic design, 1830–70', in *Planning Perspectives*, 6 (2), 1991, pp. 207–34.

38 E. Trélat, *L'École Centrale d'Architecture*. Paris: A. Morel, 1864, pp. 9–10.

39 See Trélat, *L'école centrale*.

40 See E. Trélat, *M. Charles Garnier et l'École Spéciale d'Architecture*, Paris: Ecole Spéciale d'Architecture, 1872.

41 Trélat, *L'École Centrale d'Architecture*, pp. 7–8.

CHAPTER SEVEN: AFTER HAUSSMANN: A NEW PARIS
IN AN ERA OF ALTERNATIVE ARCHITECTURES,
1870–1914

1 A. Sutcliffe, *The Autumn of Central Paris: The Defeat of Town Planning, 1850–1970*, London: Edward Arnold, 1970, p. 346.

2 G. Rousset-Charny, *Les palais parisiens de la belle époque*, Paris: Délégation à l'Action Artistique de la Ville de Paris, 1990, pp. 22–3.

3 See D. de Penanrun *et al.*, *Les architectes élèves de l'Ecole des Beaux-Arts, 1819–1894*, Paris: Imprimerie Chaix, 1895.

4 D. van Zanten, 'Architectural composition at the Ecole des Beaux-Arts from Charles Percier to Charles Garnier', in A. Drexler (ed.), *The Architecture of the Ecole des Beaux-Arts*, New York: Museum of Modern Art, 1977, p. 290 ff.

5 A. Drexler (ed.), *The Architecture of the Ecole des Beaux-Arts*, New York: Museum of Modern Art, 1977, pp. 448–9.

6 Van Zanten, 'Architectural composition', pp. 300–3.

7 *Ibid.*, p. 307.

8 De Penanrun, *Les archiectes élèves de l'Ecole des Beaux-Arts*, pp. 305–17.

9 L. Magne, *L'architecture française du siècle*, Paris: Firmin-Didot, 1889, p. 99.

10 See M.-J. Dumont, *Paris arabesques: architectures et décors arabes et orientalisants à Paris*, Paris: Editions Eric Koehler, 1988.

11 *Ibid.*, pp. 33–4.

12 B. Marrey and M.-J. Dumont, *La brique à Paris*, Paris: Picard, 1991, pp. 50–5.

13 Dumont, *Paris arabesques*, p. 35.

14 *Gabriel Davioud, architecte (1824–1881)*, Paris: Délégation à l'Action Artistique de la Ville de Paris, 1981–2, p. 89.

15 *Ibid.*, p. 27 ff.

16 *Ibid.*, pp. 93–4.

17 D. Harvey, *Consciousness and the Urban Experience: Studies in the History and Theory of Capitalist Urbanization*, Oxford: Basil Blackwell, 1985, pp. 227–9.

18 *Ibid.*, p. 239.

19 Y. Christ, *Paris des utopies*, Paris: André Balland, 1970, p. 20.

20 S. Dugast and I. Parizet, *Dictionnaire par noms d'architectes des constructions élevées à Paris aux XIXe et XXe siècles. Première série, période 1876–1899 . . . Tome 1*, Paris: Institut d'Histoire de Paris, 1990, plate 1.

21 See e.g. 26, rue François Ier, 1904, by Albert Benz, *ibid.*, plate 33.

22 F. Loyer, *Paris XIXe siècle: l'immeuble et la rue*, Paris: Hazan, 1987, p. 20.

23 Préfecture du Département de la Seine, *Documents relatifs à la révision des règlements sur les constructions et à la salubrité intérieure des bâtiments dans Paris*, Paris: Préfecture de la Seine, 1881, pp. 55–429.

24 See *Examen du projet de décret sur la hauteur, le mode de construction et la salubrité intérieure des bâtiments: observations présentées par MM. les architectes à M. le Préfet de la Seine et au Conseil municipal de Paris*, Paris: Ducher et Cie, 1882.

25 M. Bouvard and M.C. Jourdan (eds.), *Documents relatifs à la révision des décrets: (1) du 22 juillet 1882 sur les saillies permises dans la Ville de Paris; (2) du 23 juillet 1884 sur la hauteur des maisons, des combles et les lucarnes dans la Ville de Paris*, Paris: Chaix, 1900, p. 244.

26 See articles by Williot, Beltran and Vautier, in F. Caron *et al.* (eds.), *Paris et ses réseaux: naissance d'un mode de vie urbain, XIXe-XXe siècles*, Paris: Bibliothèque Historique de la Ville de Paris, 1990, pp. 213–32, 241–78.

27 See E. Cromley, *Alone Together: A History of New York's Early Apartments*, Ithaca and London: Cornell University Press, 1990.

28 Commission du Vieux Paris, *Procès-verbal*, 2, 1990, pp. 6–14.

29 See F. Borsi and E. Godoli, *Paris art nouveau: architecture et décoration*, Paris: Marc Vokar, 1989.

30 See e.g. H. Provensal, *Vers l'harmonie intégrale: l'art de demain*, Paris: Perrin, 1904.

31 M. Doumic, *L'architecture d'aujourd'hui*, Paris: Perrin, 1897.

32 See Archives Nationales, AJ[53]130, d. Guimard, and AJ[53]130, d. Guimard, p. 17.

33 Borsi and Godoli, *Paris art nouveau*, p. 179.

34 See M. Clausen, *Frantz Jourdain and the Samaritaine: Art Nouveau Theory and Criticism*, Leiden: E.J. Brill, 1987.

35 *Le seizième arrondissement mécène de l'art nouveau, 1895–1914*, Paris: Délégation à l'Action Artistique de la Ville de Paris, 1984, pp. 9–10.

36 F. Borsi and E. Godoli, *Paris art nouveau: architecture et décoration*, Paris: Marc Vokar, 1989, p. 179.

37 Clausen, *Frantz Jourdain*, p. 231.

38 See e.g. H. Guimard's lecture on 12 May 1899, in *Le Moniteur des Arts*, 44, no. 2399, 7 July 1899, pp. 1465–71.

39 Borsi and Godoli, *Paris art nouveau*, pp. 7–9.

40 *Ibid.*

41 L. Bonnier, *Les règlements de voirie*, Paris: Charles Schmid, 1903, p. 11.

42 *Construction Moderne*, 2nd series, 19, 1903–4, p. 458.

43 G. Kahn, *L'esthétique de la rue*, Paris: Bibliothèque-Charpentier, 1901.

44 *Ibid.*, p. 291.

45 *Ibid.*, p. 300.

46 *Ibid.*, pp. 303–5.

47 *Ibid.*, pp. 247–54.

48 R. de Souza, *L'art public*, Paris: H. Floury, 1901, p. 19.
49 *Ibid.*, p. 41.
50 *Ibid.*, p. 30.
51 M. Bouvard and M.C. Jourdan, *Documents relatifs à la révision des décrets: (1) du 22 juillet 1882 sur les saillies permises dans la Ville de Paris; (2) du 23 juillet 1884 sur la hauteur des maisons, les combles et les lucarnes dans la Ville de Paris*, Paris: Chaix, 1900, pp. 5–11.
52 See *Examen du projet de décret sur la hauteur, le mode de construction et la salubrité intérieure des bâtiments: observations présentées par MM. les architectes à M. le Préfet de la Seine et au Conseil municipal de Paris*, Paris: Ducher et Cie, 1882.
53 Bouvard and Jourdan, *Documents*, p. 159.
54 Conseil municipal de Paris, *Procès-verbaux*, 9 June 1909, pp. 902–5.
55 B. Marrey, *Le fer à Paris: architectures*, Paris: Picard, 1989, p. 75.
56 Bouvard and Jourdan, *Documents*, p. 58.
57 *Ibid.*, p. 58, drawings, p. 60 ff.
58 *Ibid.*, pp. 57–8.
59 *Ibid.*, p. 235.
60 *Ibid.*, pp. 359–68.
61 *Ibid.*, p. 304.
62 Conseil municipal de Paris, *Procès-verbaux*, 28 December 1899, p. 132.
63 See e.g. M. Bouvard and M.C. Jourdan, *Documents relatifs à la révision des décrets: (1) du 22 juillet 1882 sur les saillies permises dans la Ville de Paris; (2) du 23 juillet 1884 sur la hauteur des maisons, les combles et les lucarnes dans la Ville de Paris*, Paris: Chaix, 1900, pp. 131–8.
64 *Ibid.*, p. 299.
65 See L. Bonnier, *Les règlements de voirie*, Paris: Charles Schmid, 1903.
66 *Journal Officiel*, 1909, pp. 1623–4.
67 C. Magny, *Des moyens juridiques de sauvegarder les aspects esthétiques de la ville de Paris*, Paris: Bernard Tignol, 1911, p. 166; E. Hénard, *Rapports à la Commission des Perspectives Monumentales de la Ville de Paris* (from *L'Architecture*, March and April 1911), Paris, 1911, pp. 1–3; G. Meyer-Heine, 'Urbanisme et esthétique: essai pratique de réglementation d'aspect', *La Vie Urbaine*, 38, March–April 1937, pp. 83–4.
68 See Commission des Perspectives Monumentales, *Révision du décret du 13 août 1902 portant règlement sur les hauteurs et sur les saillies des bâtiments dans la Ville de Paris*, Paris: Ministère de l'Education Nationale, 1938, p. 1.
69 Magny, *Des moyens juridiques*, pp. 157–8.
70 E. Magne, *L'esthéthique des villes*, Paris: Mercure de France, 1908.
71 C. Lortsch, *La beauté de Paris et la loi*, Paris: Recueil Sirey, 1913.
72 André Hallays, 'Préface', *ibid.*, p. 9.
73 *Ibid.*, p. xii.
74 *Ibid.*, p. 12.
75 *Ibid.*, p. 19.
76 C. Magny, *Des moyens juridiques de sauvegarder les aspects esthétiques de la Ville de Paris*, Paris: Bernard Tignol, 1911, p. 2.
77 Conseil municipal de Paris, *Procès-verbaux*, 9 June 1909, p. 892.
78 *Journal Officiel*, 1909, pp. 1618–30.
79 See F. Goy-Truffaut, *Paris façade*, Paris: Hazan, 1989.
80 K. Bowie, *Les grandes gares parisiennes au XIXe siècle*, Paris: Délégation à l'Action Artistique de la Ville de Paris, n.d., p. 80.
81 *Ibid.*

82 *Ibid.*, p. 81.
83 *Ibid.*, pp. 80–6.
84 See *Victor Laloux 1850–1937: l'architecte de la Gare d'Orsay*, Paris: Réunion des Musées Nationaux, 1987.
85 A. Drexler (ed.), *The Architecture of the Ecole des Beaux-Arts*, New York: Museum of Modern Art, 1977, pp. 459–63.
86 K. Bowie, *Les grandes gares parisiennes au XIXe siècle*, Paris: Délégation à l'Action Artistique de la Ville de Paris, n.d., pp. 134–54.
87 *Ibid.*, p. 135.
88 *La Construction Moderne*, 2nd series, 7, 1901–2, p. 6.
89 G. Rousset-Charny, *Les palais parisiens de la belle époque*, Paris: Délégation à l'Action Artistique de la Ville de Paris, 1990, p. 43.
90 See F. Goy-Truffaut, *Paris façade*, Paris: Hazan, 1989.
91 Drexler (ed.), *The Architecture of the Ecole des Beaux-Arts*, pp. 454–7.
92 B. Marrey, *Les grands magasins des origines à 1939*, Paris: Picard, 1979, p. 96.
93 B. Marrey and M.-J. Dumont, *La brique à Paris*, Paris: Picard, 1991, p. 39.
94 *L'école primaire à Paris 1870–1914*, Paris: Délégation à l'Action Artistique de la Ville de Paris, 1985, p. 12.
95 *Ibid.*, pp. 12–13.
96 *La Construction Moderne*, 1, 1885–6, plate 40.
97 A. Drexler (ed.), *The Architecture of the Ecole des Beaux-Arts*, New York: Museum of Modern Art, 1977, p. 458.
98 P. Chemetov and B. Marrey, *Architectures: Paris, 1848–1914*, Paris: Dunod, 1980, pp. 112–15.
99 *Ibid.*, pp. 41–2.
100 *La Construction Moderne*, 1, 1885–6, plate 87.
101 S. Dugast and I. Parizet, *Dictionnaire par noms d'architectes des constructions élevées à Paris aux XIXe et XXe siècles. Première série, période 1876–1899 . . . Tome 1*, Paris: Institut d'Histoire de Paris, 1990, plates 73–5.
102 A. Jacques (ed.), *La carrière de l'architecte au XIXe siècle*, Paris: Editions de la Réunion des Musées Nationaux, 1986, p. 16.
103 *Ibid.*, pp. 16–17.

CHAPTER EIGHT: THE MODERNIST CHALLENGE, 1918–45

1 See A. Fourcaut (ed.), *Un siècle de banlieue parisienne (1859–1964)*, Paris: L'Harmattan, 1988, especially pp. 106–29.
2 See P. Chemetov, M.-J. Dumont and B. Marrey, *Paris-banlieue, 1919–1939; architectures domestiques*, Paris: Dunod, 1989.
3 See e.g. H. Robertson and F. Yerbury, *Examples of Modern French Architecture*, London: Ernest Benn, 1928.
4 See e.g. R. Ginsburger, *Frankreich: die Entwicklung der neuen Ideen nach Konstruktion und Form*, Vienna: Verlag von Anton Schroll, 1930.
5 J. Riches, 'Auguste Perret and his contacts with artists: Paris 1900–1914', Bartlett Scool of Architecture, MSc dissertation, 1990, pp. 28–68.
6 See *Henri Sauvage, 1873–1932*, Brussels: Archives d'Architecture Moderne, 1976.
7 F. Laisney, *Règle et règlement: la question du règlement dans l'évolution de l'urbanisme parisien, 1600–1902*, Paris: author, n.d. [1988?], appendix, unpaginated.
8 See e.g. *Henri Sauvage, 1873–1932*, p. 146.
9 M. Bouvard and M.C. Jourdan, *Documents relatifs à la*

*révision des décrets: (1) du 22 juillet 1882 sur les saillies permises dans la Ville de Paris; (2) du 23 juillet 1884 sur la hauteur des maisons, les combles et les lucarnes dans la Ville de Paris*, Paris: Chaix, 1900, pp. 240–1.

10 V. Claude, 'Sanitary engineering as a path to town planning', in *Planning Perspectives*, 4 (2), 1989, pp. 153–66.

11 A. de Baudot, *L'architecture: le passé, le présent*, Paris: Henri Laurens, 1916, p. 160.

12 *Ibid.*, p. 171.

13 E. Vitou *et al.*, *Gabriel Guévrékian, 1900–1970: une autre architecture moderne*, Paris: Connivences, 1987, pp. 21–2; R. Ginsburger, *Frankreich: die Entwicklung der neuen Ideen nach Konstruktion und Form*, Vienna: Verlag von Anton Schroll, 1930, pp. 89–92.

14 Obituary, *The Independent*, 18 February 1991.

15 Ginsburger, *Frankreich*, pp. 71–96.

16 *Rob Mallet-Stevens, architecte*, Brussels: Archives d'architecture moderne, n.d. [1980], p. 7.

17 *Ibid.*, pp. 9–12.

18 R. Becherer, 'Monumentality and the Rue Mallet-Stevens', in *Journal of the Society of Architectural Historians*, 40 (1), 1981, pp. 44–55.

19 H. Walden, 'New light on Le Corbusier's early years in Paris', in Walden (ed.), *The Open Hand: Essays on Le Corbusier*, Cambridge, Mass.: MIT Press, 1977, pp. 117–19, 122–8.

20 A. Sutcliffe, 'A vision of utopia: optimistic foundations of Le Corbusier's *doctrine d'urbanisme*', in Walden, *The Open Hand*, pp. 217–19.

21 B. Lemoine, *The Cité Internationale Universitaire de Paris*, Paris: Hervas, 1990, pp. 103–4.

22 See F. Laisney, *Règle et règlement: la question du règlement dans l'évolution de l'urbanisme parisien, 1600–1902*, Paris: author, n.d. [1988?], appendix, unpaginated.

23 B. Lemoine and P. Rivoirard, *Paris: l'architecture des Années Trente*, Lyon: La Manufacture, 1987, p. 144.

24 A. Guérard, *L'avenir de Paris*, Paris: Payot, 1929, p. 88.

25 J.-L. Cohen and A. Lortie, *Un système de projets parisiens à l'ère de la métropole: la ceinture des fortifications au périphérique*, Paris: Ecole d'Architecture Paris-Villemin, 1989, p. 290; N. Evenson, *Paris: A Century of Change*, New Haven and London: Yale University Press, 1979, pp. 41–2.

26 Evenson, *Paris: A Century of Change*, pp. 173–4; F. Borsi and E. Godoli, *Paris 1900*, London: Crosby Lockwood Staples and Granada, 1978, pp. 209–10.

27 *La Construction Moderne*, 27 March 1932, pp. 412–17.

28 Cohen and Lortie, *Un système de projets parisiens*, p. 292.

29 *La Construction Moderne*, 27 March 1932, p. 414.

30 Cohen and Lortie, *Un système de projets parisiens*, p. 295.

31 *Ibid.*, pp. 296–7.

32 See Ville de Paris et Département de la Seine, *Concours pour l'aménagement de la voie allant de la Place de l'Etoile au Rond-Point de la Défense*, Paris: Editions d'Art Charles Moreau, n.d. [1931].

33 *Ibid.*, p. 6.

34 *La Construction Moderne*, 22 May 1932, pp. 553–60, plates 121–2.

35 Ville de Paris, *Concours pour l'aménagement de la voie*, p. 9.

36 J.-L. Cohen and A. Lortie, *Un système de projets parisiens à l'ère de la métropole: la ceinture des fortifications au périphérique*, Paris: Ecole d'Architecture Paris-Villemin, 1989, p. 297.

37 Ville de Paris et Département de la Seine, *Concours*

*pour l'aménagement de la voie*, pp. 5–6.

38 Cohen and Lortie, *Un système de projets parisiens*, p. 299.

39 M. Fleury *et al.*, *Paris, de Lutèce à Beaubourg*, Paris: Flammarion, 1979, p. 31.

40 See G. Lefol, *Cinémas*, Paris: Massin, n.d. [*c.* 1920].

41 *Ibid.*, plates 14–15, 17–18.

42 *Ibid.*, plate 23.

43 J.-L. Cohen and B. Fortier (eds.), *Paris: la ville et ses projets*, Paris: Editions Babylone, 1988, p. 87.

44 H. Martin, *Guide de l'architecture moderne à Paris, 1900–1990*, Paris: Editions Alternatives, 1986, p. 14.

45 *Architecture, Mouvement, Continuité*, 43, 1977, pp. 5–25.

46 J.-L. Cohen and A. Lortie, *Un système de projets parisiens à l'ère de la métropole: la ceinture des fortifications au périphérique*, Paris: Ecole d'Architecture Paris-Villemin, 1989, p. 171.

47 *Ibid.*, p. 173.

48 G. Lefol, *Immeubles à loyers modérés entrepris par la Régie immobilière de la Ville de Paris*, Paris: Massin, n.d. [*c.* 1923], p. 3.

49 Cohen and Lortie, *Un système de projets parisiens*, pp. 185–6; F. Borsi and E. Godoli, *Paris art nouveau: architecture et décoration*, Paris: Marc Vokar, 1989, p. 76.

50 Cohen and Lortie, *Un système de projets parisiens*, p. 172.

51 *Ibid.*, pp. 173–4.

52 J.-C. Delorme and P. Chair, *L'école de Paris: dix architectes et leurs immeubles, 1905–1937*, Paris: Moniteur, 1981, p. 5.

53 P. Vago, 'Quelques immeubles nouveaux', in *L'architecture d'aujourd'hui*, 5, 1931, pp. 12–20.

54 *Ibid.*, pp. 12–13.

55 Delorme and Chair, *L'école de Paris*, p. 74.

56 *Ibid.*

57 M. Roux-Spitz, 'Entre le régionalisme et le machinisme', in *L'Architecture Française*, 28, 1943, p. 3.

58 Delorme and Chair, *L'école de Paris*, pp. 74–5.

59 Michel Raynaud, in *Architecture, Mouvement, Continuité*, 39, 1976, pp. 6–15.

60 M. Béhar and M. Salama, *Paris nouvelle/new architecture*, Paris: Regirex-France, 1985, p. 7.

61 B. Lemoine and P. Rivoirard, *Paris: l'architecture des Anneés Trente*, Lyon: La Manufacture, 1987, pp. 225–7; P. Vago, 'Quelques immeubles nouveaux', in *L'architecture d'aujourd'hui*, 1931, 5, p. 15.

62 *La Construction Moderne*, 30 August 1931, pp. 761–6.

63 B. Marrey and M.-J. Dumont, *La brique à Paris*, Paris: Picard, 1991, pp. 138–52.

64 Commission des Perspectives Monumentales, *Révision du décret du 13 août 1902 portant règlement sur les hauteurs et sur les saillies des bâtiments dans la Ville de Paris*, Paris: Ministère de l'Education Nationale, 1938, p. 1.

65 See e.g. G. Meyer-Heine. 'Urbanisme et esthéthique: essai pratique de réglementation d'aspect', in *La Vie Urbaine*, 38, March–April 1937, pp. 72–107; 39, May–June 1937, pp. 131–88.

66 Commission des Perspectives Monumentales, *Révision du décret du 13 août 1902*, pp. 19–33.

67 R. Aron, *The Vichy Regime, 1940–44*, London: Putnam, 1958, pp. 3–67.

68 W.S. Churchill, *The Second World War, 2: Their Finest Hour*, London: Cassell, 9th edn, 1967, p. 126.

69 J.-L. Cohen and H. Frank, 'Architettura dell'occupazione: Francia e Germania 1940–1950', in *Casabella*, 567, 1990, pp. 40–63.

70 See e.g. *L'Architecture Française*, 38, 1943, pp. 4–10.
71 See e.g. M. Roux-Spitz, 'Entre le régionalisme et le machinisme', in *L'Architecture Française*, 1943, 28, pp. 3–5.
72 See A. Sutcliffe, *The Autumn of Central Paris*, London: Edward Arnold, 1970, p. 253.
73 See e.g. L. Dorléac, *Histoire de l'art: Paris 1940–1944: ordre national, traditions et modernités*, Paris: Publications de la Sorbonne, 1986, p. 33.
74 *Ibid.*, p. 12; B. Lemoine and P. Rivoirard, *Paris: l'architecture des Anneés Trente*, Lyon: La Manufacture, 1987, pp. 114–19.
75 A. le Donné, *L'architecte dans la cité*, Paris: Editions du Seuil, 1945.

CHAPTER NINE: THE VITAL ENCOUNTER: MODERNITY VERSUS TRADITION IN POST-WAR PARIS

1 B. Vayssière, *Reconstruction, déconstruction: le hard french ou l'architecture française des trente glorieuses*, Paris: Picard, 1988, p. 58.
2 See e.g. the summary of the Paris case in J. Bastié, *Paris en l'an 2000*, Paris: Sédimo, n.d. [1965], pp. 13–14, 121–2.
3 For a convenient and very authoritative summary of the new growth strategy, see Bastié, *Paris en l'an 2000*.
4 *Paris-Projet*, 13/14, 1975, p. 38; Préfecture de la Seine, *Plan d'urbanisme directeur de Paris*, Paris: Imprimerie Municipale, 1960, pp. 3–33.
5 *Ibid.*, pp. 61–100.
6 *Ibid.*, pp. 3–5.
7 Conseil Municipal, *Session extraordinaire des 26 et 27 octobre 1959. Compte-rendu des débats relatifs au Plan d'Urbanisme Directeur de Paris*, Paris: Imprimerie Municipale, 1960.
8 *Ibid.*, pp. 4–6.
9 *Ibid.*, p. 8.
10 Préfecture de la Seine, *Plan d'urbanisme directeur*, pp. 9–13.
11 *Paris-Projet*, 13/14, 1975, p. 36.
12 *Ibid.*, pp. 40–1.
13 Préfecture de la Seine, *Plan d'urbanisme directeur de Paris*, Paris: Imprimerie Municipale, 1960, pp. 96–7.
14 F. Laisney, 'Paris: les règlements du XXe siècle', in F. Laisney and X. Malverti (eds), *La ville régulière, II: formes urbaines et règlements*, Paris: Ecole d'Architecture de Paris Belleville, 1990, p. 47.
15 Préfecture de la Seine, *Plan d'urbanisme directeur*, p. 97.
16 B. Vayssière, *Reconstruction, déconstruction: le hard french ou l'architecture française des trente glorieuses*, Paris: Picard, 1988, p. 58.
17 I. Schein, *Paris construit*, Paris: Editions Vincent Fréal, 1970, p. 2.
18 M. Besset, *New French Architecture*, London: The Architectural Press, 1967, pp. 6–7.
19 J.-P. Epron, 'Expert et l'école', in Institut Français d'Architecture, *Roger-Henri Expert 1882–1955*, Paris: Moniteur, 1983, p. 35.
20 Article by (Sir) Richard Rogers in *The Independent*, 13 February 1991.
21 Besset, *New French Architecture*, pp. 6–7.
22 N. Evenson, *Paris: A Century of Change. 1878–1978*, New Haven and London: Yale University Press, 1979, p. 63.
23 *Ibid.*, p. 59.
24 *Ibid.*, pp. 191–2.
25 *Ibid.*, pp. 193–4.
26 See e.g. M. Besset, *New French Architecture*, London: The Architectural Press, 1967.
27 See G. Weill (ed.), *La perspective de la Défense dans l'art et l'histoire*, Nanterre: Archives Départementales des Hauts-de-Seine, 1983.
28 *L'Architecture d'Aujourd'hui*, 118, 1965, pp. 14–19.
29 Evenson, *Paris: A Century of Change*, p. 300.
30 *The Times*, 14 September 1972.
31 *Ibid.*, 2 October 1972.
32 He probably had in mind the consulting architects A. Epstein and Sons. See N. Evenson, *Paris: A Century of Change, 1878–1978*, New Haven and London: Yale University Press, 1979, p. 194.
33 *Le Monde*, 17 October 1972.
34 Evenson, *Paris: A Century of Change*, pp. 186–92.
35 A. Sutcliffe, *The Autumn of Central Paris: The Defeat of Town Planning, 1850–1970*, London: Edward Arnold, 1970, p. 317.
36 Association pour la Consultation Internationale pour l'Aménagement du Quartier des Halles, *600 contreprojets pour les Halles*, Paris: Moniteur, 1981, p. 76 ff.
37 *Mémoires du Préfet de Paris*, 1968, no. 2, p. 28.
38 A. Sutcliffe, *The Autumn of Central Paris: The Defeat of Town Planning, 1850–1970*, London: Edward Arnold, 1970, p. 318.
39 J. de Sacy, *Le quartier des Halles*, Paris: Editions du Temps, 1969.
40 *The Times*, 2 May 1975.
41 See B. Marrey, *Le fer à Paris: architecture*, Paris: Picard, 1989.
42 *600 contreprojets pour les Halles*, p. 16.
43 *Ibid.*, p. 27 ff.
44 Marrey, *Le fer à Paris*, p. 177.
45 See R. Piano and R. Rogers, *Centre Beaubourg, Paris, France, 1972–1977*, Tokyo: A.D.A. Edita, 1977.
46 Marrey, *Le fer à Paris*, p. 174.
47 J.-L. Cohen *et al.*, *The Twentieth Century: Architecture and Urbanism: Paris*, Tokyo: Architecture and Urbanism Publishing Co., 1990, p. 152.
48 B. Appleyard, *Richard Rogers*, London: Faber and Faber, 1986, p. 162.
49 See e.g. *ibid.*, pp. 166–85.
50 B. Marrey, *Le fer à Paris: architecture*, Paris: Picard, 1989, p. 174.
51 Appleyard, *Richard Rogers*, p. 201.
52 Piano and Rogers, *Centre Beaubourg*, n.p.; Appleyard, *Richard Rogers*, pp. 215–16.
53 H. Martin, *Guide de l'architecture moderne à Paris, 1900–1989*, Paris: Editions Alternatives, 1986, p. 24.
54 *Paris-Projet*, 10/11, 1975, pp. 9, 121.
55 *Ibid.*, p. 121.
56 *Ibid.*
57 *Ibid.*, pp. 126–8.
58 Préfecture de Paris, *Plan d'occupation des sols de la Ville de Paris*, Paris: Préfecture de Paris, 1976.
59 *Le Monde*, 26 November 1985.
60 *Paris-Projet*, 13/14, 1975, pp. 4–89.
61 Préfecture de Paris, *Plan d'occupation des sols*, p. 7.
62 *Ibid.*, pp. 1–2.
63 *Ibid.*, p. 8.
64 *Ibid.*, p. 22.
65 *Ibid.*, p. 19.
66 See e.g. *Bulletin Municipal Officiel*, 2 December 1974, pp. 835–47.
67 M. Béhar and M. Salama, *Paris nouvelle/new architecture*, Paris: Regirex France, 1985, p. 6.
68 M. Bertrand, *Architecture de l'habitat urbain: la maison, le quartier, la ville*, Paris: Dunod, 1980.

69 Béhar and Salama, *Paris nouvelle*, p. 10.
70 *L'Architecture d'Aujourd'hui*, 215, 1981, pp. 26–30.
71 H. Martin, *Guide de l'architecture moderne à Paris, 1900–1990*, Paris: Editions Alternatives, 1986, p. 238.
72 See e.g. A.-M. Chatelet, 'Vues de Paris', in *Bulletin d'Informations Architecturales*, 90, supplement, December 1984.
73 Béhar and Salama, *Paris nouvelle*, p. 6.
74 J. Chirac, 'Préface', in *Concours d'architecture, 1980–1986*, Paris: Ville de Paris, Direction de l'Architecture, 1986.
75 *1977–1983: Architecture*, Paris: Régie Immobilière de la Ville de Paris, 1982, p. 1.
76 J.-M. Hoyet, 'Avant-propos', in M. Béhar and M. Salama, *Paris nouvelle/new architecture*, Paris: Regirex France, 1985, p. 3.
77 See e.g. *Paris avenir*, 106, February 1989.
78 The fullest review is to be found in *Paris 1979–1989*, New York: Rizzoli, 1988.
79 *Paris Tomorrow: Architecture, Town Planning, Preservation, Renovation*, London: Ambassade de France, 1985.
80 See e.g. interview in *Le Nouvel Observateur*, 14 December 1984.
81 *Architecture d'Aujourd'hui*, 256, 1988, p. 14.
82 *Architecture d'Aujourd'hui*, 225, 1983, pp. 72–83; 227, 1983, pp. 90–114.
83 *Concours international d'architecture pour tête Défense*, Paris: Etablissement Public d'Aménagement de la Défense, 1982; *Architecture d'Aujourd'hui*, 264, 1989, p. 18.
84 *Architecture d'Aujourd'hui*, 264, 1989, p. 18.
85 *L'événement du jeudi*, 26 June–2 July 1986.
86 *Le Nouvel Observateur*, 14 December 1984.
87 B. Marrey, *Le fer à Paris: architecture*, Paris: Picard, 1989, p. 188.
88 *Paris 1979–1989*, New York: Rizzoli, 1988, p. 42.
89 *Architecture d'Aujourd'hui*, 256, 1988, pp. 14–15.
90 *Architecture d'Aujourd'hui*, 263, 1989, pp. 8–16.
91 *Ibid.*
92 *Ibid.*, p. 12.
93 *Ibid.*, 231, 1984, pp. 23–9.
94 *Ibid.*, 233, 1984, pp. v–xii.
95 G. Charlet, *L'Opéra de la Bastille: genèse et réalisation*, Milan and Paris: Electa France, 1989, pp. 18–19.
96 *Ibid.*, pp. 31–2.
97 P. Woolf, '"Le caprice du prince": the problem of the Bastille Opéra', in *Planning Perspectives*, 2 (1), 1987, pp. 53–69.
98 Charlet, *L'Opéra de la Bastille*, pp. 40–1.
99 *Ibid.*, pp. 42–5.
100 'Concours Opéra-Bastille', in *Architecture, Mouvement, Continuité*, 1984, 3, pp. 87–104.
101 Charlet, *L'Opéra de la Bastille*, p. 47.
102 *Ibid.*, p. 79.
103 *Ibid.*, p. 88.
104 See Woolf, '"Le caprice du prince"'.
105 *Le Monde*, 26 November 1985; *Libération*, 9 April 1986.
106 *Paris-Projet*, 29, n.d., p. 12.
107 *Ibid.*, p. 5.
108 *Ibid.*
109 *Ibid.*
110 *Ibid.*, p. 13.
111 *Architecture d'Aujourd'hui*, 265, 1989, pp. 184–93.
112 *Architecture d'Aujourd'hui*, 273, 1991, pp. 12–20.
113 *Independent on Sunday, Review*, 11 November 1990.
114 *Architecture d'Aujourd'hui*, 269, 1990, pp. 114–23.
115 *Architecture d'Aujourd'hui*, 265, 1989, pp. 212–25.
116 A. Papadakis (ed.), *Post-Modernism on Trial*, London: Academy Editions, 1991, p. 10.

# Selected Bibliography

Androuet du Cerceau, Jacques. *Les plus excellents bastiments de France* (introduction by David Thomson), Paris: Sand et Conti, 1988

Androuet du Cerceau, Jacques. *Livre d'architecture*, Paris: B. Prévost, 1559

Appleyard, Bryan. *Richard Rogers*, London: Faber and Faber, 1986

Babelon, Jean-Pierre. *Demeures parisiennes sous Henri IV et Louis XIII*, Paris: Le Temps, 1965

Babelon, Jean-Pierre. *Paris au XVIe siècle*, Paris: Hachette, 1986

Ballon, Hilary. *The Paris of Henri IV: Architecture and Urbanism*, New York and Cambridge, Mass.: The Architectural History Foundation and MIT Press, 1991

Becherer, Richard. 'Monumentality and the Rue Mallet-Stevens', in *Journal of the Society of Architectural Historians*, 40 (1), 1981, pp. 44–55

Béhar, Michèle and Salama, Manuelle. *Paris nouvelle/new architecture*, Paris: Regirex-France, 1985

Bergeron, Louis (ed.). *Paris: genèse d'un paysage*, Paris: Picard, 1989

Bernard, Leon. *The Emerging City: Paris in the Age of Louis XIV*, Durham, N.C.: Duke University Press, 1970

Bertrand, Michel. *Architecture de l'habitat urbain: la maison, le quartier, la ville*, Paris: Dunod, 1980

Besset, Maurice. *New French Architecture*, London: The Architectural Press, 1967

Biver, Marie-Louise. *Pierre Fontaine: premier architecte de l'Empereur*, Paris: Plon, 1964

Biver, Paul and Marie-Louise. *Abbayes, monastères et couvents de Paris des origines à la fin du XVIIIe siècle*, Paris: Editions d'Histoire de d'Art, 1970

Blondel, François. *Cours d'architecture enseigné dans l'Académie Royale d'Architecture* (3 vols.), Paris: Lambert Roulland, 1675; author, 1683

Blondel, Jacques-François. *Architecture française* (4 vols.), Paris: Jombert, 1752–6

Blunt, Anthony. *François Mansart and the Origins of French Classical Architecture*, London: The Warburg Institute, 1941

Blunt, Anthony. *Philibert de l'Orme*, London: Zwemmer, 1958

Bonnier, Louis. *Les règlements de voirie*, Paris: Charles Schmid, 1903

Boudon, Françoise *et al. Système de l'architecture urbaine: le quartier des Halles à Paris* (2 vols.), Paris: CNRS, 1977

Bourget, Pierre. 'Essai sur l'implantation d'immeubles tours de prestige', in *Urbanisme*, 39 (117), 1970, pp. 28–9

Braham, Allan and Smith, Peter. *François Mansart* (2 vols.), London: Zwemmer, 1973

Calliat, Victor. *Parallèle des maisons de Paris construites depuis 1830 jusqu'à nos jours*, Paris: Bance, 1850

Calliat, Victor. *Parallèle des maisons de Paris construites depuis 1850 jusqu'à nos jours*, Paris: Morel, 1864

Castex, J. *et al. Formes urbaines: de l'ilot à la barre*, Paris: Dunod Bordas, 1977

Charlet, Gérard. *L'Opéra de la Bastille: genèse et réalisation*, Milan and Paris: Electa France, 1989

Chaslin, François. *Les Paris de François Mitterrand: histoire des grands projets architecturaux*, Paris: Gallimard, 1985

Chemetov, Paul and Marrey, Bernard. *Architectures: Paris, 1848–1914*, Paris: Dunod, 1980

Chemetov, Paul *et al. Paris-banlieue, 1919–1939: architectures domestiques*, Paris: Dunod, 1989

Christ, Yvan. *Paris des utopies*, Paris: André Balland, 1970

Clausen, Meredith. *Frantz Jourdain and the Samaritaine: Art Nouveau Theory and Criticism*, Leiden: E.J. Brill, 1987

Cobb, Richard. *The Streets of Paris*, London: Duckworth, 1980

Cohen, Jean-Louis and Fortier, Bruno (eds.). *Paris: la ville et ses projets*, Paris: Editions Babylone, 1988

Cornu, Marcel. *La conquête de Paris*, Paris: Mercure de France, 1972

Couperie, Pierre. *Paris Through the Ages: An Illustrated Historical Atlas of Urbanism and Architecture*, London: Barrie and Jenkins, 1970

Daly, César. *L'architecture privée au XIXe siècle sous Napoléon III: nouvelles maisons de Paris et des environs* (3 vols.), Paris: Morel, 1864

De Brunhoff, Jacques. *La Place Dauphine et l'Île de la Cité*, Paris: La Manufacture, 1987

De Sacy, Jacques. *Le quartier des Halles*, Paris: Editions du Temps, 1969

De Souza, Robert. *L'art public*, Paris: H. Floury, 1901

Delorme, Jean-Claude and Chair, Philippe. *L'école de Paris: dix architectes et leurs immeubles, 1905–1937*, Paris: Moniteur, 1981

Doumic, Max. *L'architecture d'aujourd'hui*, Paris: Perrin, 1897

Drexler, Arthur (ed.). *The Architecture of the Ecole des Beaux-Arts*, New York: Museum of Modern Art, 1977

Egbert, Donald. *The Beaux-Arts Tradition in French Architecture*, Princeton: Princeton University Press, 1980

Evenson, Norma. *Paris: A Century of Change, 1878–1978*, New Haven and London: Yale University Press, 1979

Favier, Jean. *Paris au XVe siècle, 1380–1500*, Paris: Hachette, 1974

Fermigier, André. *La bataille de Paris: des Halles à la Pyramide, chroniques d'urbanisme*, Paris: Gallimard, 1991

Francastel, Pierre (ed.). *L'urbanisme de Paris et l'Europe, 1600–1680*, Paris: Klincksieck, 1969

Gallet, Michel. *Paris Domestic Architecture of the Eighteenth Century*, London: Barrie and Jenkins, 1972

Ginsburger, Roger. *Frankreich: die Entwicklung der neuen Ideen nach Konstruktion und Form*, Vienna: Verlag von Anton Schroll, 1930

Granet, André. *Architecture contemporaine: construction et décoration*, Paris: De Brunoff, 1922

Hamon, Françoise. 'Les églises parisiennes du XVIIIe siècle: théorie et pratique de l'architecture cultuelle', in *Revue de l'Art*, 32, 1976, pp. 7–14.

Harouel, Jean-Louis. *Histoire de l'urbanisme*, Paris: Presses Universitaires de France, 1981

Herrmann, Wolfgang. *Laugier and Eighteenth Century French Theory*, London: A. Zwemmer, 1962

Herrmann, Wolfgang. *The Theory of Claude Perrault*, London: A. Zwemmer, 1973

Jacques, Annie (ed.). *La carrière de l'architecte au XIXe siècle*, Paris: Editions de la Réunion des Musées Nationaux, 1986

Josephson, Ragnar. *Kungarnas Paris*, Stockholm: Bokförlaget Natur och Kultur, 1943

Laugier, Marc-Antoine. *Essai sur l'architecture. Observations sur l'architecture* (new edn), Brussels: Pierre Mardaga, 1979

Lavedan, Pierre. *Nouvelle histoire de Paris: histoire de l'urbanisme à Paris*, Paris: Hachette, 1975

Le Moël, Michel. *L'architecture privée à Paris au Grand Siècle*, Paris: Commission des Travaux Historiques de la Ville de Paris, 1990

Lemoine, Bertrand and Rivoirard, Philippe. *Paris: l'architecture des Années Trente*, Lyon: La Manufacture, 1987

Lortsch, Charles. *La beauté de Paris et la loi*, Paris: Recueil Sirey, 1913

Loyer, François. *Paris XIXe siècle: l'immeuble et la rue*, Paris: Hazan, 1987

Magne, Emile. *L'esthétique des villes*, Paris: Mercure de France, 1908

Magne, Lucien. *L'architecture française du siècle*, Paris: Firmin-Didot, 1889

Marrey, Bernard. *Le fer à Paris: architectures*, Paris: Picard, 1989

Marrey, Bernard. *Les grands magasins des origines à 1939*, Paris: Picard, 1979

Marrey, Bernard. *Louis Bonnier 1856–1946*, Liège: Pierre Mardaga, 1988

Middleton, Robin (ed.). *The Beaux-Arts and Nineteenth-Century French Architecture*, London: Thames and Hudson, 1982

Olsen, Donald. *The City as a Work of Art: London, Paris, Vienna*, New Haven and London: Yale University Press, 1986

*Paris 1979–1989*. New York: Rizzoli, 1988

Patte, Pierre. *Mémoires sur les objets les plus importans de l'architecture*, Paris: Rozet, 1769

Pérouse de Montclos, Jean-Marie. *Histoire de l'architecture française de la Renaissance à la Révolution*, Paris: Mengès, 1989

Pinkney, David. *Napoleon III and the Rebuilding of Paris*, Princeton: Princeton University Press, 1958

Ragon, Michel. *L'architecture des gares*, Paris: Denöel, 1984

Raynaud, Michel (ed.). *Michel Roux-Spitz: architecte 1888–1957*, Brussels: Pierre Mardaga, n.d. [1983]

Salvadori, Renzo. *Architect's Guide to Paris*, Sevenoaks: Butterworth Architecture, 1990

Schein, I. *Paris construit*, Paris: Vincent Fréal, 1961 and 1970

Sutcliffe, A. *The Autumn of Central Paris: The Defeat of Town Planning, 1850–1970*, London: Edward Arnold, 1970

Thomson, David. *Renaissance Paris: Architecture and Growth, 1475–1600*, London: A. Zwemmer, 1984

Van Zanten, David. *Designing Paris: The Architecture of Duban, Labrouste, Duc, and Vaudoyer*, Cambridge, Mass.: MIT Press, 1987

Viollet-le-Duc, Eugène. *Entretiens sur l'architecture*, Paris: Mardaga, 1977

# Index